◄ KAMOME ►
SHIRAHAMA

Witch Hat Atelier

◄ VOLUME ►

5

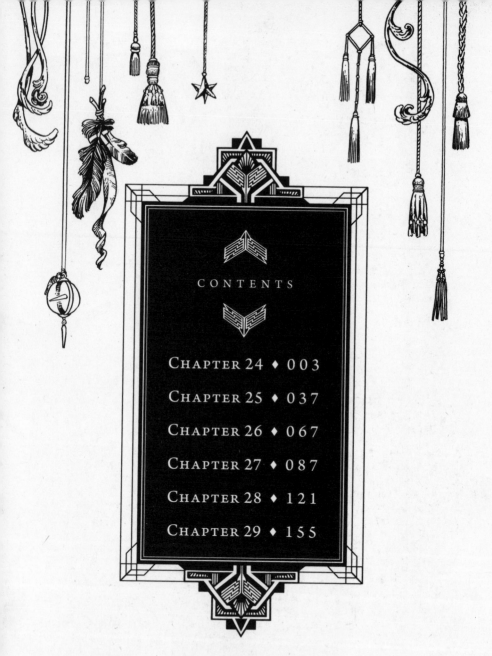

CONTENTS

WITCH HAT ATELIER

♦

KAMOME
SHIRAHAMA

Chapter 24

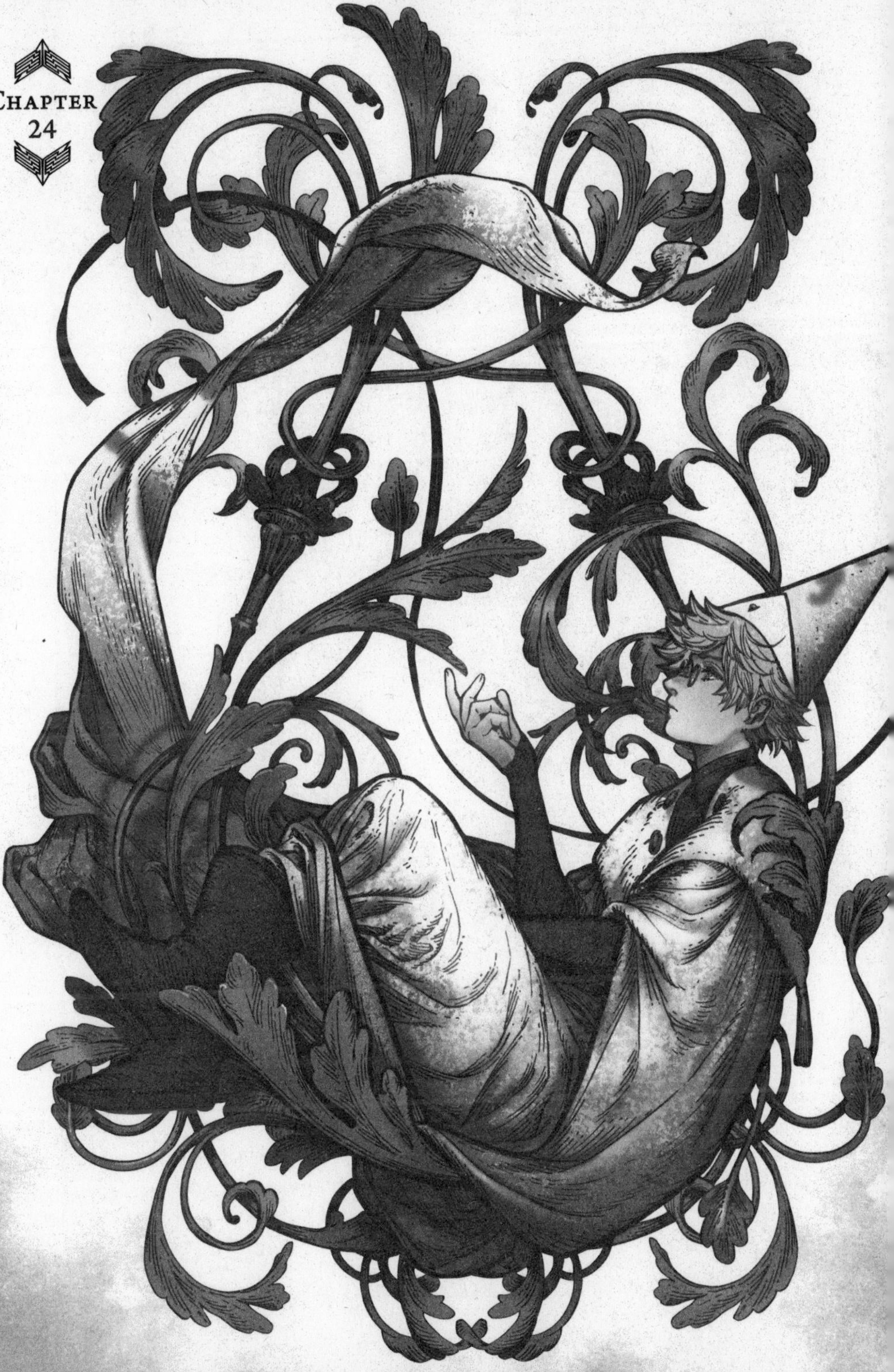

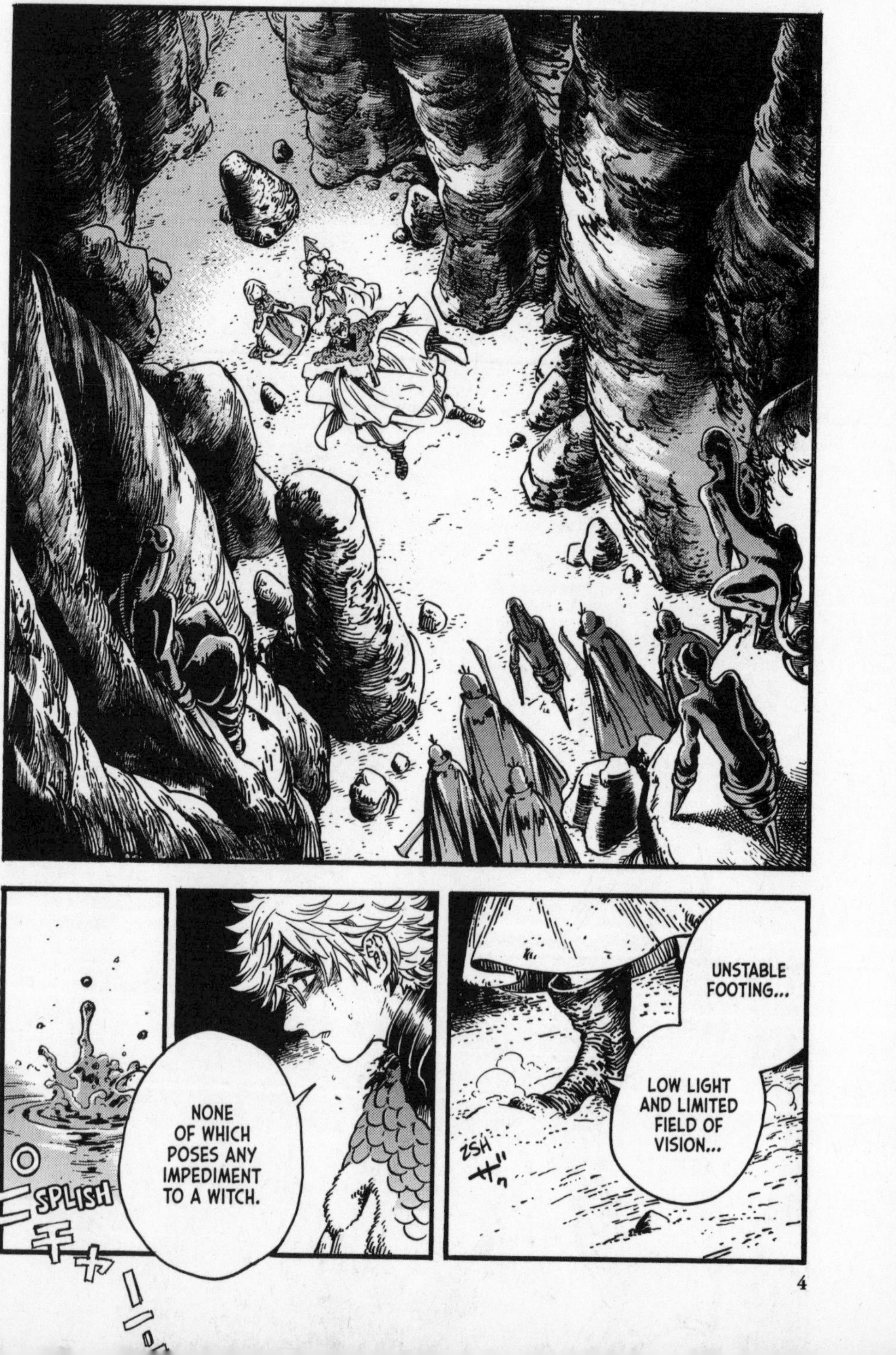
UNSTABLE FOOTING...
LOW LIGHT AND LIMITED FIELD OF VISION...
ZSH
NONE OF WHICH POSES ANY IMPEDIMENT TO A WITCH.
SPLISH

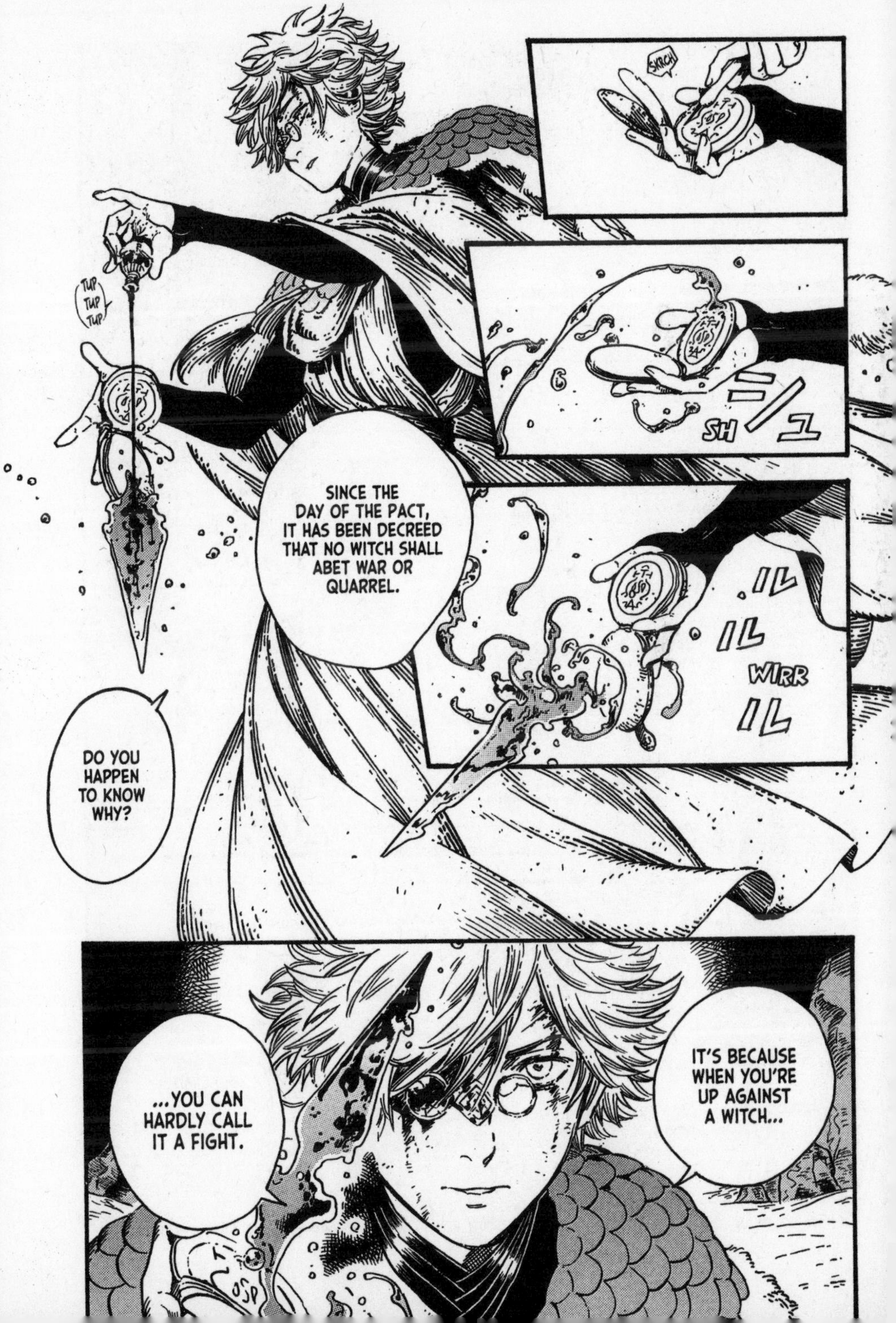
SKRCH
SH
WIRR
TUP TUP TUP
SINCE THE DAY OF THE PACT, IT HAS BEEN DECREED THAT NO WITCH SHALL ABET WAR OR QUARREL.
DO YOU HAPPEN TO KNOW WHY?
IT'S BECAUSE WHEN YOU'RE UP AGAINST A WITCH...
...YOU CAN HARDLY CALL IT A FIGHT.

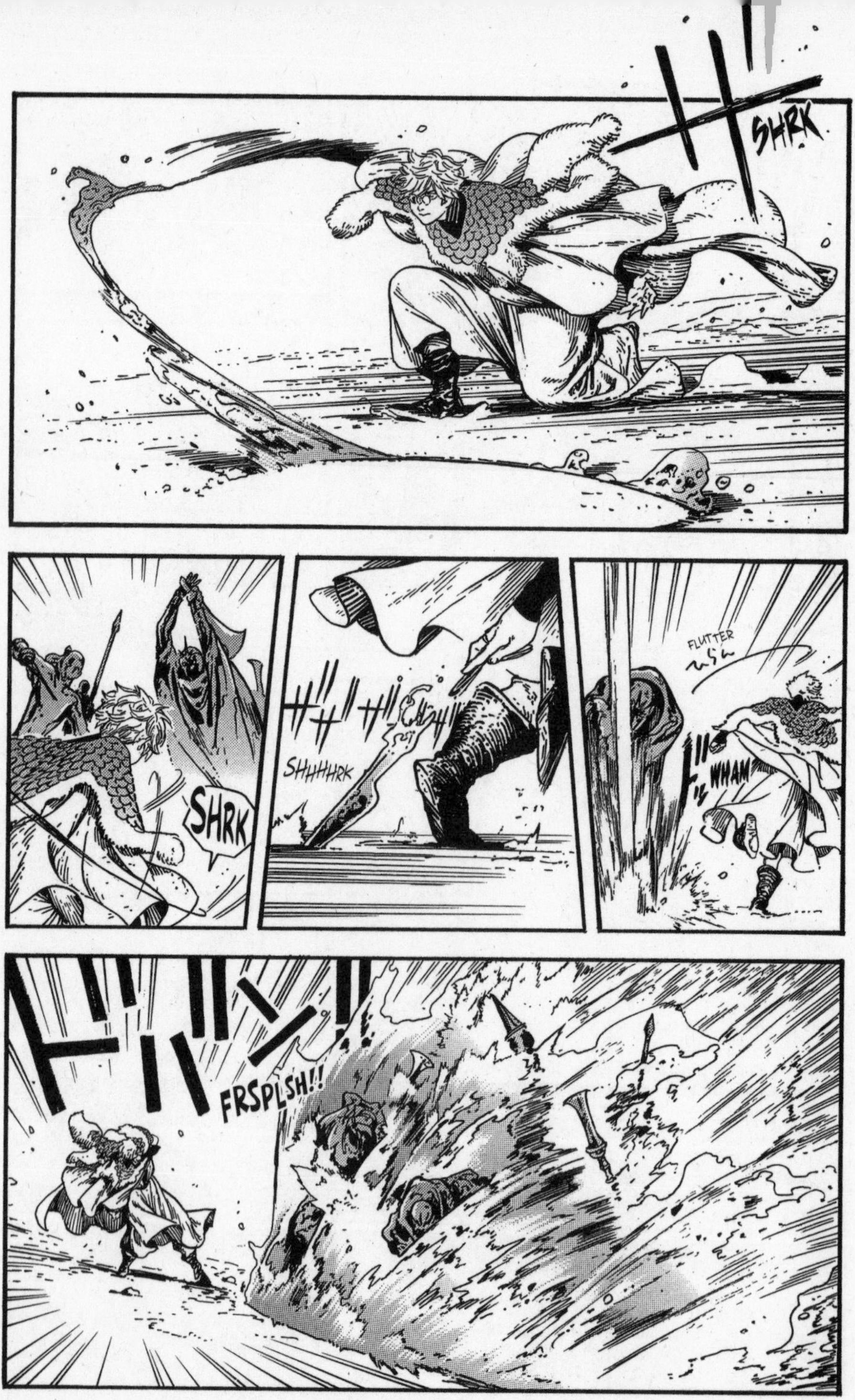
SHRK
FLUTTER
WHAM
SHHHHRK
SHRK
FRSPLSH!!

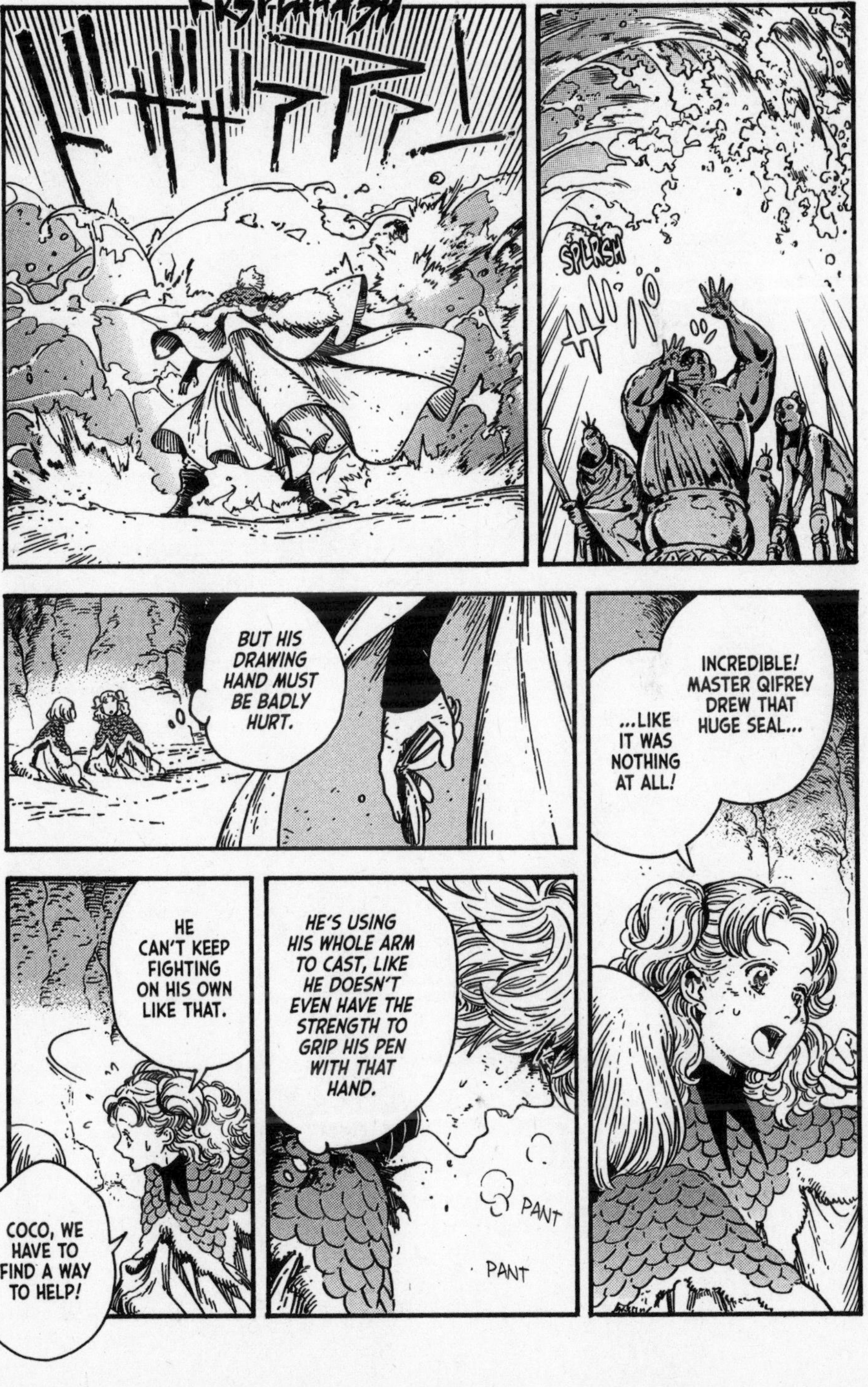
SPLRSH
KRSPLAAASH
ドザザアアー
INCREDIBLE! MASTER QIFREY DREW THAT HUGE SEAL...
...LIKE IT WAS NOTHING AT ALL!
BUT HIS DRAWING HAND MUST BE BADLY HURT.
HE'S USING HIS WHOLE ARM TO CAST, LIKE HE DOESN'T EVEN HAVE THE STRENGTH TO GRIP HIS PEN WITH THAT HAND.
PANT
PANT
HE CAN'T KEEP FIGHTING ON HIS OWN LIKE THAT.
COCO, WE HAVE TO FIND A WAY TO HELP!

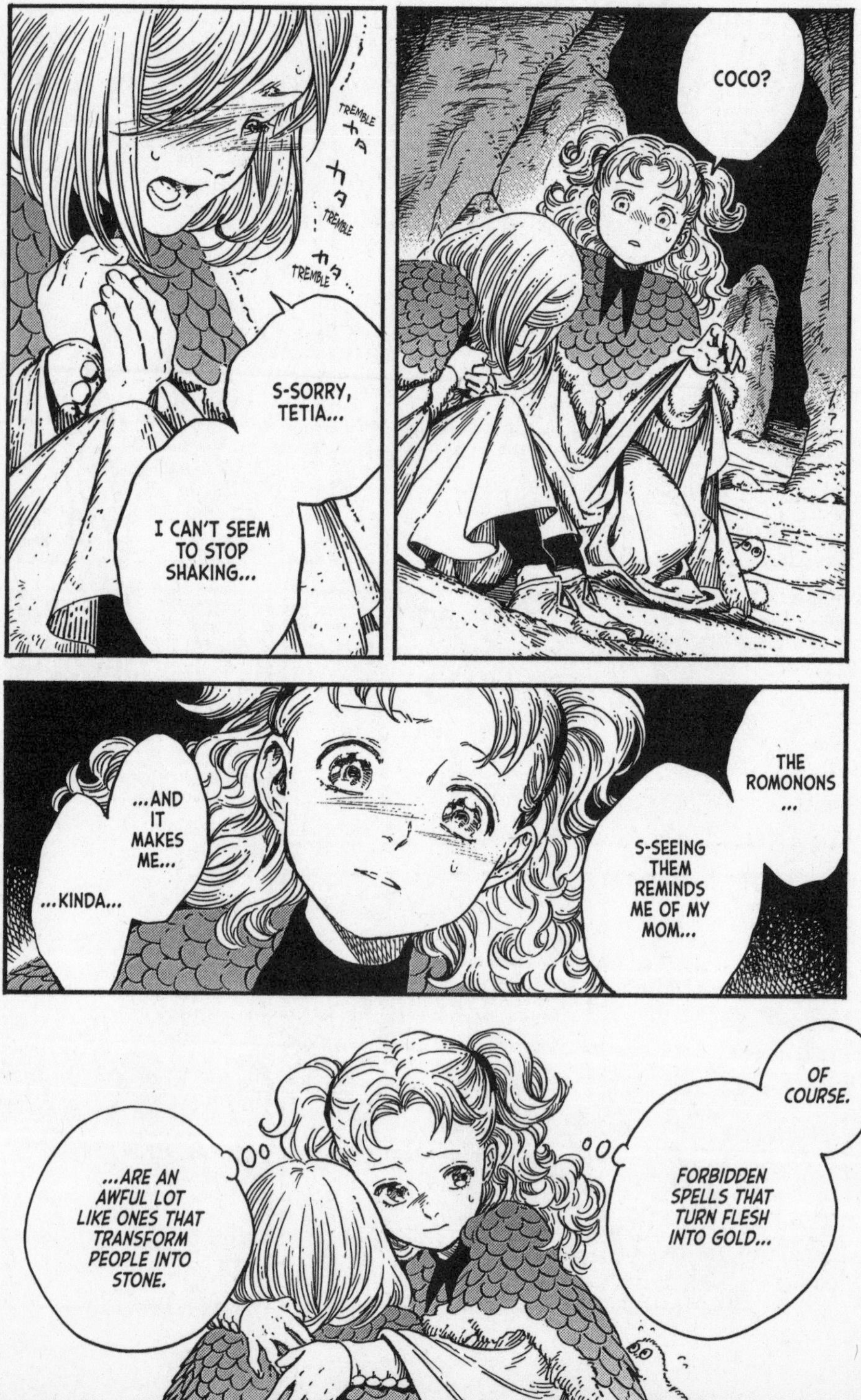
COCO?
TREMBLE カタ
TREMBLE カタ
TREMBLE カタ...
S-SORRY, TETIA...
I CAN'T SEEM TO STOP SHAKING...
THE ROMONONS ...
S-SEEING THEM REMINDS ME OF MY MOM...
...AND IT MAKES ME...
...KINDA...
OF COURSE.
FORBIDDEN SPELLS THAT TURN FLESH INTO GOLD...
...ARE AN AWFUL LOT LIKE ONES THAT TRANSFORM PEOPLE INTO STONE.

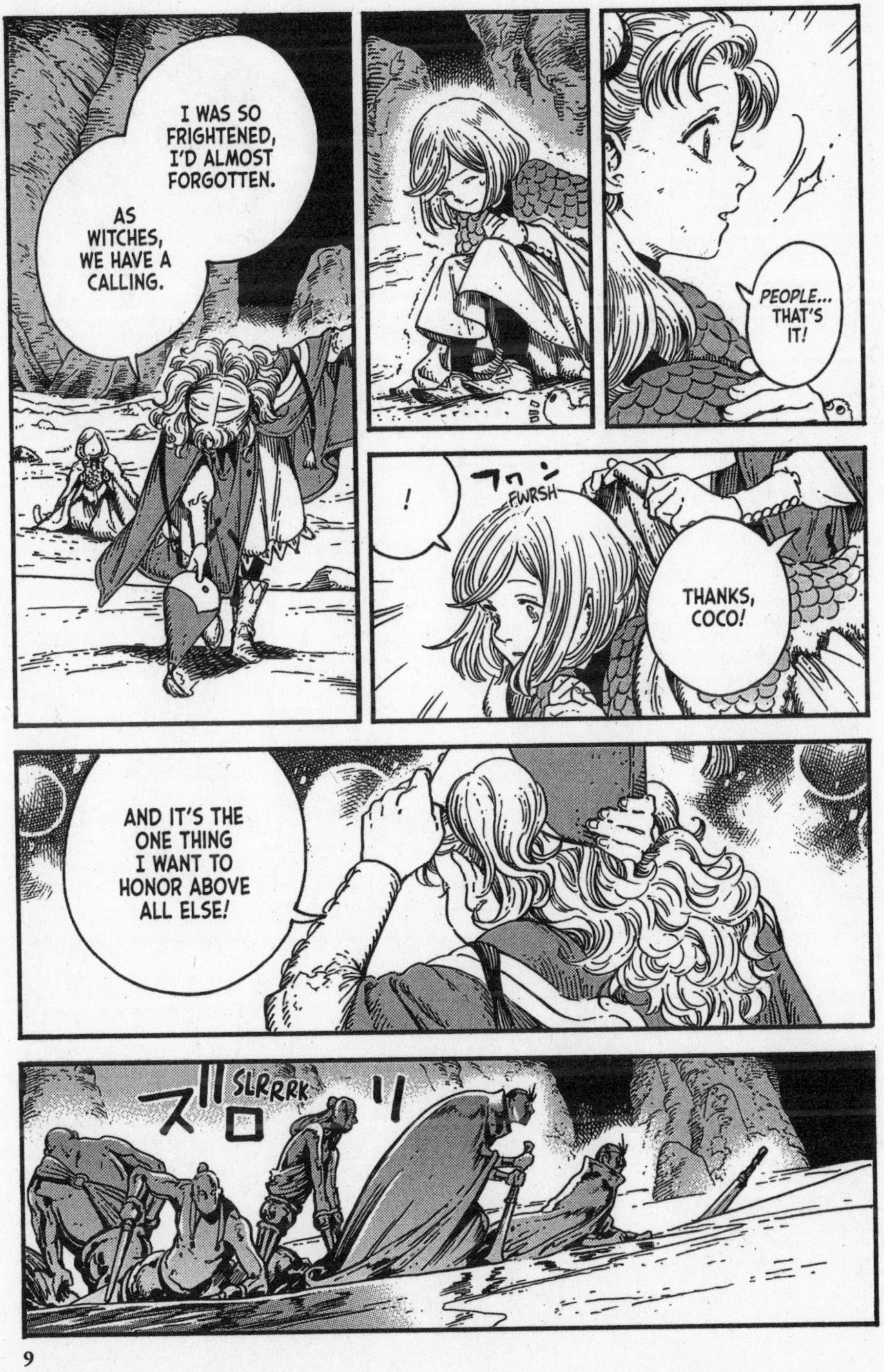
PEOPLE... THAT'S IT!
フワン
FWRSH
!
THANKS, COCO!
I WAS SO FRIGHTENED, I'D ALMOST FORGOTTEN.
AS WITCHES, WE HAVE A CALLING.
AND IT'S THE ONE THING I WANT TO HONOR ABOVE ALL ELSE!
ズロリ
SLRRRK

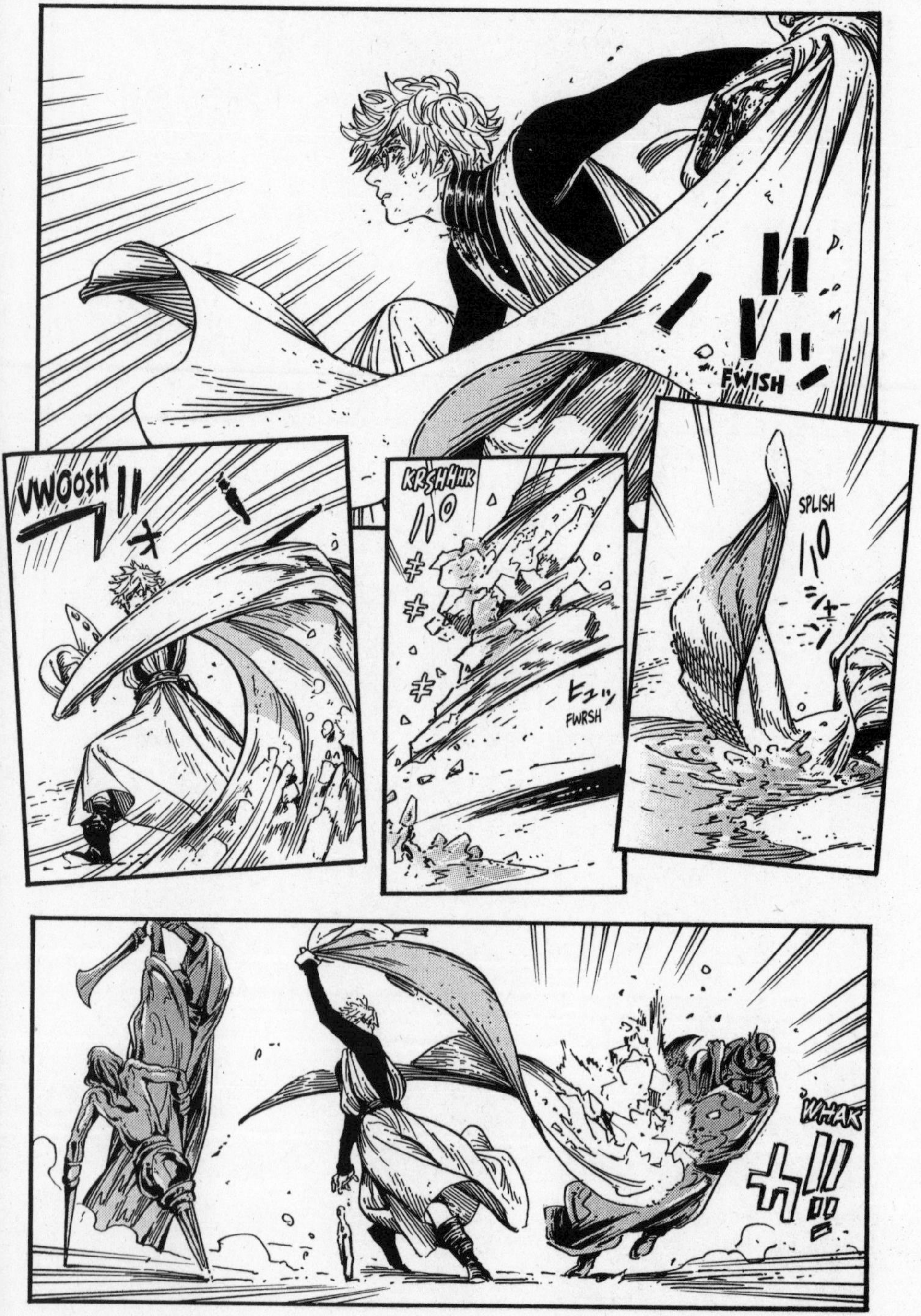
FWISH
SPLISH
KRSHHHK
FWRSH
VWOOSH
WHAK

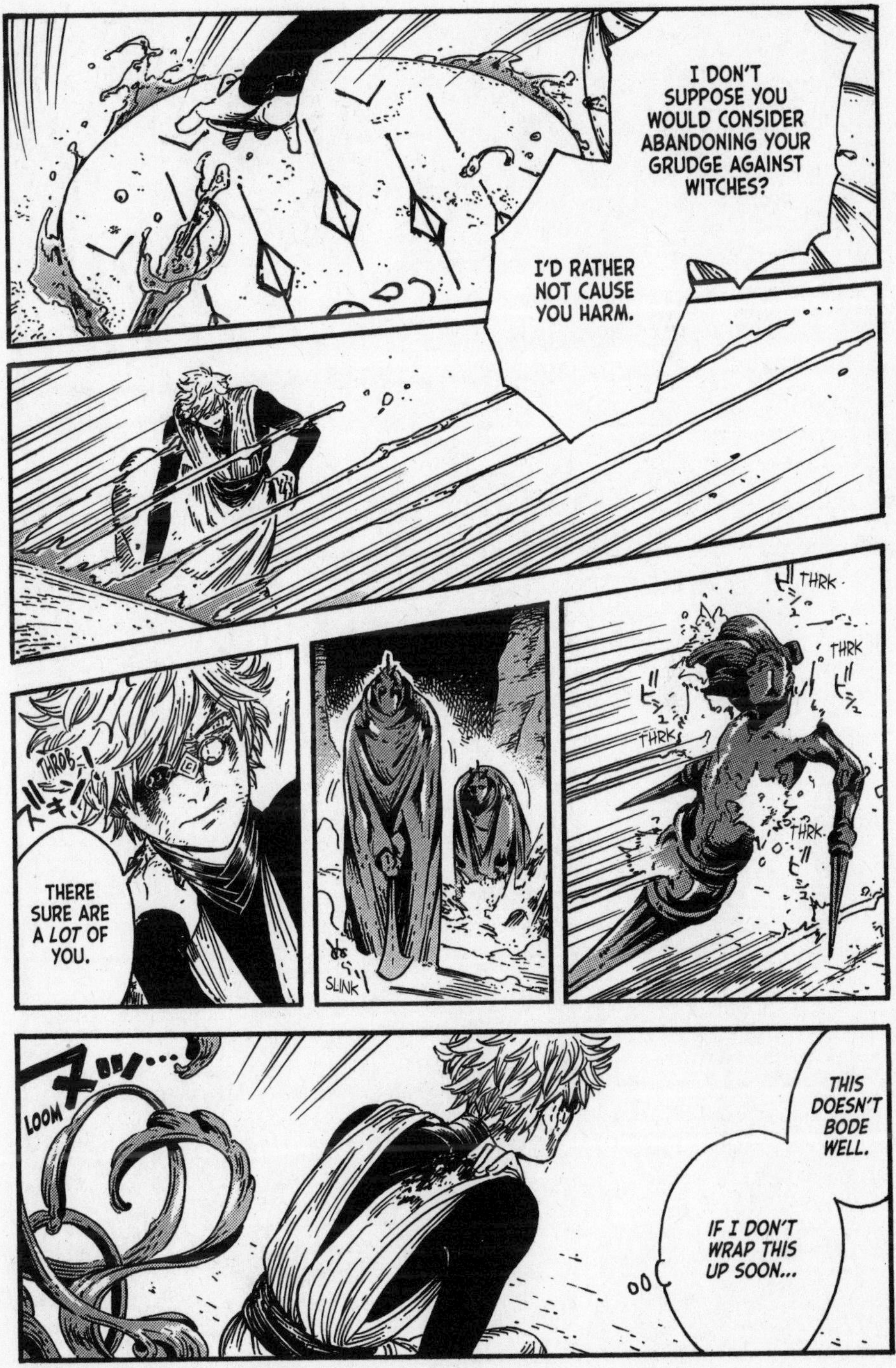
I DON'T SUPPOSE YOU WOULD CONSIDER ABANDONING YOUR GRUDGE AGAINST WITCHES?
I'D RATHER NOT CAUSE YOU HARM.
THRK
THRK
THRK
THRK
SLINK
THROB
THERE SURE ARE A LOT OF YOU.
THIS DOESN'T BODE WELL.
IF I DON'T WRAP THIS UP SOON...
LOOM

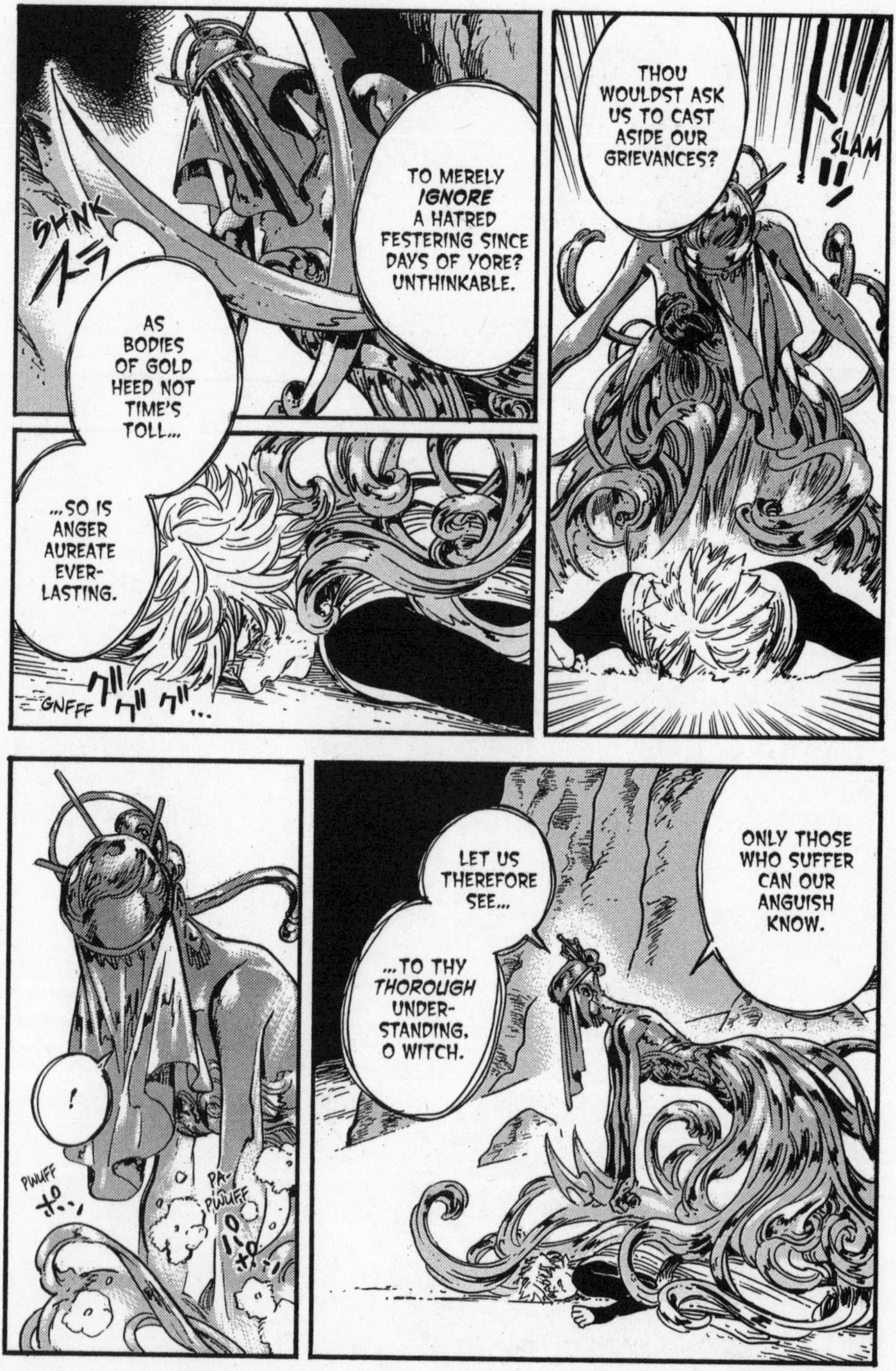
THOU WOULDST ASK US TO CAST ASIDE OUR GRIEVANCES?
SLAM
TO MERELY *IGNORE* A HATRED FESTERING SINCE DAYS OF YORE? UNTHINKABLE.
SHNK
AS BODIES OF GOLD HEED NOT TIME'S TOLL...
...SO IS ANGER AUREATE EVER-LASTING.
GNFFF
ONLY THOSE WHO SUFFER CAN OUR ANGUISH KNOW.
LET US THEREFORE SEE...
...TO THY *THOROUGH* UNDER-STANDING, O WITCH.
!
PWUFF
PA-PWUFF

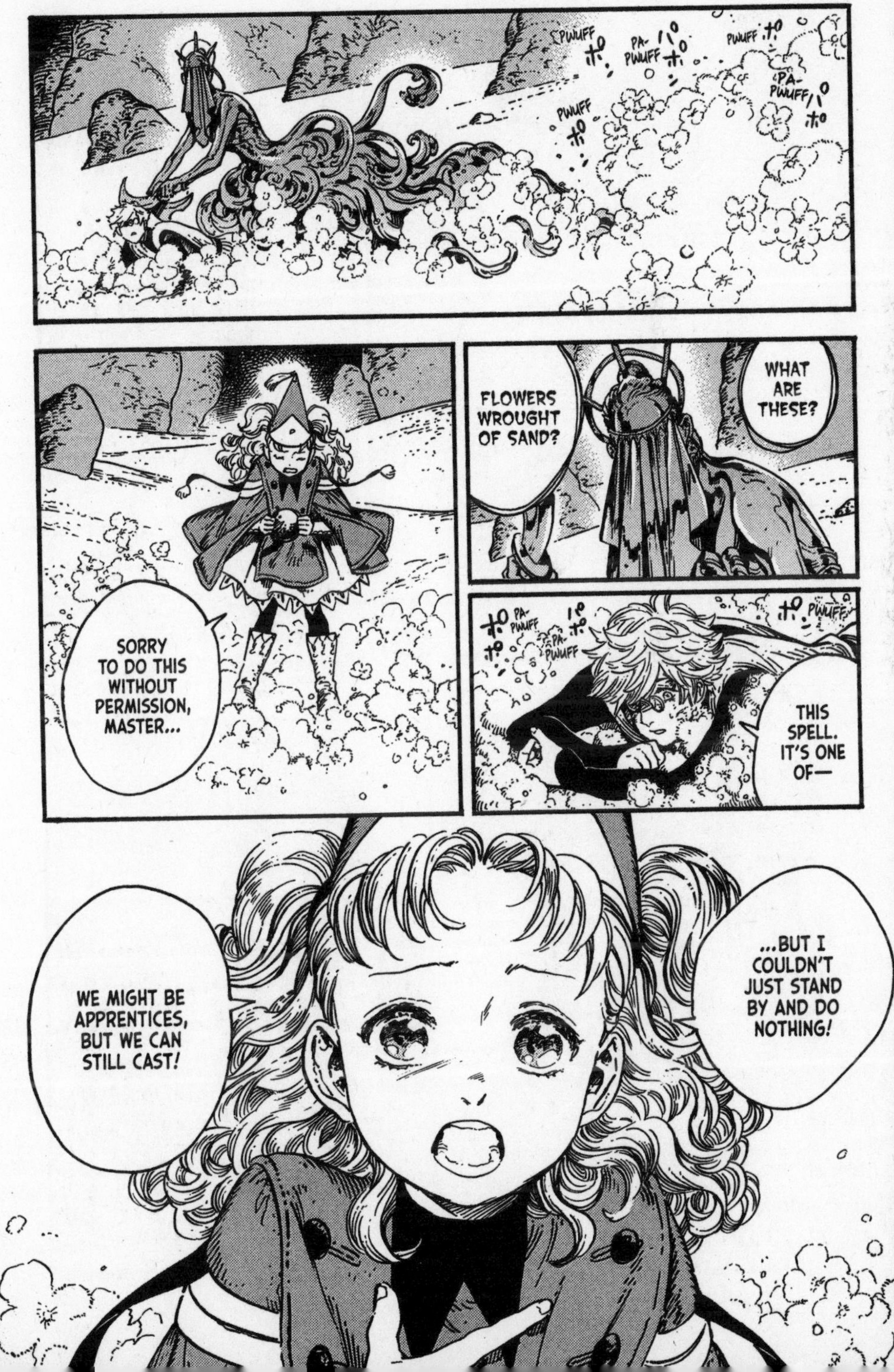
PWUFF
PA-PWUFF
PWUFF
PA-PWUFF
PWUFF
WHAT ARE THESE?
FLOWERS WROUGHT OF SAND?
PA-PWUFF
PA-PWUFF
PWUFF
THIS SPELL. IT'S ONE OF—
SORRY TO DO THIS WITHOUT PERMISSION, MASTER...
...BUT I COULDN'T JUST STAND BY AND DO NOTHING!
WE MIGHT BE APPRENTICES, BUT WE CAN STILL CAST!

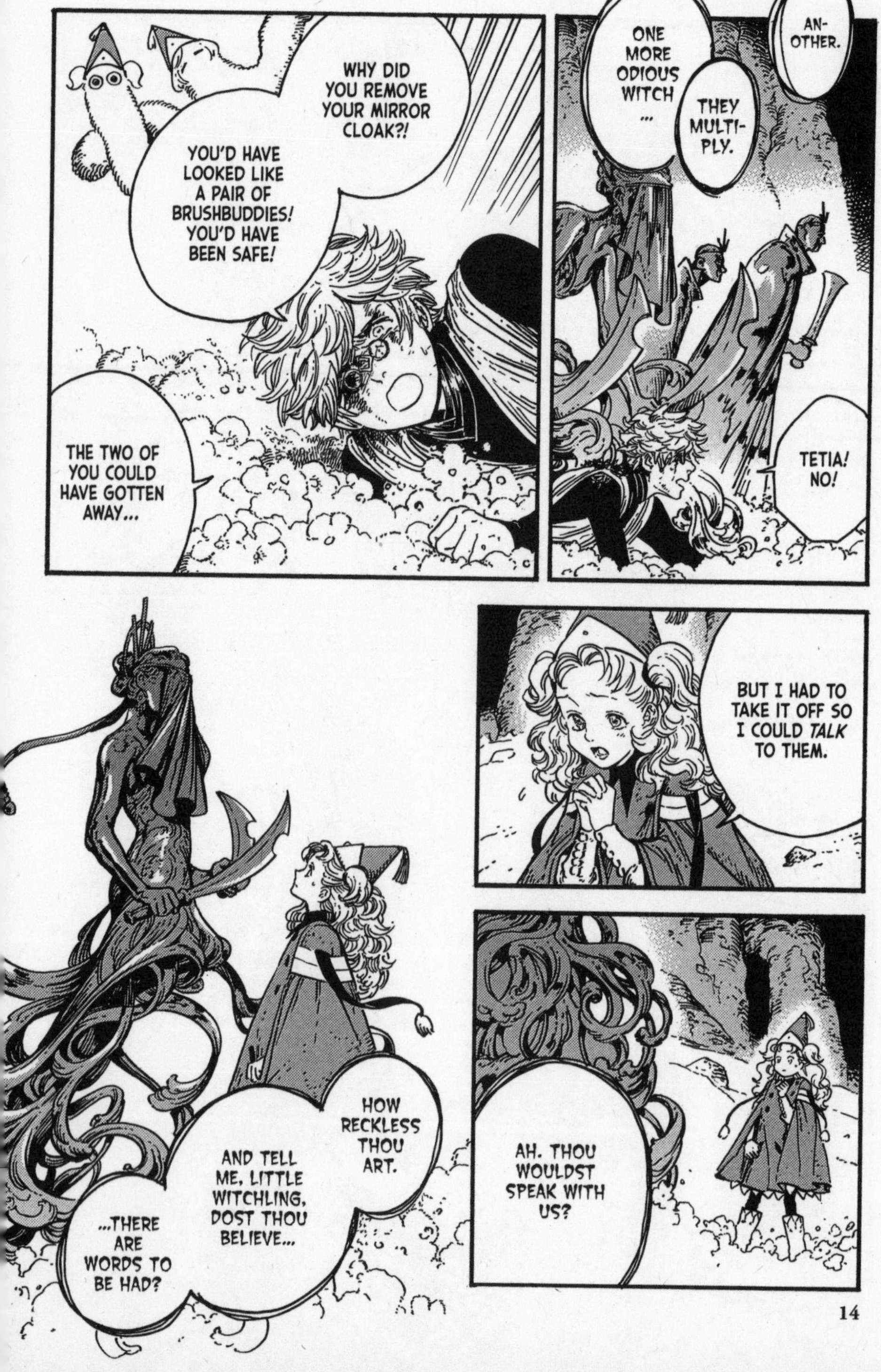
AN-OTHER.
ONE MORE ODIOUS WITCH ...
THEY MULTI-PLY.
TETIA! NO!
WHY DID YOU REMOVE YOUR MIRROR CLOAK?!
YOU'D HAVE LOOKED LIKE A PAIR OF BRUSHBUDDIES! YOU'D HAVE BEEN SAFE!
THE TWO OF YOU COULD HAVE GOTTEN AWAY...
BUT I HAD TO TAKE IT OFF SO I COULD *TALK* TO THEM.
AH. THOU WOULDST SPEAK WITH US?
HOW RECKLESS THOU ART.
AND TELL ME, LITTLE WITCHLING, DOST THOU BELIEVE...
...THERE ARE WORDS TO BE HAD?

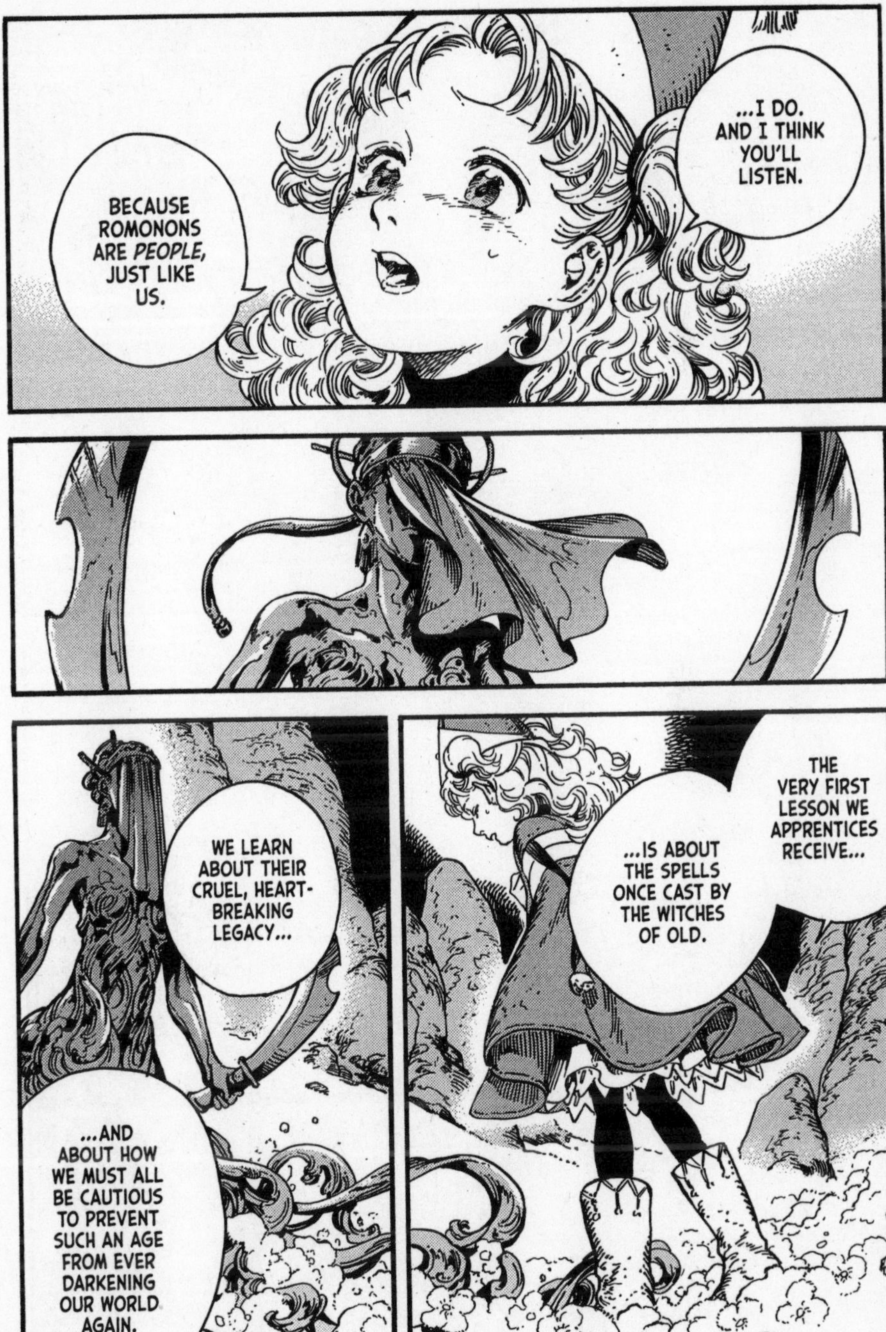
...I DO. AND I THINK YOU'LL LISTEN.
BECAUSE ROMONONS ARE *PEOPLE*, JUST LIKE US.
THE VERY FIRST LESSON WE APPRENTICES RECEIVE...
...IS ABOUT THE SPELLS ONCE CAST BY THE WITCHES OF OLD.
WE LEARN ABOUT THEIR CRUEL, HEART-BREAKING LEGACY...
...AND ABOUT HOW WE MUST ALL BE CAUTIOUS TO PREVENT SUCH AN AGE FROM EVER DARKENING OUR WORLD AGAIN.

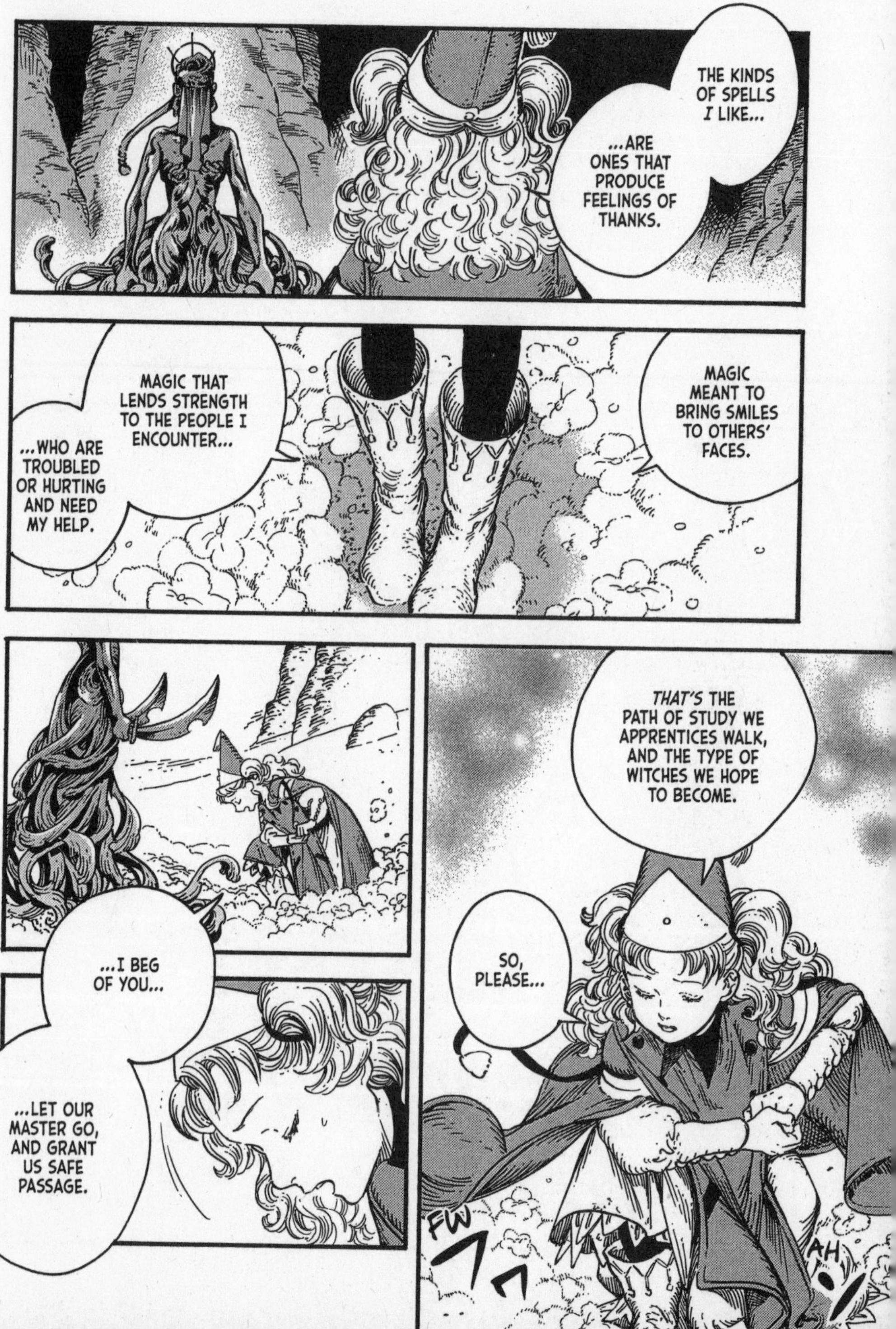
THE KINDS OF SPELLS *I* LIKE...
...ARE ONES THAT PRODUCE FEELINGS OF THANKS.
MAGIC MEANT TO BRING SMILES TO OTHERS' FACES.
MAGIC THAT LENDS STRENGTH TO THE PEOPLE I ENCOUNTER...
...WHO ARE TROUBLED OR HURTING AND NEED MY HELP.
THAT'S THE PATH OF STUDY WE APPRENTICES WALK, AND THE TYPE OF WITCHES WE HOPE TO BECOME.
SO, PLEASE...
FW
AH!
...I BEG OF YOU...
...LET OUR MASTER GO, AND GRANT US SAFE PASSAGE.

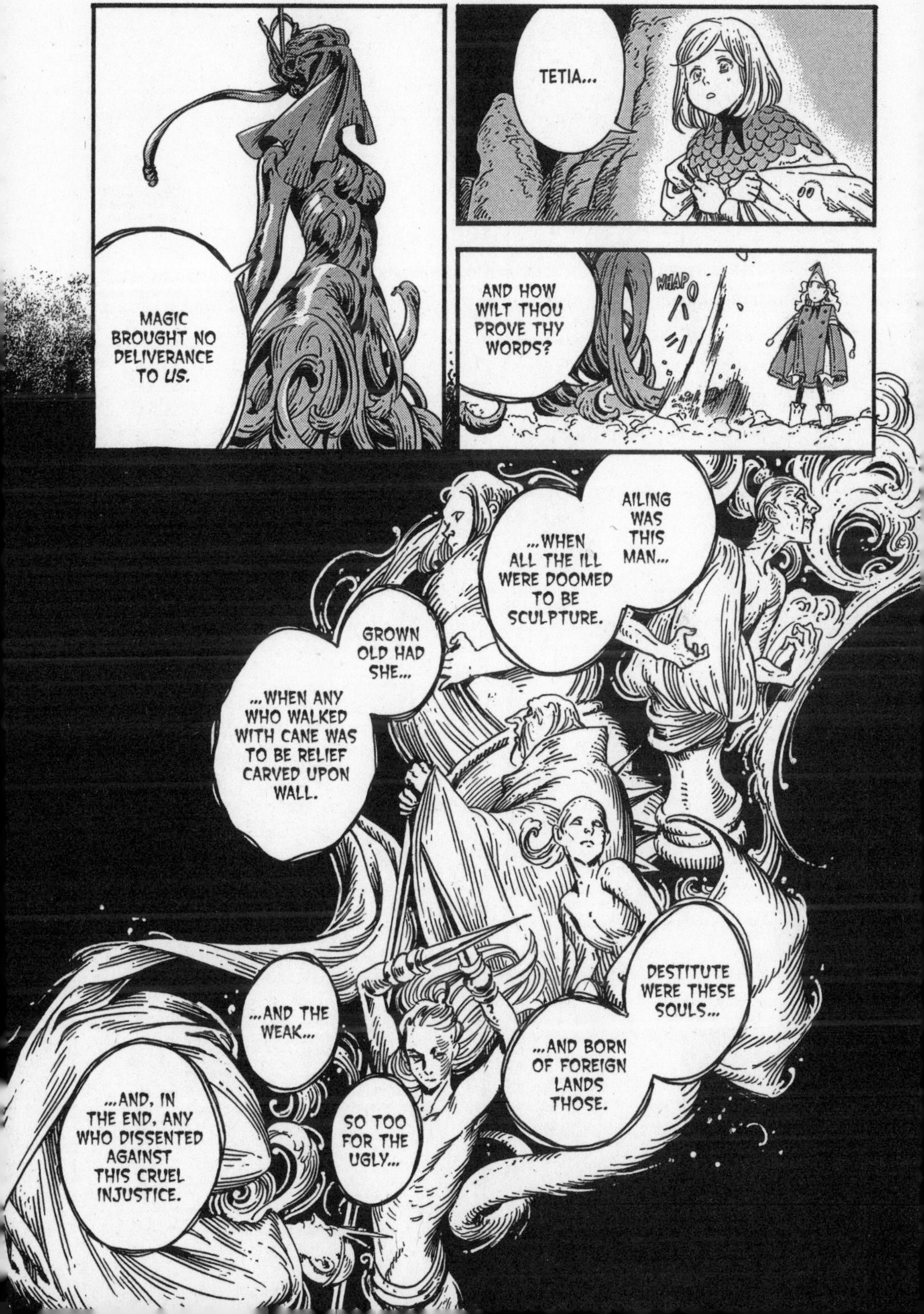
TETIA...
AND HOW WILT THOU PROVE THY WORDS?
WHAP
MAGIC BROUGHT NO DELIVERANCE TO US.
AILING WAS THIS MAN...
...WHEN ALL THE ILL WERE DOOMED TO BE SCULPTURE.
GROWN OLD HAD SHE...
...WHEN ANY WHO WALKED WITH CANE WAS TO BE RELIEF CARVED UPON WALL.
DESTITUTE WERE THESE SOULS...
...AND BORN OF FOREIGN LANDS THOSE.
...AND THE WEAK...
SO TOO FOR THE UGLY...
...AND, IN THE END, ANY WHO DISSENTED AGAINST THIS CRUEL INJUSTICE.

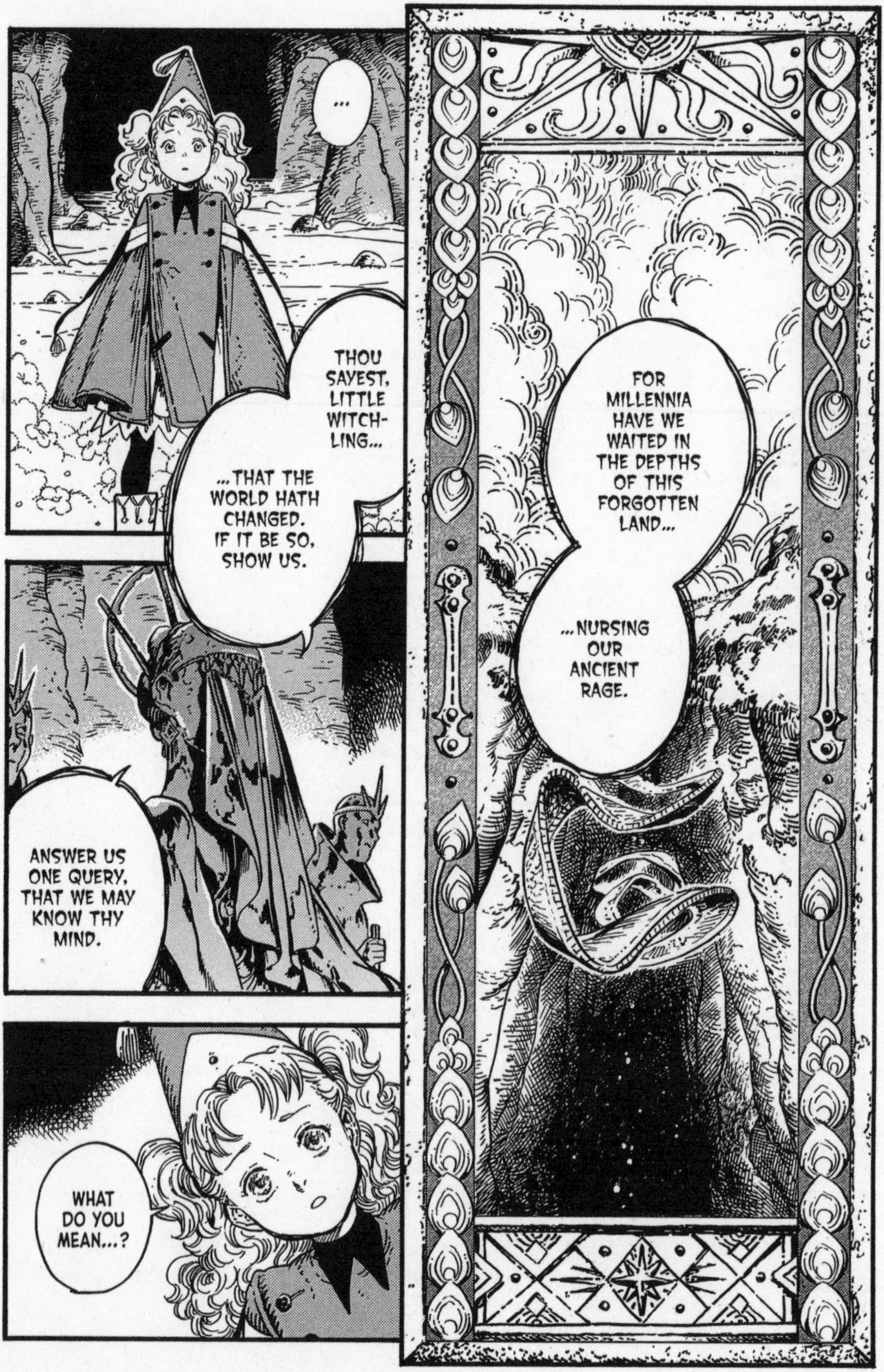
FOR MILLENNIA HAVE WE WAITED IN THE DEPTHS OF THIS FORGOTTEN LAND...
...NURSING OUR ANCIENT RAGE.
...
THOU SAYEST, LITTLE WITCHLING...
...THAT THE WORLD HATH CHANGED. IF IT BE SO, SHOW US.
ANSWER US ONE QUERY, THAT WE MAY KNOW THY MIND.
WHAT DO YOU MEAN...?

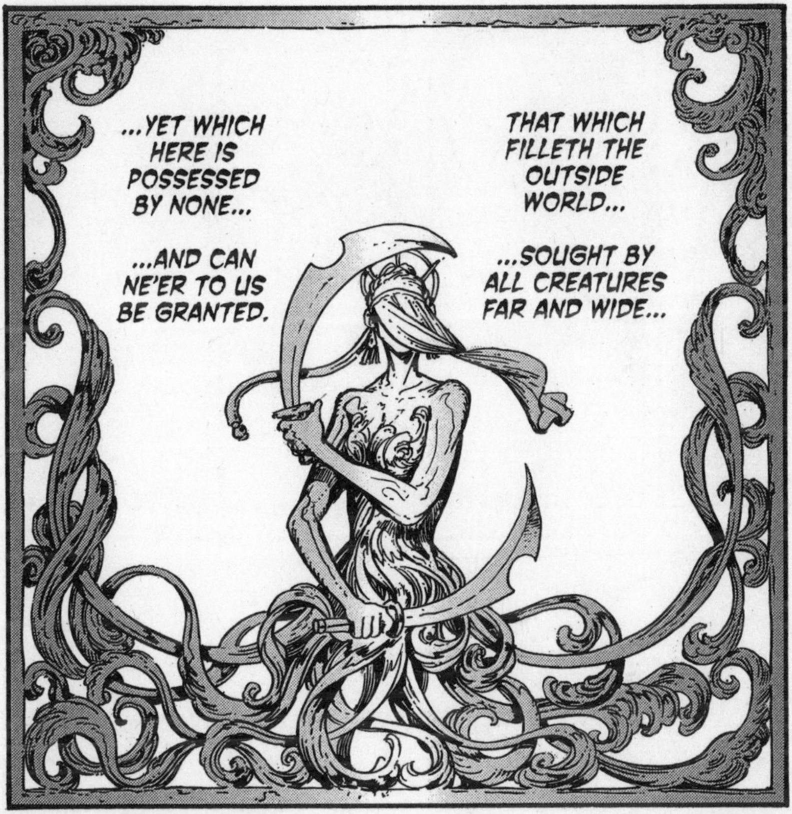
THAT WHICH FILLETH THE OUTSIDE WORLD...
...SOUGHT BY ALL CREATURES FAR AND WIDE...
...YET WHICH HERE IS POSSESSED BY NONE...
...AND CAN NE'ER TO US BE GRANTED.
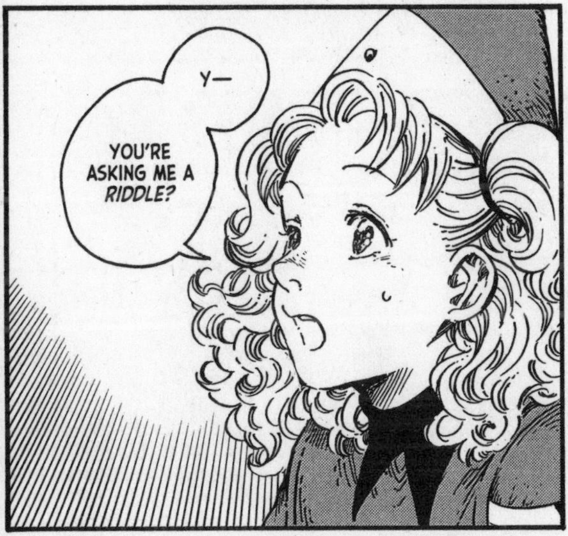
Y—
YOU'RE ASKING ME A *RIDDLE?*
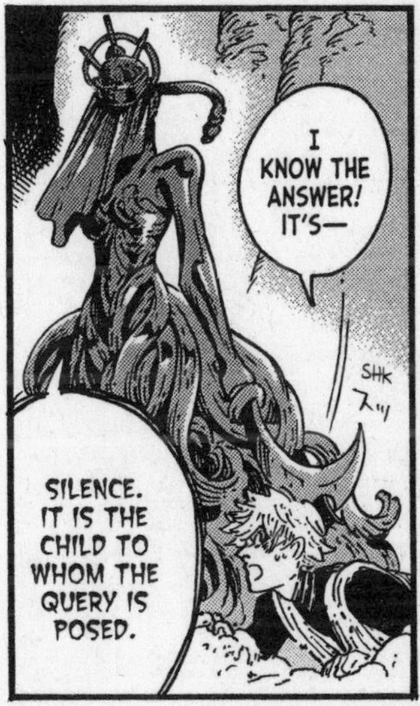
I KNOW THE ANSWER! IT'S—
SHK スッ
SILENCE. IT IS THE CHILD TO WHOM THE QUERY IS POSED.

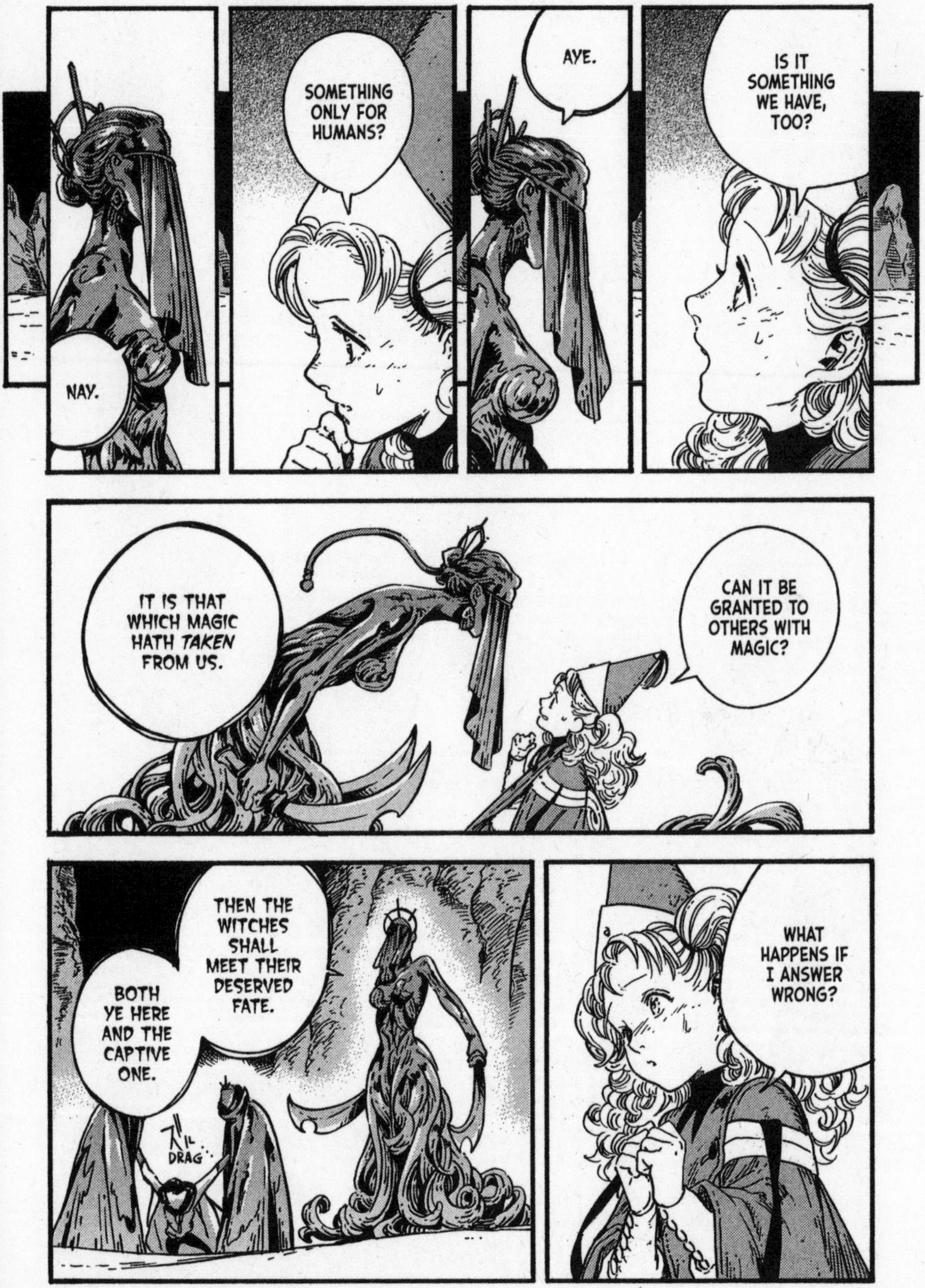
IS IT SOMETHING WE HAVE, TOO?
AYE.
SOMETHING ONLY FOR HUMANS?
NAY.
IT IS THAT WHICH MAGIC HATH *TAKEN* FROM US.
CAN IT BE GRANTED TO OTHERS WITH MAGIC?
WHAT HAPPENS IF I ANSWER WRONG?
THEN THE WITCHES SHALL MEET THEIR DESERVED FATE.
BOTH YE HERE AND THE CAPTIVE ONE.
DRAG

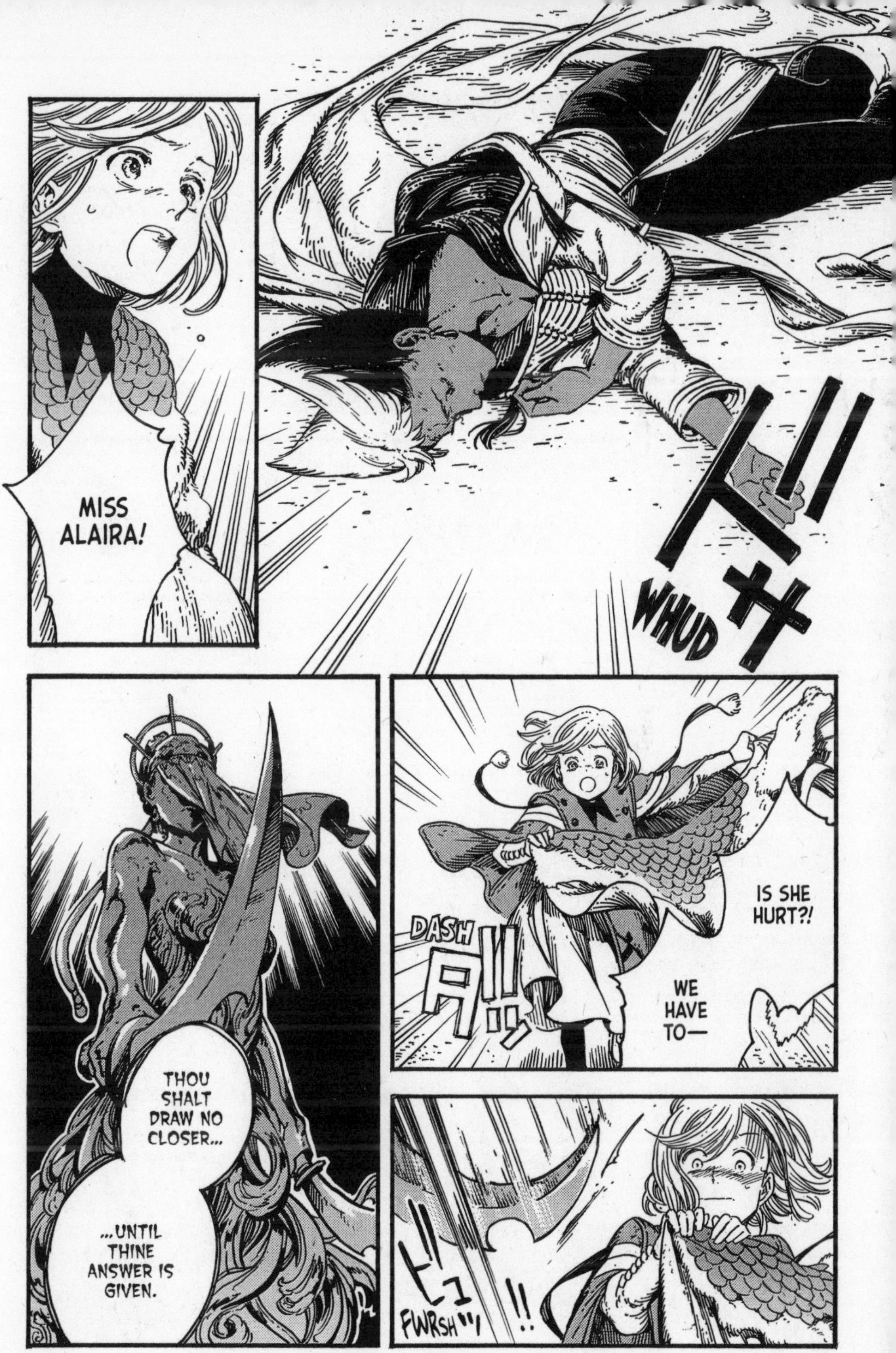
WHUD
MISS ALAIRA!
IS SHE HURT?!
WE HAVE TO—
DASH
FWRSH
THOU SHALT DRAW NO CLOSER...
...UNTIL THINE ANSWER IS GIVEN.

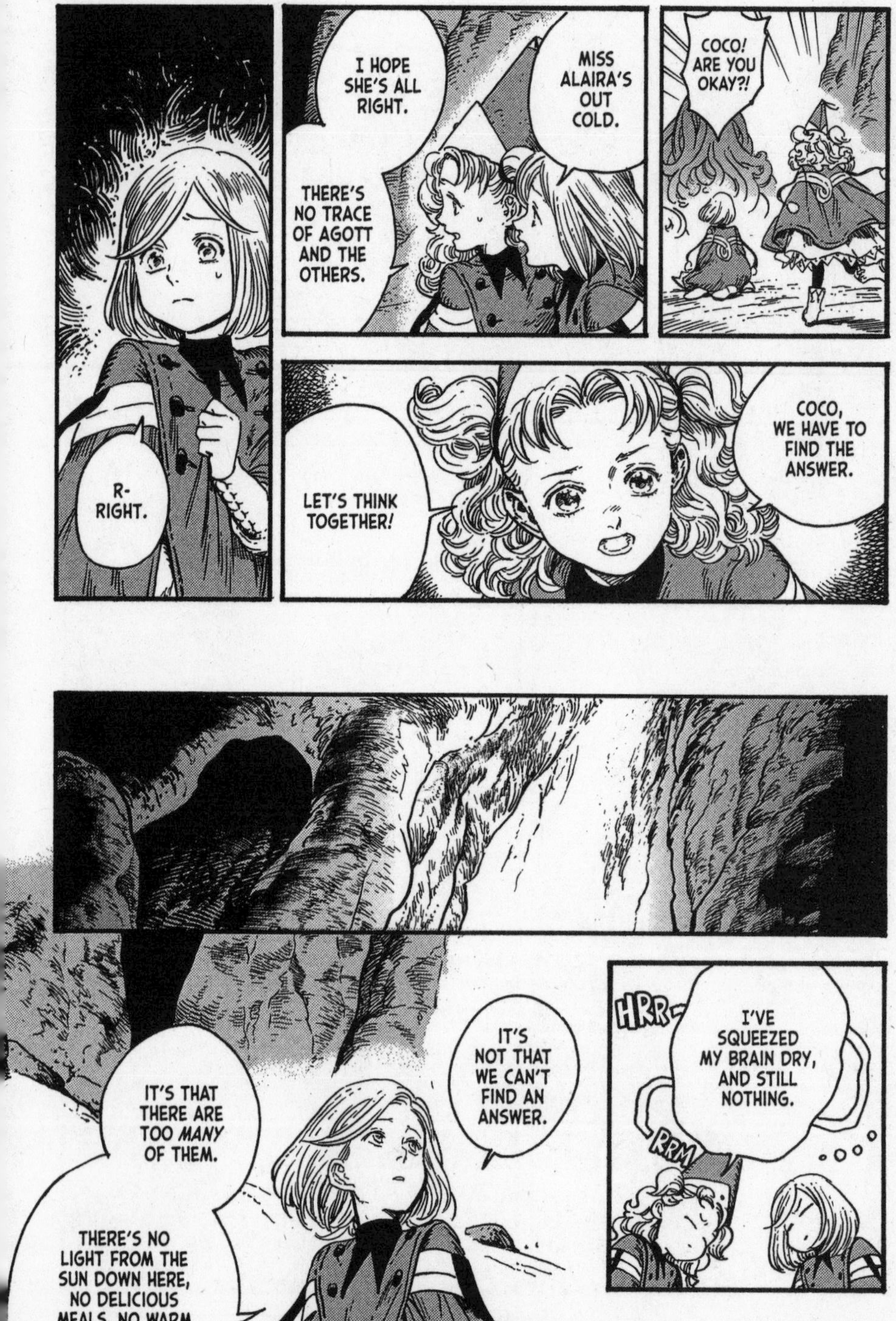
COCO! ARE YOU OKAY?!
MISS ALAIRA'S OUT COLD.
I HOPE SHE'S ALL RIGHT.
THERE'S NO TRACE OF AGOTT AND THE OTHERS.
COCO, WE HAVE TO FIND THE ANSWER.
LET'S THINK TOGETHER!
R- RIGHT.
HRR-
RRM
I'VE SQUEEZED MY BRAIN DRY, AND STILL NOTHING.
IT'S NOT THAT WE CAN'T FIND AN ANSWER.
IT'S THAT THERE ARE TOO *MANY* OF THEM.
THERE'S NO LIGHT FROM THE SUN DOWN HERE, NO DELICIOUS MEALS, NO WARM BEDS...

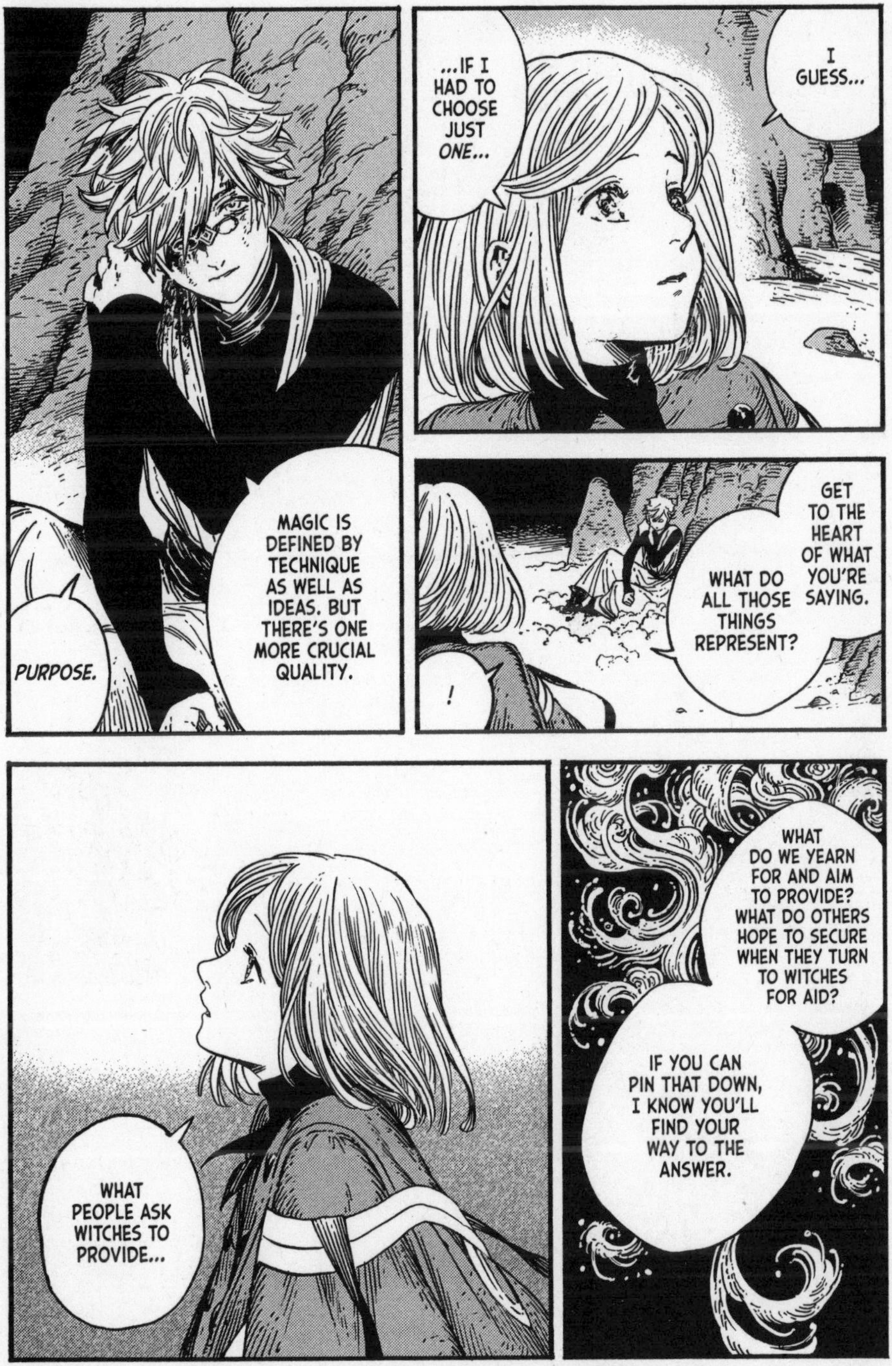
I GUESS...
...IF I HAD TO CHOOSE JUST *ONE*...
GET TO THE HEART OF WHAT YOU'RE SAYING.
WHAT DO ALL THOSE THINGS REPRESENT?
!
MAGIC IS DEFINED BY TECHNIQUE AS WELL AS IDEAS. BUT THERE'S ONE MORE CRUCIAL QUALITY.
PURPOSE.
WHAT DO WE YEARN FOR AND AIM TO PROVIDE? WHAT DO OTHERS HOPE TO SECURE WHEN THEY TURN TO WITCHES FOR AID?
IF YOU CAN PIN THAT DOWN, I KNOW YOU'LL FIND YOUR WAY TO THE ANSWER.
WHAT PEOPLE ASK WITCHES TO PROVIDE...

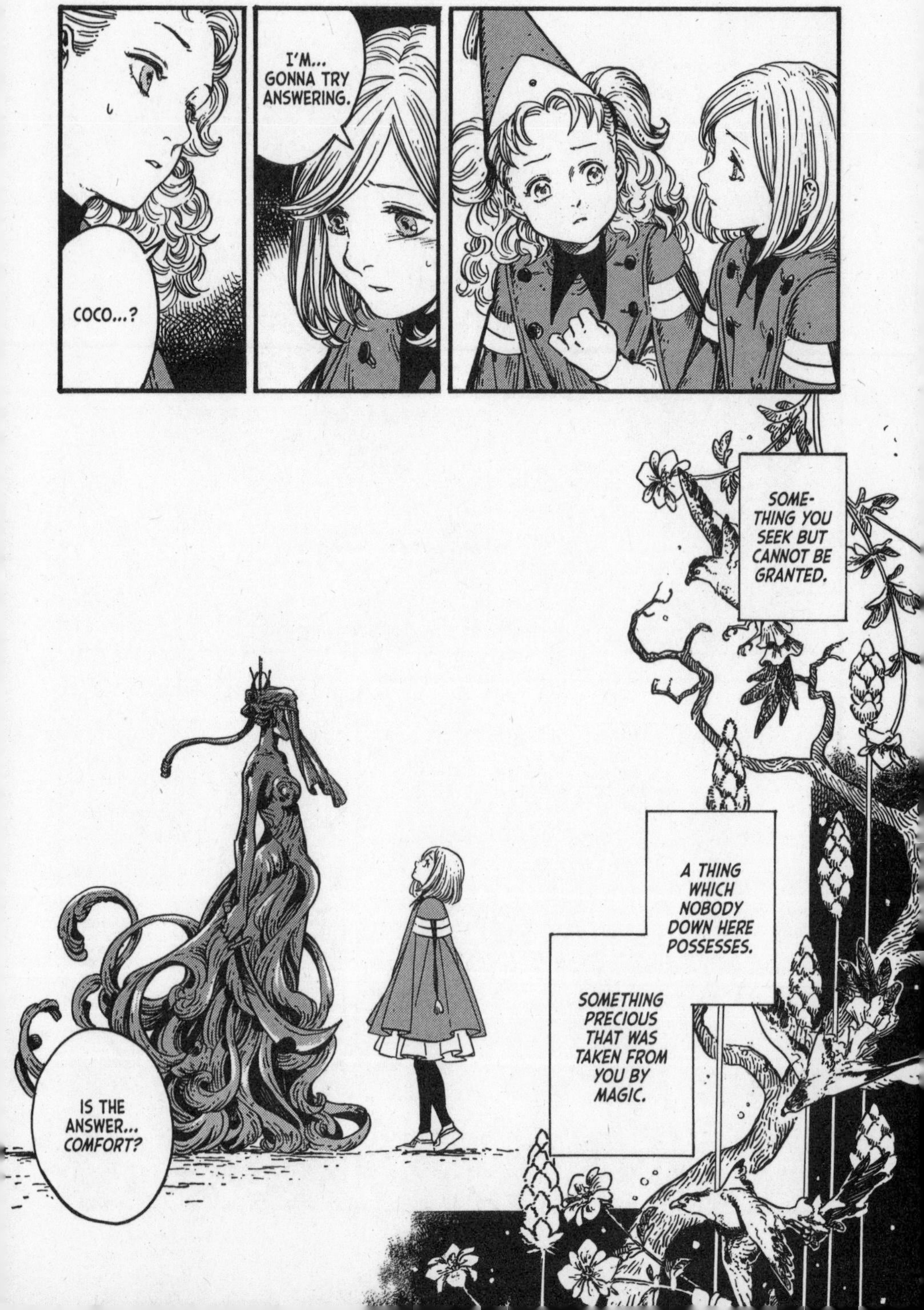
I'M... GONNA TRY ANSWERING.
COCO...?
SOME-THING YOU SEEK BUT CANNOT BE GRANTED.
A THING WHICH NOBODY DOWN HERE POSSESSES.
SOMETHING PRECIOUS THAT WAS TAKEN FROM YOU BY MAGIC.
IS THE ANSWER... COMFORT?

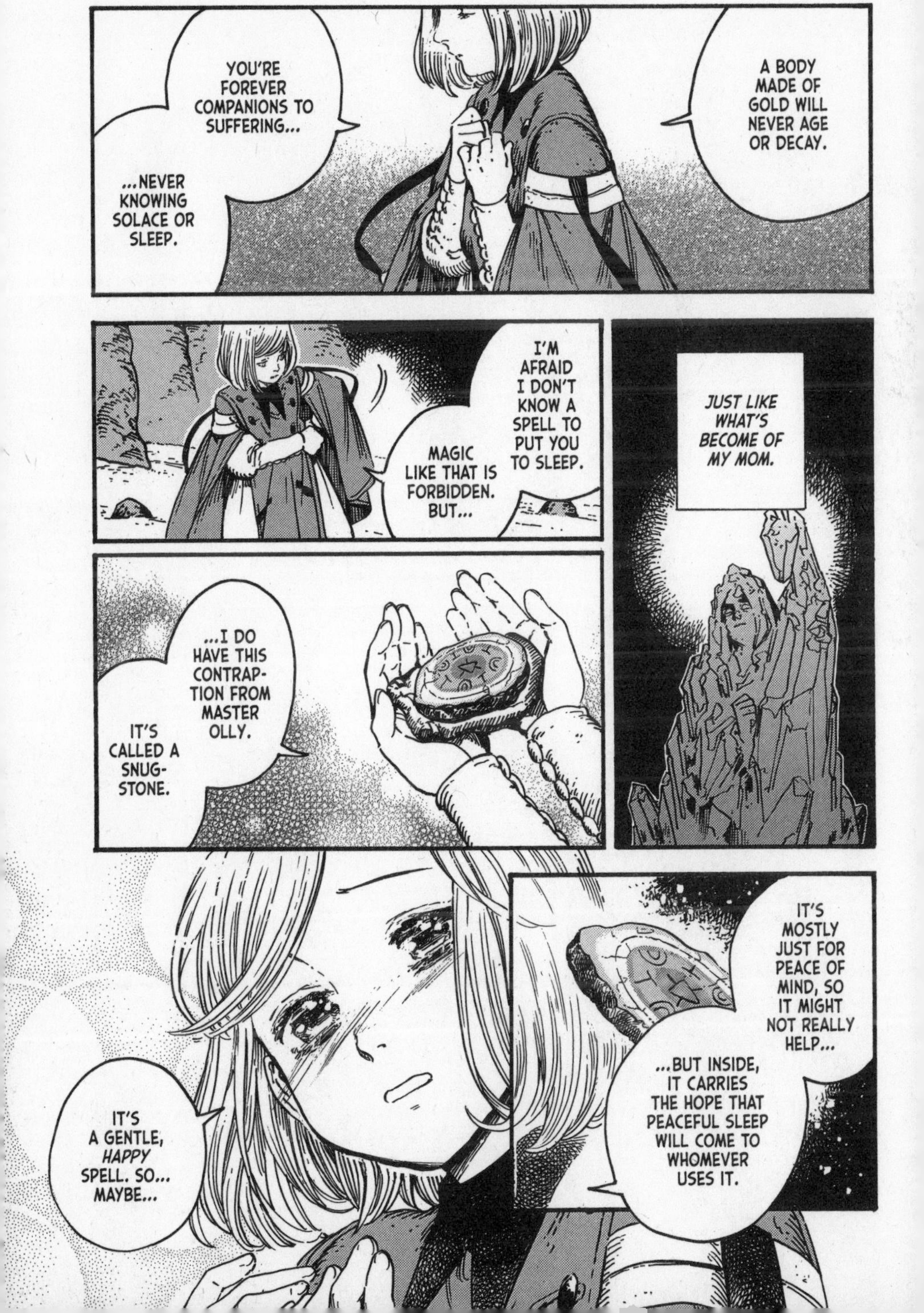
A BODY MADE OF GOLD WILL NEVER AGE OR DECAY.
YOU'RE FOREVER COMPANIONS TO SUFFERING...
...NEVER KNOWING SOLACE OR SLEEP.
JUST LIKE WHAT'S BECOME OF MY MOM.
I'M AFRAID I DON'T KNOW A SPELL TO PUT YOU TO SLEEP.
MAGIC LIKE THAT IS FORBIDDEN. BUT...
...I DO HAVE THIS CONTRAP-TION FROM MASTER OLLY.
IT'S CALLED A SNUG-STONE.
IT'S MOSTLY JUST FOR PEACE OF MIND, SO IT MIGHT NOT REALLY HELP...
...BUT INSIDE, IT CARRIES THE HOPE THAT PEACEFUL SLEEP WILL COME TO WHOMEVER USES IT.
IT'S A GENTLE, *HAPPY* SPELL. SO... MAYBE...

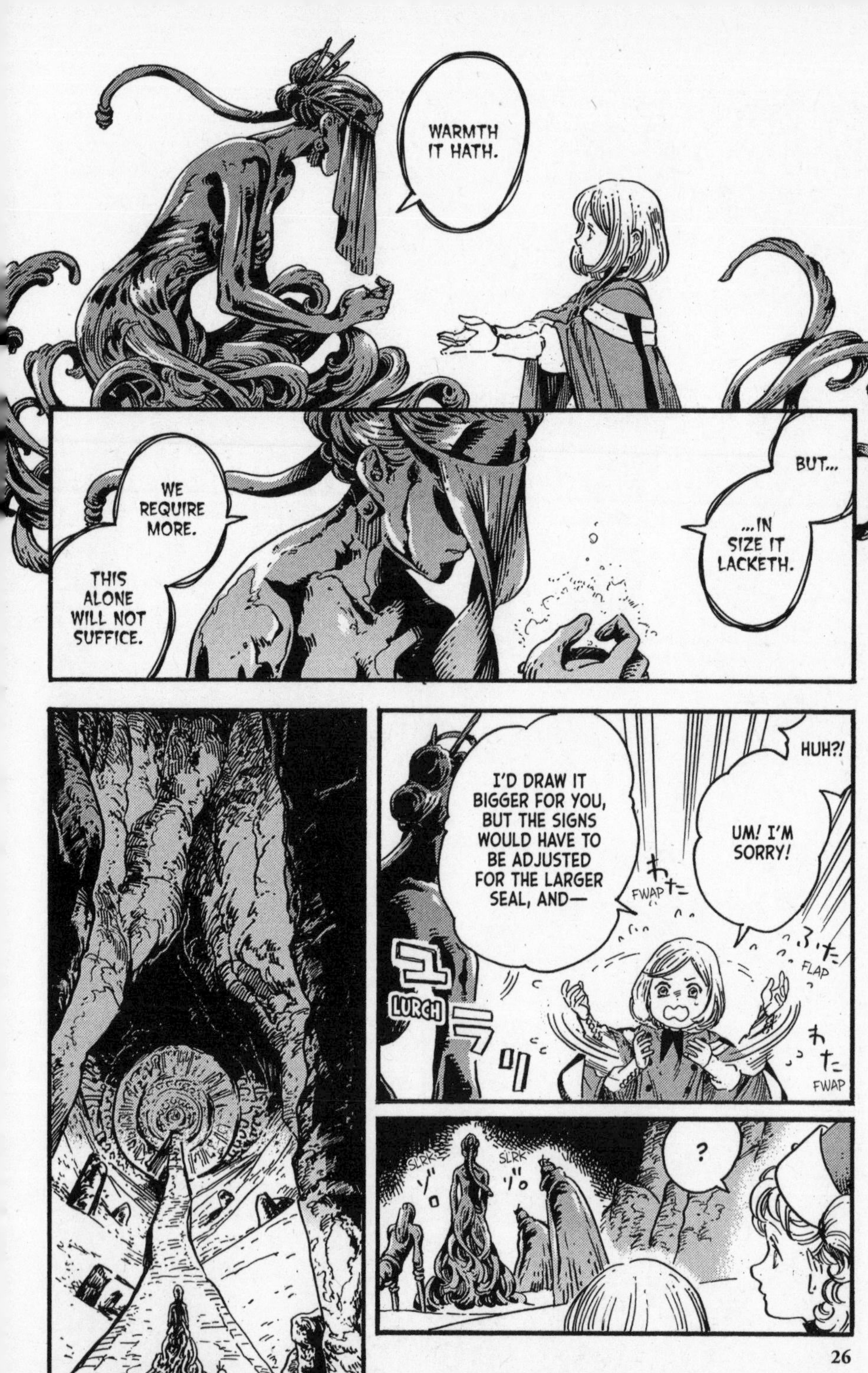
WARMTH IT HATH.
BUT...
...IN SIZE IT LACKETH.
WE REQUIRE MORE.
THIS ALONE WILL NOT SUFFICE.
HUH?!
UM! I'M SORRY!
FLAP
FWAP
FWAP
I'D DRAW IT BIGGER FOR YOU, BUT THE SIGNS WOULD HAVE TO BE ADJUSTED FOR THE LARGER SEAL, AND—
LURCH
?
SLRK
SLRK

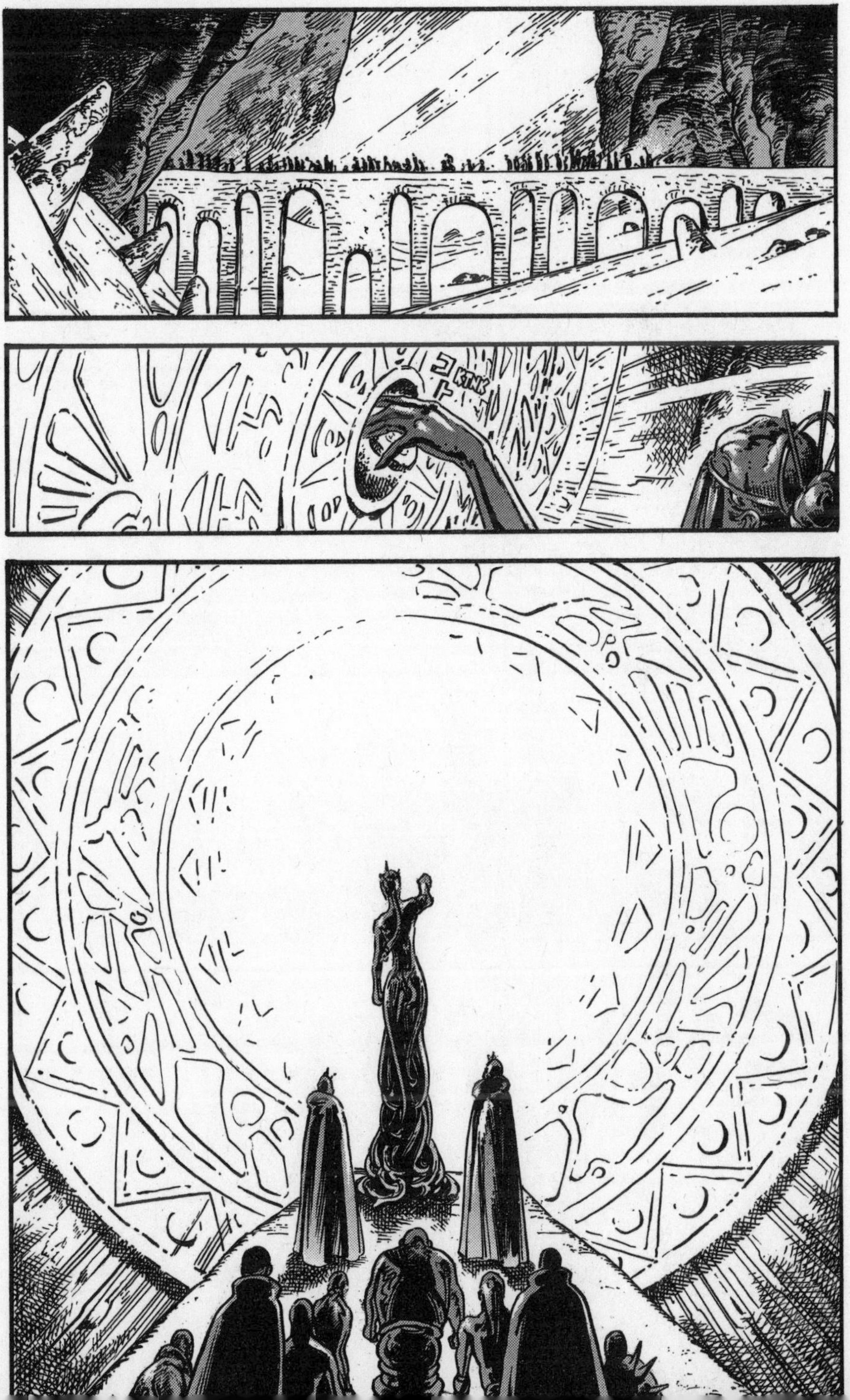
コト
KTNK

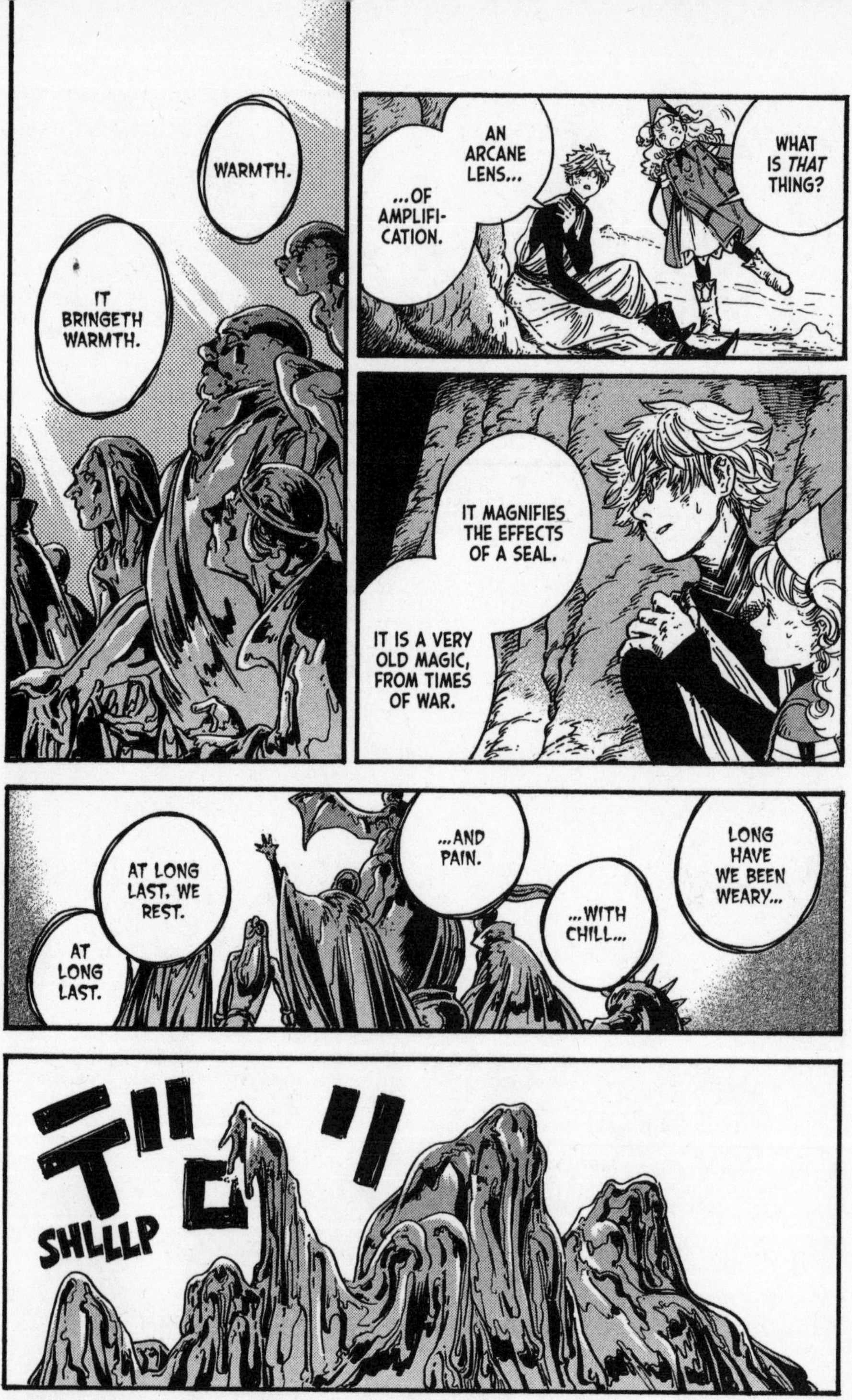
WHAT IS *THAT* THING?
AN ARCANE LENS...
...OF AMPLIFICATION.
IT MAGNIFIES THE EFFECTS OF A SEAL.
IT IS A VERY OLD MAGIC, FROM TIMES OF WAR.
WARMTH.
IT BRINGETH WARMTH.
LONG HAVE WE BEEN WEARY...
...WITH CHILL...
...AND PAIN.
AT LONG LAST, WE REST.
AT LONG LAST.
SHLLLP

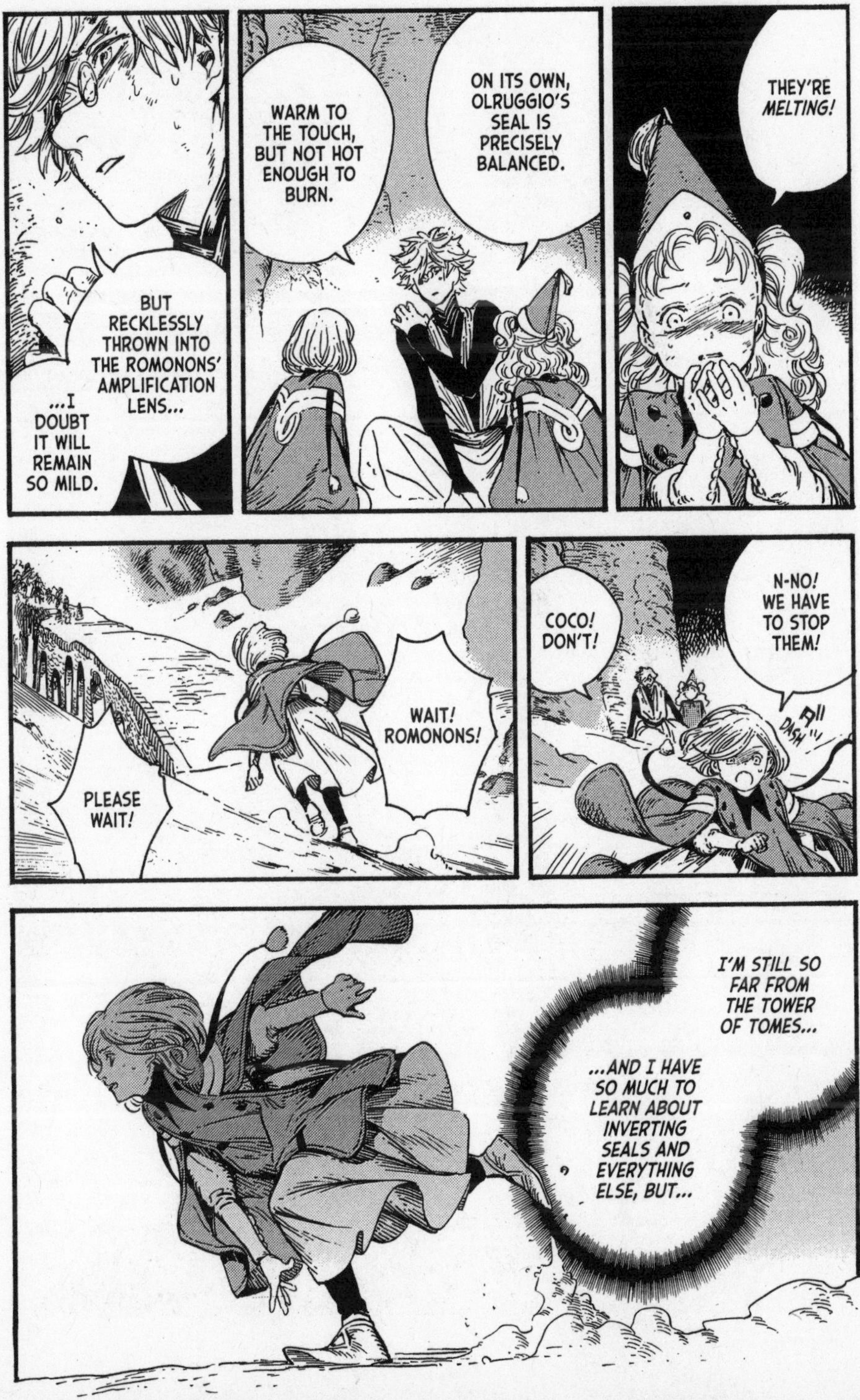
THEY'RE MELTING!
ON ITS OWN, OLRUGGIO'S SEAL IS PRECISELY BALANCED.
WARM TO THE TOUCH, BUT NOT HOT ENOUGH TO BURN.
BUT RECKLESSLY THROWN INTO THE ROMONONS' AMPLIFICATION LENS...
...I DOUBT IT WILL REMAIN SO MILD.
N-NO! WE HAVE TO STOP THEM!
COCO! DON'T!
DASH
WAIT! ROMONONS!
PLEASE WAIT!
I'M STILL SO FAR FROM THE TOWER OF TOMES...
...AND I HAVE SO MUCH TO LEARN ABOUT INVERTING SEALS AND EVERYTHING ELSE, BUT...

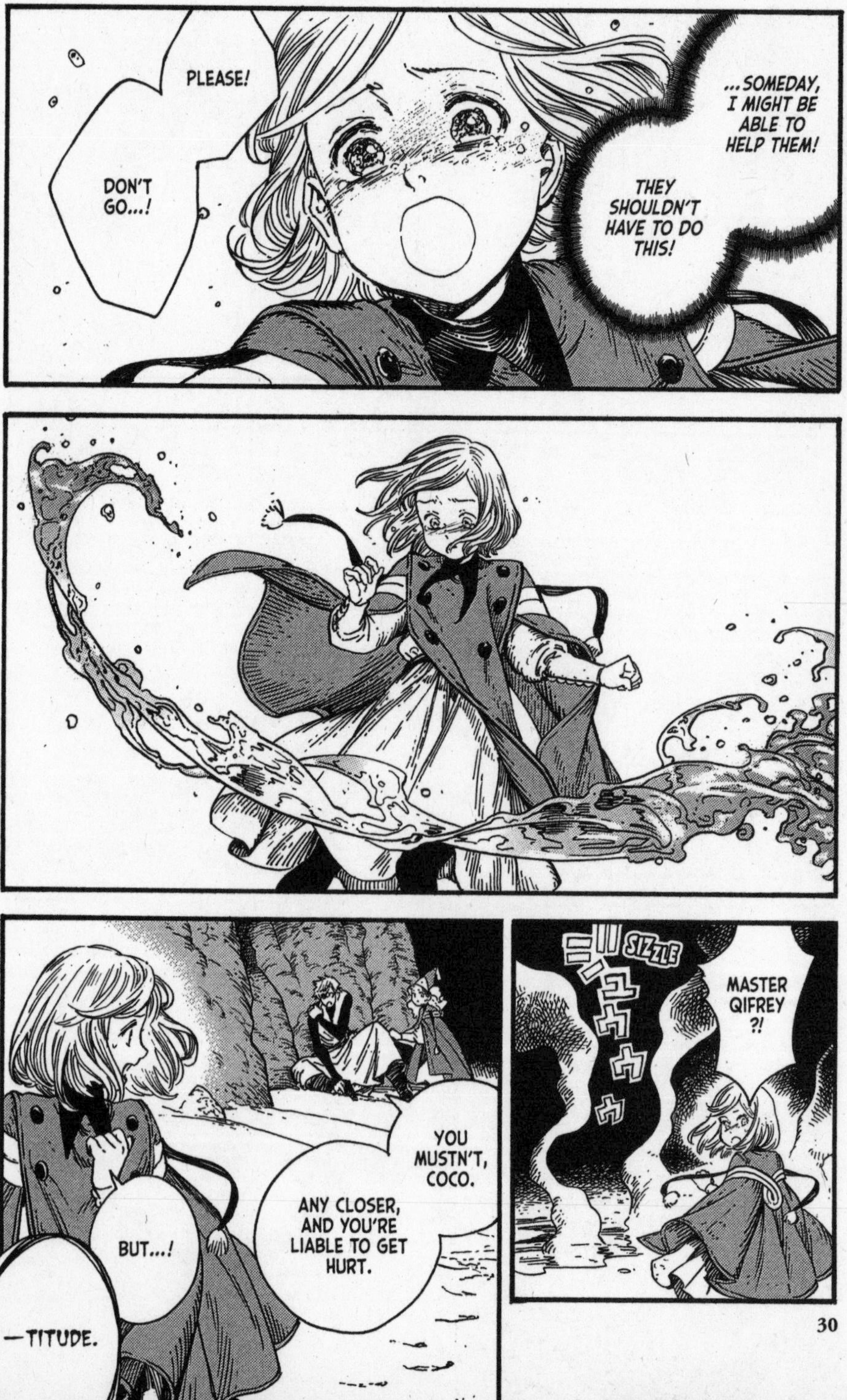
...SOMEDAY, I MIGHT BE ABLE TO HELP THEM!
THEY SHOULDN'T HAVE TO DO THIS!
PLEASE!
DON'T GO...!
SIZZLE
MASTER QIFREY?!
YOU MUSTN'T, COCO.
ANY CLOSER, AND YOU'RE LIABLE TO GET HURT.
BUT...!
—TITUDE.

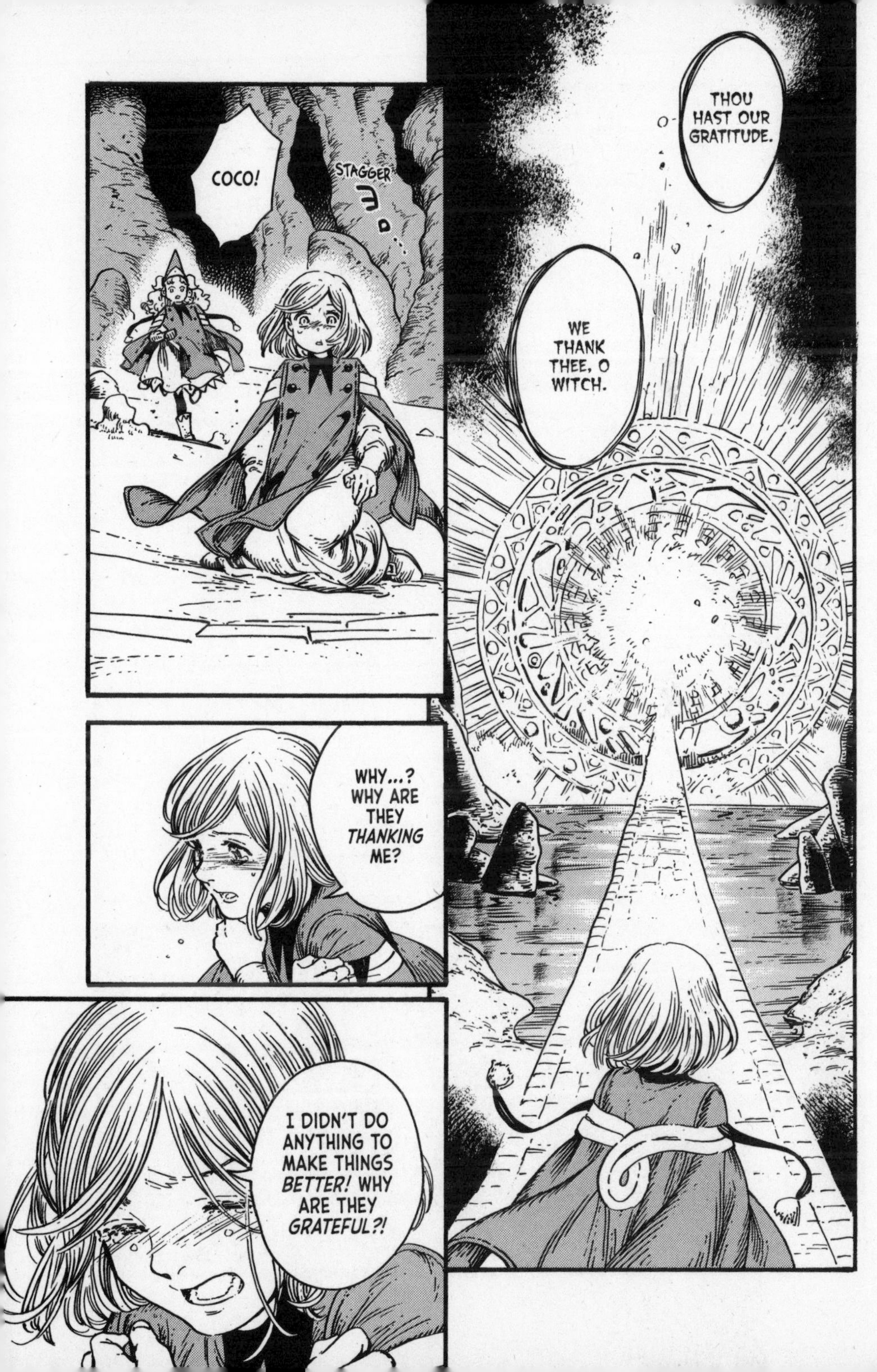
THOU HAST OUR GRATITUDE.
WE THANK THEE, O WITCH.
COCO!
STAGGER
WHY...? WHY ARE THEY *THANKING* ME?
I DIDN'T DO ANYTHING TO MAKE THINGS *BETTER!* WHY ARE THEY *GRATEFUL?!*

I CAN'T EXPLAIN IT EITHER, COCO.
BUT I'M SURE OF ONE THING.
I HOPE I NEVER HAVE TO HEAR...
...ANOTHER THANK YOU THAT SOUNDS SO *SAD.*
...I KNOW.
ME, TOO.

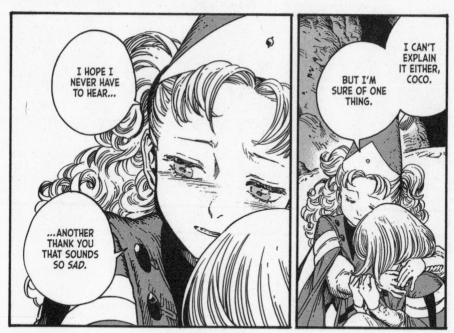

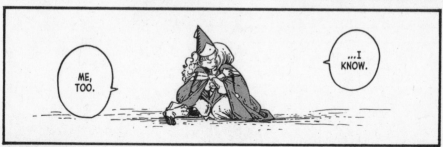

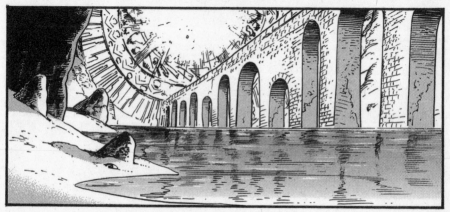

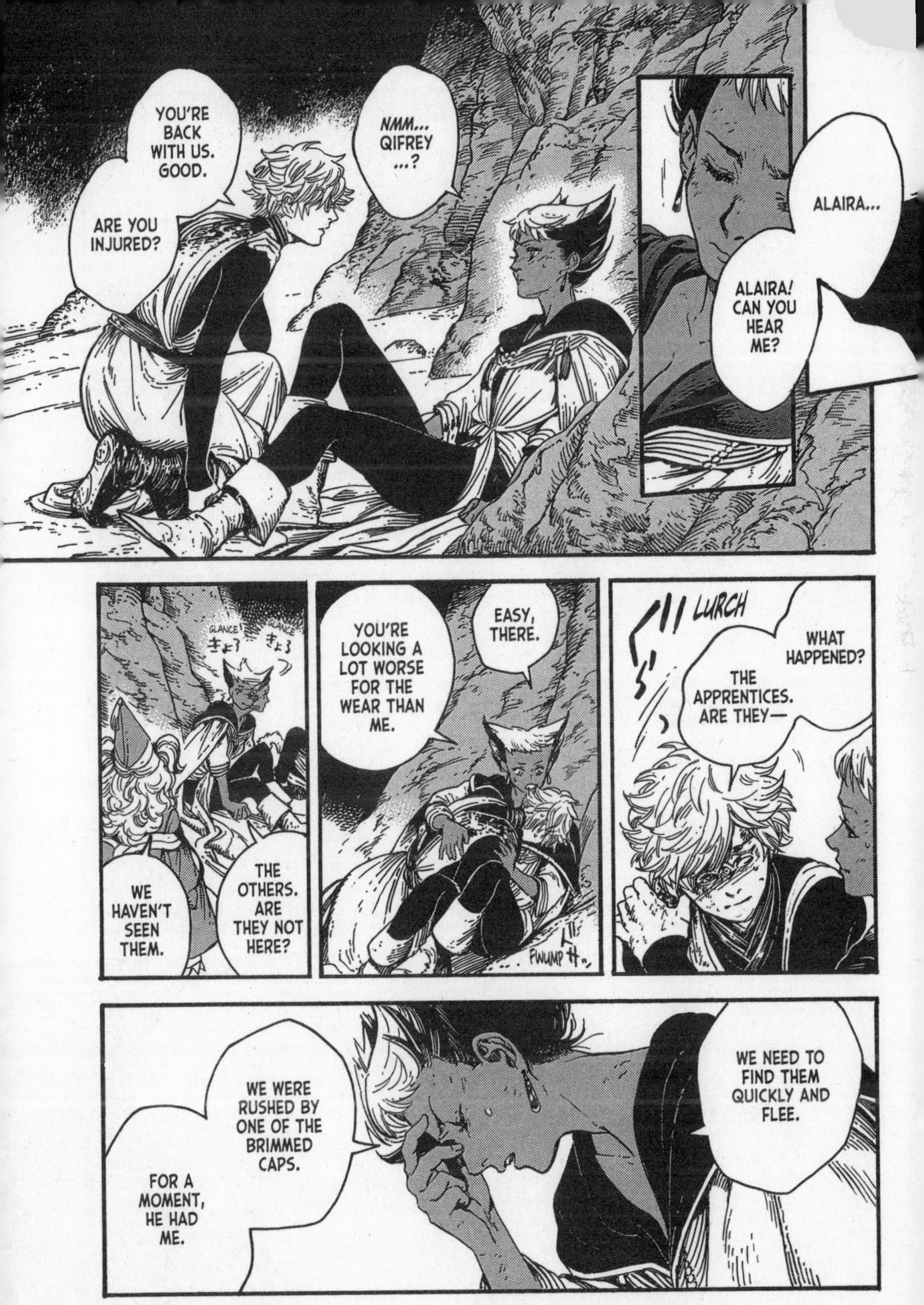
ALAIRA...
ALAIRA! CAN YOU HEAR ME?
NMM... QIFREY ...?
YOU'RE BACK WITH US. GOOD.
ARE YOU INJURED?
LURCH
WHAT HAPPENED?
THE APPRENTICES. ARE THEY—
EASY, THERE.
YOU'RE LOOKING A LOT WORSE FOR THE WEAR THAN ME.
FWUMP
GLANCE!
GLANCE
THE OTHERS. ARE THEY NOT HERE?
WE HAVEN'T SEEN THEM.
WE NEED TO FIND THEM QUICKLY AND FLEE.
WE WERE RUSHED BY ONE OF THE BRIMMED CAPS.
FOR A MOMENT, HE HAD ME.

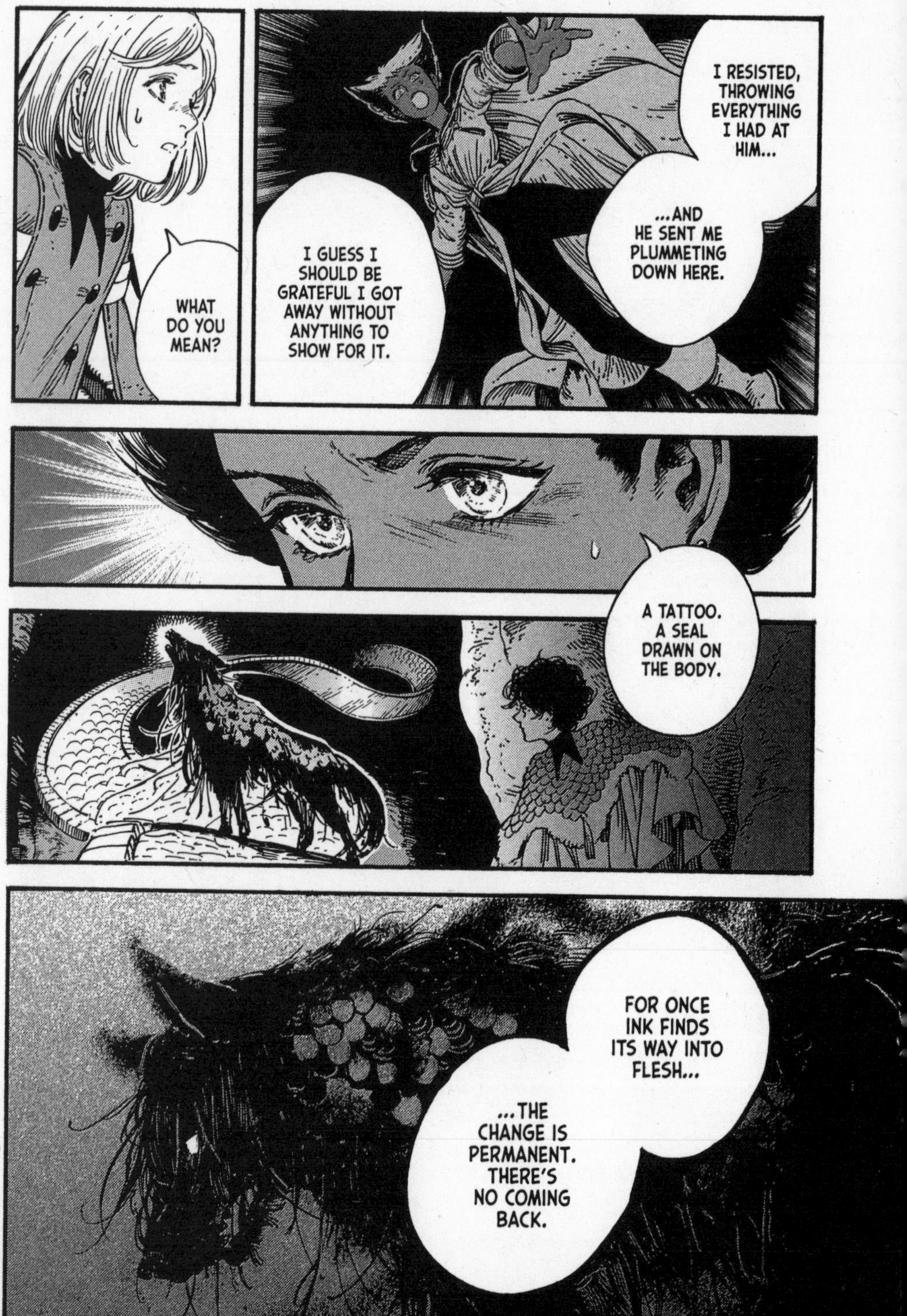
I RESISTED, THROWING EVERYTHING I HAD AT HIM...
...AND HE SENT ME PLUMMETING DOWN HERE.
I GUESS I SHOULD BE GRATEFUL I GOT AWAY WITHOUT ANYTHING TO SHOW FOR IT.
WHAT DO YOU MEAN?
A TATTOO. A SEAL DRAWN ON THE BODY.
FOR ONCE INK FINDS ITS WAY INTO FLESH...
...THE CHANGE IS PERMANENT. THERE'S NO COMING BACK.

CHAPTER 24 ♦ END

Witch Hat Atelier

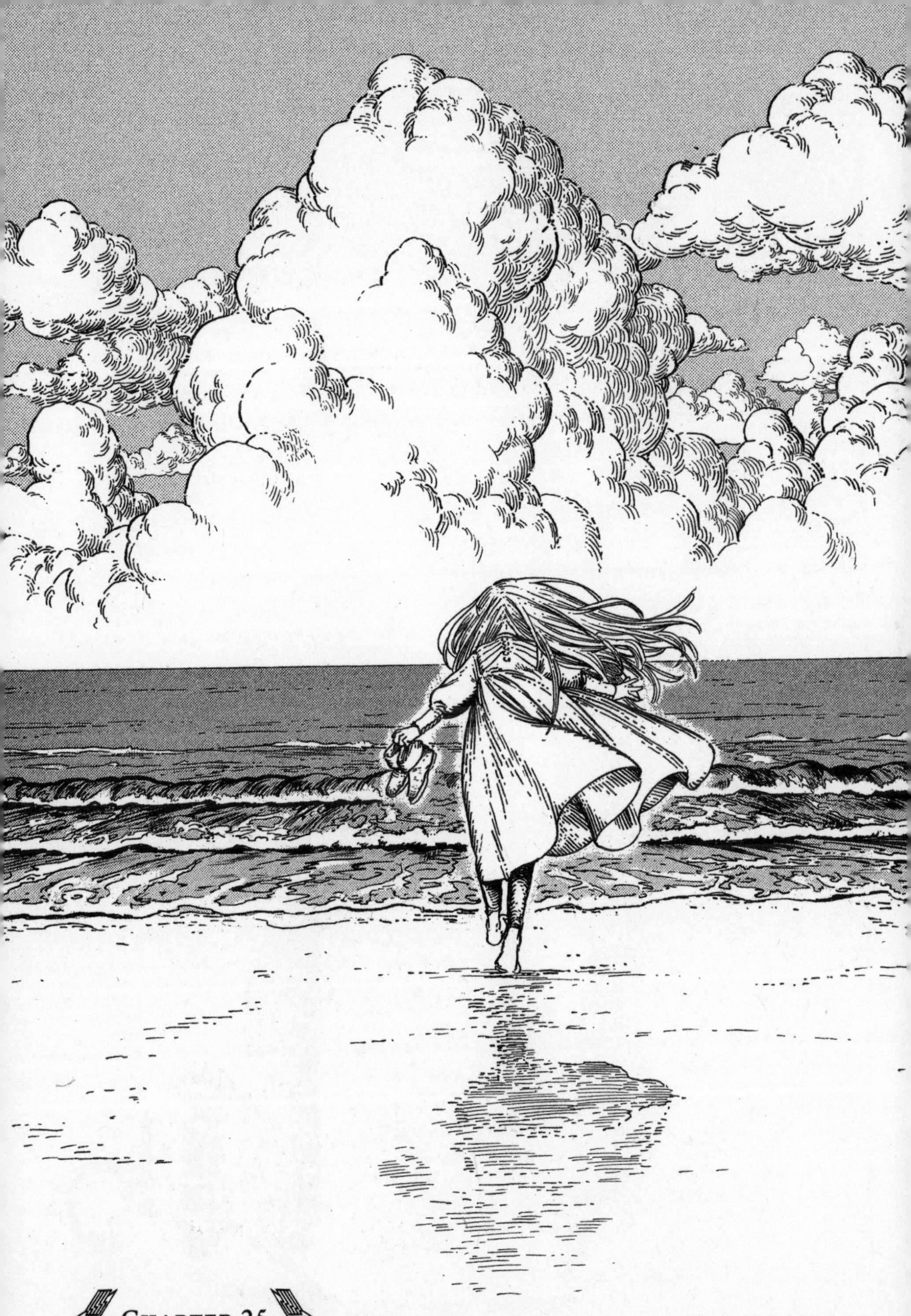

Chapter 25

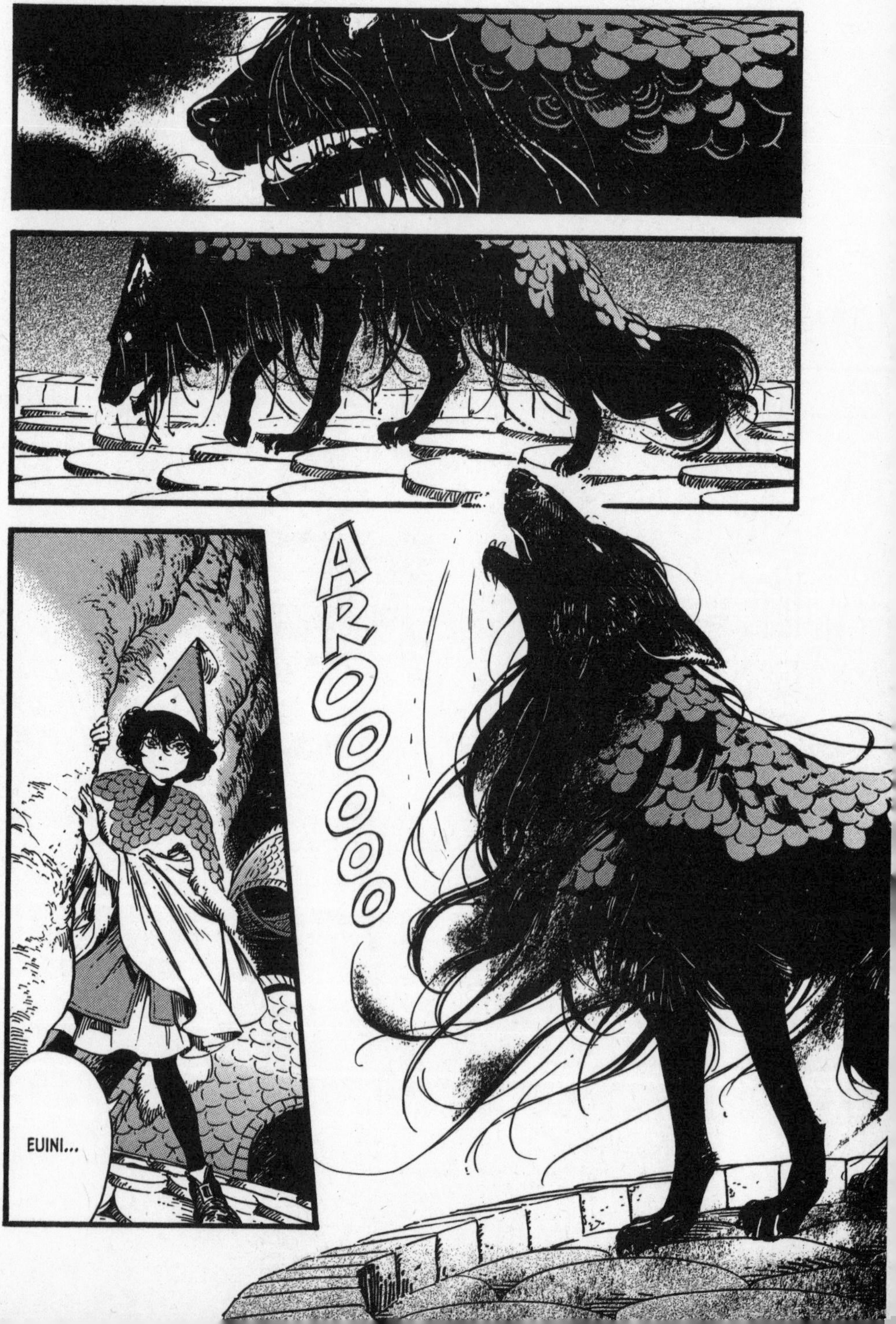
AROOOOOO
EUINI...

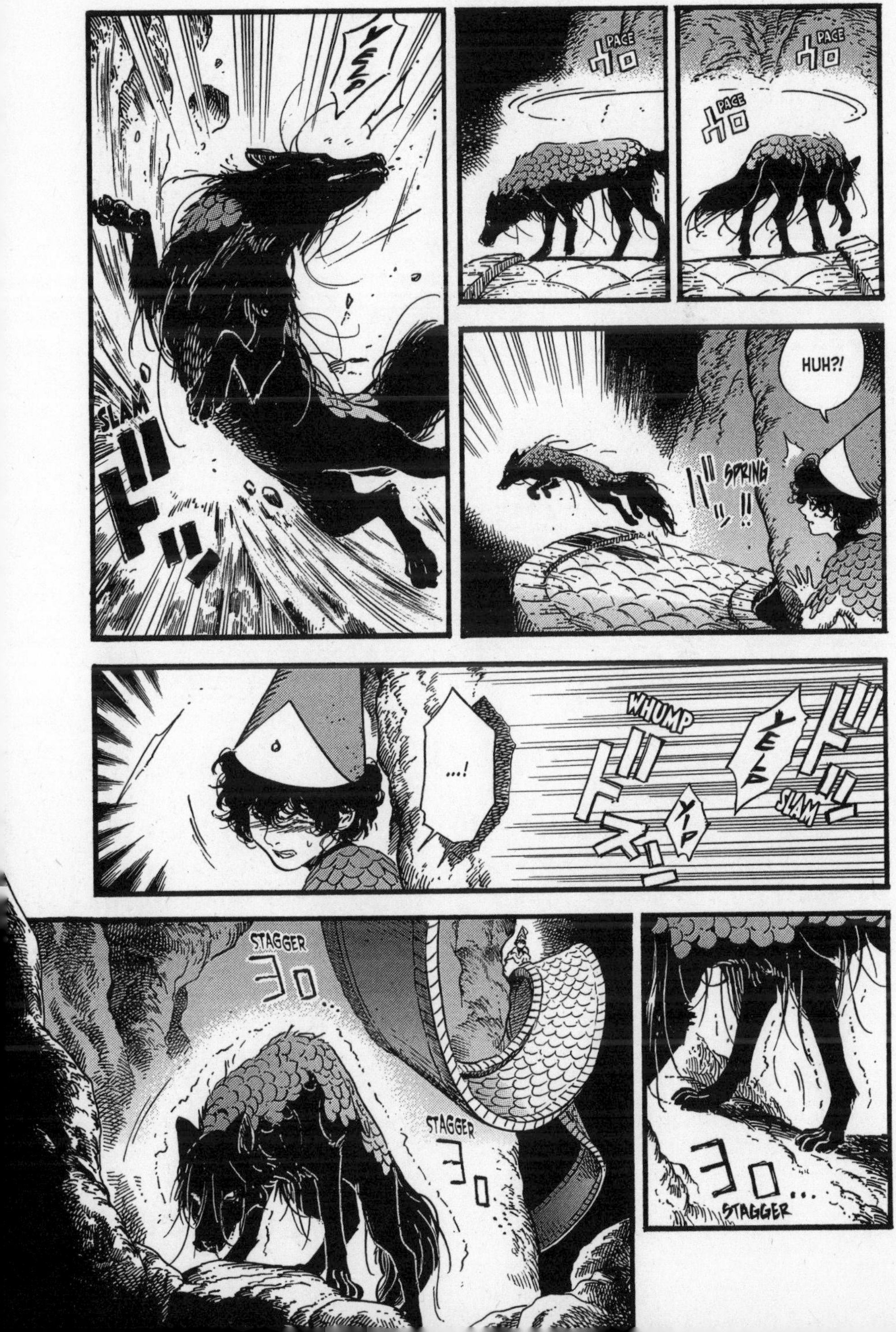

PACE
PACE
PACE
PACE
HUH?!
SPRING
YELP
SLAM
SLAM
YELP
YIP
WHUMP
...!
STAGGER
STAGGER
STAGGER

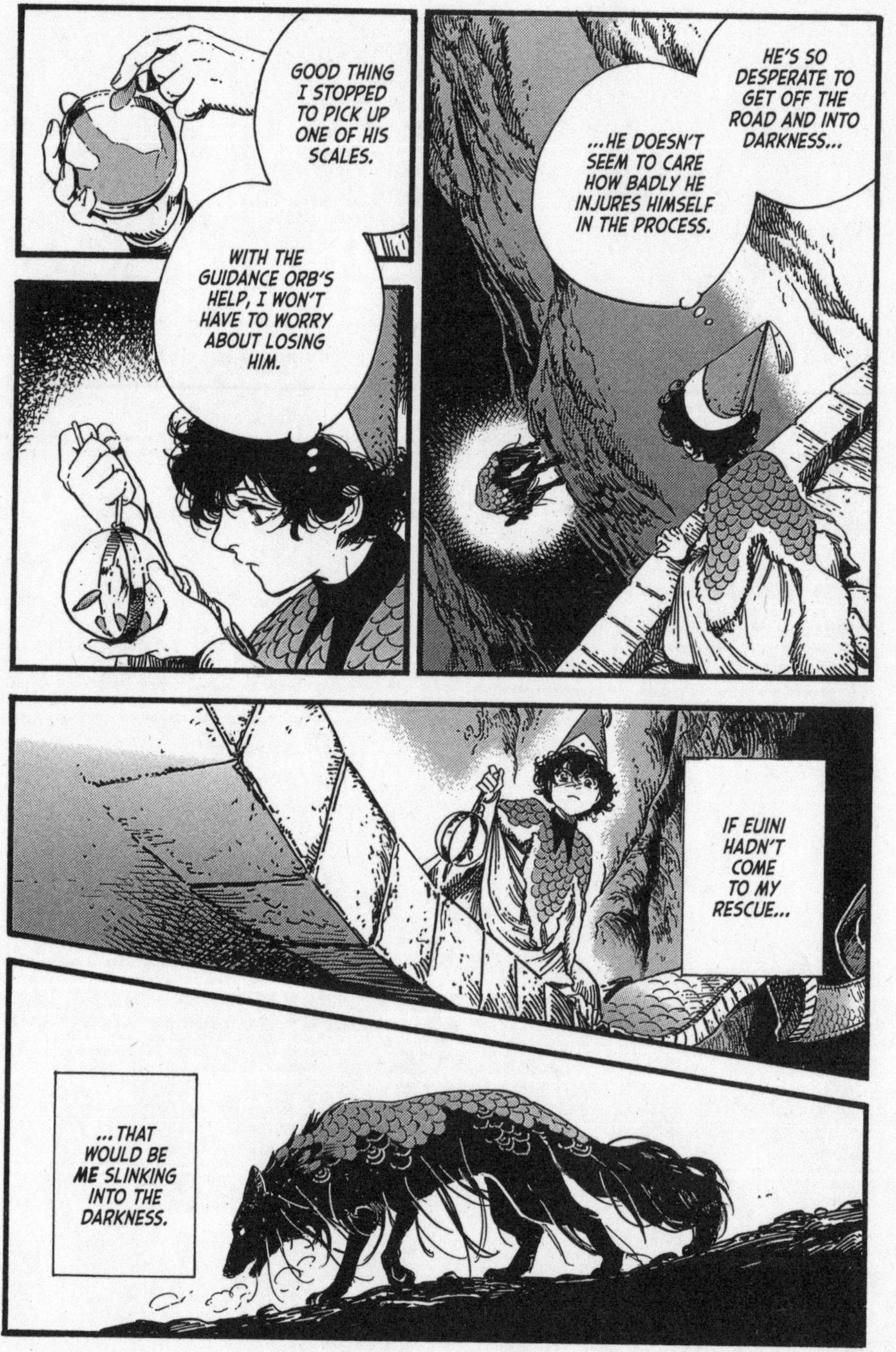
HE'S SO DESPERATE TO GET OFF THE ROAD AND INTO DARKNESS...
...HE DOESN'T SEEM TO CARE HOW BADLY HE INJURES HIMSELF IN THE PROCESS.
GOOD THING I STOPPED TO PICK UP ONE OF HIS SCALES.
WITH THE GUIDANCE ORB'S HELP, I WON'T HAVE TO WORRY ABOUT LOSING HIM.
IF EUINI HADN'T COME TO MY RESCUE...
...THAT WOULD BE **ME** SLINKING INTO THE DARKNESS.

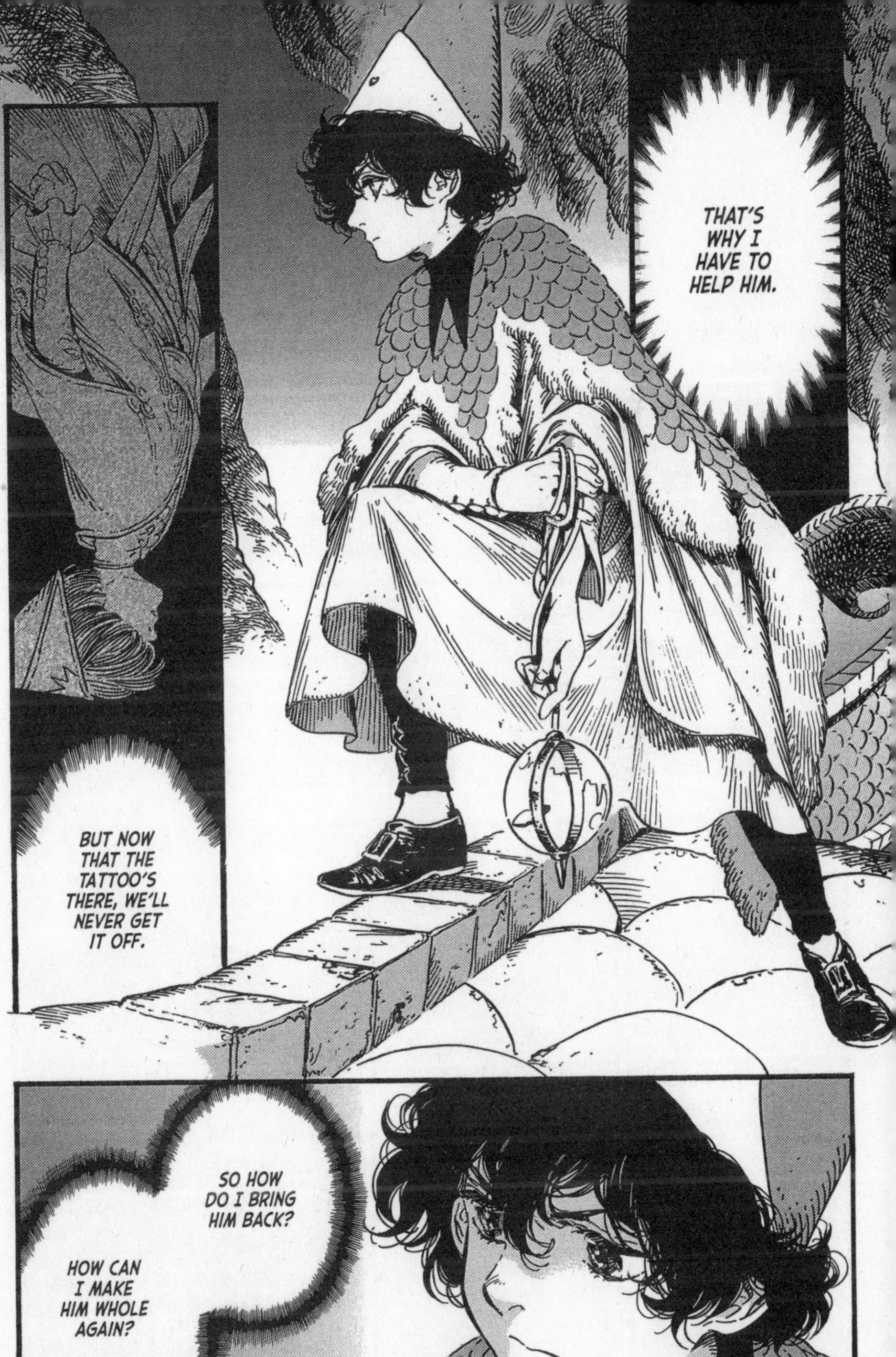
THAT'S WHY I HAVE TO HELP HIM.
BUT NOW THAT THE TATTOO'S THERE, WE'LL NEVER GET IT OFF.
SO HOW DO I BRING HIM BACK?
HOW CAN I MAKE HIM WHOLE AGAIN?

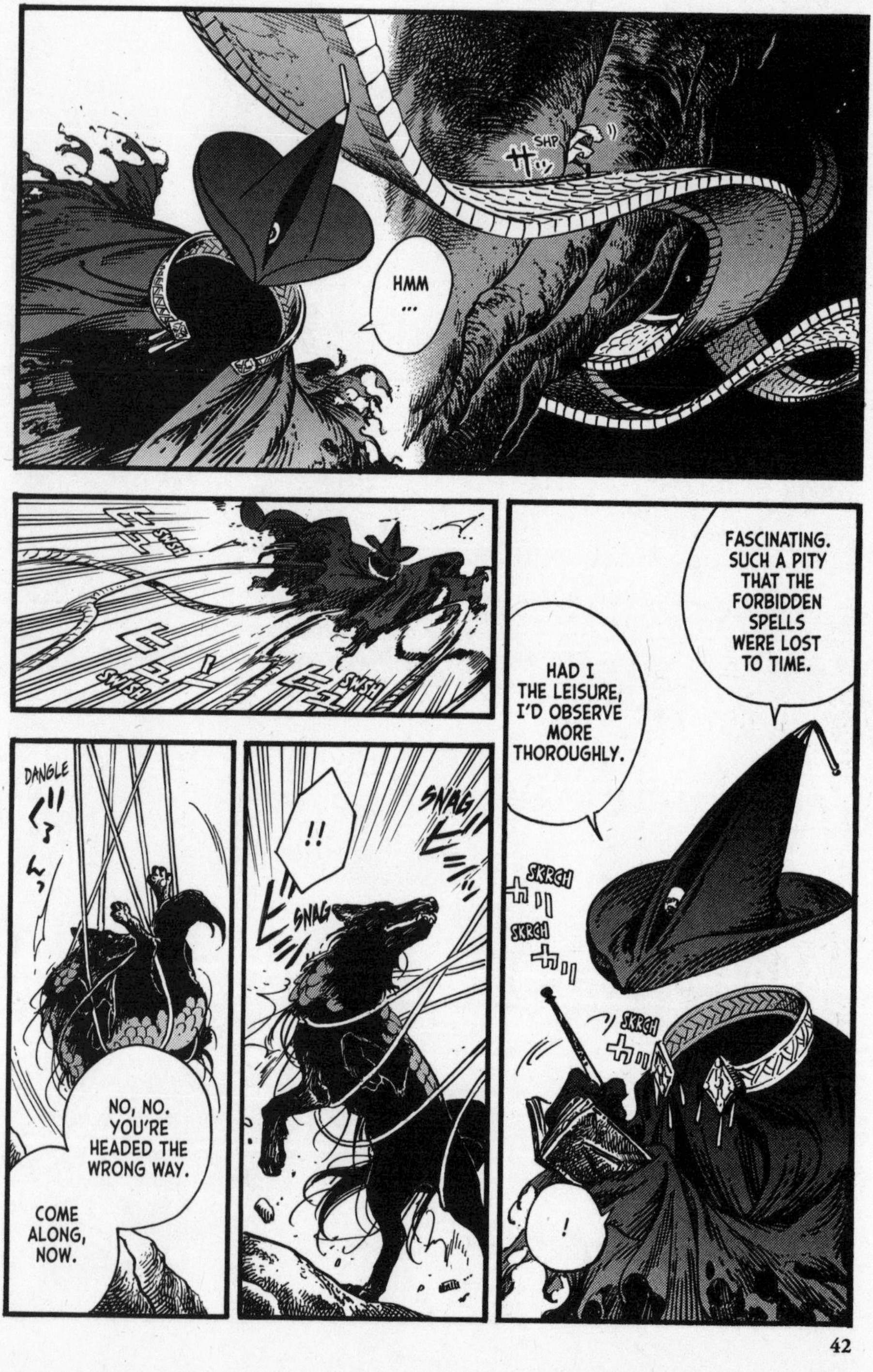
SHP
HMM ...
FASCINATING. SUCH A PITY THAT THE FORBIDDEN SPELLS WERE LOST TO TIME.
HAD I THE LEISURE, I'D OBSERVE MORE THOROUGHLY.
SKRCH
SKRCH
SKRCH
!
SWSH
SWSH
SWSH
SNAG
!!
SNAG
DANGLE
NO, NO. YOU'RE HEADED THE WRONG WAY.
COME ALONG, NOW.

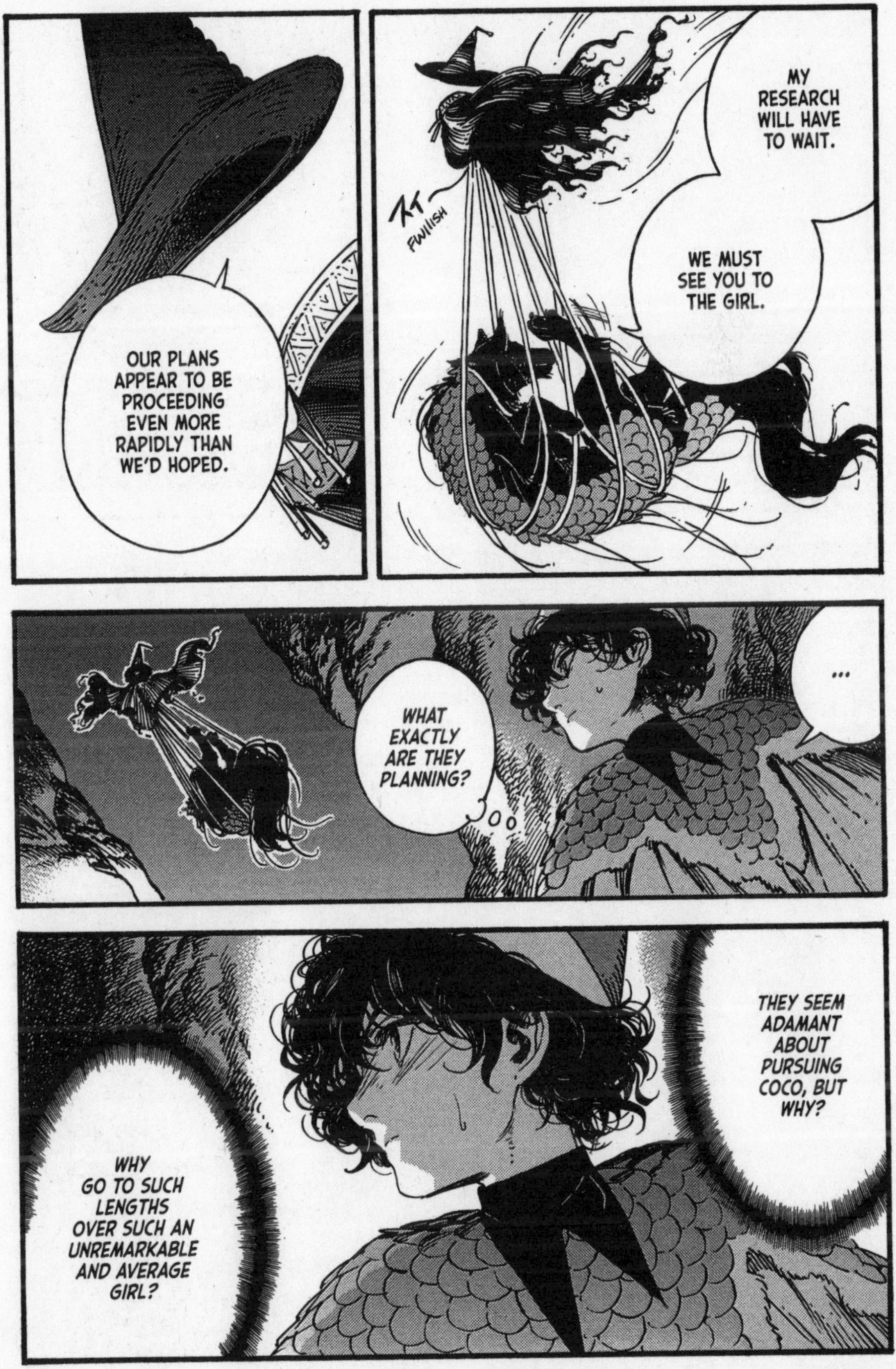
MY RESEARCH WILL HAVE TO WAIT.
WE MUST SEE YOU TO THE GIRL.
FWIISH
OUR PLANS APPEAR TO BE PROCEEDING EVEN MORE RAPIDLY THAN WE'D HOPED.
...
WHAT EXACTLY ARE THEY PLANNING?
THEY SEEM ADAMANT ABOUT PURSUING COCO, BUT WHY?
WHY GO TO SUCH LENGTHS OVER SUCH AN UNREMARKABLE AND AVERAGE GIRL?

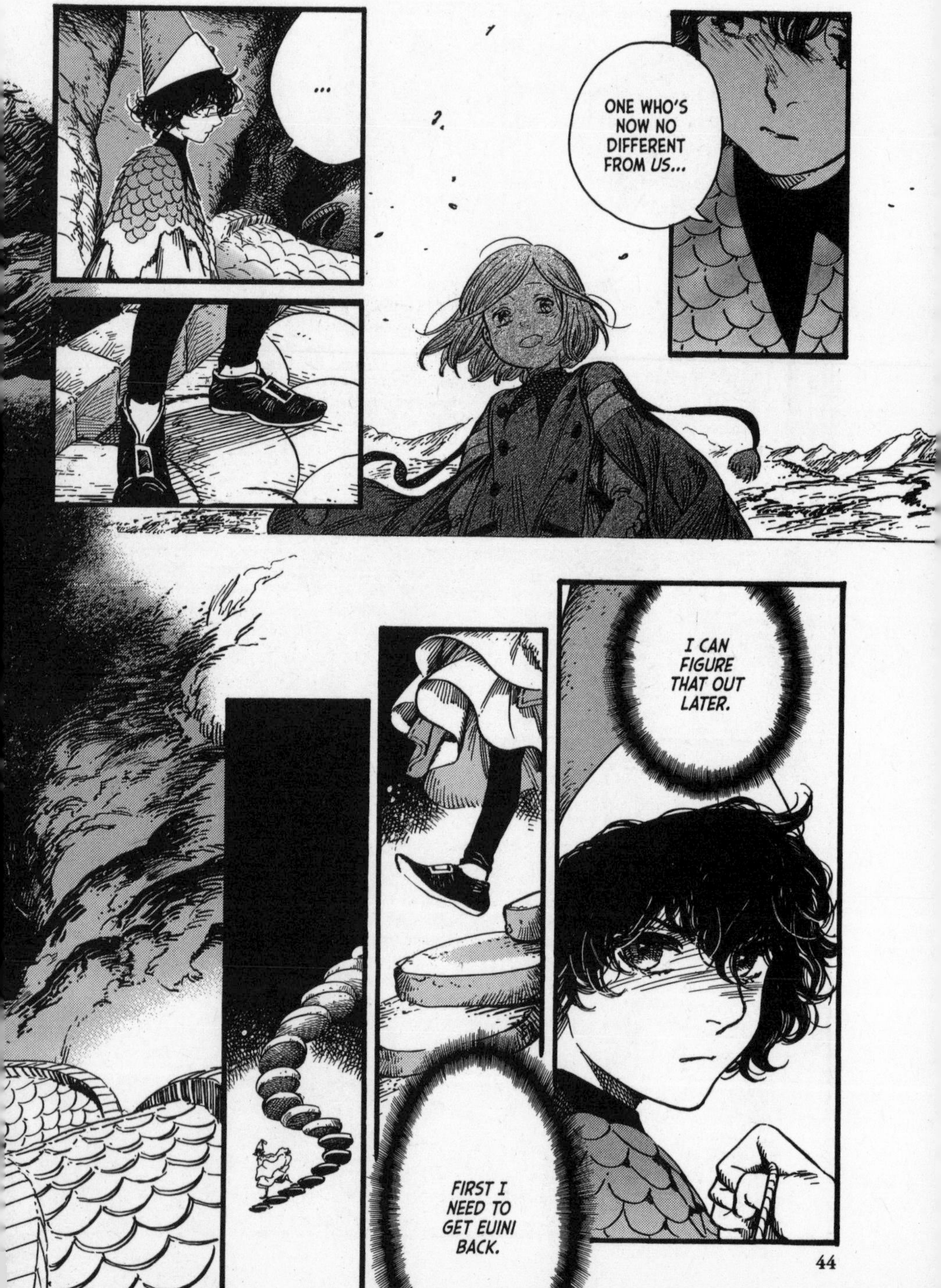
ONE WHO'S NOW NO DIFFERENT FROM US...
...
I CAN FIGURE THAT OUT LATER.
FIRST I NEED TO GET EUINI BACK.

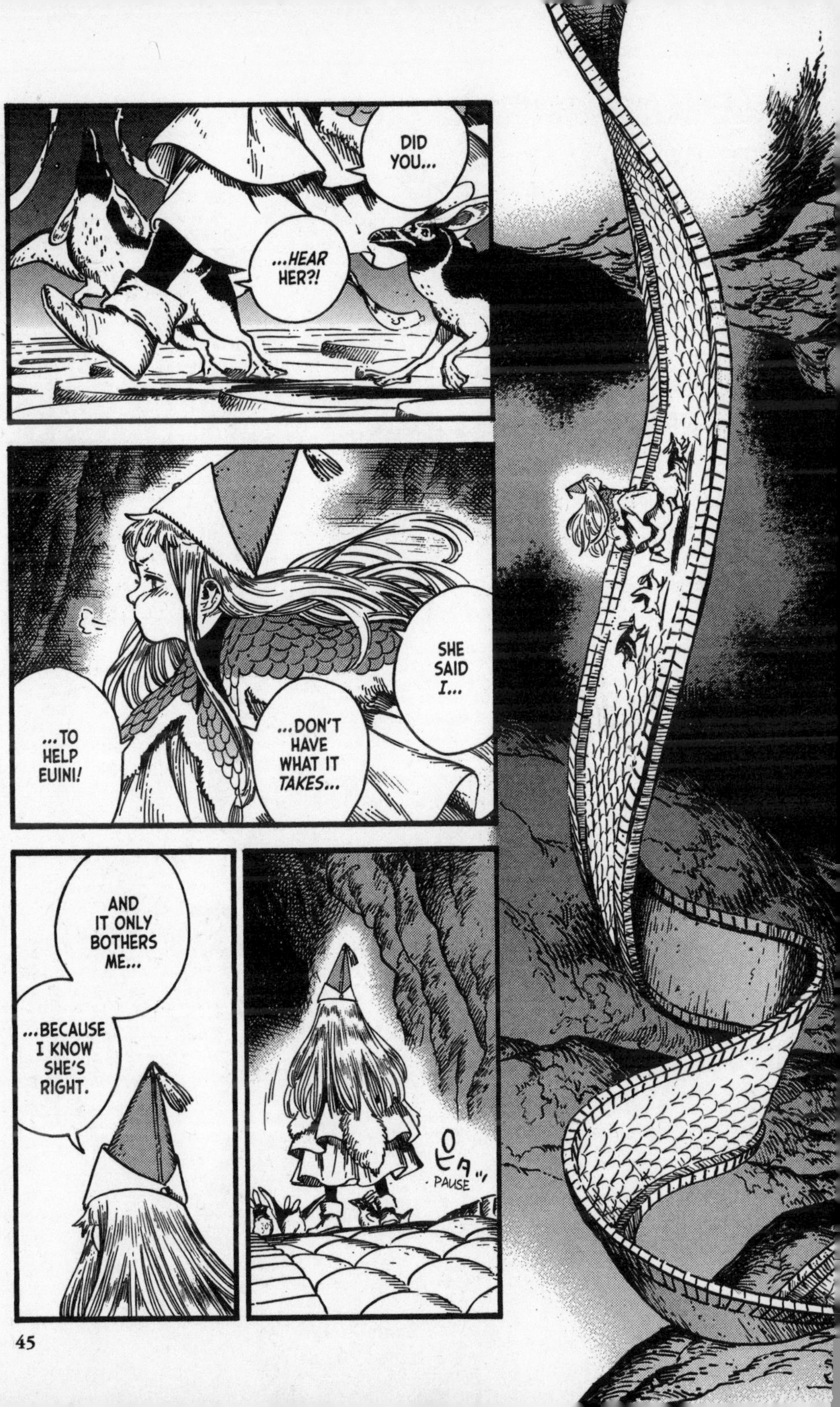
DID YOU...
...HEAR HER?!
SHE SAID I...
...DON'T HAVE WHAT IT TAKES...
...TO HELP EUINI!
ピタッ
PAUSE
AND IT ONLY BOTHERS ME...
...BECAUSE I KNOW SHE'S RIGHT.

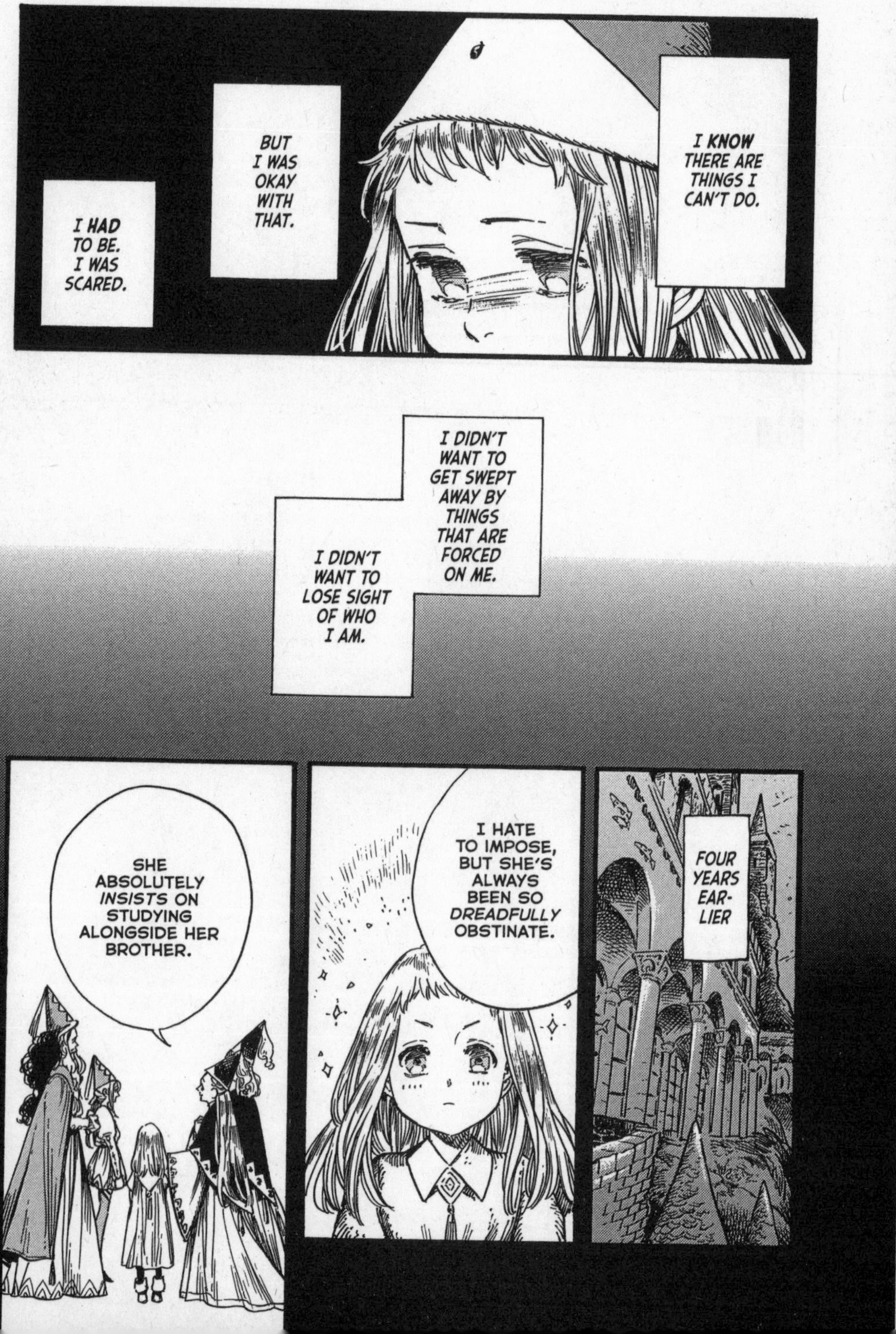
I KNOW THERE ARE THINGS I CAN'T DO.
BUT I WAS OKAY WITH THAT.
I HAD TO BE. I WAS SCARED.
I DIDN'T WANT TO GET SWEPT AWAY BY THINGS THAT ARE FORCED ON ME.
I DIDN'T WANT TO LOSE SIGHT OF WHO I AM.
FOUR YEARS EAR-LIER
I HATE TO IMPOSE, BUT SHE'S ALWAYS BEEN SO *DREADFULLY* OBSTINATE.
SHE ABSOLUTELY *INSISTS* ON STUDYING ALONGSIDE HER BROTHER.

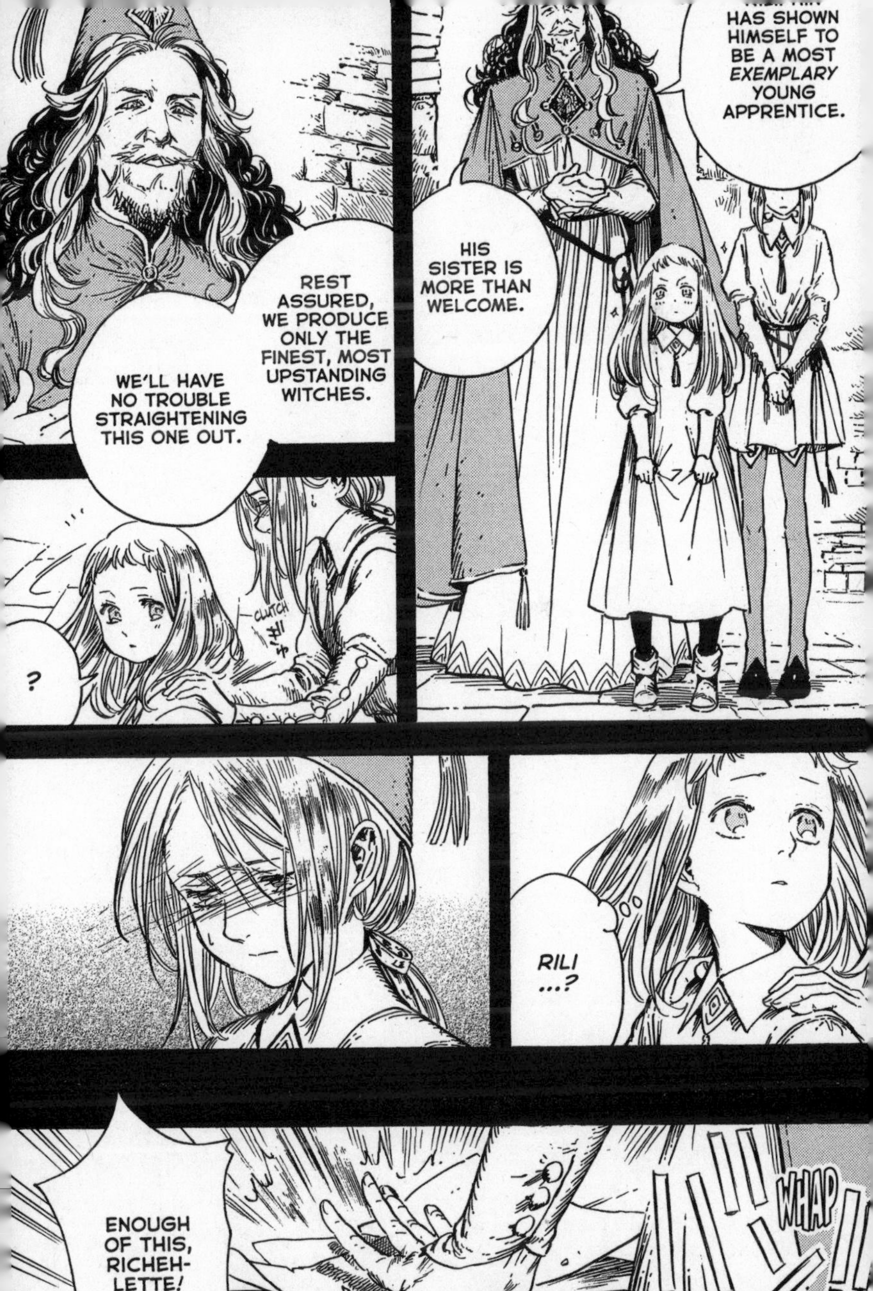
HAS SHOWN HIMSELF TO BE A MOST *EXEMPLARY* YOUNG APPRENTICE.
HIS SISTER IS MORE THAN WELCOME.
REST ASSURED, WE PRODUCE ONLY THE FINEST, MOST UPSTANDING WITCHES.
WE'LL HAVE NO TROUBLE STRAIGHTENING THIS ONE OUT.
CLUTCH
?
RILI ...?
WHAP!!
ENOUGH OF THIS, RICHEH-LETTE!

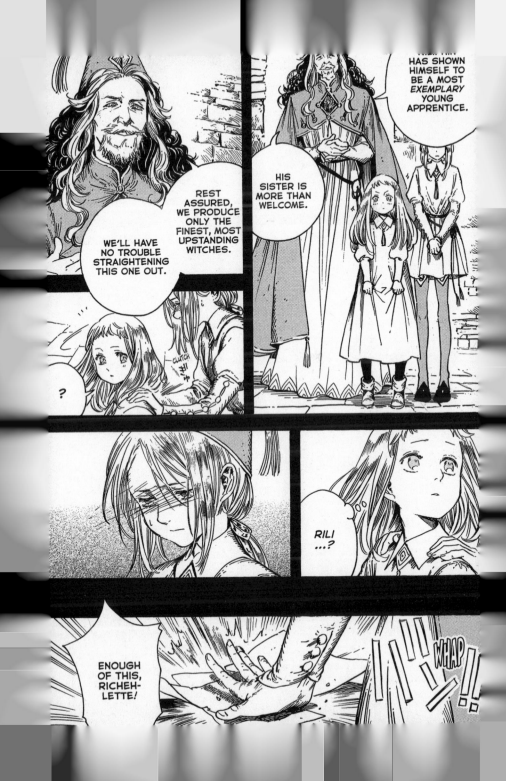

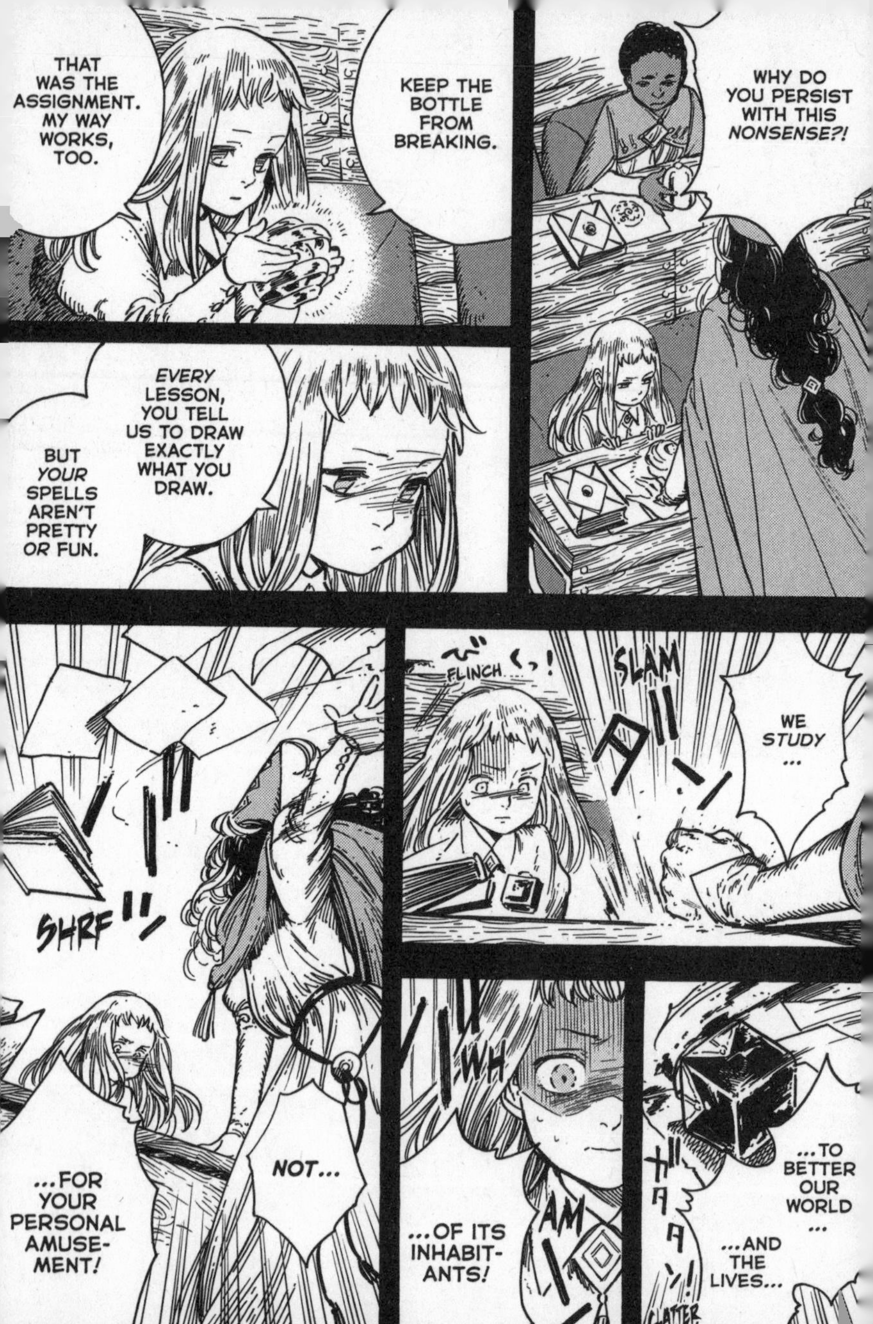
WHY DO YOU PERSIST WITH THIS *NONSENSE?!*
KEEP THE BOTTLE FROM BREAKING.
THAT WAS THE ASSIGNMENT. MY WAY WORKS, TOO.
EVERY LESSON, YOU TELL US TO DRAW EXACTLY WHAT YOU DRAW.
BUT *YOUR* SPELLS AREN'T PRETTY *OR* FUN.
びくっ!
FLINCH
SLAM
ダンッ
WE *STUDY* ...
...TO BETTER OUR WORLD ...
...AND THE LIVES...
カタタンッ!
CLATTER
WH
...OF ITS INHABIT-ANTS!
AM
SHRF
NOT...
...FOR YOUR PERSONAL AMUSE-MENT!

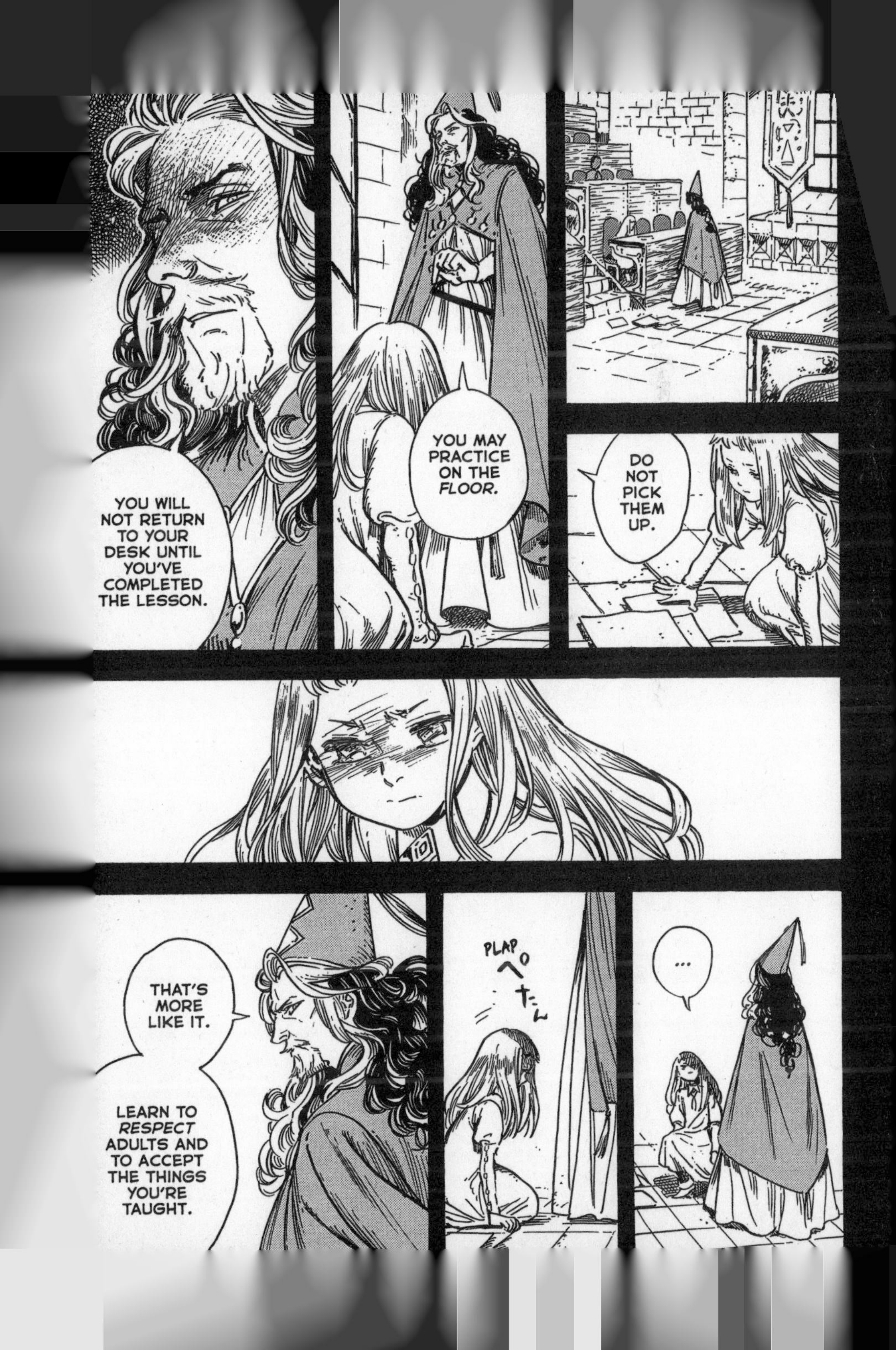
DO NOT PICK THEM UP.
YOU MAY PRACTICE ON THE *FLOOR*.
YOU WILL NOT RETURN TO YOUR DESK UNTIL YOU'VE COMPLETED THE LESSON.
...
PLAP
へたん
THAT'S MORE LIKE IT.
LEARN TO *RESPECT* ADULTS AND TO ACCEPT THE THINGS YOU'RE TAUGHT.

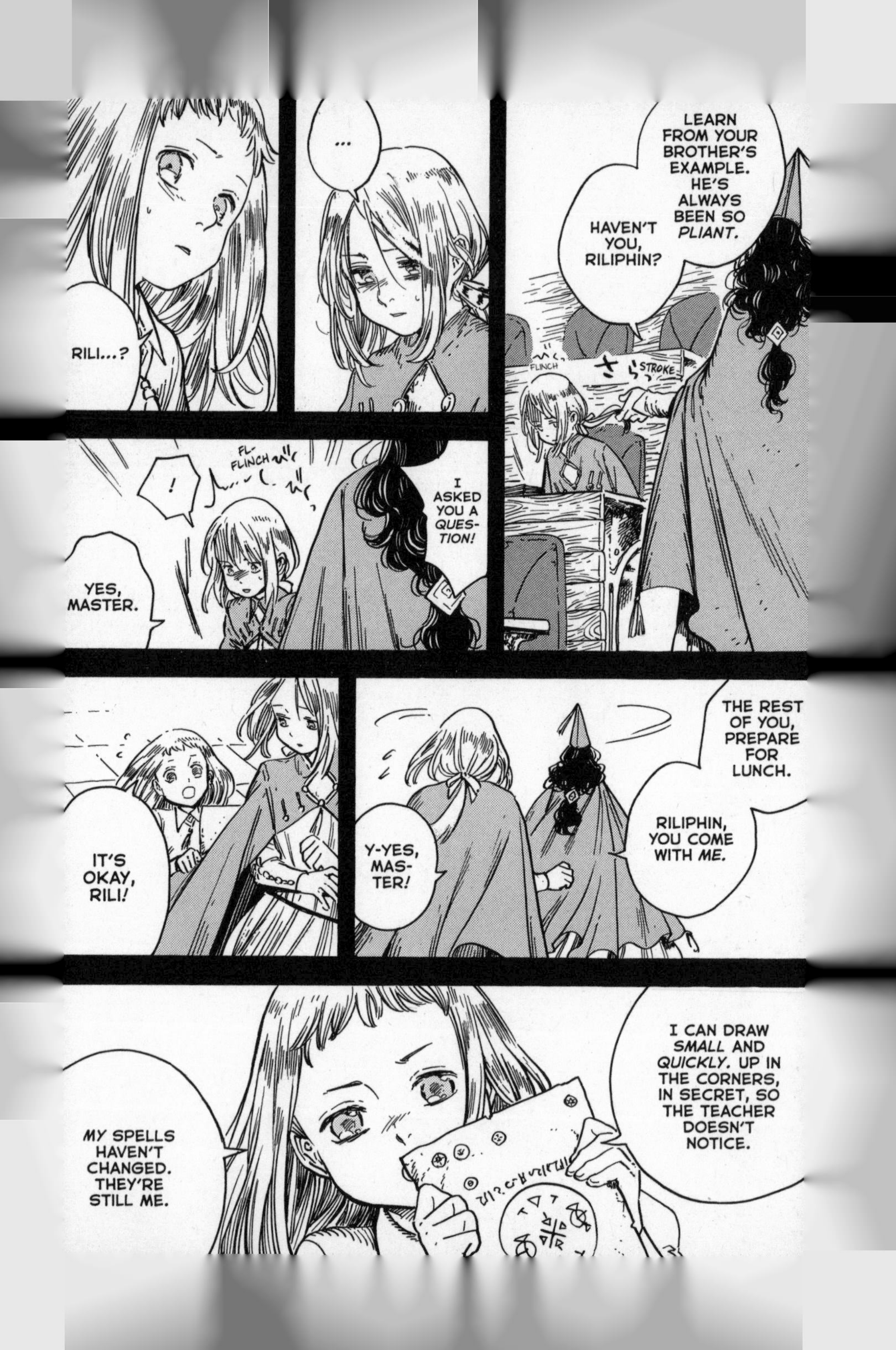
LEARN FROM YOUR BROTHER'S EXAMPLE. HE'S ALWAYS BEEN SO *PLIANT*.
HAVEN'T YOU, RILIPHIN?
FLINCH
STROKE
...
RILI...?
I ASKED YOU A *QUES-TION!*
FL-FLINCH
!
YES, MASTER.
THE REST OF YOU, PREPARE FOR LUNCH.
RILIPHIN, YOU COME WITH *ME*.
Y-YES, MAS-TER*!*
IT'S OKAY, RILI*!*
I CAN DRAW *SMALL* AND *QUICKLY*. UP IN THE CORNERS, IN SECRET, SO THE TEACHER DOESN'T NOTICE.
MY SPELLS HAVEN'T CHANGED. THEY'RE STILL ME.

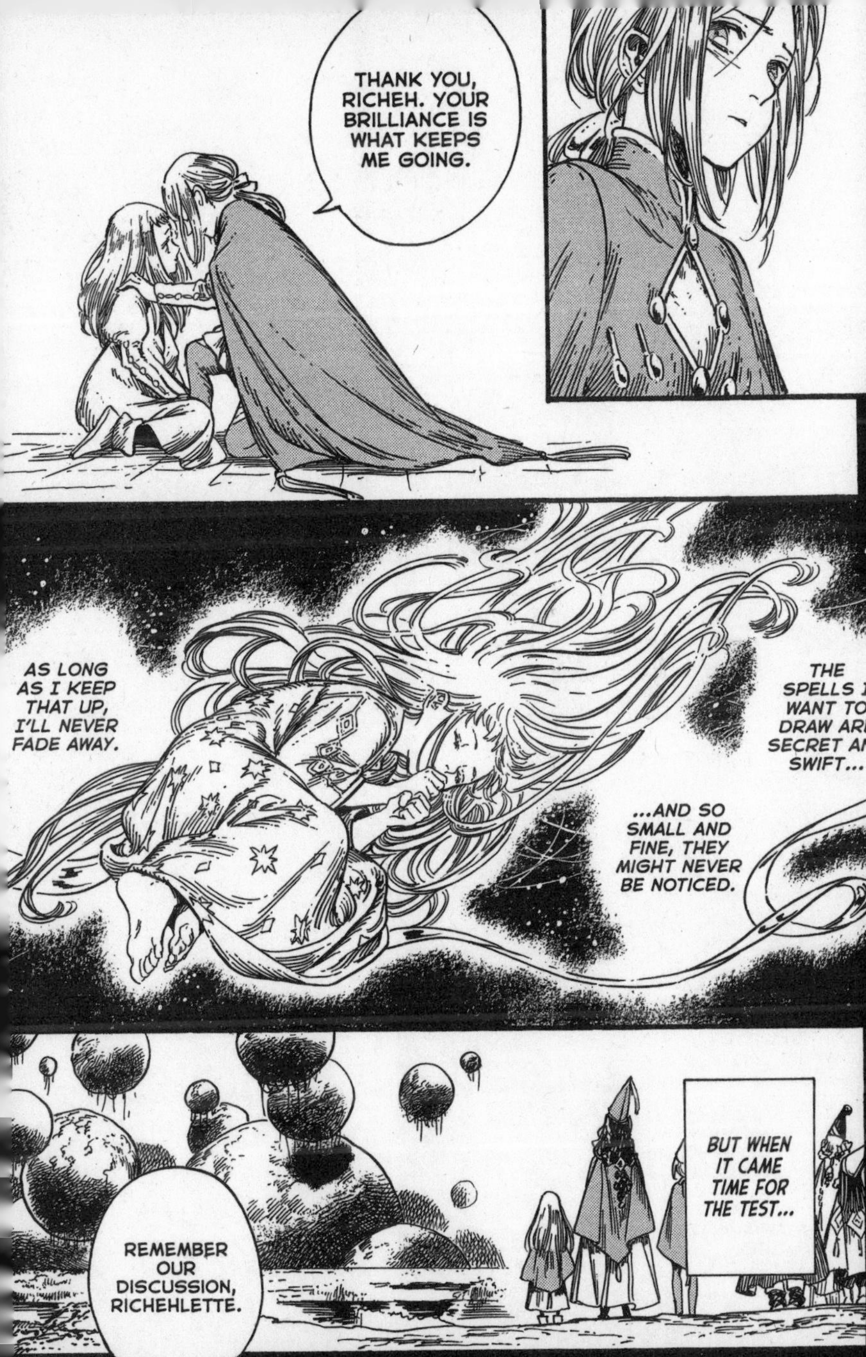
THANK YOU, RICHEH. YOUR BRILLIANCE IS WHAT KEEPS ME GOING.
THE SPELLS I WANT TO DRAW ARE SECRET AND SWIFT...
...AND SO SMALL AND FINE, THEY MIGHT NEVER BE NOTICED.
AS LONG AS I KEEP THAT UP, I'LL NEVER FADE AWAY.
BUT WHEN IT CAME TIME FOR THE TEST...
REMEMBER OUR DISCUSSION, RICHEHLETTE.

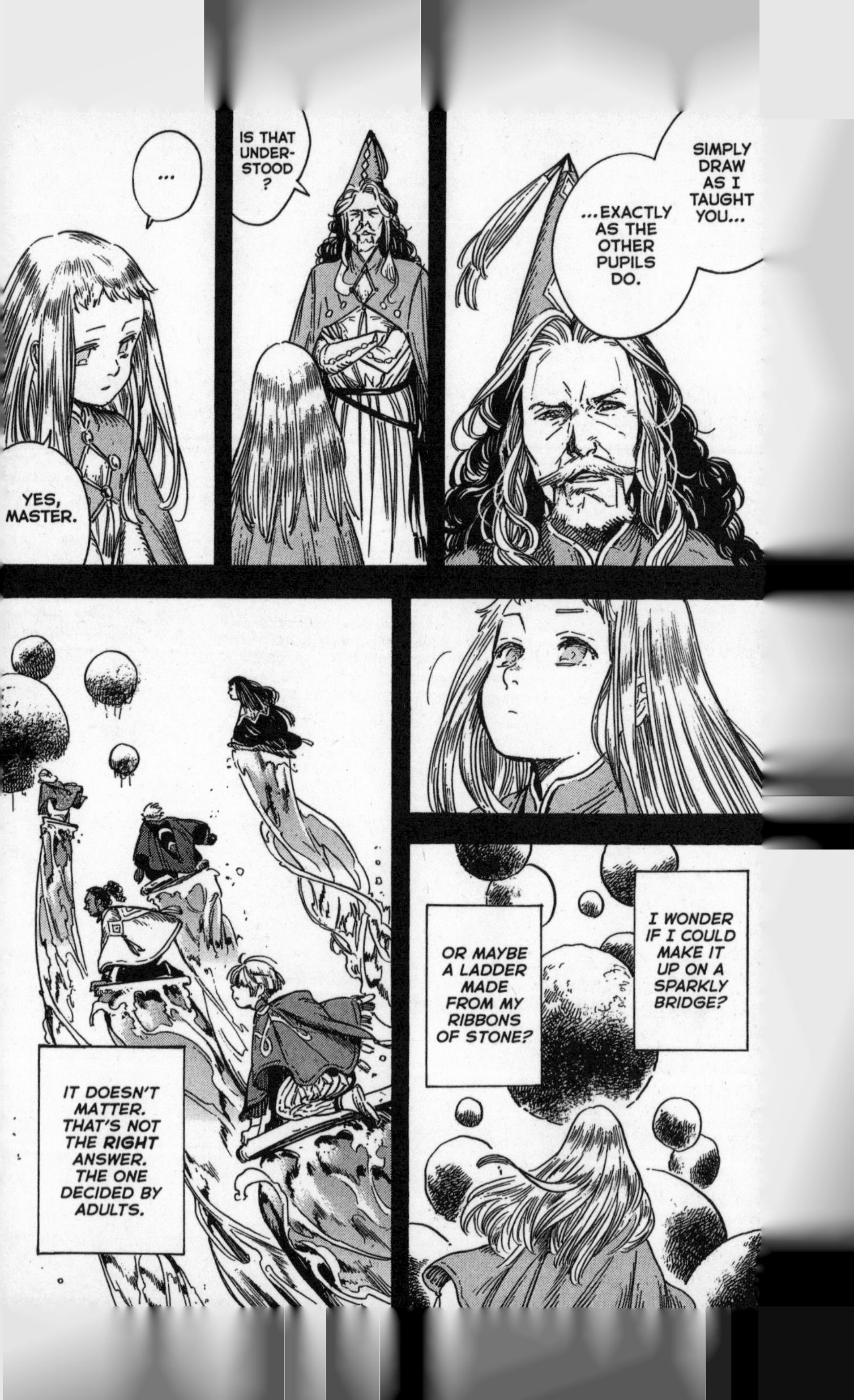
SIMPLY DRAW AS I TAUGHT YOU...
...EXACTLY AS THE OTHER PUPILS DO.
IS THAT UNDER-STOOD?
...
YES, MASTER.
I WONDER IF I COULD MAKE IT UP ON A SPARKLY BRIDGE?
OR MAYBE A LADDER MADE FROM MY RIBBONS OF STONE?
IT DOESN'T MATTER. THAT'S NOT THE RIGHT ANSWER. THE ONE DECIDED BY ADULTS.

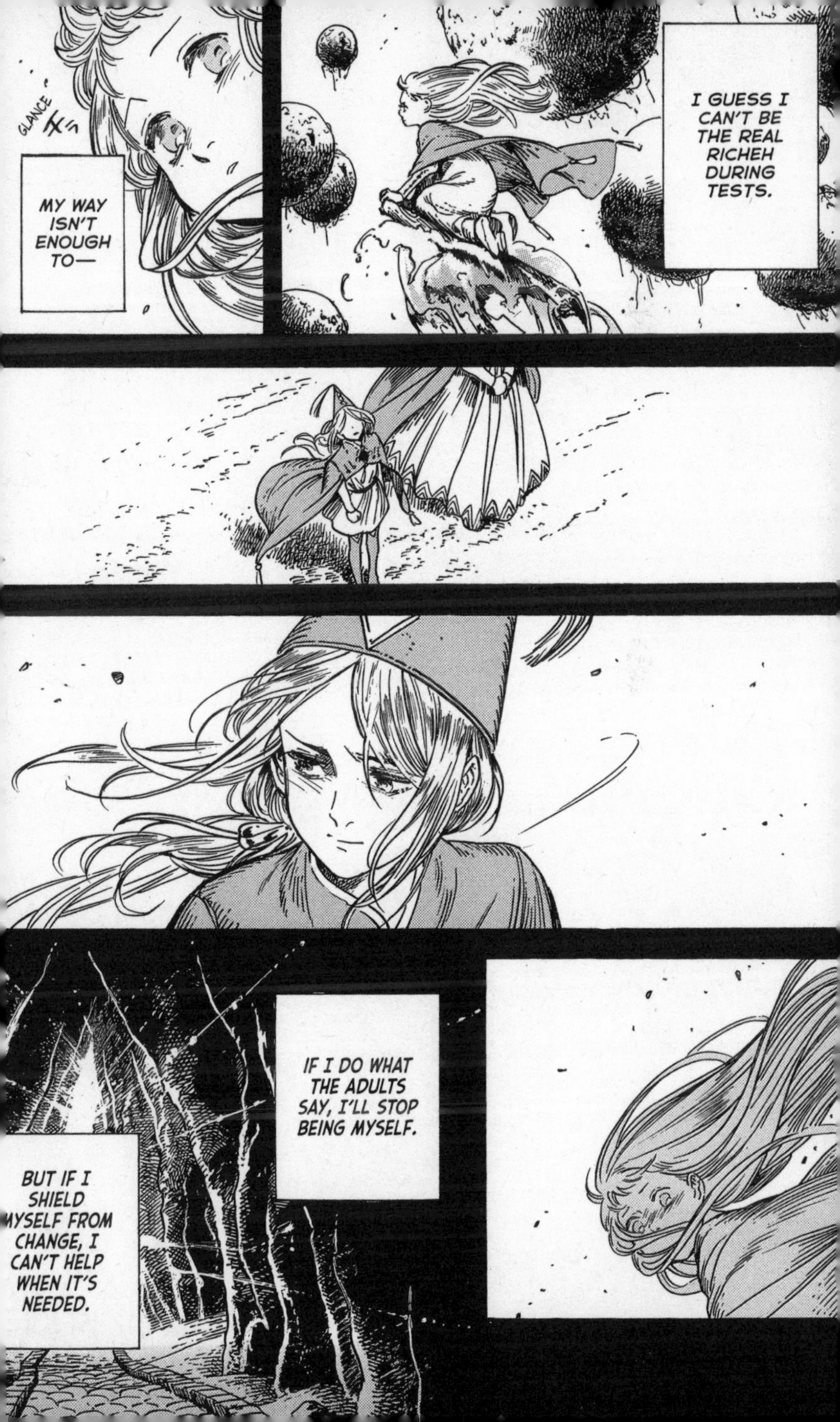
I GUESS I CAN'T BE THE REAL RICHEH DURING TESTS.
GLANCE
MY WAY ISN'T ENOUGH TO—
IF I DO WHAT THE ADULTS SAY, I'LL STOP BEING MYSELF.
BUT IF I SHIELD MYSELF FROM CHANGE, I CAN'T HELP WHEN IT'S NEEDED.

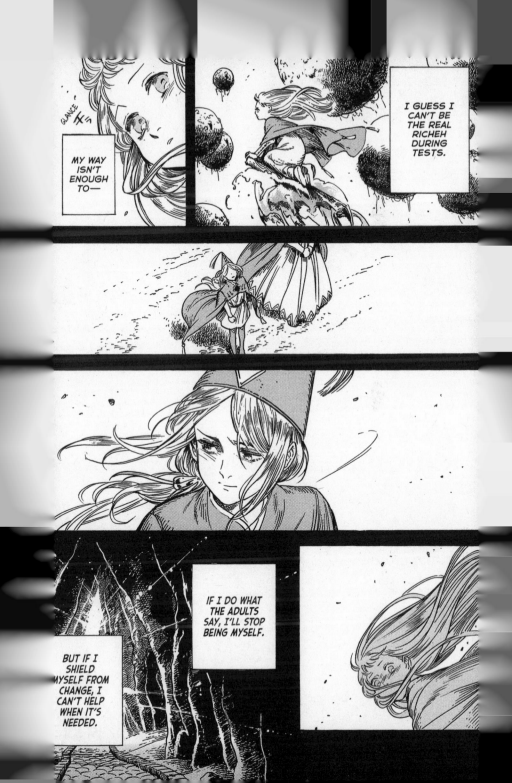

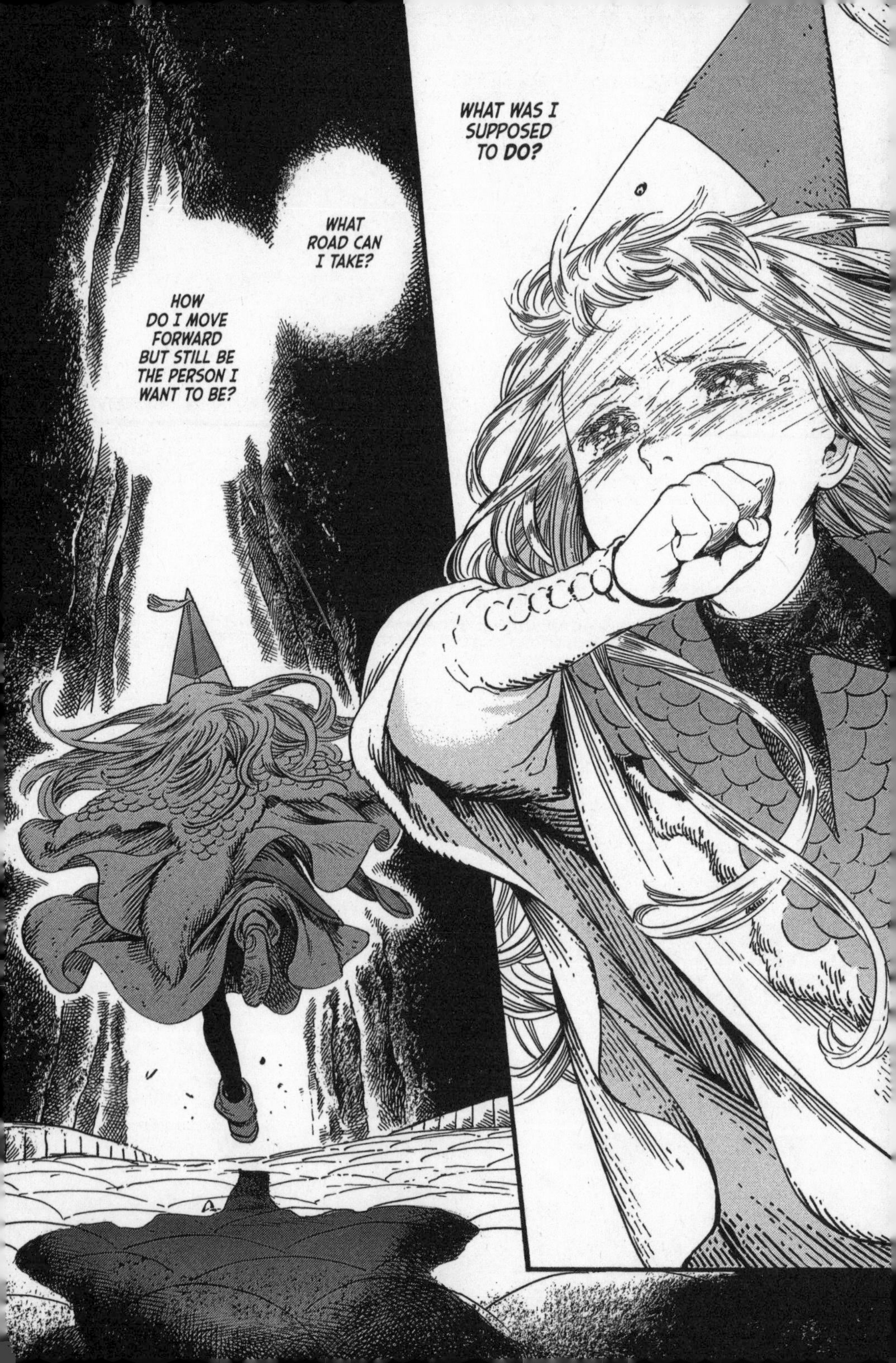
WHAT WAS I SUPPOSED TO DO?
WHAT ROAD CAN I TAKE?
HOW DO I MOVE FORWARD BUT STILL BE THE PERSON I WANT TO BE?

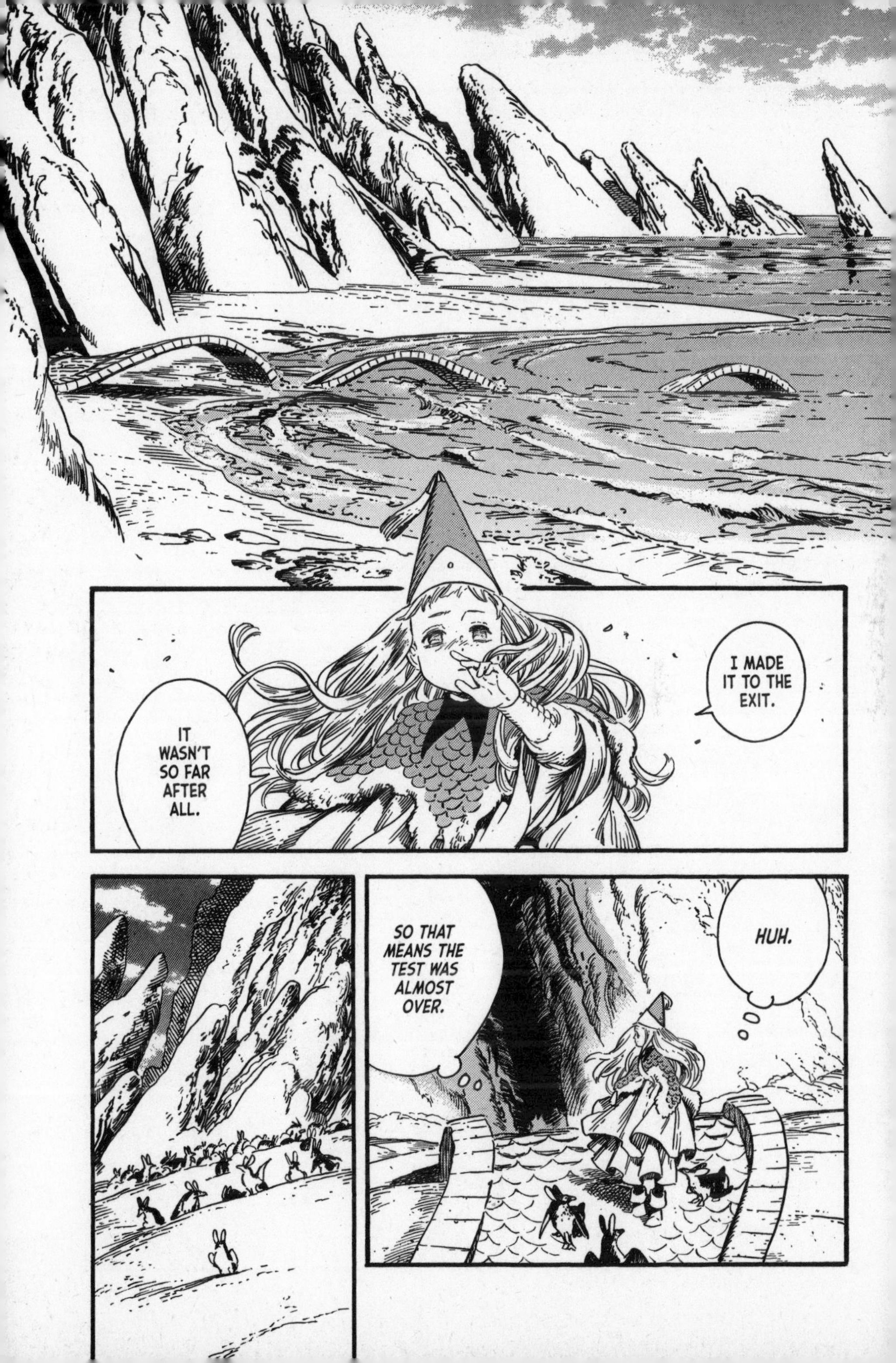
I MADE IT TO THE EXIT.
IT WASN'T SO FAR AFTER ALL.
HUH.
SO THAT MEANS THE TEST WAS ALMOST OVER.

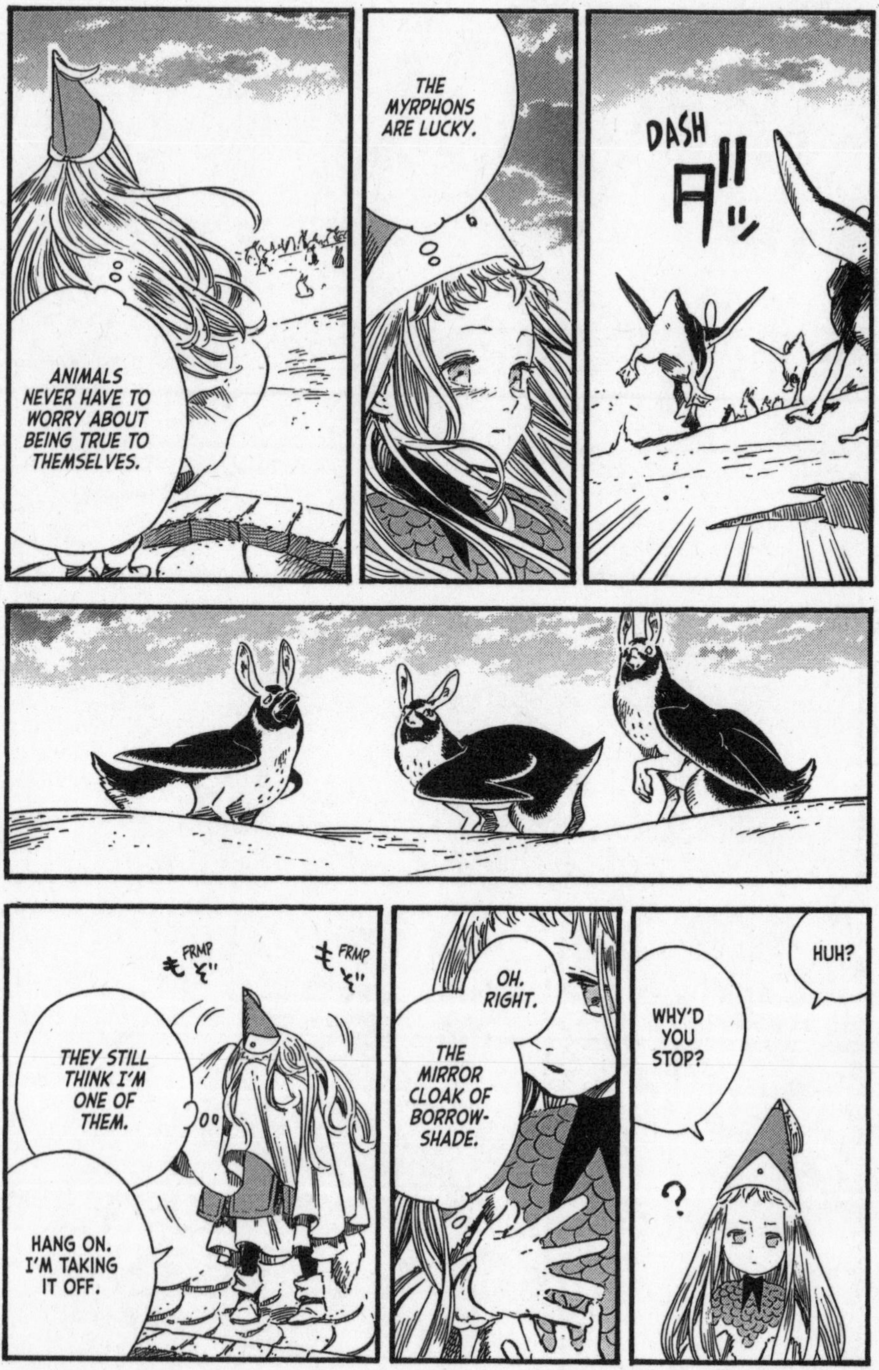
DASH
ダッ
THE MYRPHONS ARE LUCKY.
ANIMALS NEVER HAVE TO WORRY ABOUT BEING TRUE TO THEMSELVES.
HUH?
WHY'D YOU STOP?
?
OH. RIGHT.
THE MIRROR CLOAK OF BORROW-SHADE.
FRMP もぞ
FRMP もぞ
THEY STILL THINK I'M ONE OF THEM.
HANG ON. I'M TAKING IT OFF.

IT'S EUINI'S PALM QUIRE.

HEY...

PLUNK

HUH? THAT'S WEIRD.

PWAFF

PWAFF

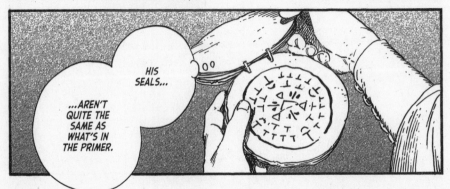

HIS SEALS...

...AREN'T QUITE THE SAME AS WHAT'S IN THE PRIMER.

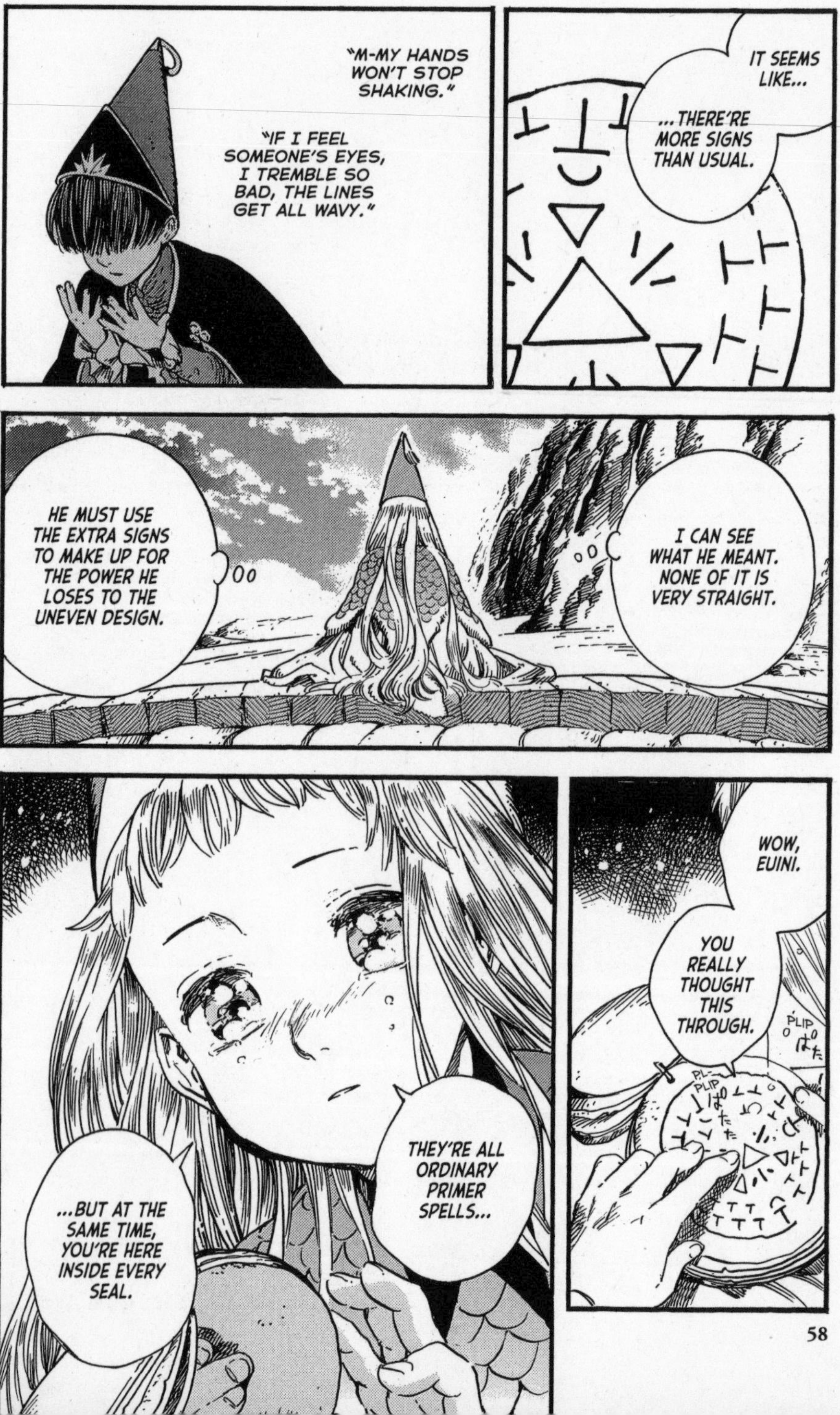
IT SEEMS LIKE...
...THERE'RE MORE SIGNS THAN USUAL.
"M-MY HANDS WON'T STOP SHAKING."
"IF I FEEL SOMEONE'S EYES, I TREMBLE SO BAD, THE LINES GET ALL WAVY."
I CAN SEE WHAT HE MEANT. NONE OF IT IS VERY STRAIGHT.
HE MUST USE THE EXTRA SIGNS TO MAKE UP FOR THE POWER HE LOSES TO THE UNEVEN DESIGN.
WOW, EUINI.
YOU REALLY THOUGHT THIS THROUGH.
PLIP ぱた
PL- PLIP ぱたた
THEY'RE ALL ORDINARY PRIMER SPELLS...
...BUT AT THE SAME TIME, YOU'RE HERE INSIDE EVERY SEAL.

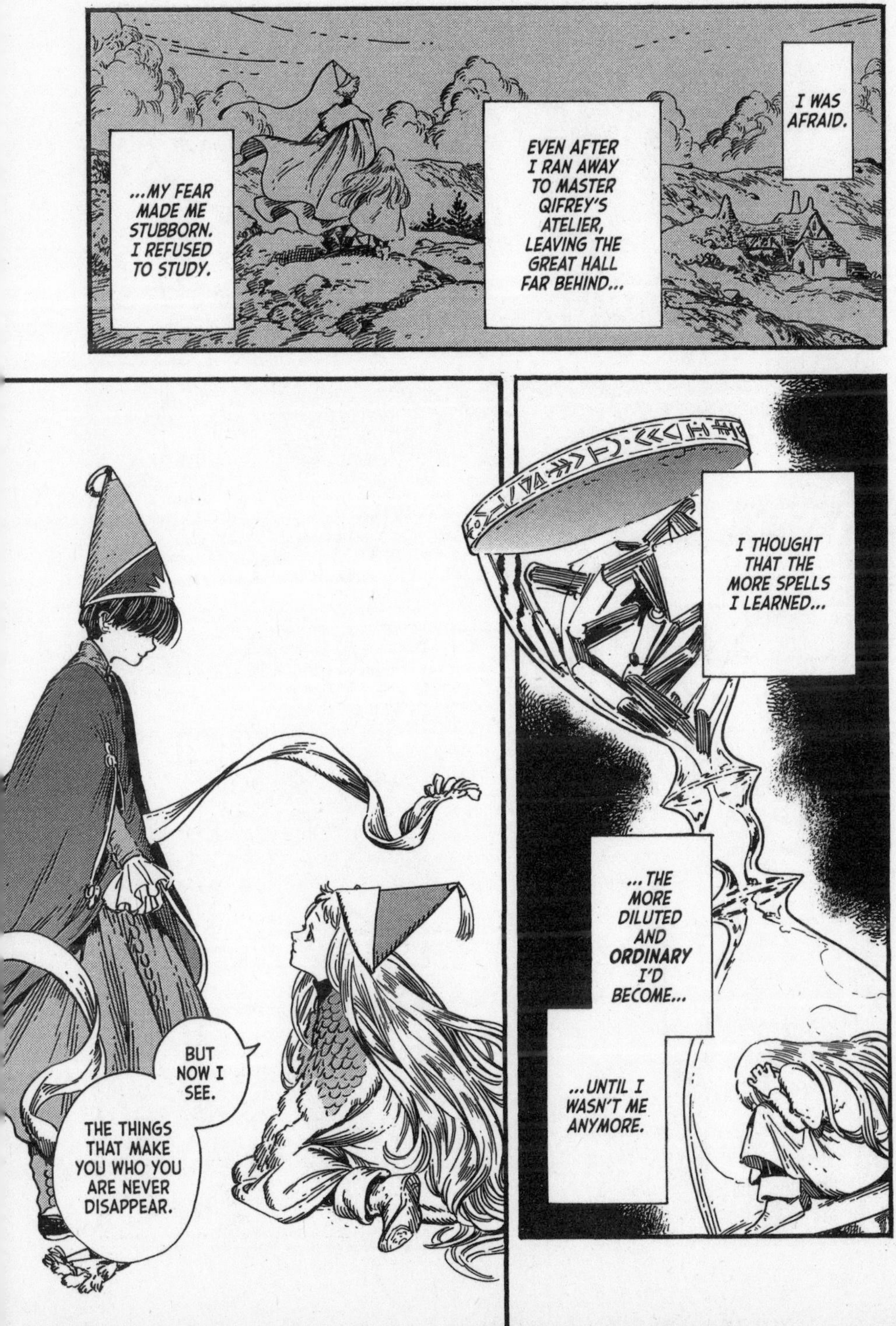
I WAS AFRAID.
EVEN AFTER I RAN AWAY TO MASTER QIFREY'S ATELIER, LEAVING THE GREAT HALL FAR BEHIND...
...MY FEAR MADE ME STUBBORN. I REFUSED TO STUDY.
I THOUGHT THAT THE MORE SPELLS I LEARNED...
...THE MORE DILUTED AND ORDINARY I'D BECOME...
...UNTIL I WASN'T ME ANYMORE.
BUT NOW I SEE.
THE THINGS THAT MAKE YOU WHO YOU ARE NEVER DISAPPEAR.

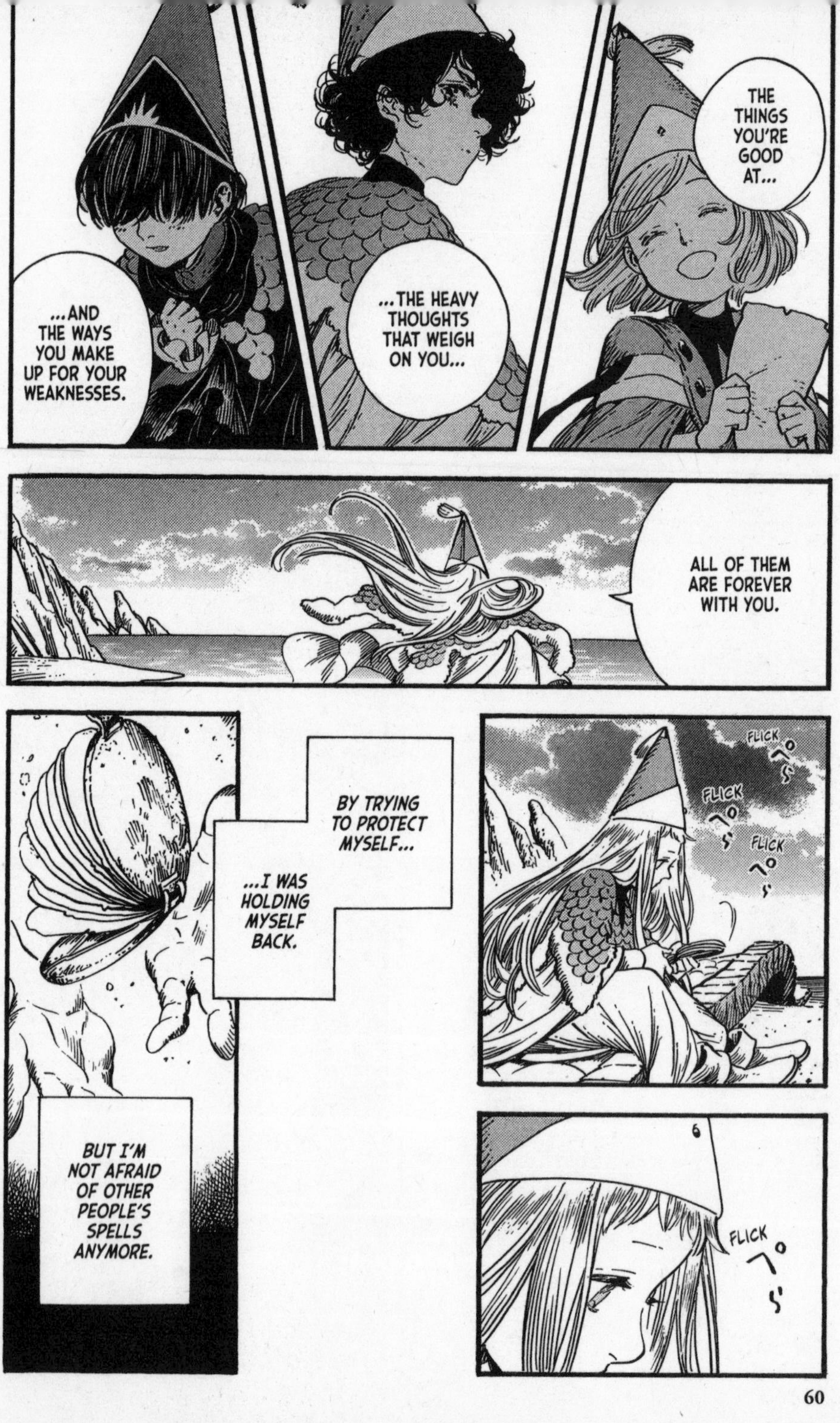
THE THINGS YOU'RE GOOD AT...
...THE HEAVY THOUGHTS THAT WEIGH ON YOU...
...AND THE WAYS YOU MAKE UP FOR YOUR WEAKNESSES.
ALL OF THEM ARE FOREVER WITH YOU.
FLICK
FLICK
FLICK
FLICK
BY TRYING TO PROTECT MYSELF...
...I WAS HOLDING MYSELF BACK.
BUT I'M NOT AFRAID OF OTHER PEOPLE'S SPELLS ANYMORE.

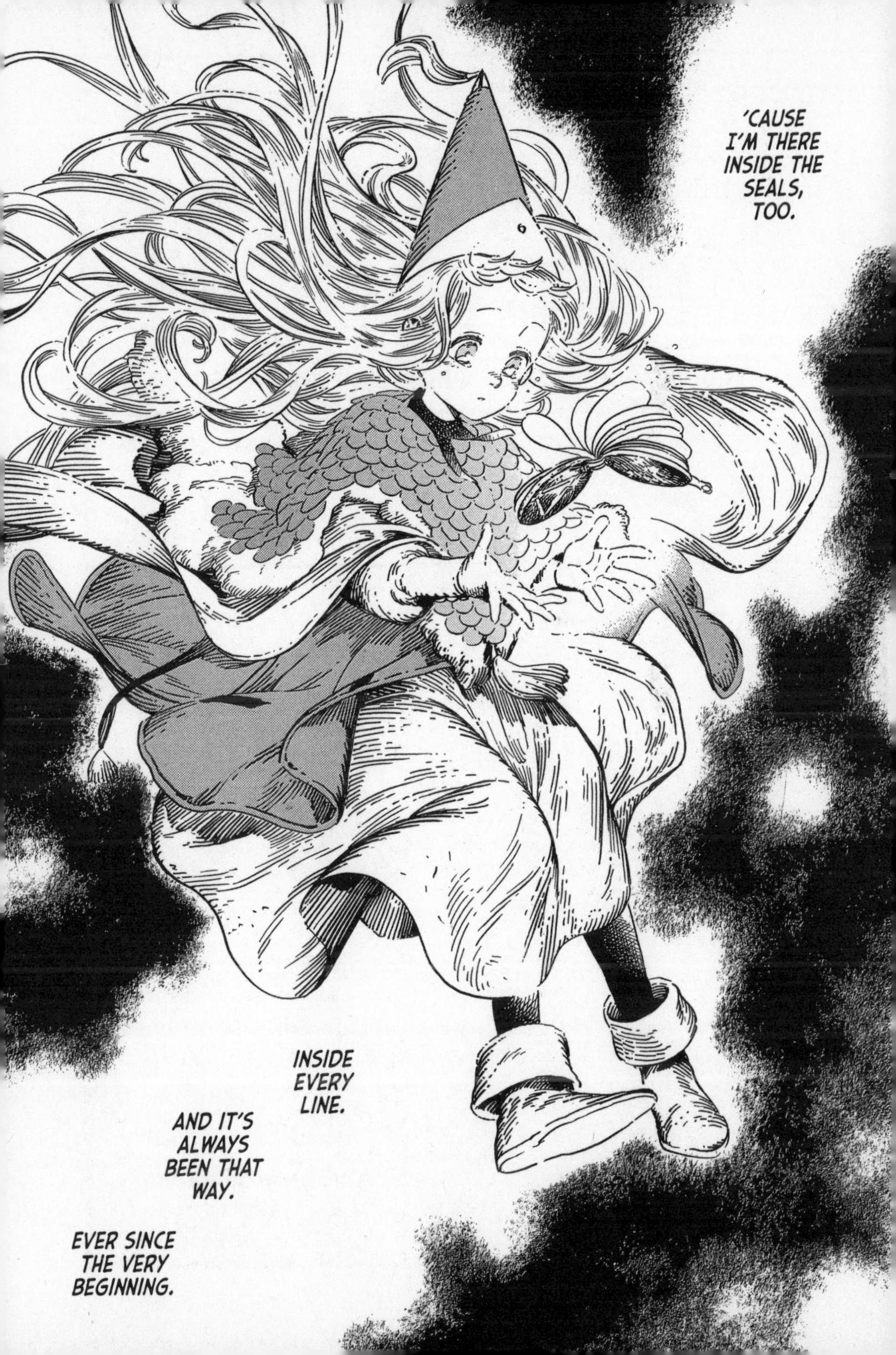
'CAUSE I'M THERE INSIDE THE SEALS, TOO.
INSIDE EVERY LINE.
AND IT'S ALWAYS BEEN THAT WAY.
EVER SINCE THE VERY BEGINNING.

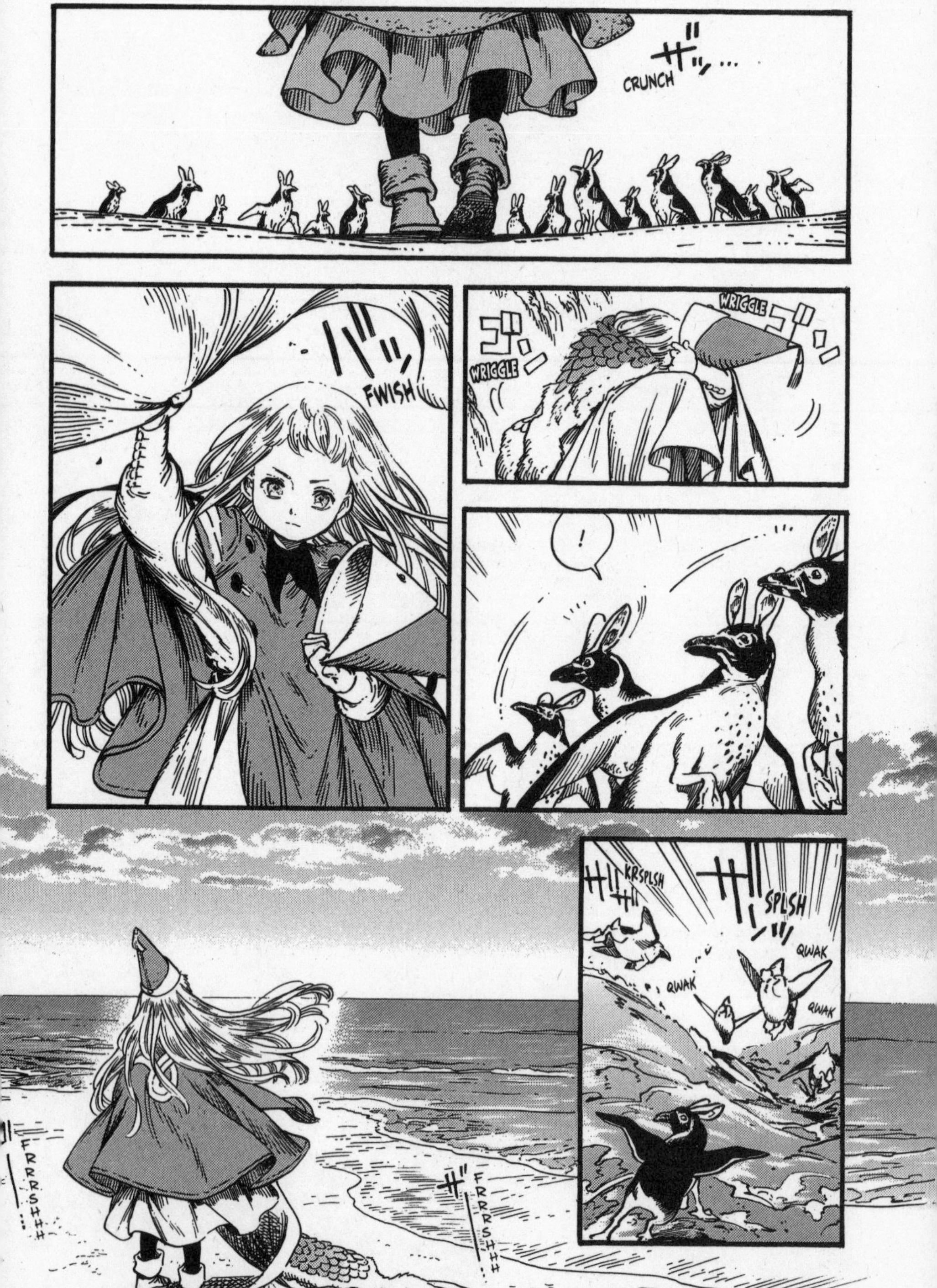

CRUNCH
WRIGGLE
WRIGGLE
!
FWISH
KRSPLSH
SPLSH
QWAK
QWAK
QWAK
FRRRSHHH
FRRRSHHH

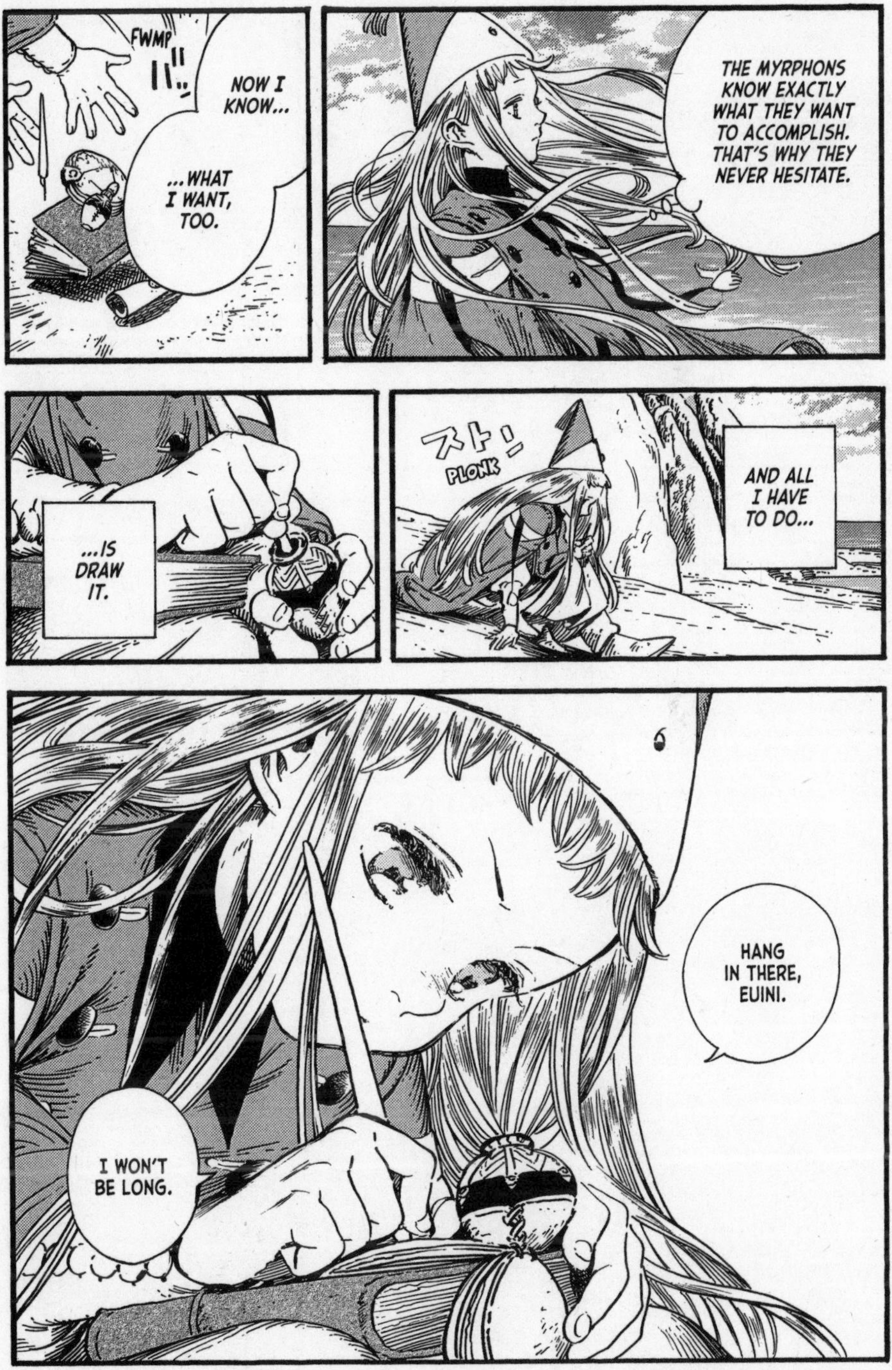
THE MYRPHONS KNOW EXACTLY WHAT THEY WANT TO ACCOMPLISH. THAT'S WHY THEY NEVER HESITATE.
FWMP
NOW I KNOW...
...WHAT I WANT, TOO.
ストン
PLONK
AND ALL I HAVE TO DO...
...IS DRAW IT.
HANG IN THERE, EUINI.
I WON'T BE LONG.

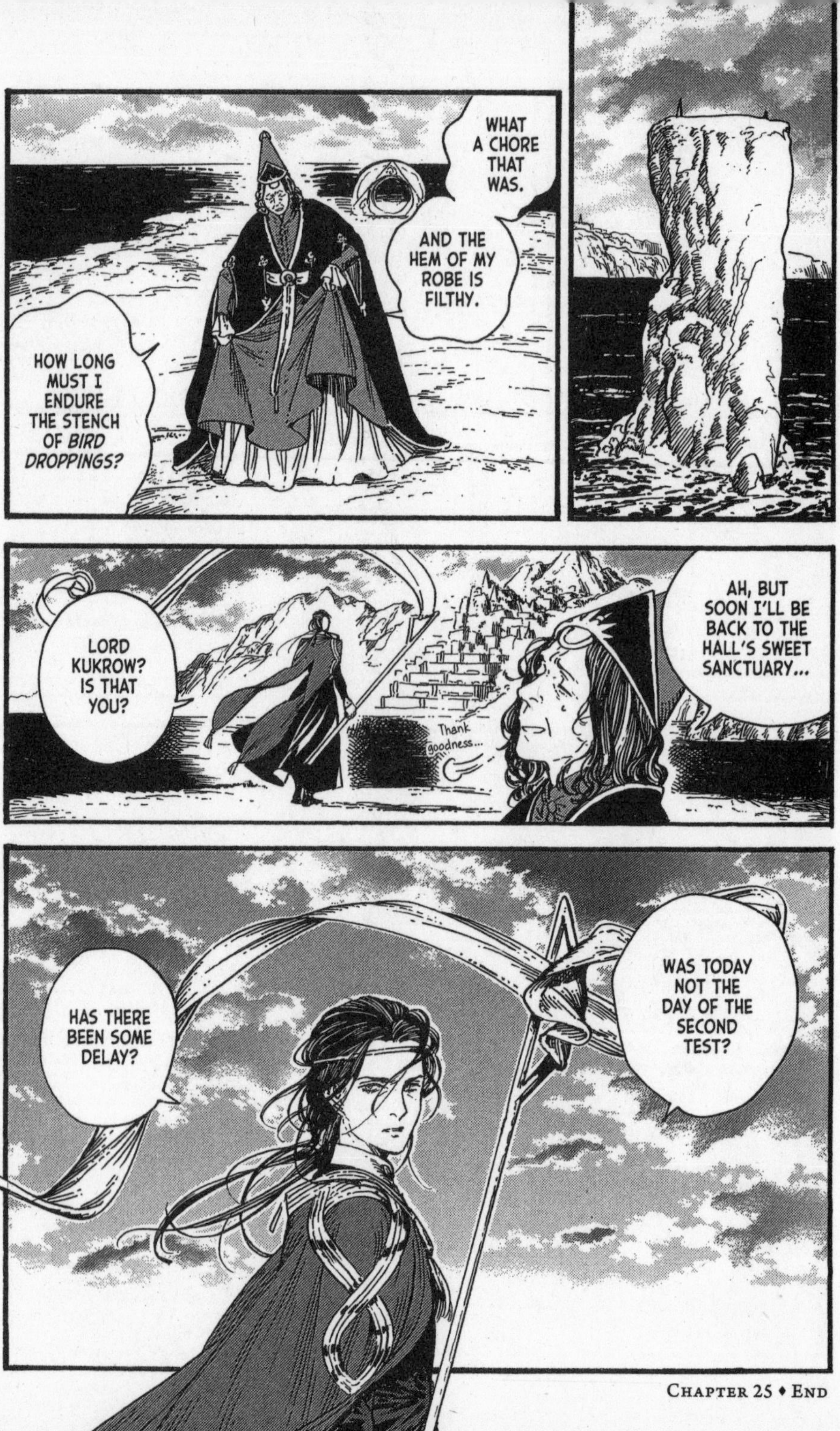
WHAT A CHORE THAT WAS.
AND THE HEM OF MY ROBE IS FILTHY.
HOW LONG MUST I ENDURE THE STENCH OF *BIRD DROPPINGS?*
AH, BUT SOON I'LL BE BACK TO THE HALL'S SWEET SANCTUARY...
Thank goodness...
LORD KUKROW? IS THAT YOU?
WAS TODAY NOT THE DAY OF THE SECOND TEST?
HAS THERE BEEN SOME DELAY?

CHAPTER 25 ♦ END

Witch Hat Atelier

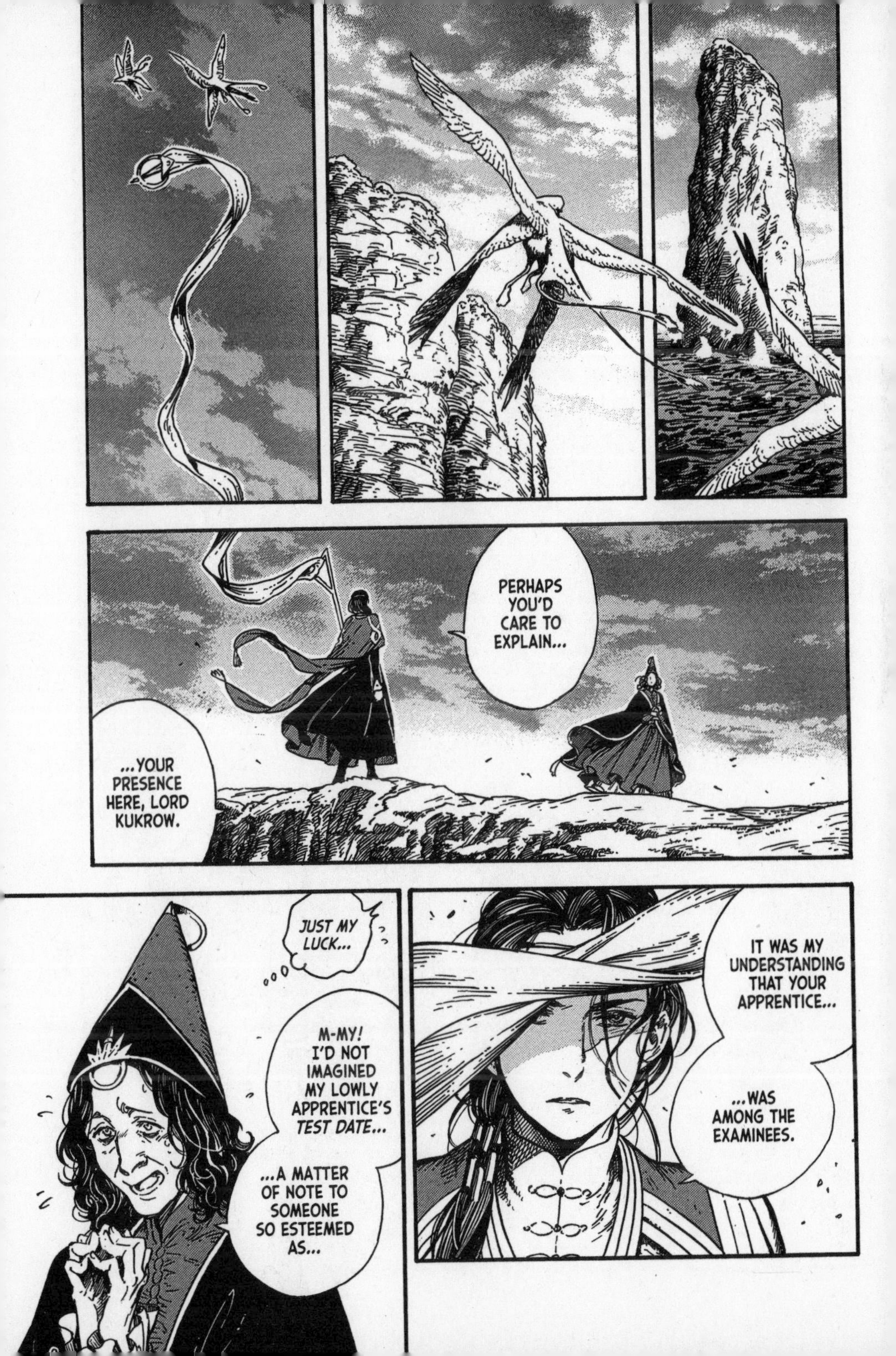
PERHAPS YOU'D CARE TO EXPLAIN...
...YOUR PRESENCE HERE, LORD KUKROW.
IT WAS MY UNDERSTANDING THAT YOUR APPRENTICE...
...WAS AMONG THE EXAMINEES.
JUST MY LUCK...
M-MY! I'D NOT IMAGINED MY LOWLY APPRENTICE'S *TEST DATE*...
...A MATTER OF NOTE TO SOMEONE SO ESTEEMED AS...

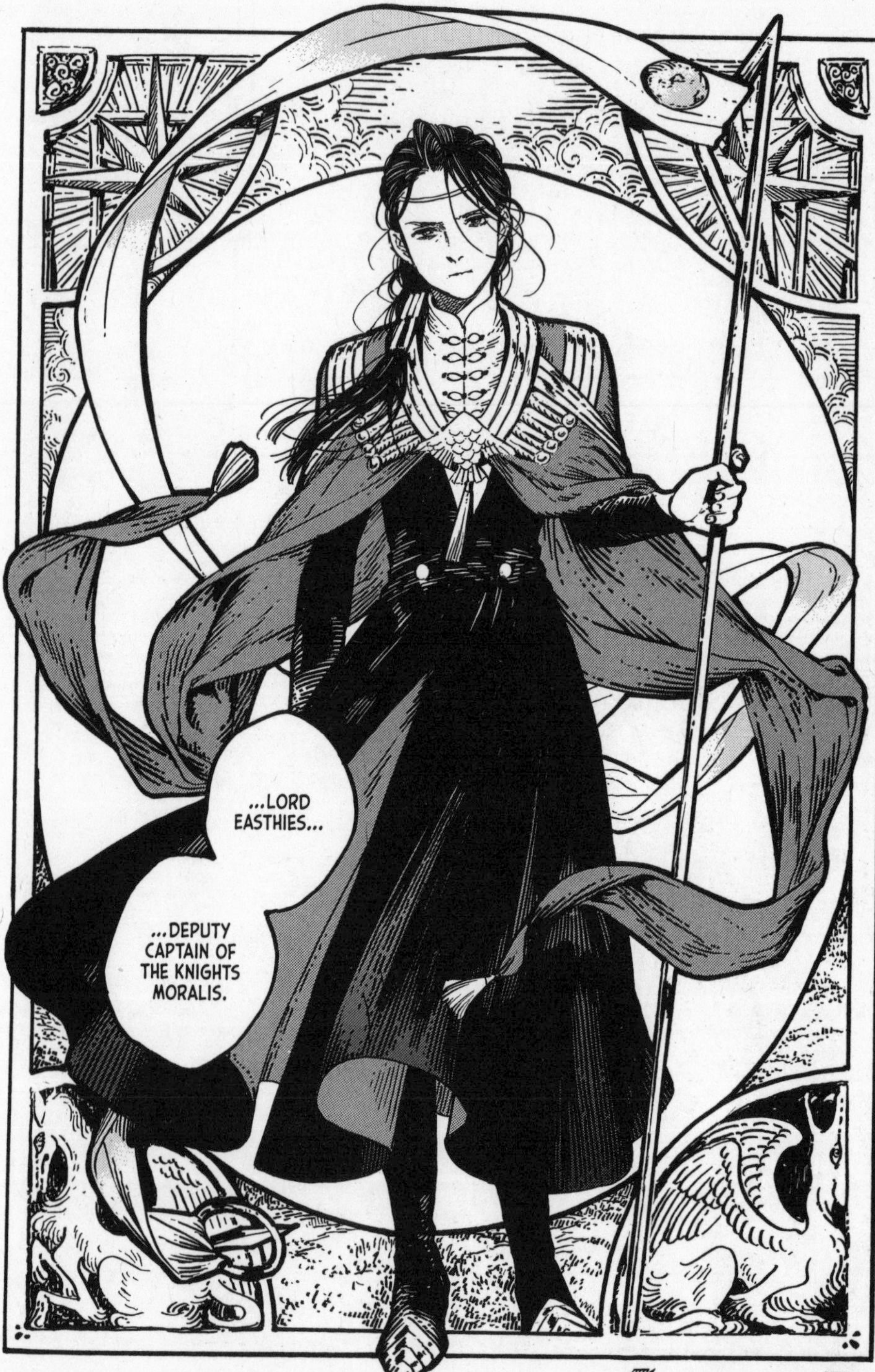
...LORD EASTHIES...
...DEPUTY CAPTAIN OF THE KNIGHTS MORALIS.

CHAPTER 26

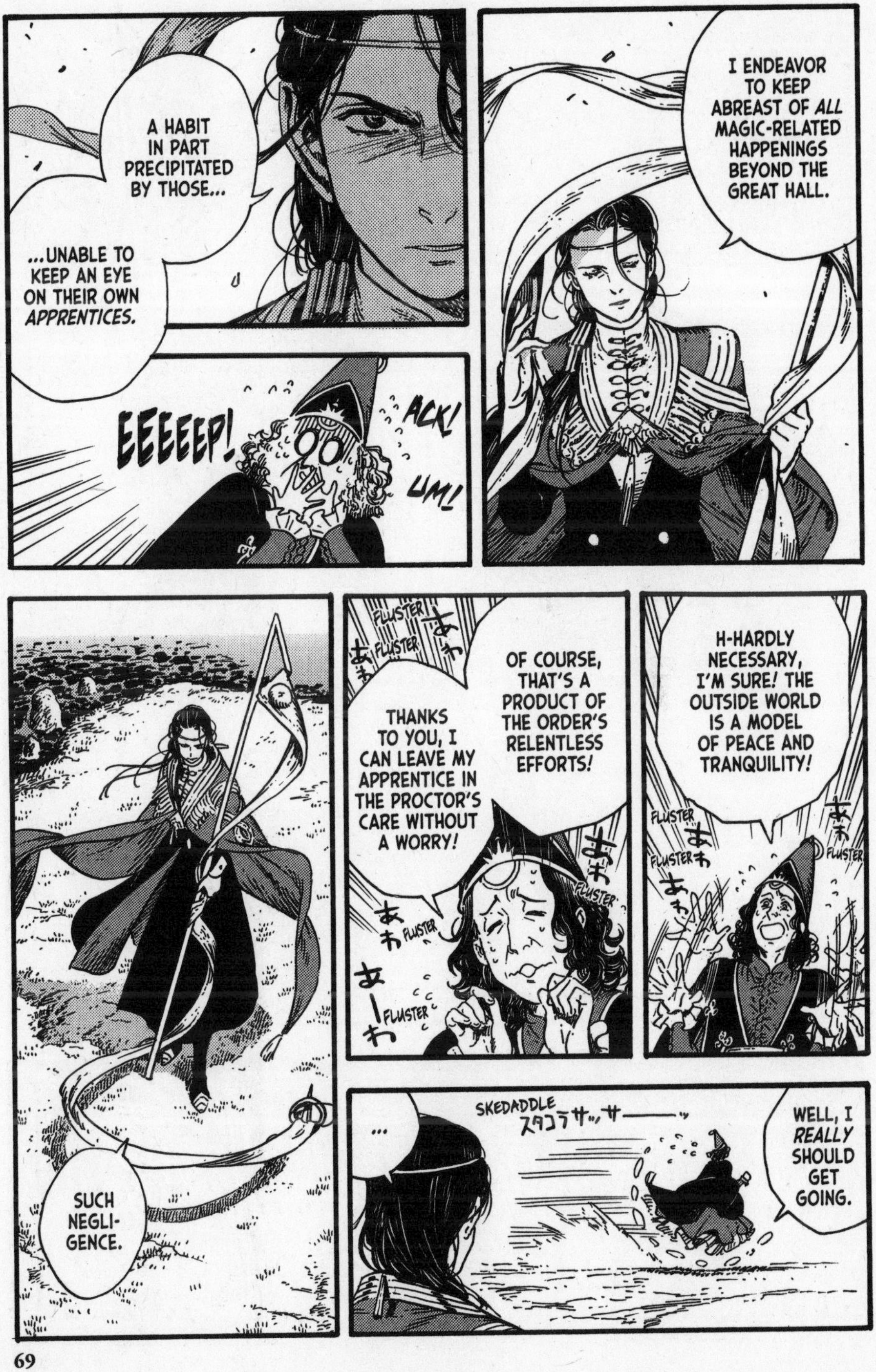
I ENDEAVOR TO KEEP ABREAST OF *ALL* MAGIC-RELATED HAPPENINGS BEYOND THE GREAT HALL.
A HABIT IN PART PRECIPITATED BY THOSE...
...UNABLE TO KEEP AN EYE ON THEIR OWN *APPRENTICES.*
EEEEEP!
ACK!
UM!
H-HARDLY NECESSARY, I'M SURE! THE OUTSIDE WORLD IS A MODEL OF PEACE AND TRANQUILITY!
FLUSTER あわ
FLUSTER あわ
FLUSTER あわ
OF COURSE, THAT'S A PRODUCT OF THE ORDER'S RELENTLESS EFFORTS!
THANKS TO YOU, I CAN LEAVE MY APPRENTICE IN THE PROCTOR'S CARE WITHOUT A WORRY!
FLUSTER あわ
FLUSTER あわ
FLUSTER あわ
FLUSTER あわ
FLUSTER あーわ
WELL, I *REALLY* SHOULD GET GOING.
SKEDADDLE スタコラサッサーーッ
...
SUCH NEGLI-GENCE.

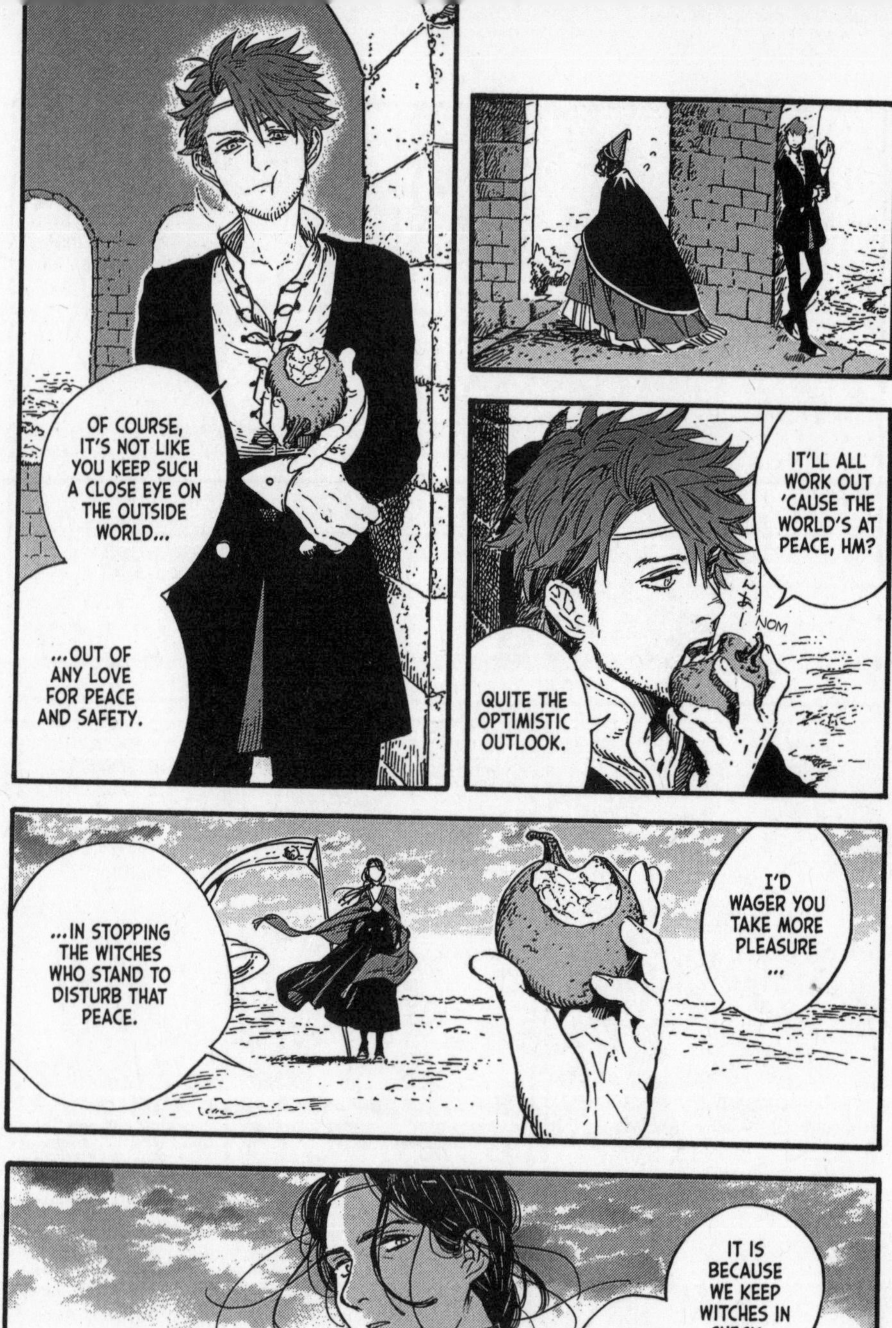
IT'LL ALL WORK OUT 'CAUSE THE WORLD'S AT PEACE, HM?
NOM
QUITE THE OPTIMISTIC OUTLOOK.
OF COURSE, IT'S NOT LIKE YOU KEEP SUCH A CLOSE EYE ON THE OUTSIDE WORLD...
...OUT OF ANY LOVE FOR PEACE AND SAFETY.
I'D WAGER YOU TAKE MORE PLEASURE ...
...IN STOPPING THE WITCHES WHO STAND TO DISTURB THAT PEACE.
IT IS BECAUSE WE KEEP WITCHES IN CHECK...
...THAT PEACE IS MAINTAINED, UTOWIN.

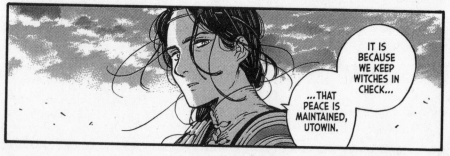

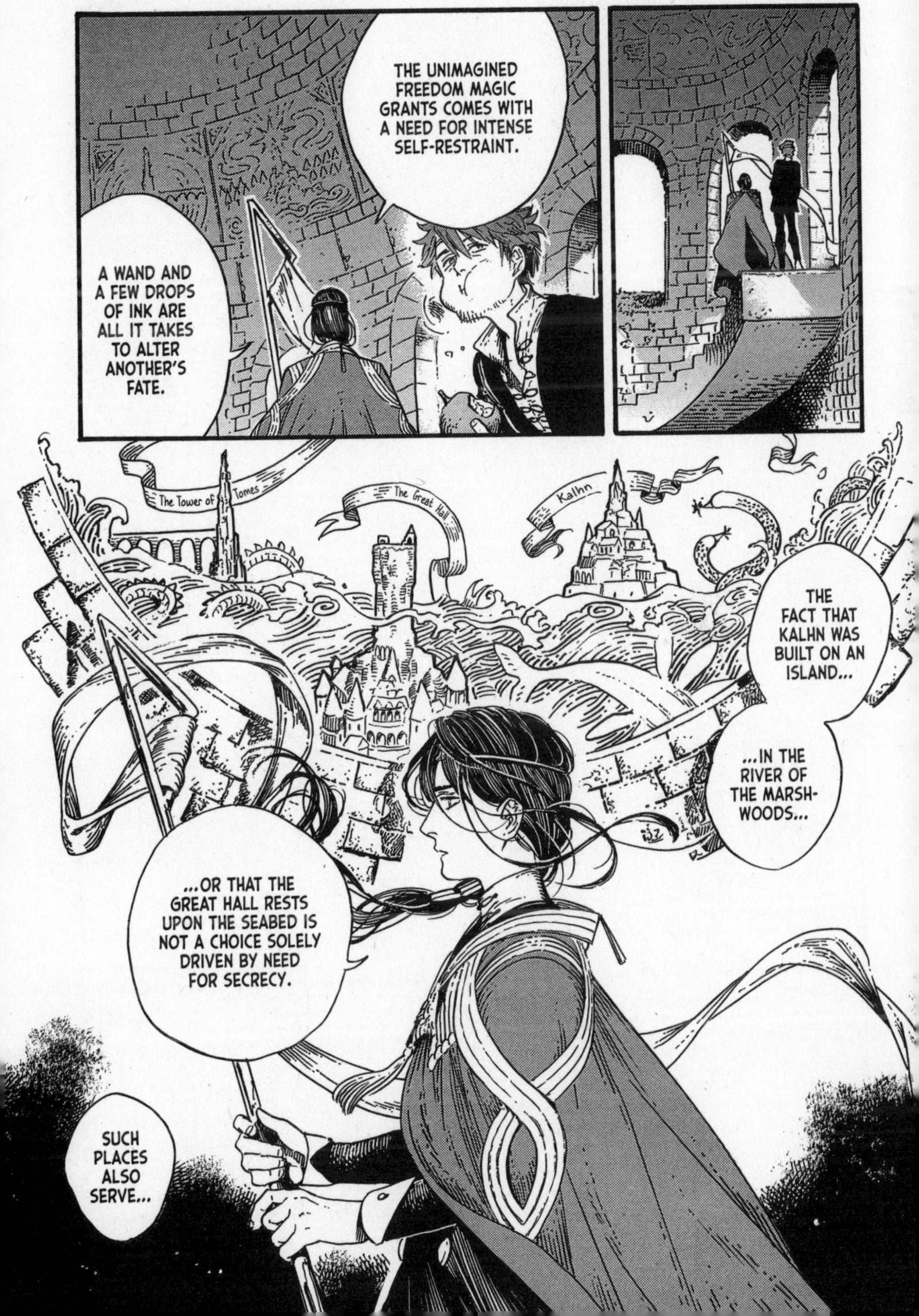
THE UNIMAGINED FREEDOM MAGIC GRANTS COMES WITH A NEED FOR INTENSE SELF-RESTRAINT.
A WAND AND A FEW DROPS OF INK ARE ALL IT TAKES TO ALTER ANOTHER'S FATE.
Kalhn
The Great Hall
The Tower of Tomes
THE FACT THAT KALHN WAS BUILT ON AN ISLAND...
...IN THE RIVER OF THE MARSH-WOODS...
...OR THAT THE GREAT HALL RESTS UPON THE SEABED IS NOT A CHOICE SOLELY DRIVEN BY NEED FOR SECRECY.
SUCH PLACES ALSO SERVE...

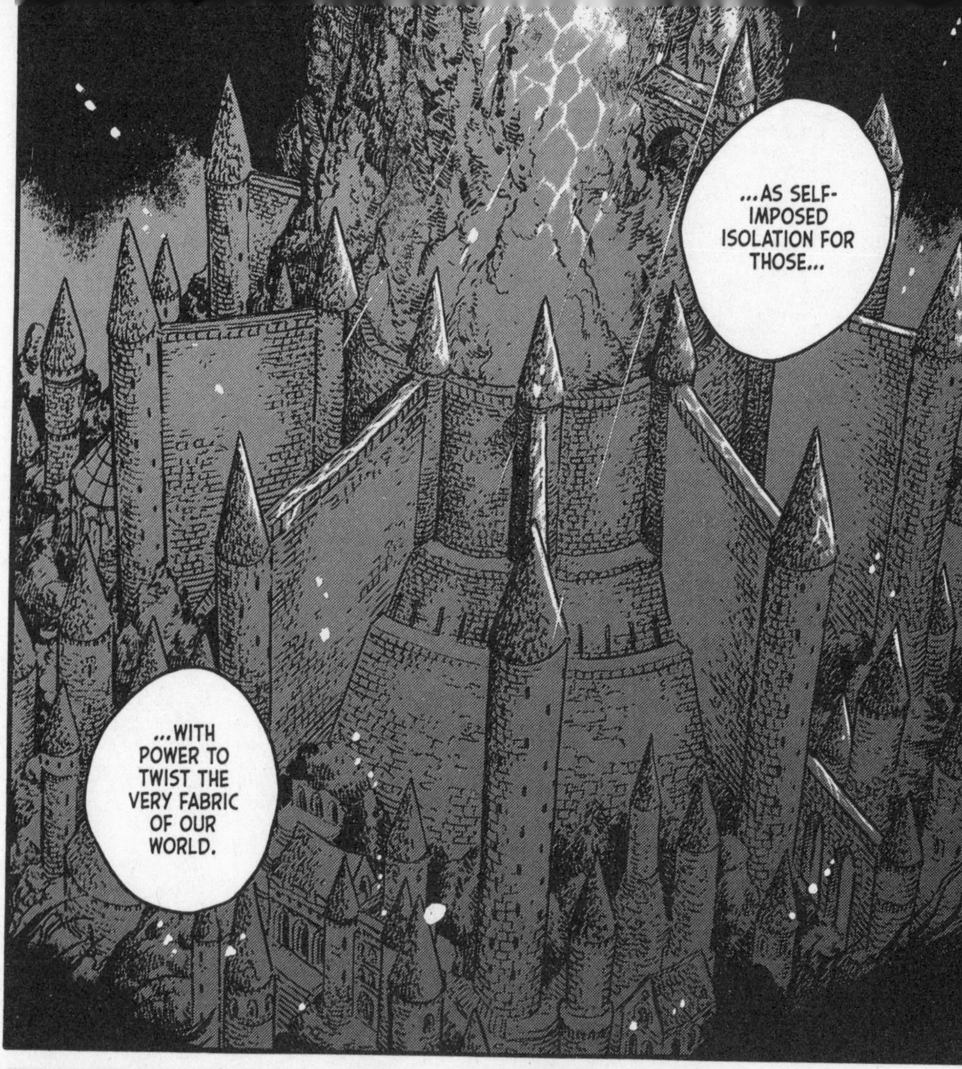
...AS SELF-IMPOSED ISOLATION FOR THOSE...
...WITH POWER TO TWIST THE VERY FABRIC OF OUR WORLD.

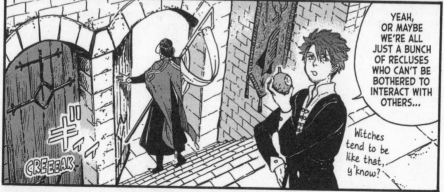

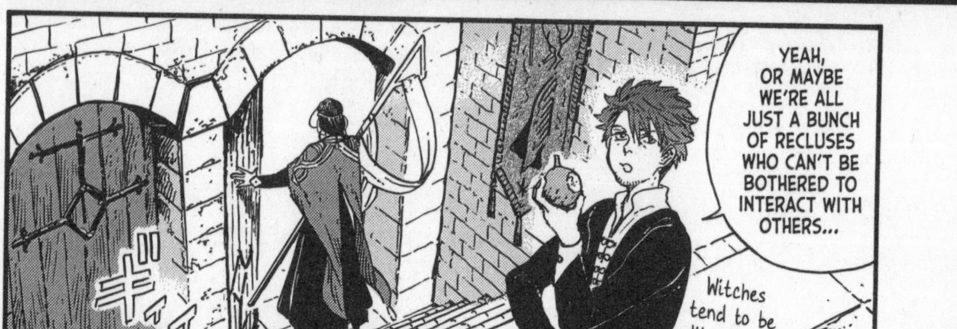
YEAH, OR MAYBE WE'RE ALL JUST A BUNCH OF RECLUSES WHO CAN'T BE BOTHERED TO INTERACT WITH OTHERS...
Witches tend to be like that, y'know?
ギィィ
CREEEAK

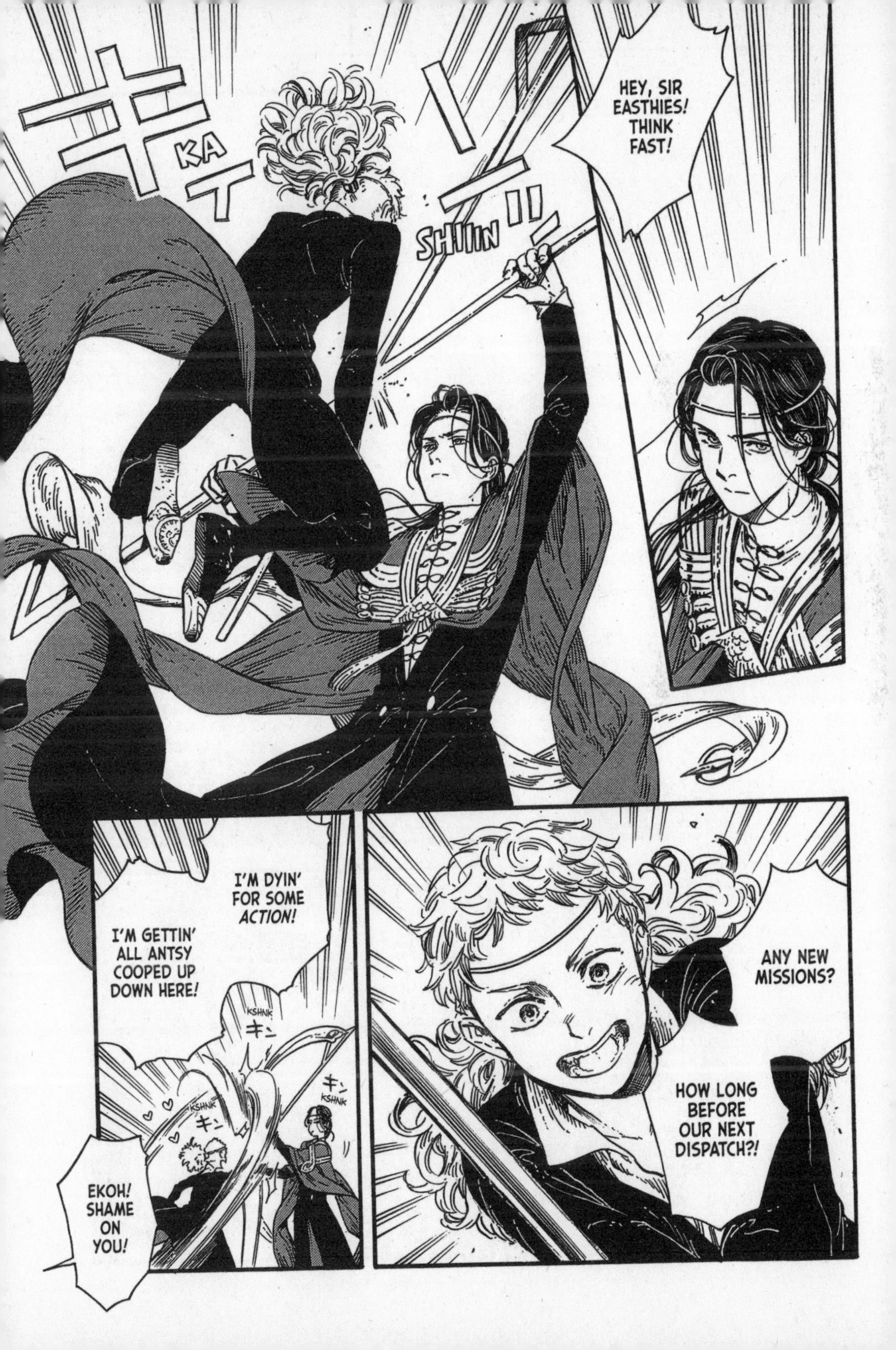
HEY, SIR EASTHIES! THINK FAST!
KA
SHIIIN
ANY NEW MISSIONS?
HOW LONG BEFORE OUR NEXT DISPATCH?!
I'M DYIN' FOR SOME *ACTION!*
I'M GETTIN' ALL ANTSY COOPED UP DOWN HERE!
KSHNK
キン
キン
KSHNK
KSHNK
キン
EKOH! SHAME ON YOU!

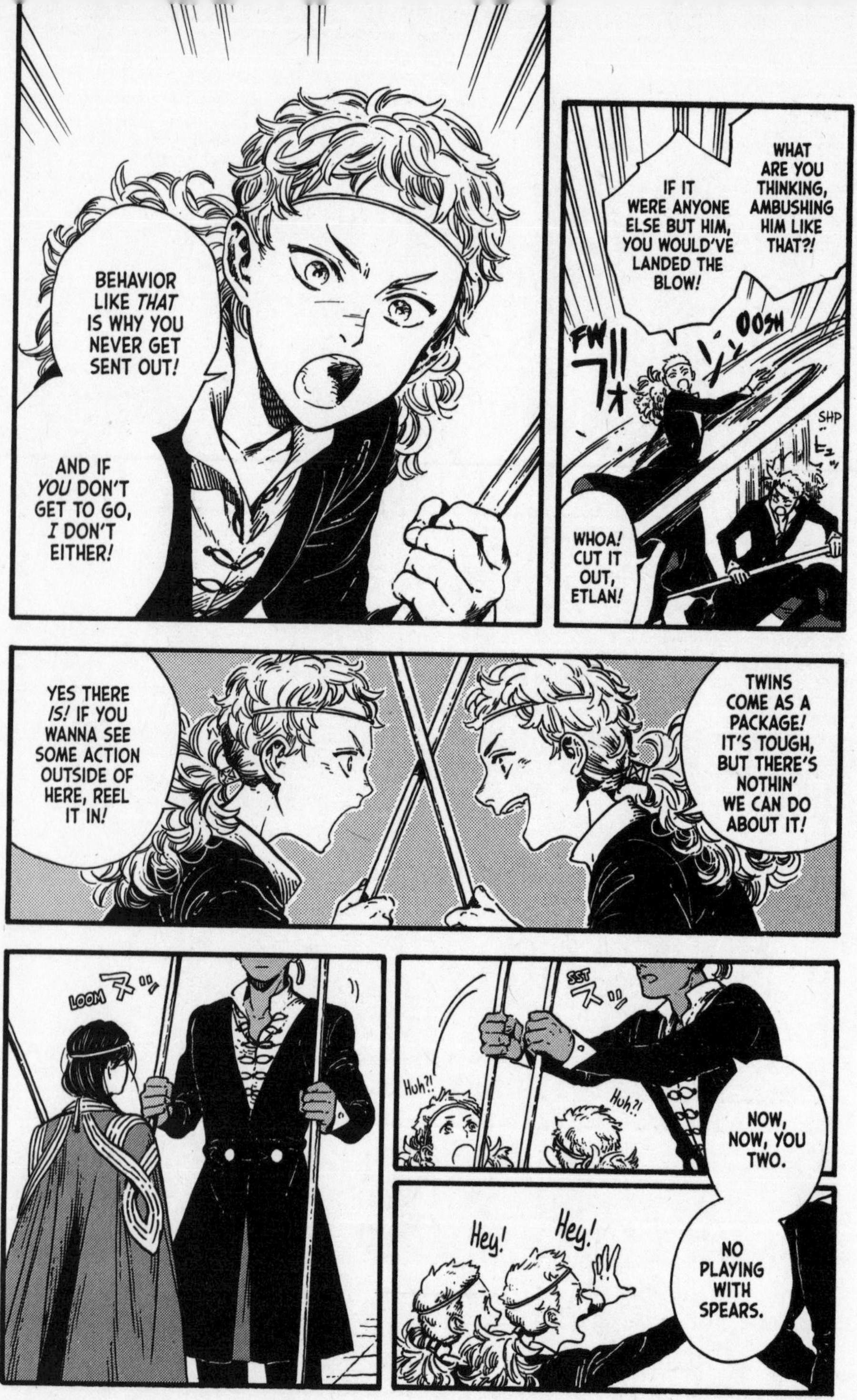
WHAT ARE YOU THINKING, AMBUSHING HIM LIKE THAT?!
IF IT WERE ANYONE ELSE BUT HIM, YOU WOULD'VE LANDED THE BLOW!
FW
OOSH
SHP
WHOA! CUT IT OUT, ETLAN!
BEHAVIOR LIKE *THAT* IS WHY YOU NEVER GET SENT OUT!
AND IF *YOU* DON'T GET TO GO, *I* DON'T EITHER!
TWINS COME AS A PACKAGE! IT'S TOUGH, BUT THERE'S NOTHIN' WE CAN DO ABOUT IT!
YES THERE *IS!* IF YOU WANNA SEE SOME ACTION OUTSIDE OF HERE, REEL IT IN!
SST
Huh?!
Huh?!
NOW, NOW, YOU TWO.
Hey!
Hey!
NO PLAYING WITH SPEARS.
LOOM

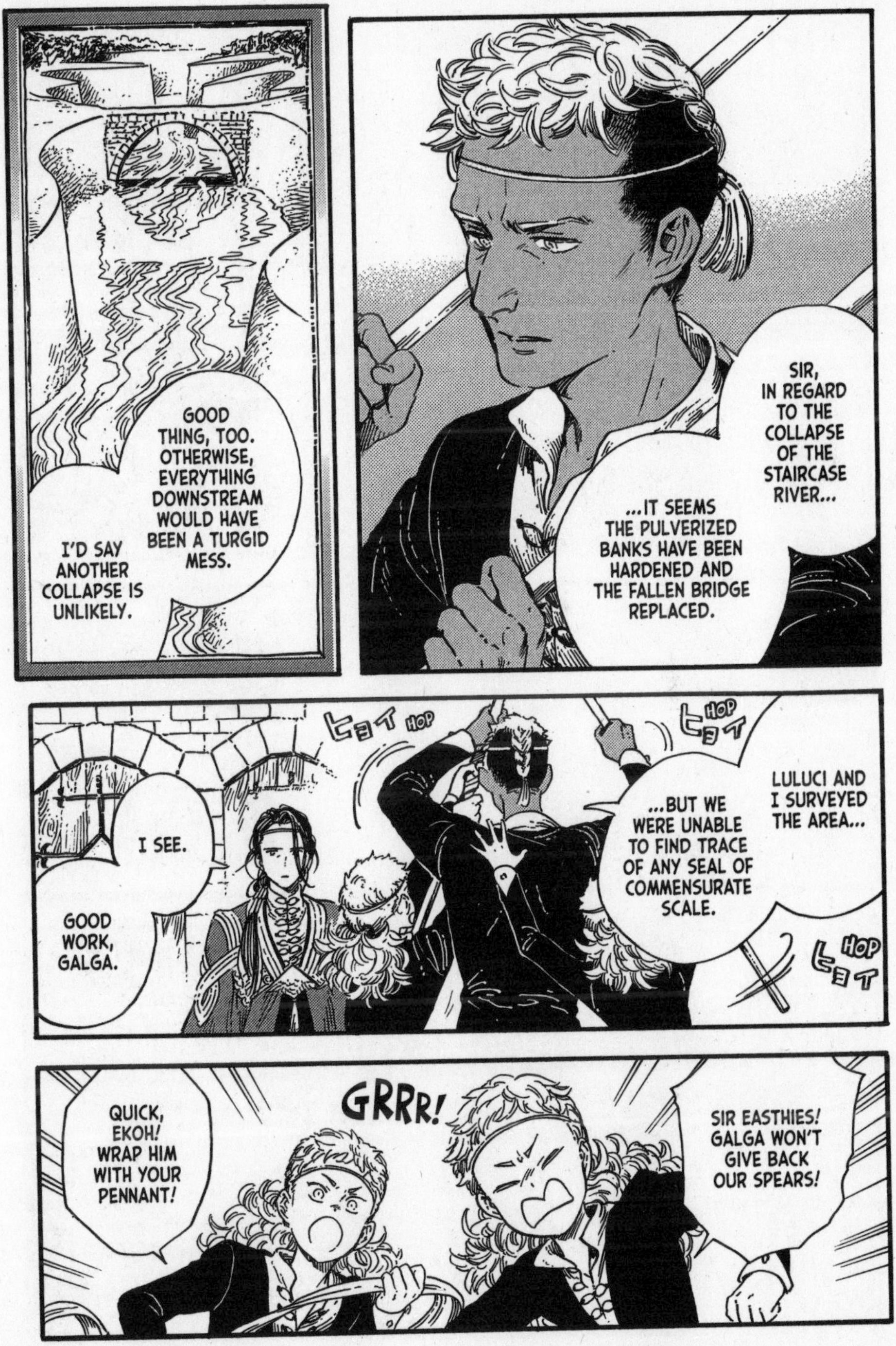
SIR, IN REGARD TO THE COLLAPSE OF THE STAIRCASE RIVER...
...IT SEEMS THE PULVERIZED BANKS HAVE BEEN HARDENED AND THE FALLEN BRIDGE REPLACED.
GOOD THING, TOO. OTHERWISE, EVERYTHING DOWNSTREAM WOULD HAVE BEEN A TURGID MESS.
I'D SAY ANOTHER COLLAPSE IS UNLIKELY.
ヒョイ HOP
ヒョイ HOP
LULUCI AND I SURVEYED THE AREA...
...BUT WE WERE UNABLE TO FIND TRACE OF ANY SEAL OF COMMENSURATE SCALE.
ヒョイ HOP
I SEE.
GOOD WORK, GALGA.
SIR EASTHIES! GALGA WON'T GIVE BACK OUR SPEARS!
GRRR!
QUICK, EKOH! WRAP HIM WITH YOUR PENNANT!

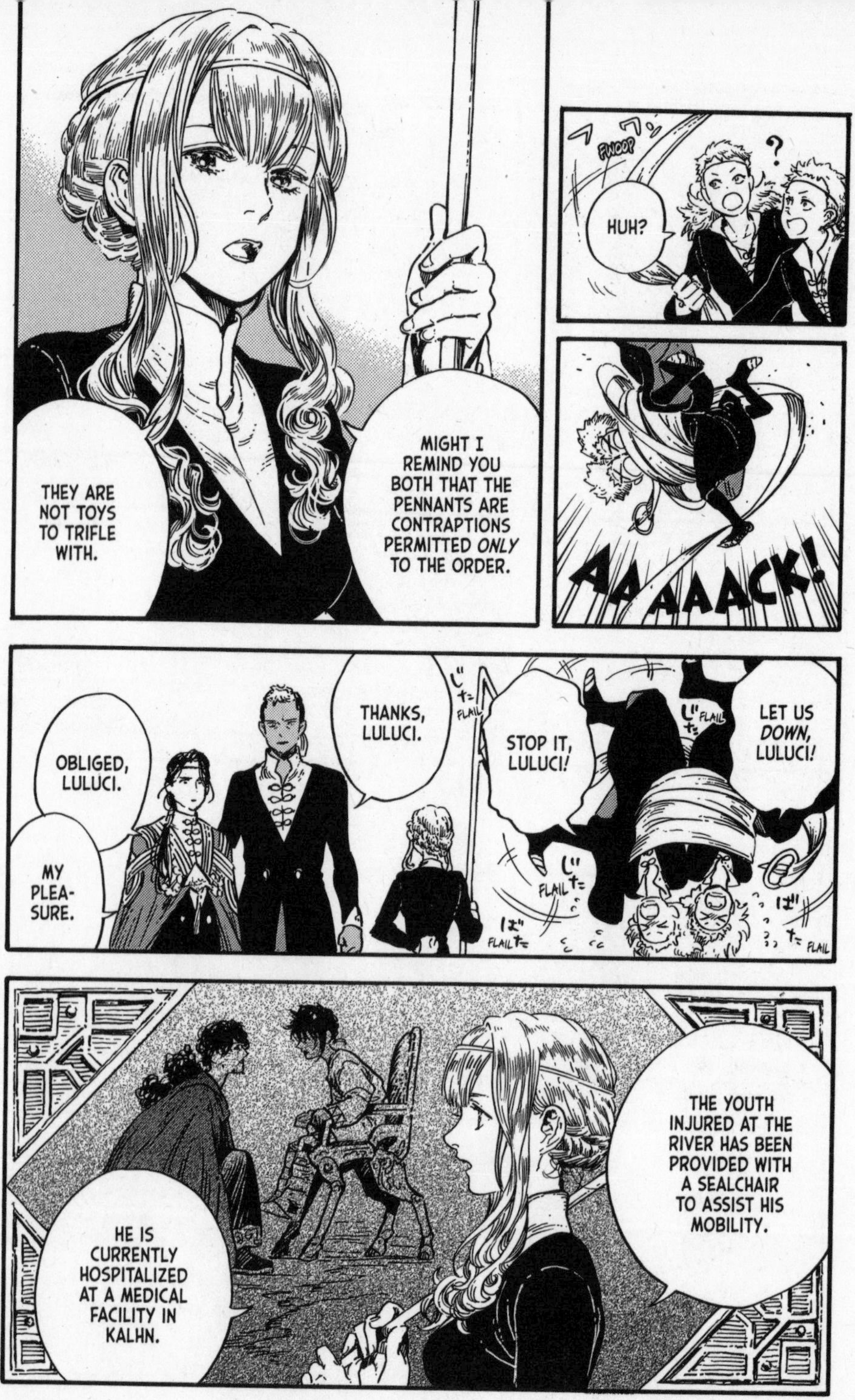

FWOOP
?
HUH?
AAAACK!
MIGHT I REMIND YOU BOTH THAT THE PENNANTS ARE CONTRAPTIONS PERMITTED *ONLY* TO THE ORDER.
THEY ARE NOT TOYS TO TRIFLE WITH.
LET US *DOWN*, LULUCI!
FLAIL
STOP IT, LULUCI!
FLAIL
FLAIL
FLAIL
FLAIL
THANKS, LULUCI.
OBLIGED, LULUCI.
MY PLEA-SURE.
THE YOUTH INJURED AT THE RIVER HAS BEEN PROVIDED WITH A SEALCHAIR TO ASSIST HIS MOBILITY.
HE IS CURRENTLY HOSPITALIZED AT A MEDICAL FACILITY IN KALHN.

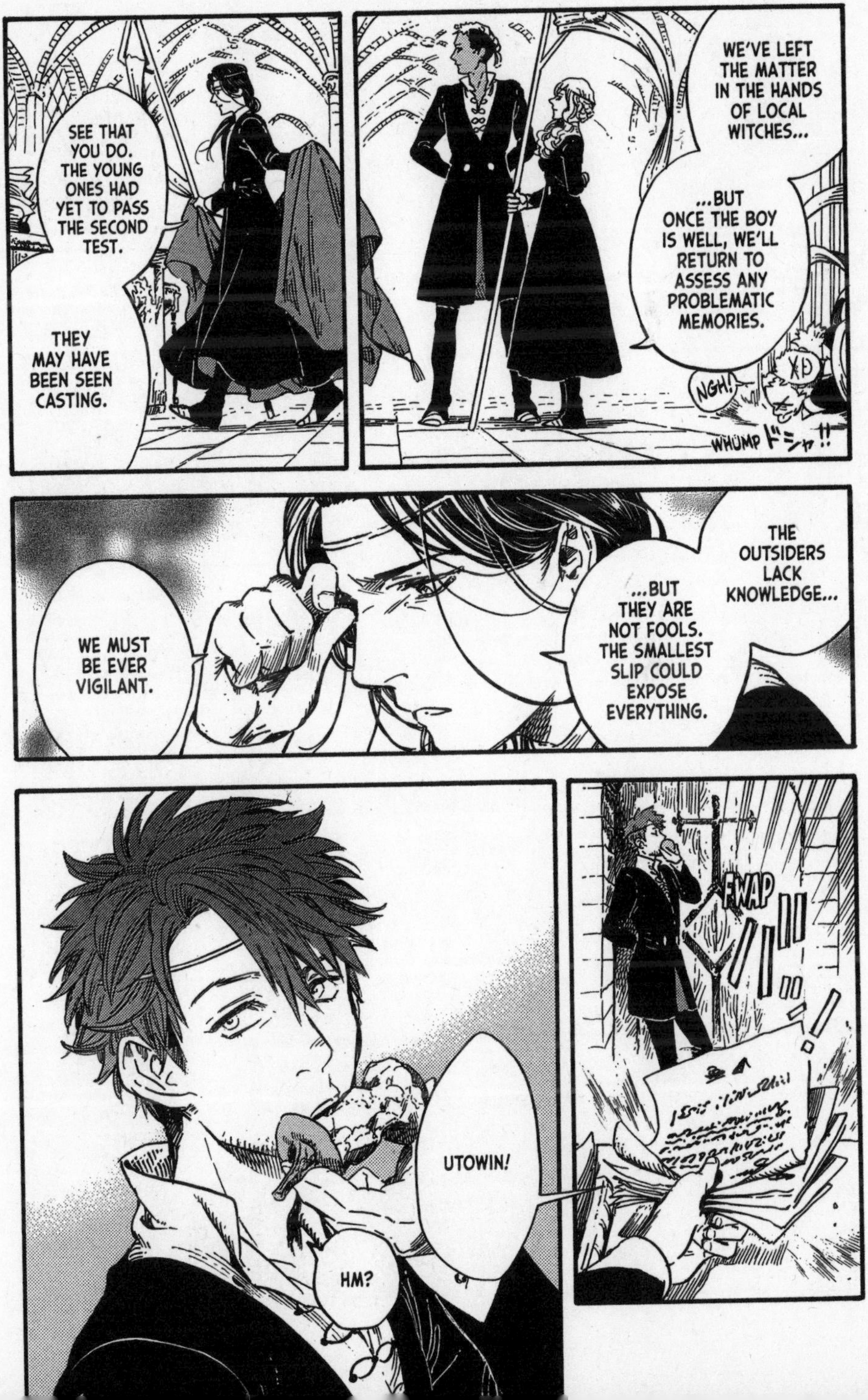
WE'VE LEFT THE MATTER IN THE HANDS OF LOCAL WITCHES...
...BUT ONCE THE BOY IS WELL, WE'LL RETURN TO ASSESS ANY PROBLEMATIC MEMORIES.
NGH!
WHUMP ドシャ!!
SEE THAT YOU DO. THE YOUNG ONES HAD YET TO PASS THE SECOND TEST.
THEY MAY HAVE BEEN SEEN CASTING.
THE OUTSIDERS LACK KNOWLEDGE...
...BUT THEY ARE NOT FOOLS. THE SMALLEST SLIP COULD EXPOSE EVERYTHING.
WE MUST BE EVER VIGILANT.
FWAP
UTOWIN!
HM?

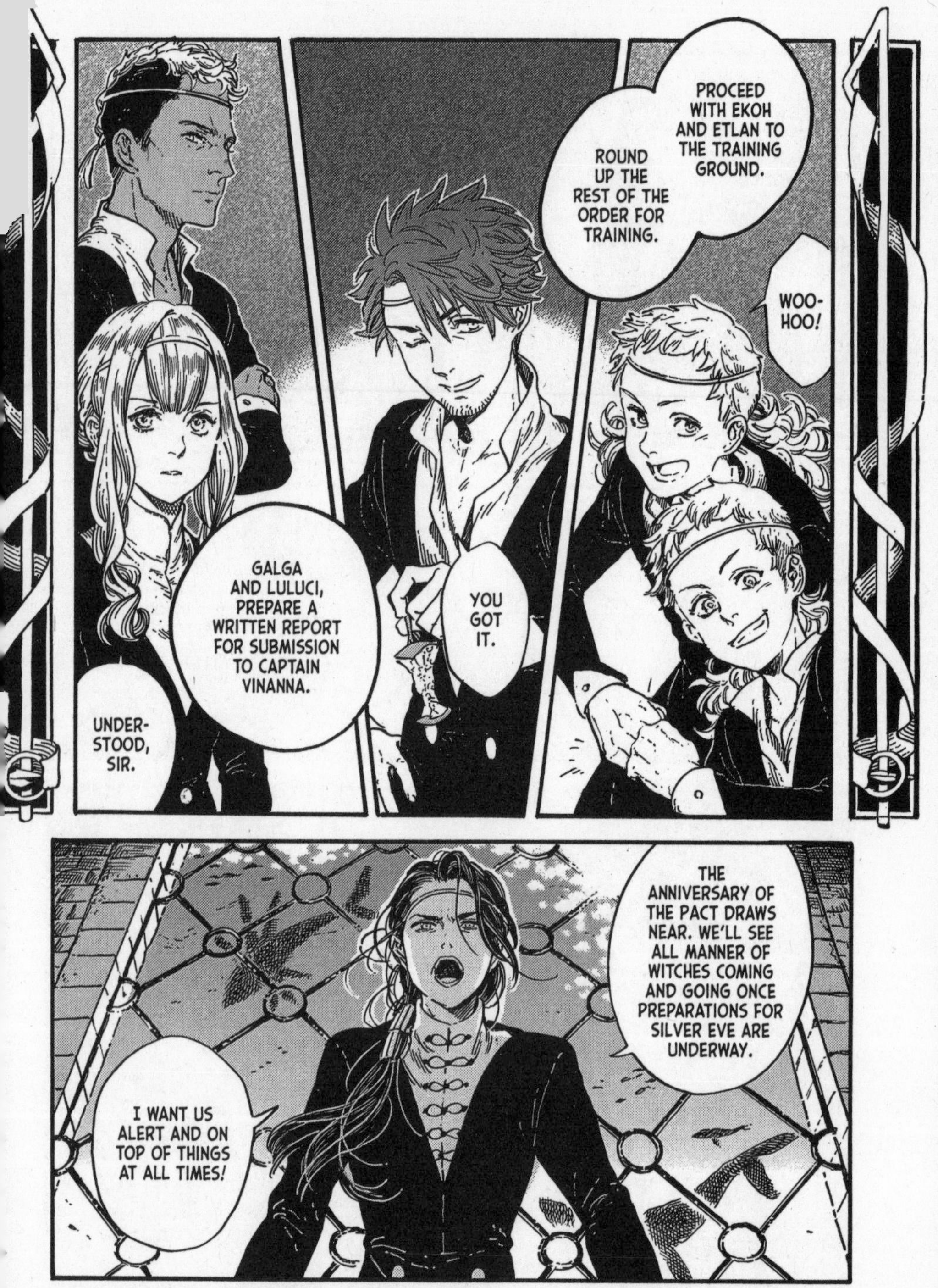
PROCEED WITH EKOH AND ETLAN TO THE TRAINING GROUND.
WOO-HOO!
ROUND UP THE REST OF THE ORDER FOR TRAINING.
YOU GOT IT.
GALGA AND LULUCI, PREPARE A WRITTEN REPORT FOR SUBMISSION TO CAPTAIN VINANNA.
UNDER-STOOD, SIR.
THE ANNIVERSARY OF THE PACT DRAWS NEAR. WE'LL SEE ALL MANNER OF WITCHES COMING AND GOING ONCE PREPARATIONS FOR SILVER EVE ARE UNDERWAY.
I WANT US ALERT AND ON TOP OF THINGS AT ALL TIMES!

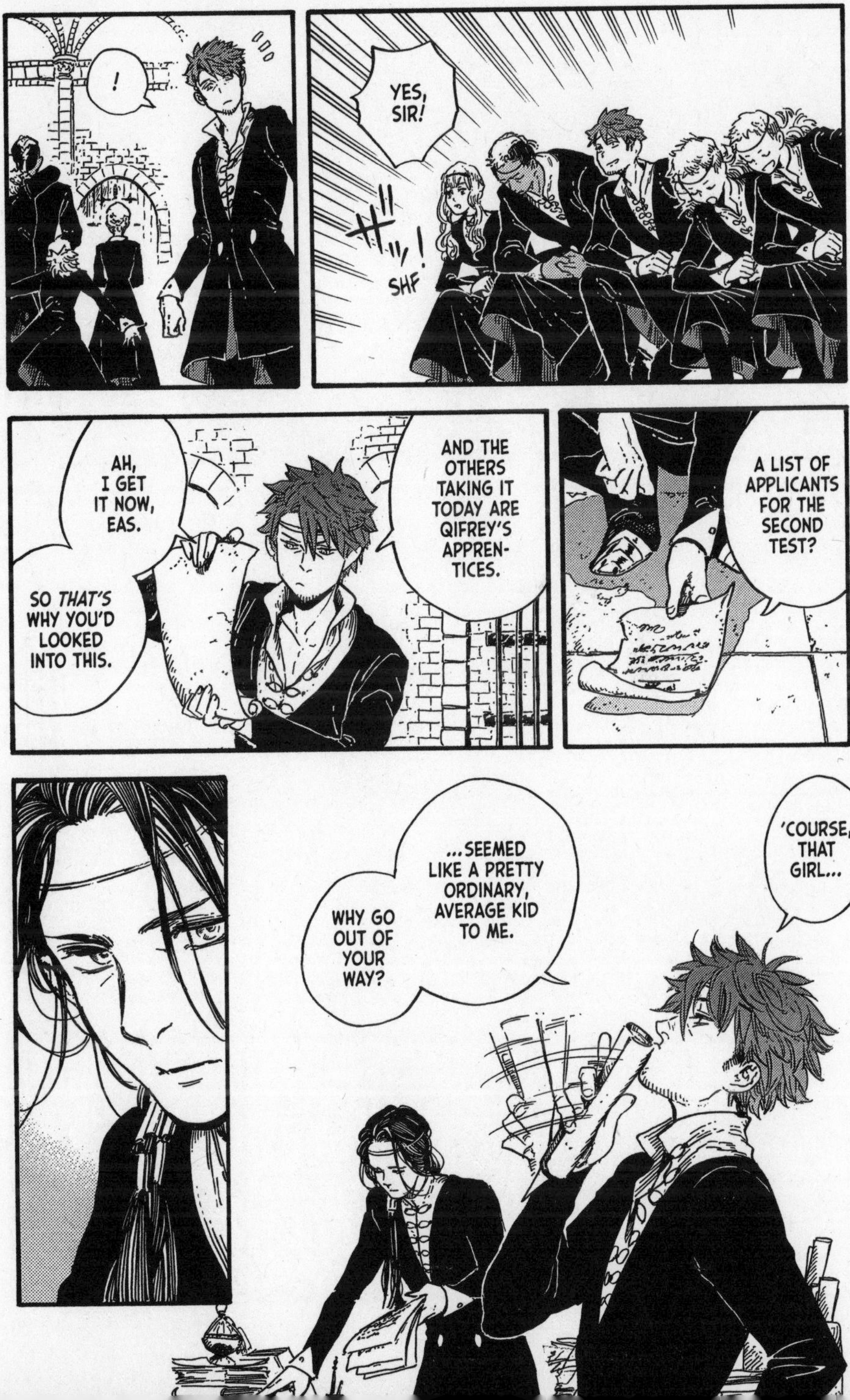
YES, SIR!
SHF
!
A LIST OF APPLICANTS FOR THE SECOND TEST?
AND THE OTHERS TAKING IT TODAY ARE QIFREY'S APPREN-TICES.
AH, I GET IT NOW, EAS.
SO *THAT'S* WHY YOU'D LOOKED INTO THIS.
'COURSE, THAT GIRL...
...SEEMED LIKE A PRETTY ORDINARY, AVERAGE KID TO ME.
WHY GO OUT OF YOUR WAY?

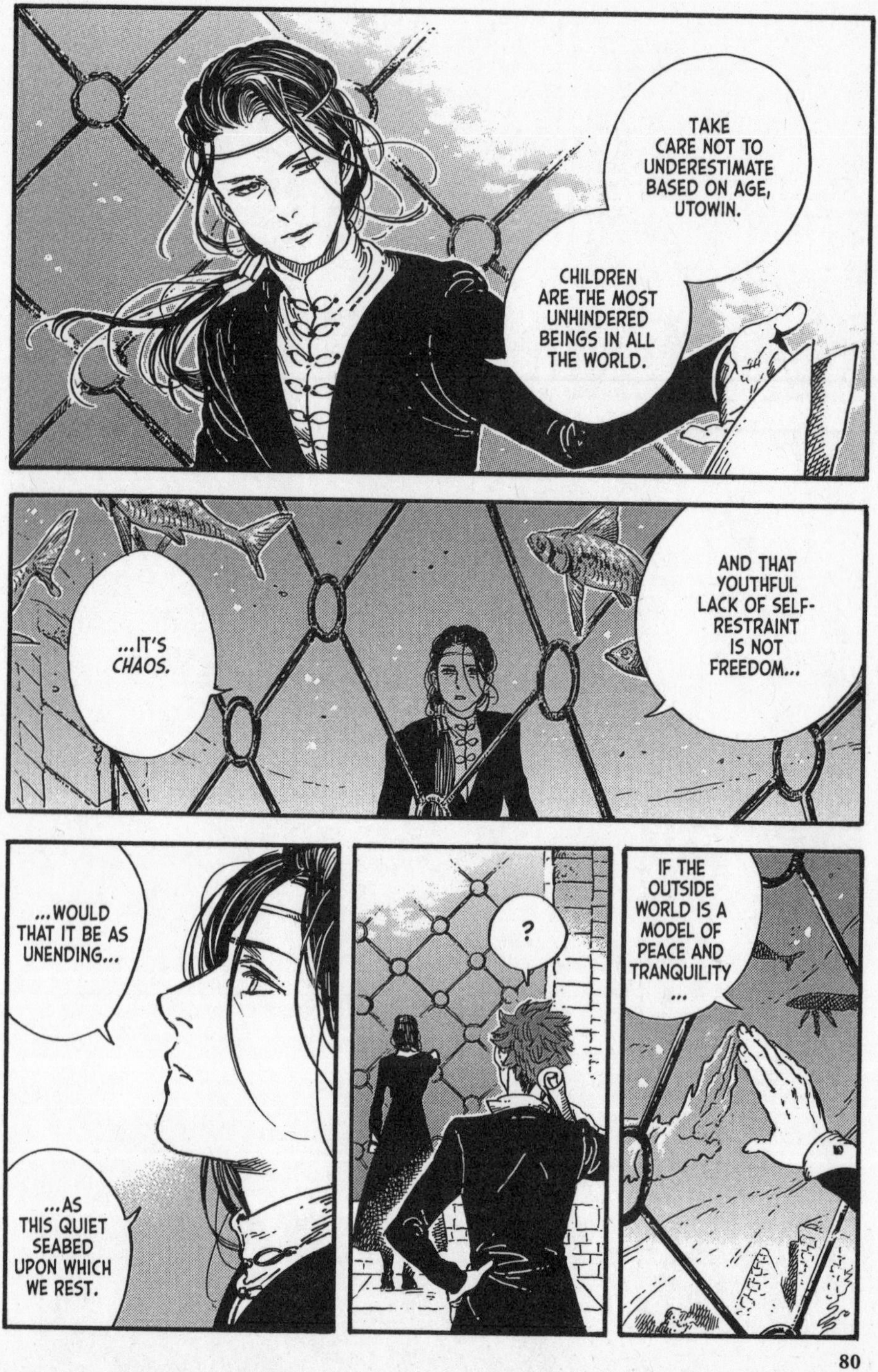
TAKE CARE NOT TO UNDERESTIMATE BASED ON AGE, UTOWIN.
CHILDREN ARE THE MOST UNHINDERED BEINGS IN ALL THE WORLD.
AND THAT YOUTHFUL LACK OF SELF-RESTRAINT IS NOT FREEDOM...
...IT'S CHAOS.
IF THE OUTSIDE WORLD IS A MODEL OF PEACE AND TRANQUILITY ...
?
...WOULD THAT IT BE AS UNENDING...
...AS THIS QUIET SEABED UPON WHICH WE REST.

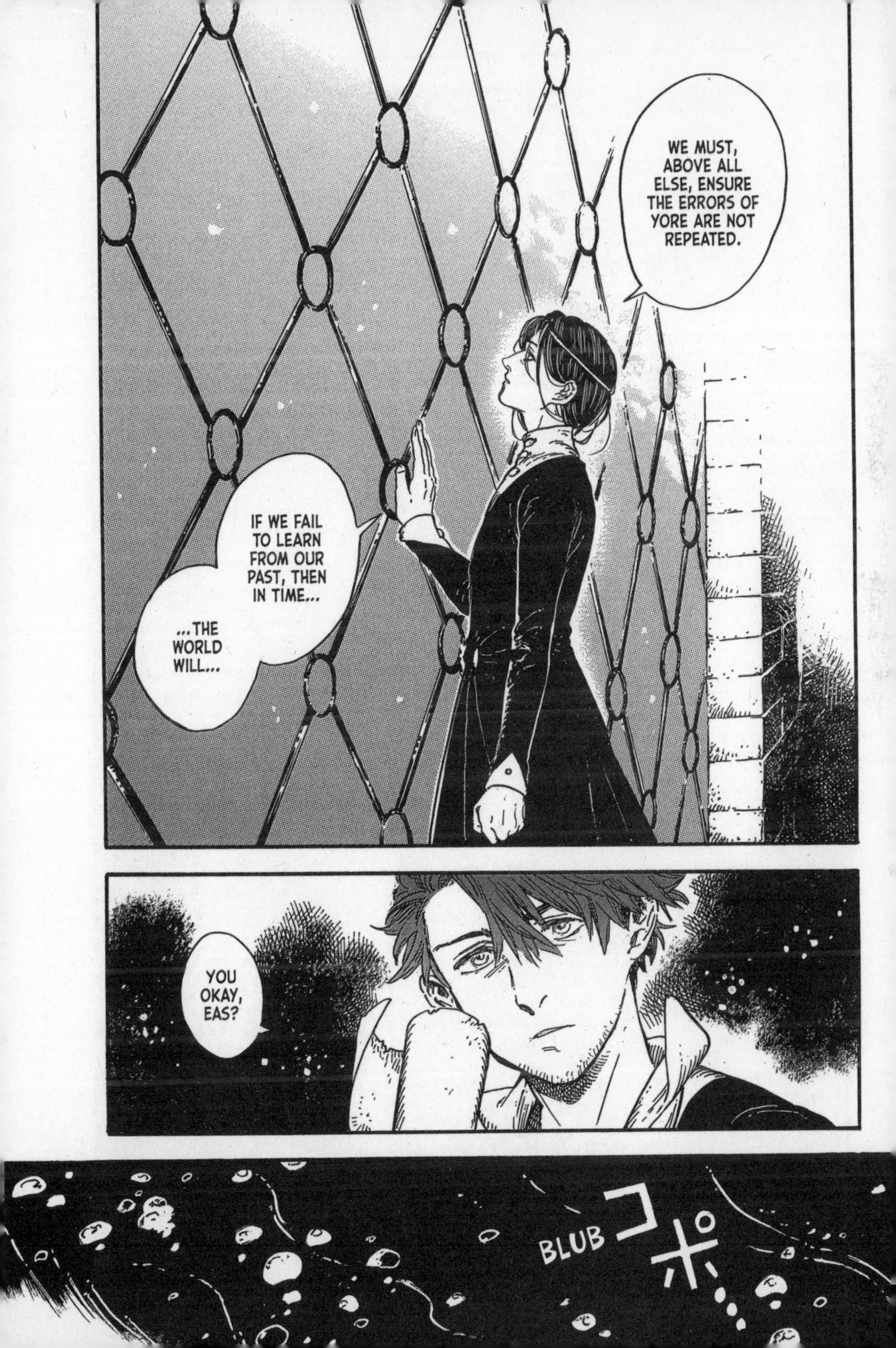
WE MUST, ABOVE ALL ELSE, ENSURE THE ERRORS OF YORE ARE NOT REPEATED.
IF WE FAIL TO LEARN FROM OUR PAST, THEN IN TIME...
...THE WORLD WILL...
YOU OKAY, EAS?
BLUB
コポ

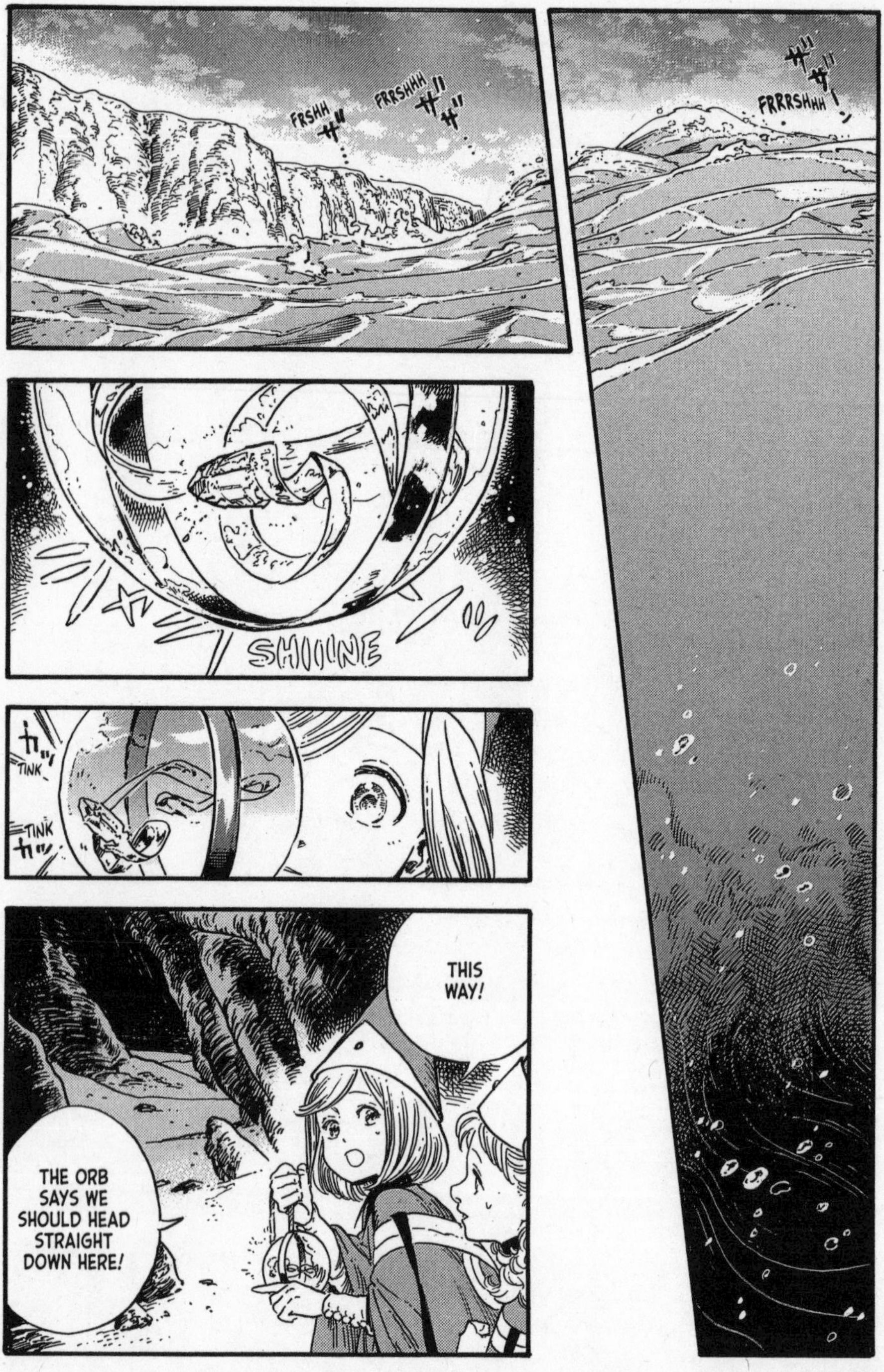
FRRRSHHH
FRSHH
FRRSHHH
SHIIINE
TINK
TINK
THIS WAY!
THE ORB SAYS WE SHOULD HEAD STRAIGHT DOWN HERE!

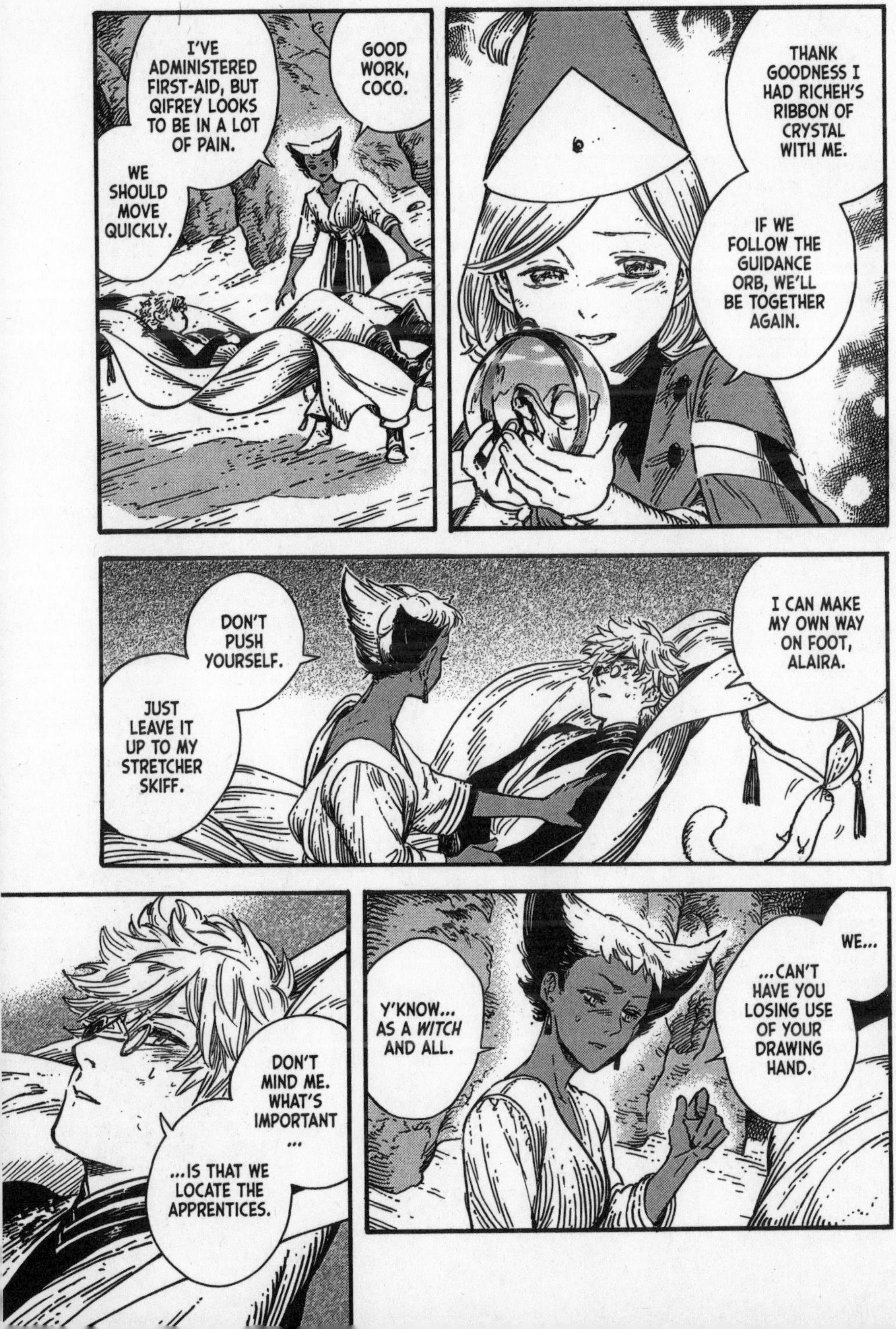
THANK GOODNESS I HAD RICHEH'S RIBBON OF CRYSTAL WITH ME.
IF WE FOLLOW THE GUIDANCE ORB, WE'LL BE TOGETHER AGAIN.
GOOD WORK, COCO.
I'VE ADMINISTERED FIRST-AID, BUT QIFREY LOOKS TO BE IN A LOT OF PAIN.
WE SHOULD MOVE QUICKLY.
I CAN MAKE MY OWN WAY ON FOOT, ALAIRA.
DON'T PUSH YOURSELF.
JUST LEAVE IT UP TO MY STRETCHER SKIFF.
WE...
...CAN'T HAVE YOU LOSING USE OF YOUR DRAWING HAND.
Y'KNOW... AS A *WITCH* AND ALL.
DON'T MIND ME. WHAT'S IMPORTANT...
...IS THAT WE LOCATE THE APPRENTICES.

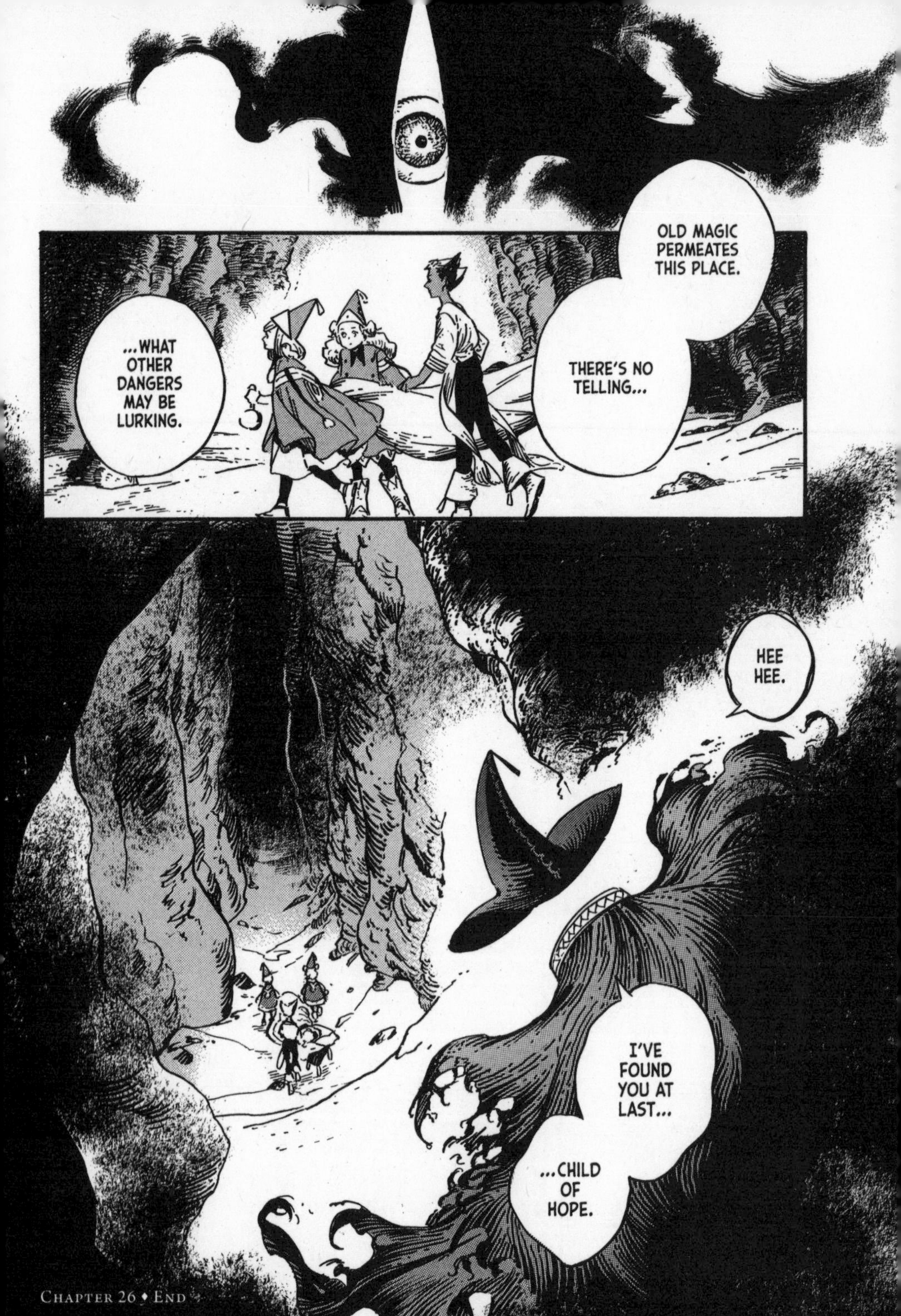
OLD MAGIC PERMEATES THIS PLACE.
THERE'S NO TELLING...
...WHAT OTHER DANGERS MAY BE LURKING.
HEE HEE.
I'VE FOUND YOU AT LAST...
...CHILD OF HOPE.

Chapter 26 • End

Witch Hat Atelier

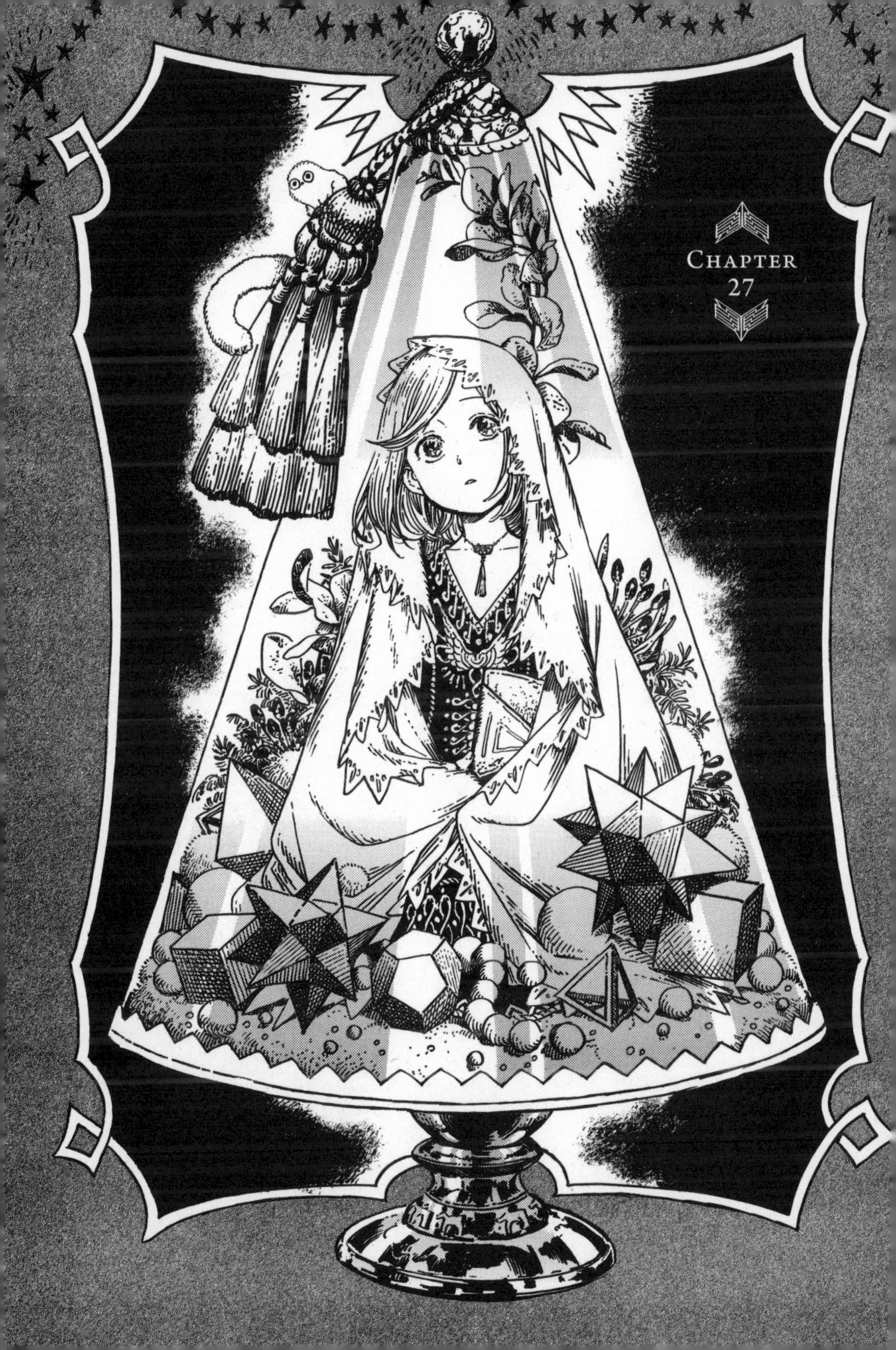
CHAPTER
27

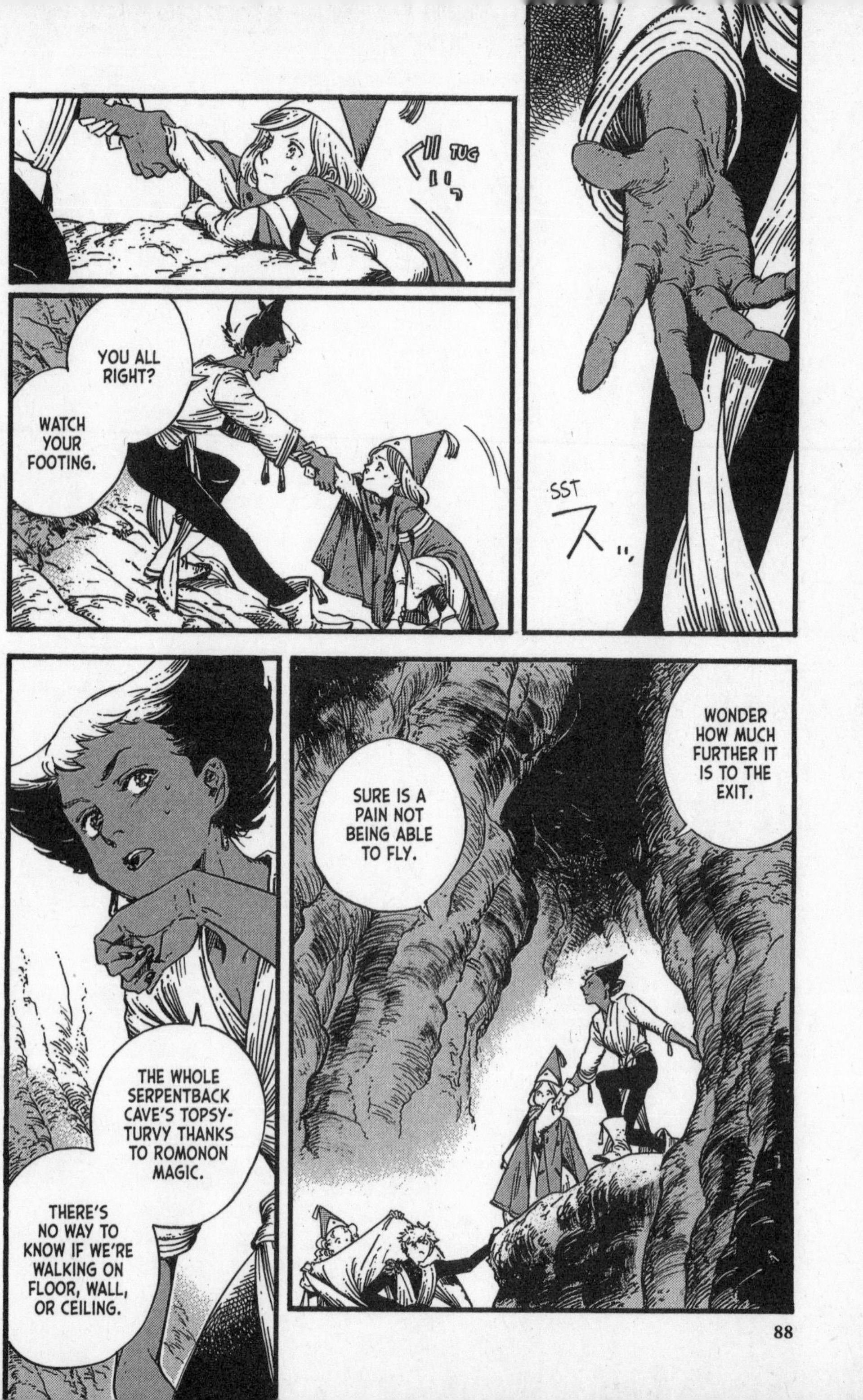
SST
ス
ぐい TUG
YOU ALL RIGHT?
WATCH YOUR FOOTING.
WONDER HOW MUCH FURTHER IT IS TO THE EXIT.
SURE IS A PAIN NOT BEING ABLE TO FLY.
THE WHOLE SERPENTBACK CAVE'S TOPSY-TURVY THANKS TO ROMONON MAGIC.
THERE'S NO WAY TO KNOW IF WE'RE WALKING ON FLOOR, WALL, OR CEILING.

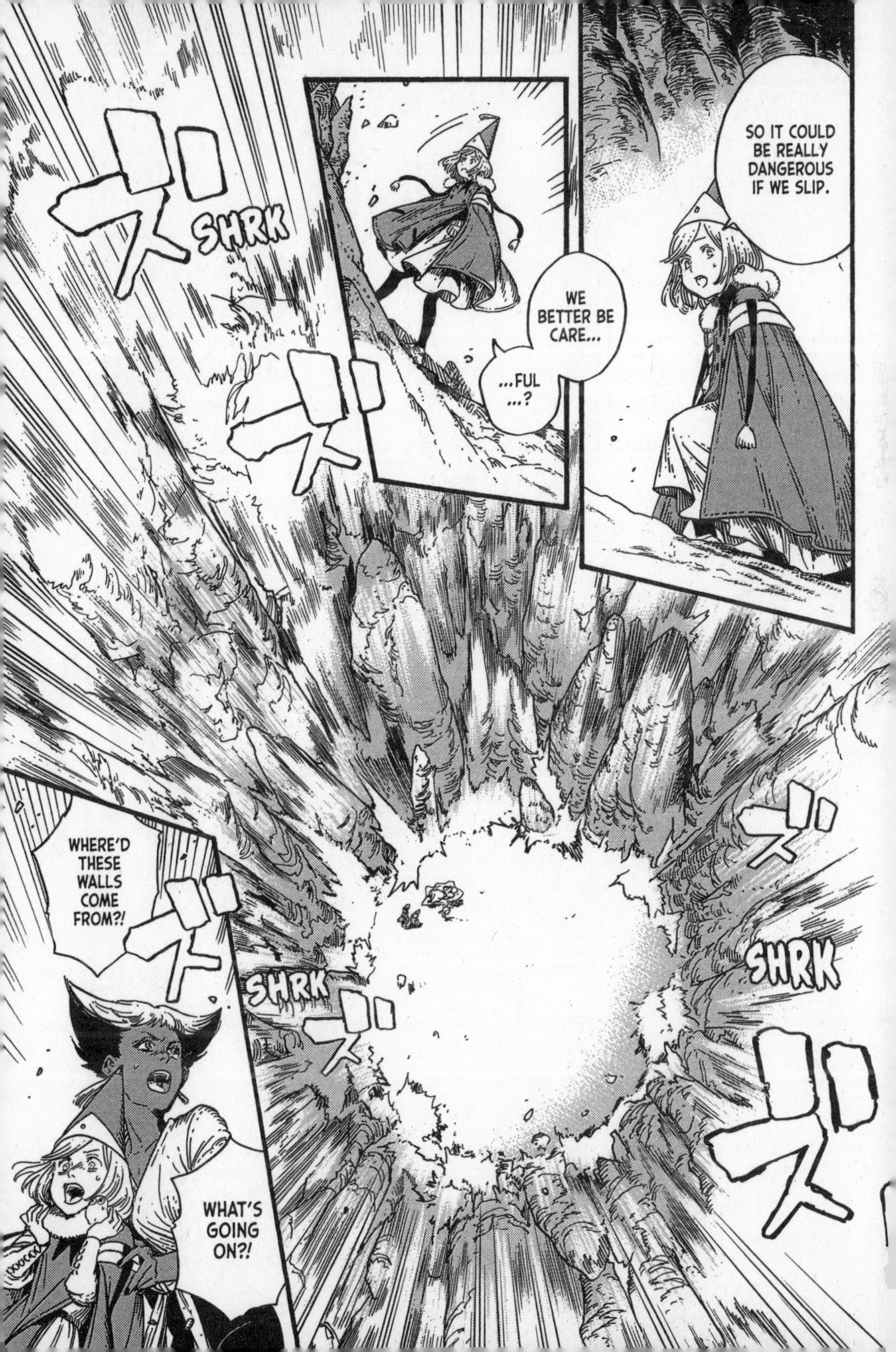
SO IT COULD BE REALLY DANGEROUS IF WE SLIP.
WE BETTER BE CARE...
...FUL ...?
SHRK
SHRK
SHRK
WHERE'D THESE WALLS COME FROM?!
WHAT'S GOING ON?!

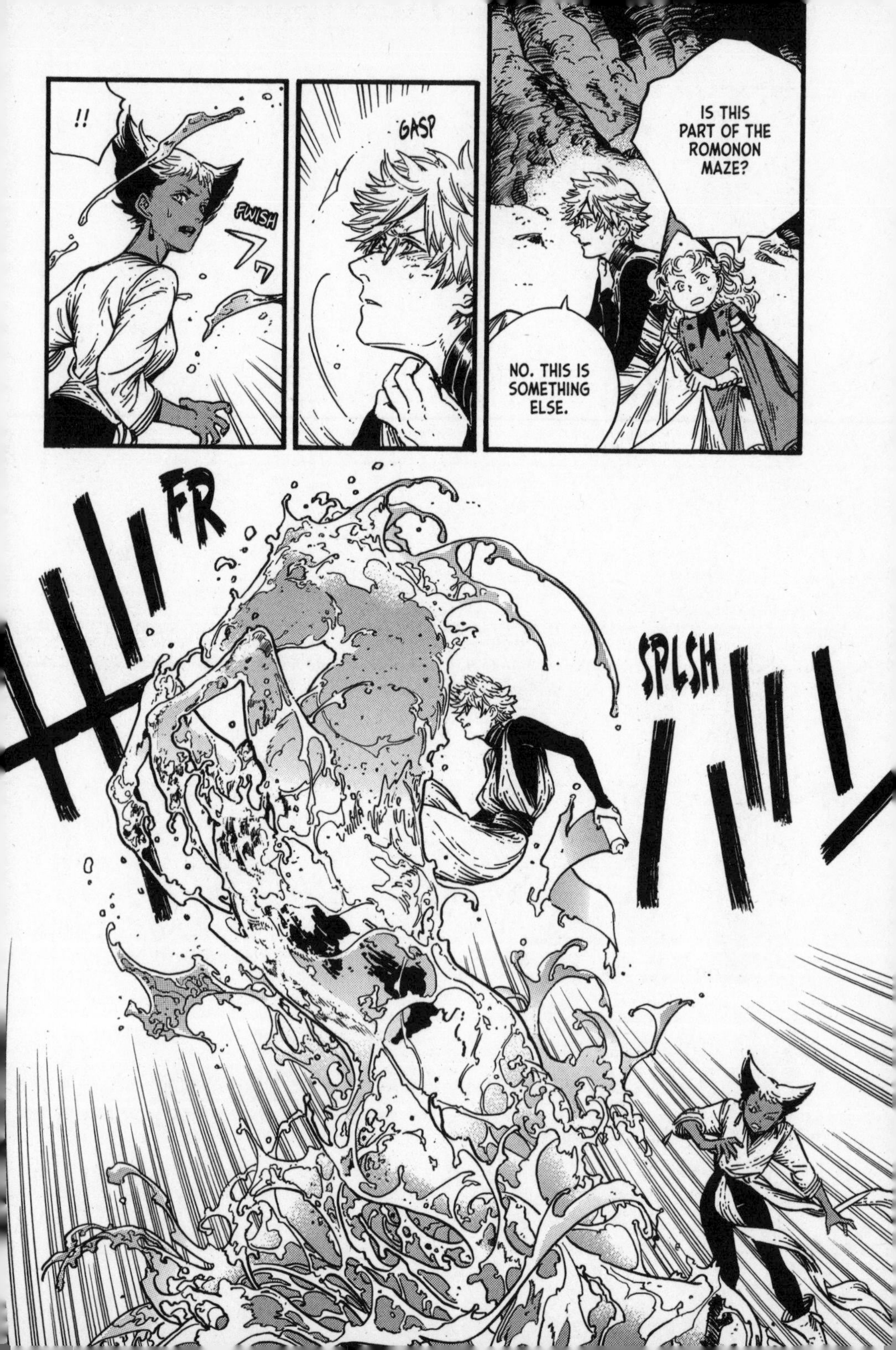
IS THIS PART OF THE ROMONON MAZE?
...
NO. THIS IS SOMETHING ELSE.
GASP
!!
FWISH
SPLSH
FR

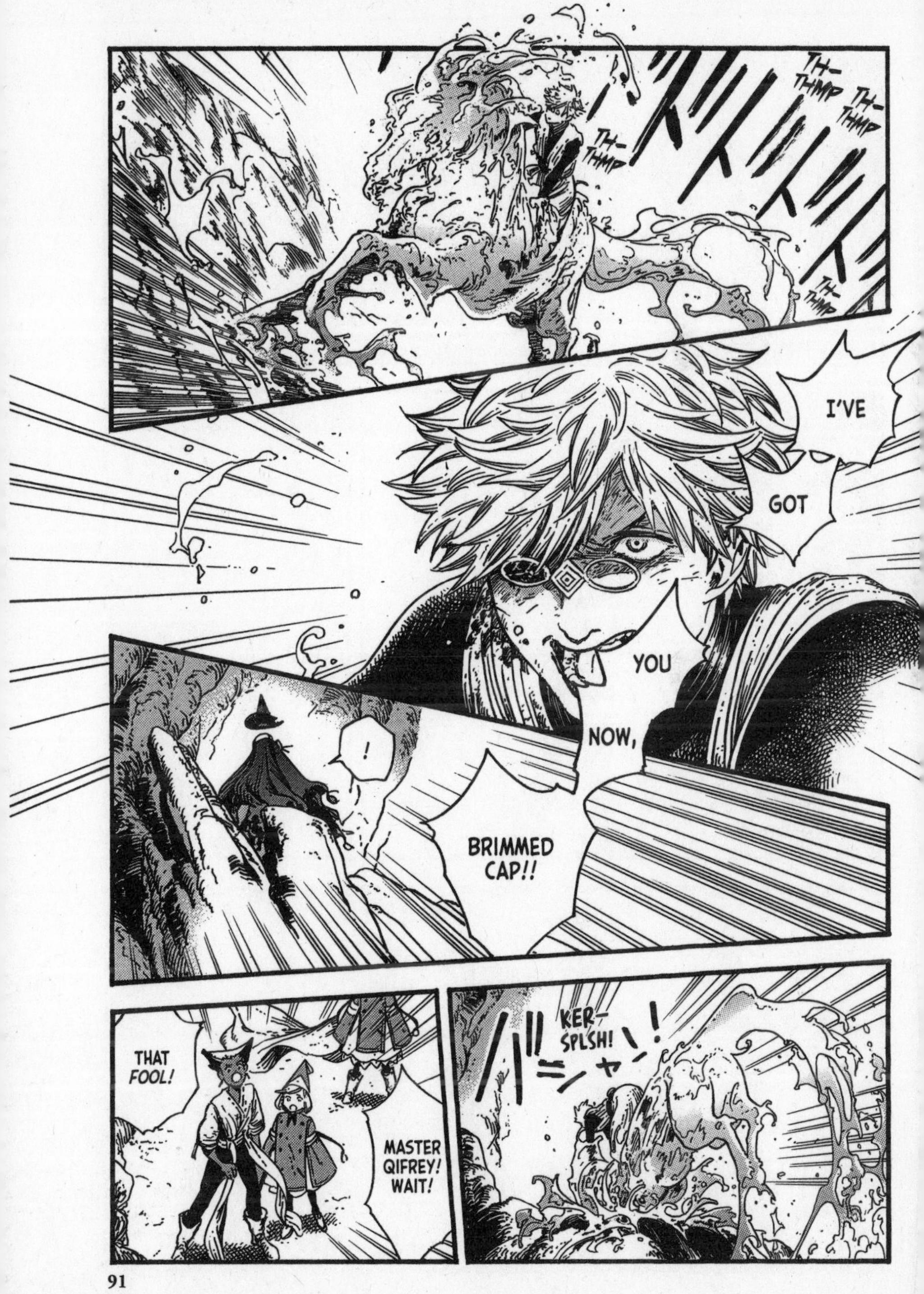
TH-THMP
TH-THMP
TH-THMP
TH-THMP
I'VE GOT YOU NOW, BRIMMED CAP!!
!
KER-SPLSH!
MASTER QIFREY! WAIT!
THAT FOOL!

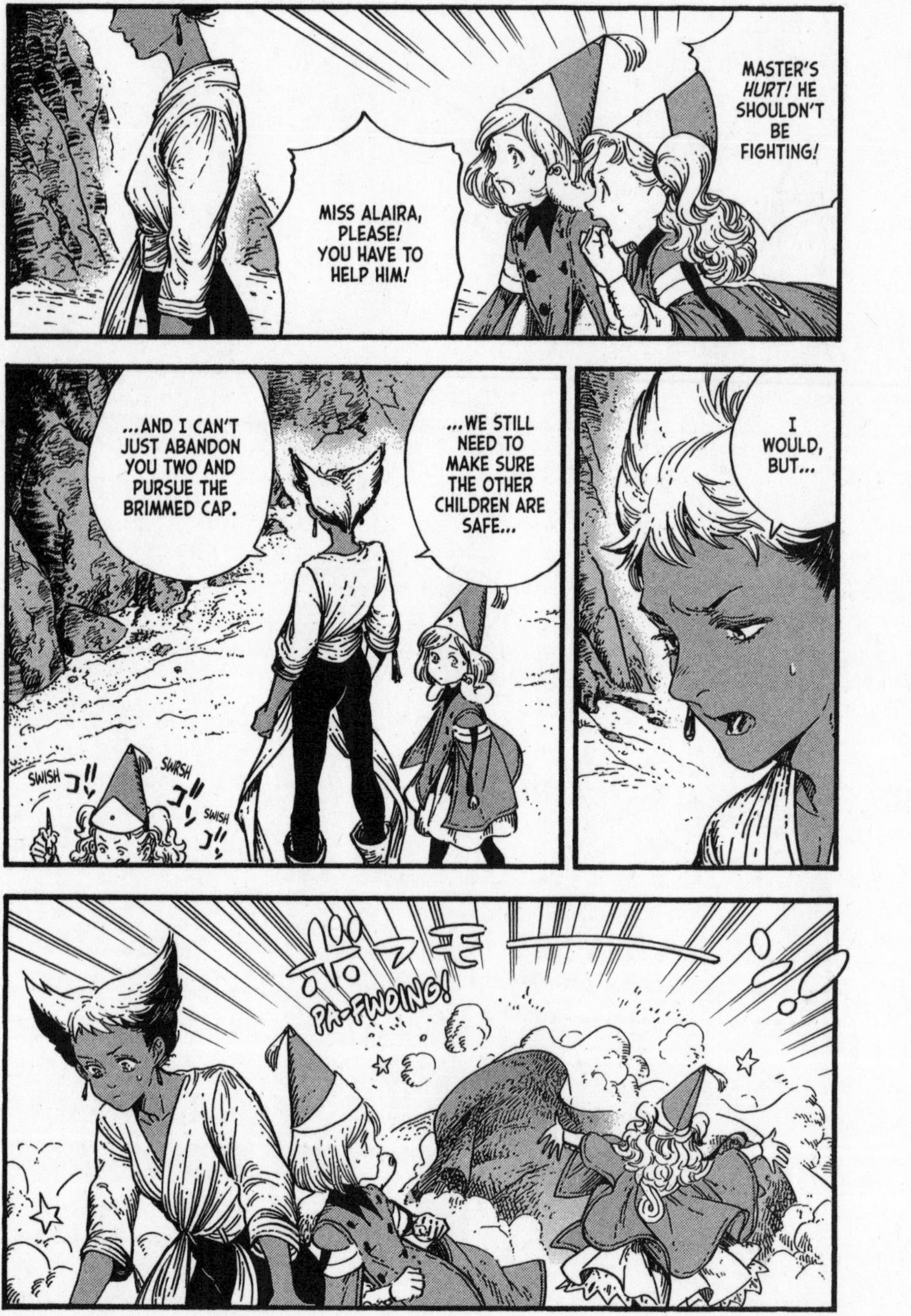
MASTER'S *HURT!* HE SHOULDN'T BE FIGHTING!
MISS ALAIRA, PLEASE! YOU HAVE TO HELP HIM!
I WOULD, BUT...
...WE STILL NEED TO MAKE SURE THE OTHER CHILDREN ARE SAFE...
...AND I CAN'T JUST ABANDON YOU TWO AND PURSUE THE BRIMMED CAP.
SWISH
SWRSH
SWISH
PA-FWOING!

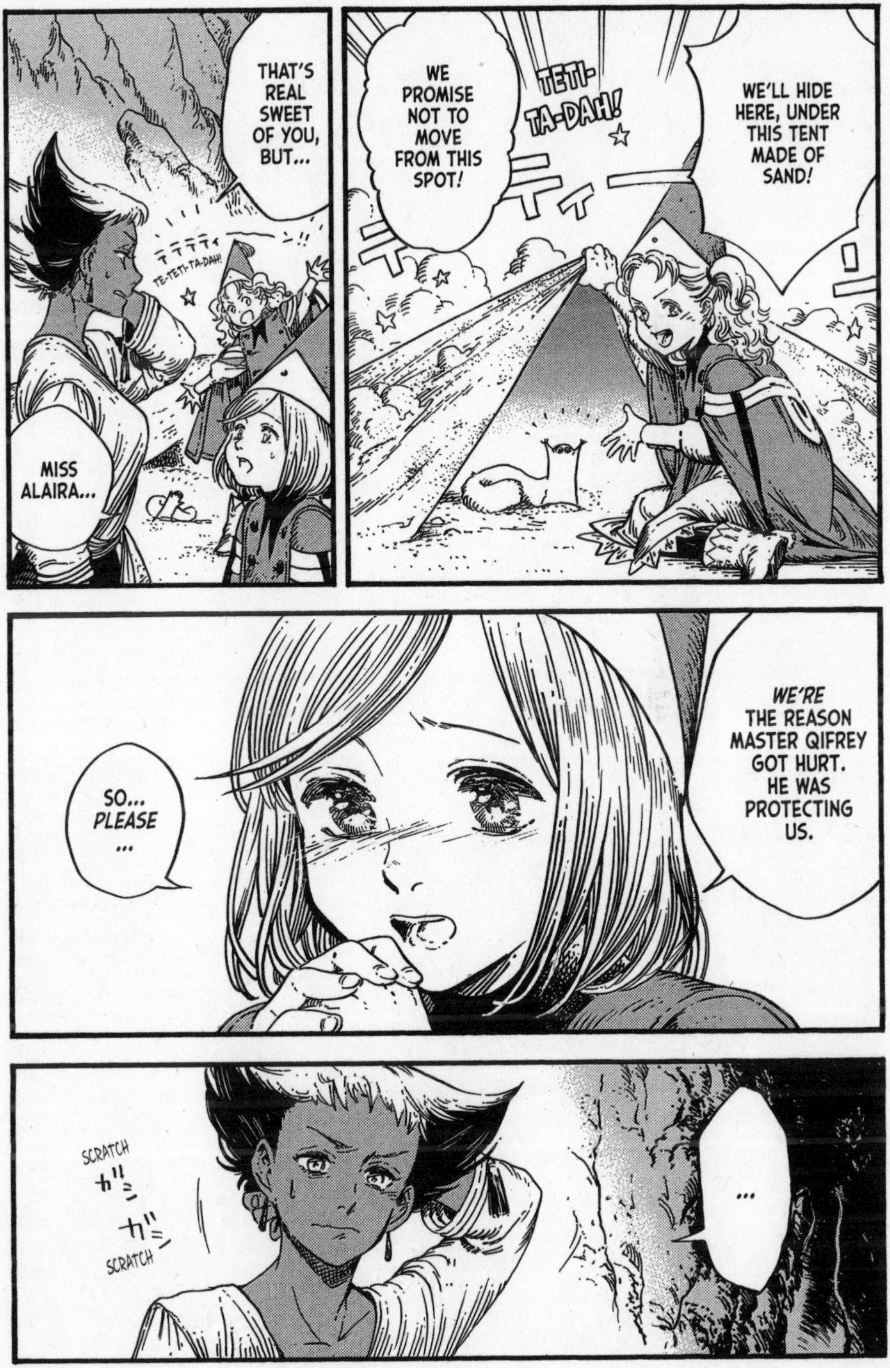
WE'LL HIDE HERE, UNDER THIS TENT MADE OF SAND!
TETI-TA-DAH!
WE PROMISE NOT TO MOVE FROM THIS SPOT!
THAT'S REAL SWEET OF YOU, BUT...
テテテティ
TE-TETI-TA-DAH!
MISS ALAIRA...
WE'RE THE REASON MASTER QIFREY GOT HURT. HE WAS PROTECTING US.
SO... PLEASE ...
...
SCRATCH
SCRATCH

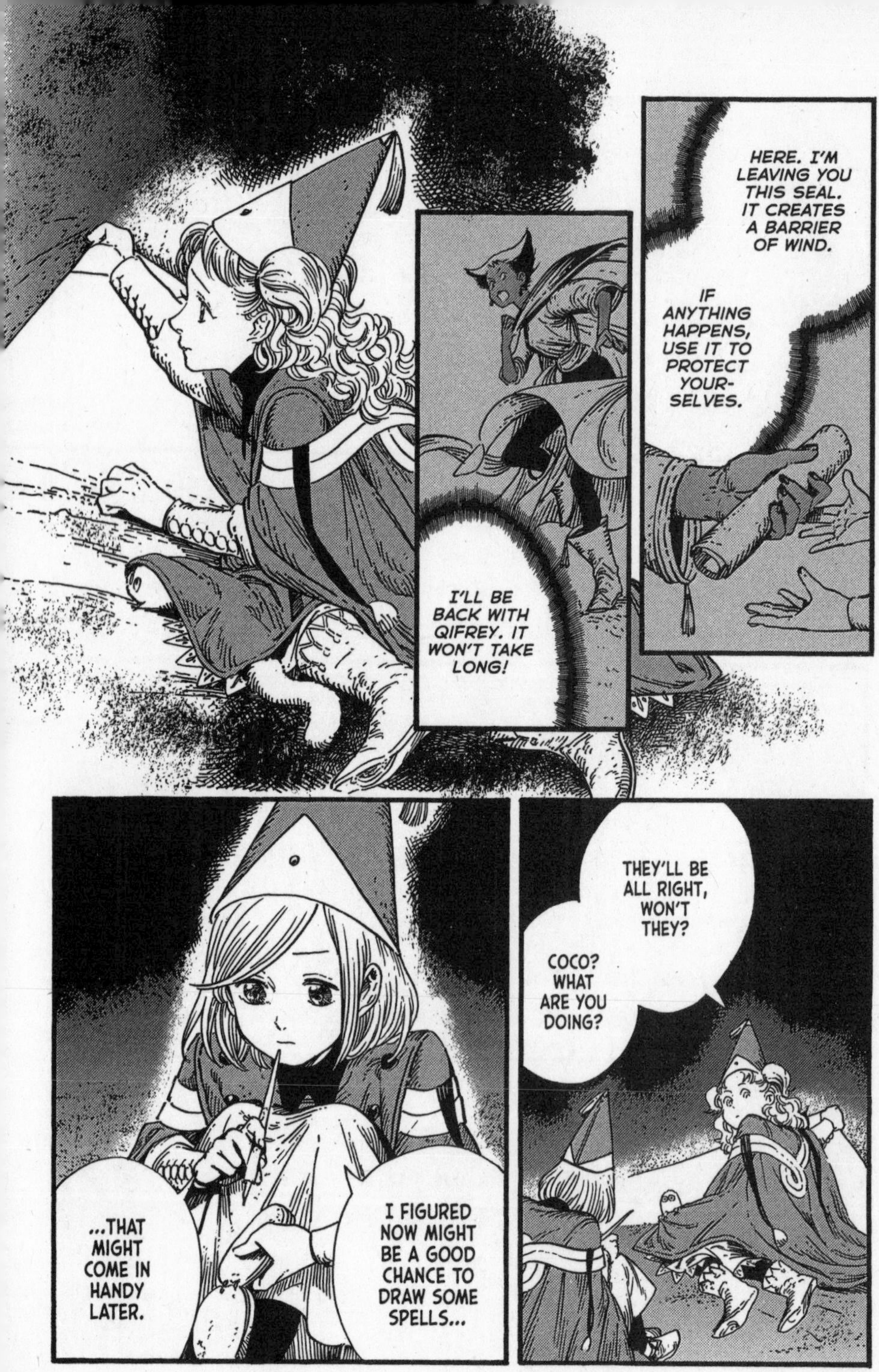
HERE. I'M LEAVING YOU THIS SEAL. IT CREATES A BARRIER OF WIND.
IF ANYTHING HAPPENS, USE IT TO PROTECT YOUR-SELVES.
I'LL BE BACK WITH QIFREY. IT WON'T TAKE LONG!
THEY'LL BE ALL RIGHT, WON'T THEY?
COCO? WHAT ARE YOU DOING?
I FIGURED NOW MIGHT BE A GOOD CHANCE TO DRAW SOME SPELLS...
...THAT MIGHT COME IN HANDY LATER.

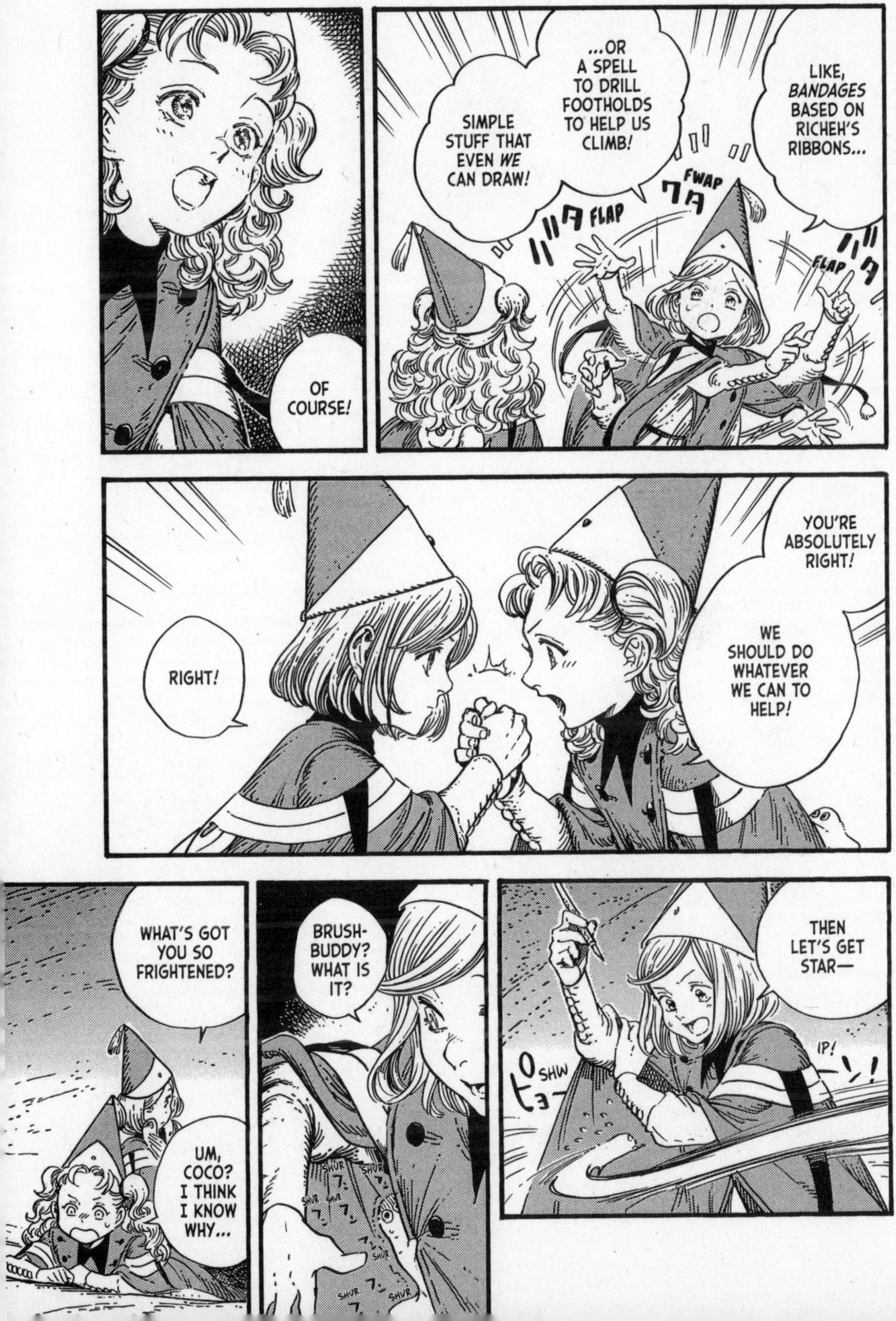
LIKE, BANDAGES BASED ON RICHEH'S RIBBONS...
...OR A SPELL TO DRILL FOOTHOLDS TO HELP US CLIMB!
SIMPLE STUFF THAT EVEN WE CAN DRAW!
FLAP
FWAP
FLAP
OF COURSE!
YOU'RE ABSOLUTELY RIGHT!
WE SHOULD DO WHATEVER WE CAN TO HELP!
RIGHT!
THEN LET'S GET STAR—
IP!
SHW
BRUSH-BUDDY? WHAT IS IT?
SHUR
SHUR
SHUR
SHUR
SHUR
SHUR
WHAT'S GOT YOU SO FRIGHTENED?
UM, COCO? I THINK I KNOW WHY...

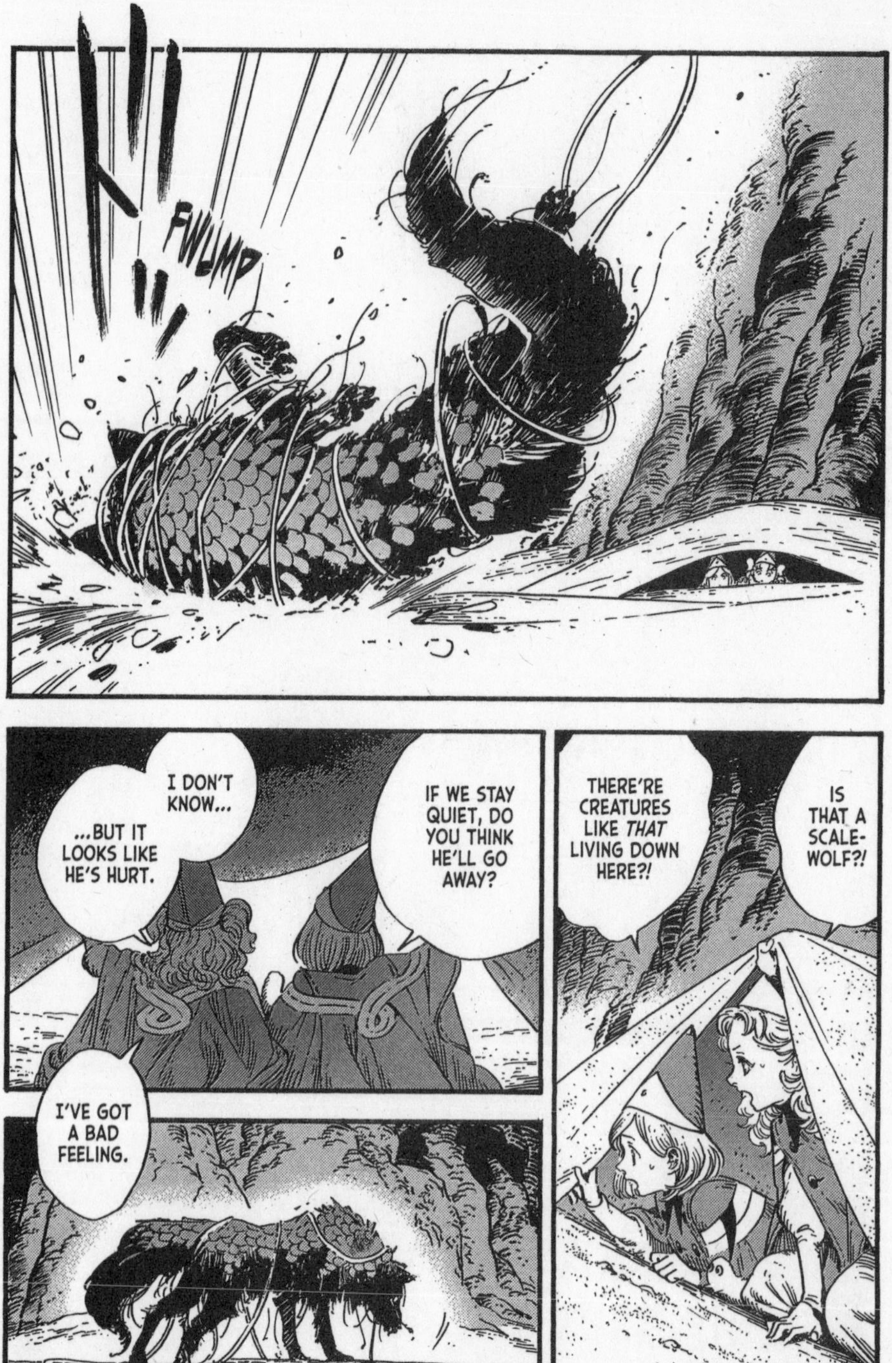
FWUMP
IS THAT A SCALE-WOLF?!
THERE'RE CREATURES LIKE *THAT* LIVING DOWN HERE?!
IF WE STAY QUIET, DO YOU THINK HE'LL GO AWAY?
I DON'T KNOW...
...BUT IT LOOKS LIKE HE'S HURT.
I'VE GOT A BAD FEELING.

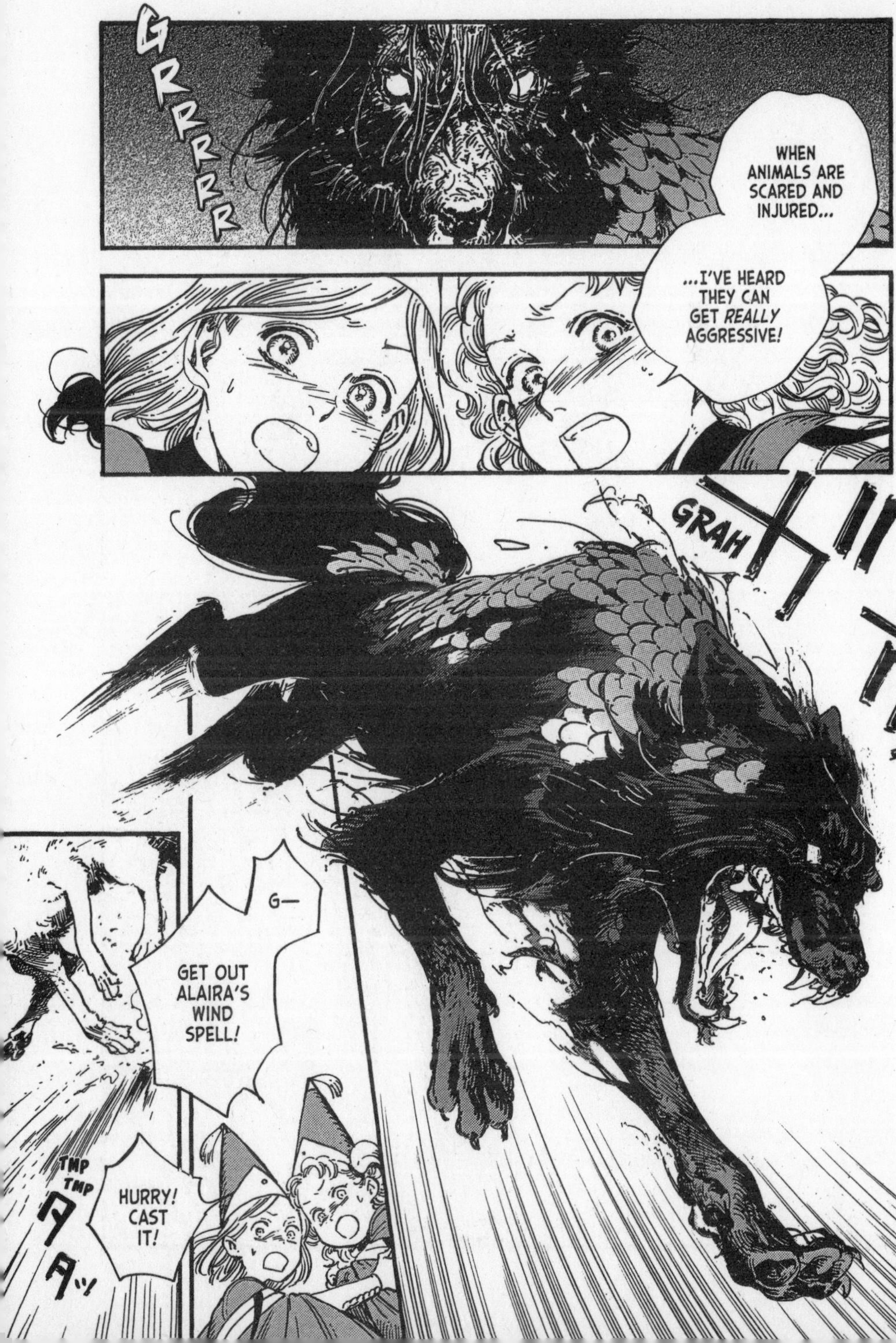
WHEN ANIMALS ARE SCARED AND INJURED...
GRRRRR
...I'VE HEARD THEY CAN GET *REALLY* AGGRESSIVE!
GRAH
G—
GET OUT ALAIRA'S WIND SPELL!
HURRY! CAST IT!
TMP TMP

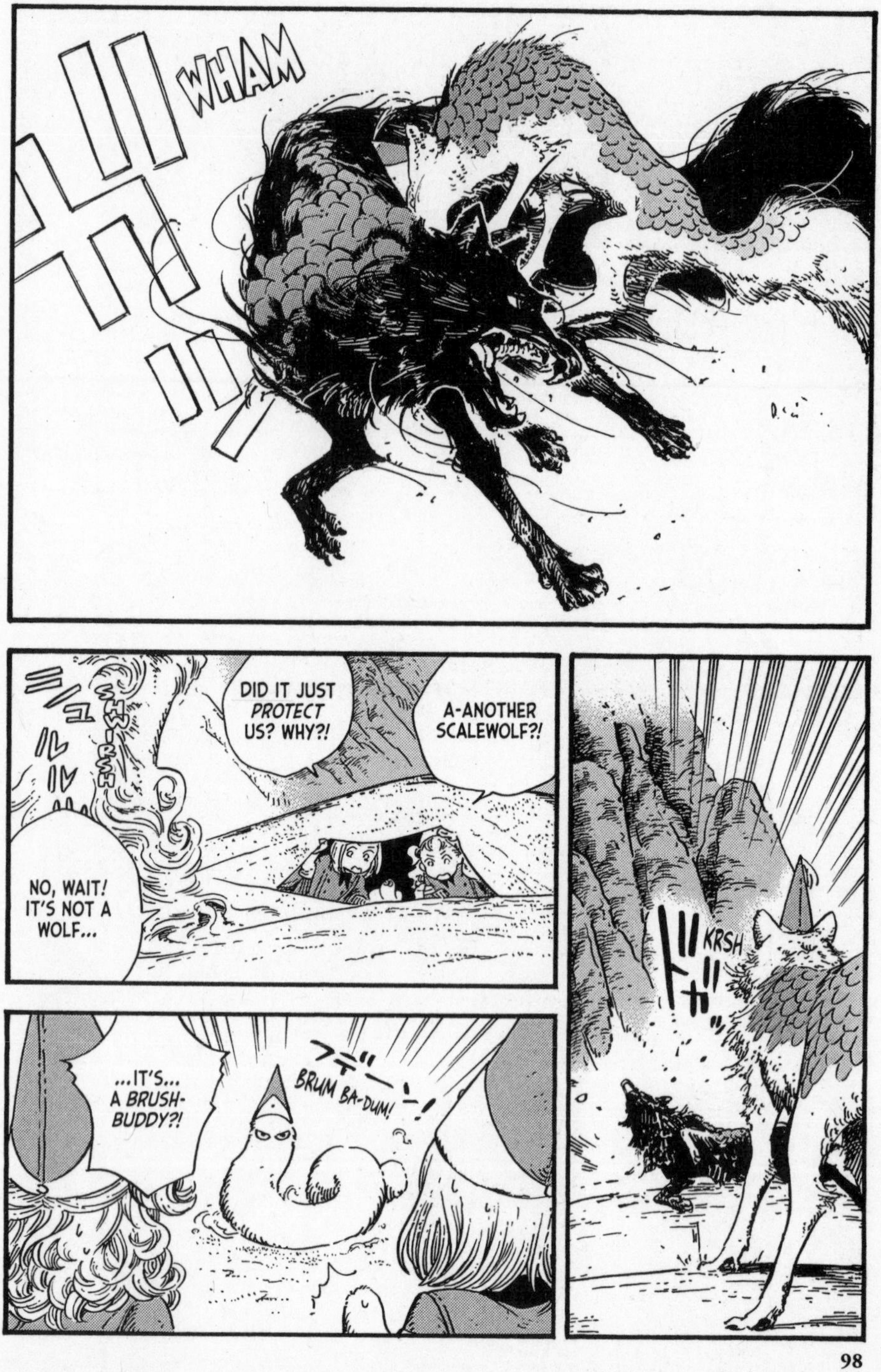
WHAM
KRSH
A-ANOTHER SCALEWOLF?!
DID IT JUST *PROTECT* US? WHY?!
SHWIRSH
NO, WAIT! IT'S NOT A WOLF...
BRUM BA-DUM!
...IT'S... A *BRUSH-BUDDY*?!

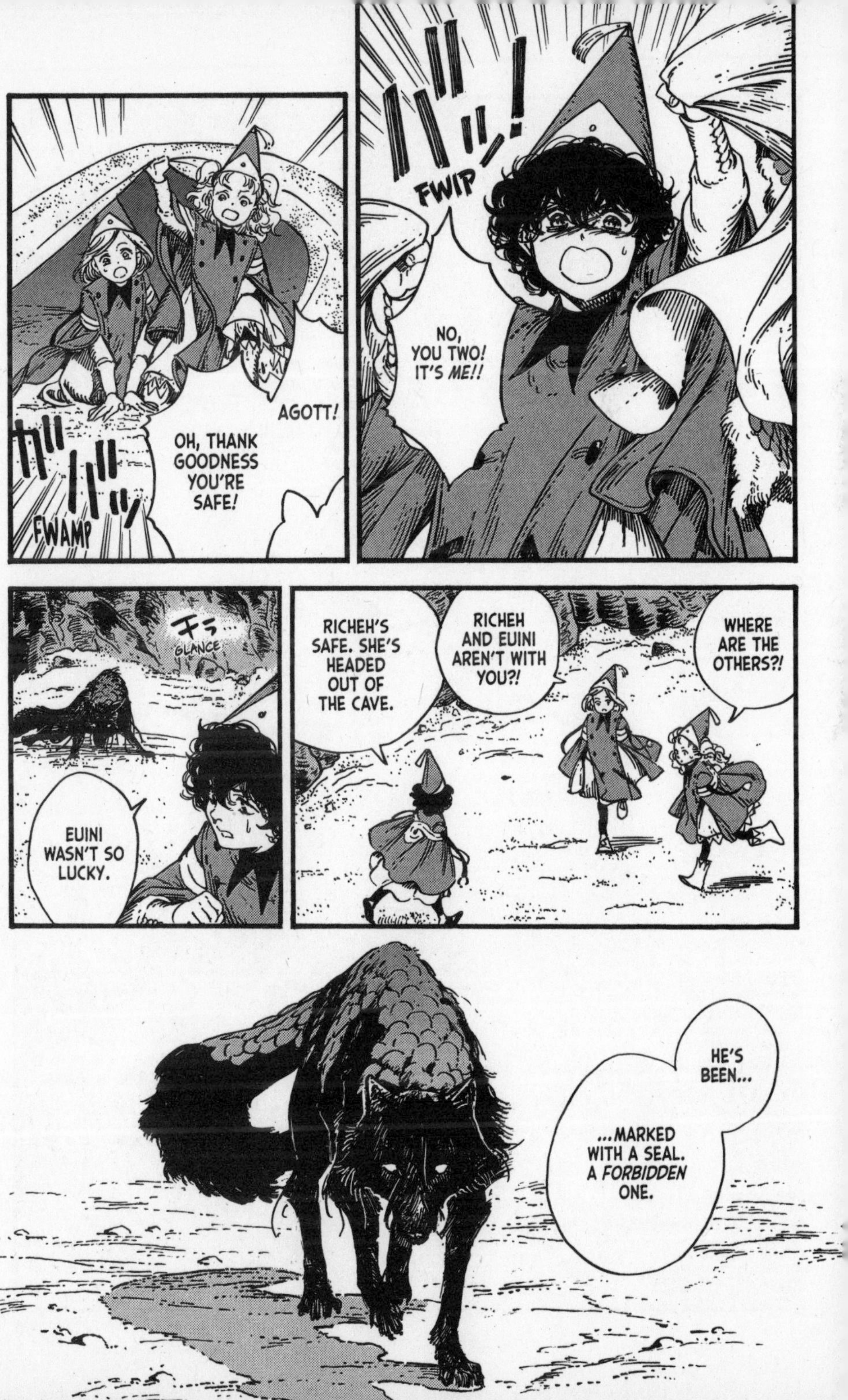
FWIP
NO, YOU TWO! IT'S *ME*!!
AGOTT!
OH, THANK GOODNESS YOU'RE SAFE!
FWAMP
WHERE ARE THE OTHERS?!
RICHEH AND EUINI AREN'T WITH YOU?!
RICHEH'S SAFE. SHE'S HEADED OUT OF THE CAVE.
チラ…
GLANCE
EUINI WASN'T SO LUCKY.
HE'S BEEN...
...MARKED WITH A SEAL. A *FORBIDDEN* ONE.

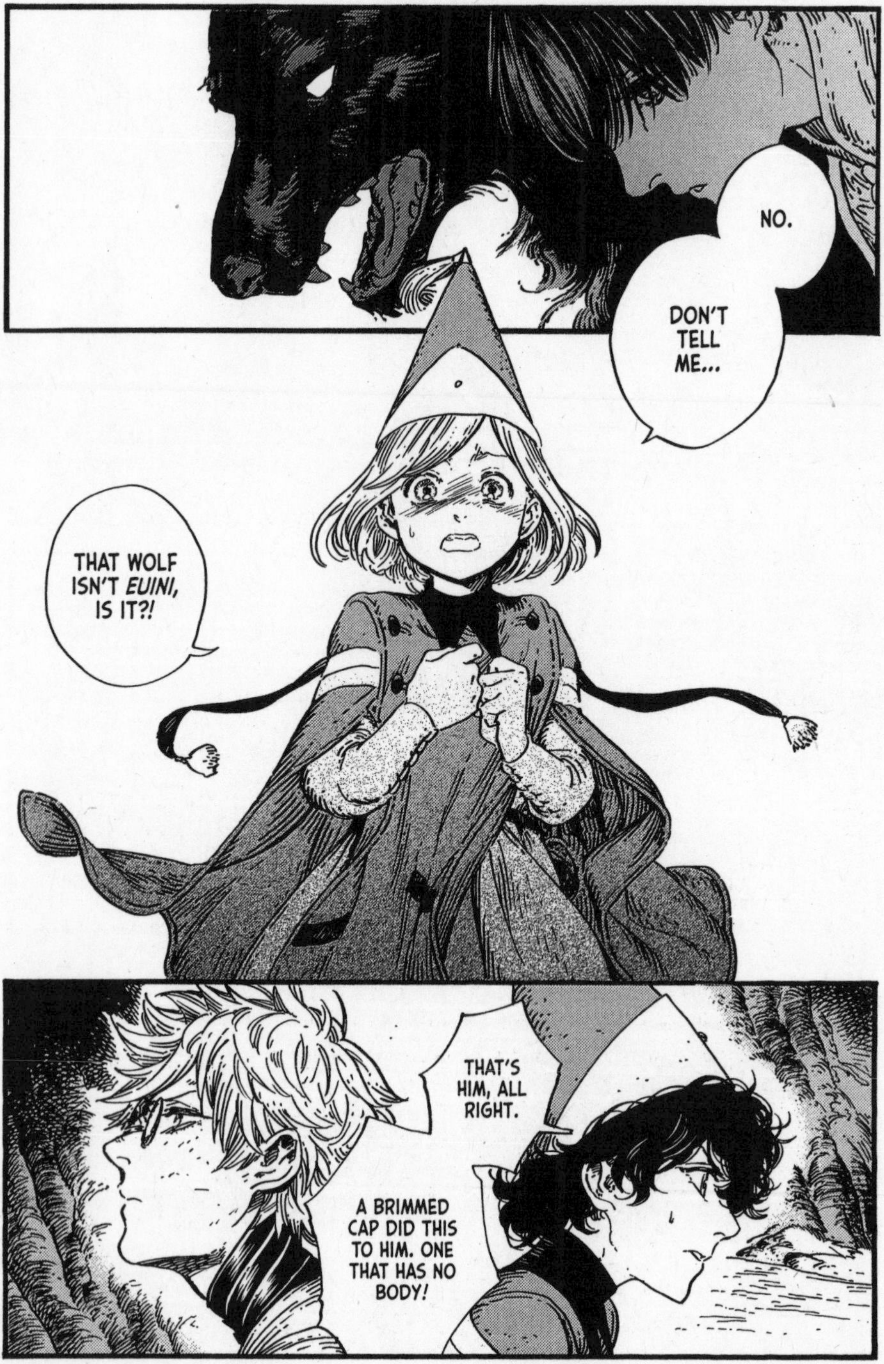
NO.
DON'T TELL ME...
THAT WOLF ISN'T *EUINI*, IS IT?!
THAT'S HIM, ALL RIGHT.
A BRIMMED CAP DID THIS TO HIM. ONE THAT HAS NO BODY!

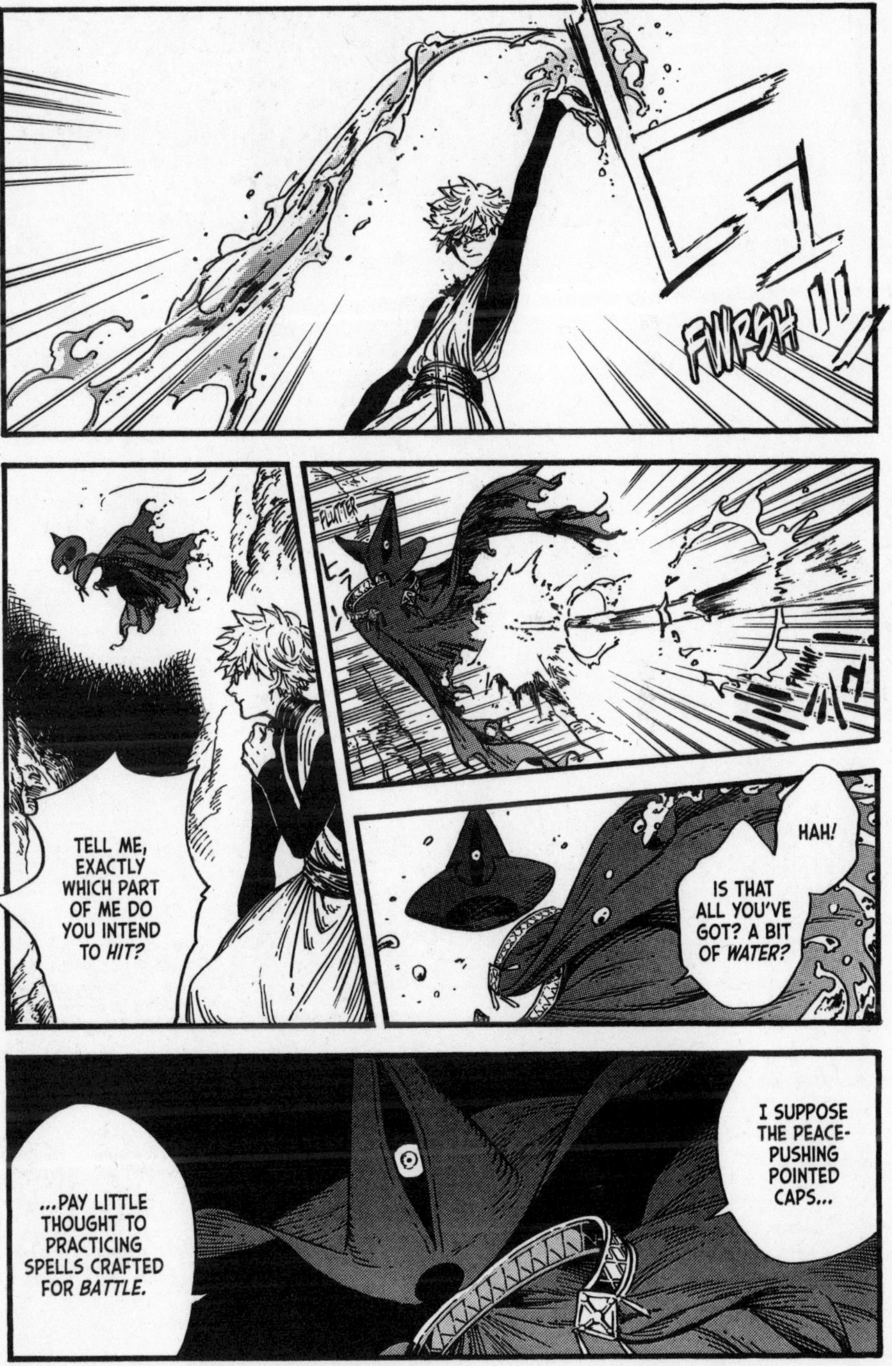
FWRSH
FWAM!
FLUTTER
HAH!
IS THAT ALL YOU'VE GOT? A BIT OF *WATER?*
TELL ME, EXACTLY WHICH PART OF ME DO YOU INTEND TO *HIT?*
I SUPPOSE THE PEACE-PUSHING POINTED CAPS...
...PAY LITTLE THOUGHT TO PRACTICING SPELLS CRAFTED FOR *BATTLE.*

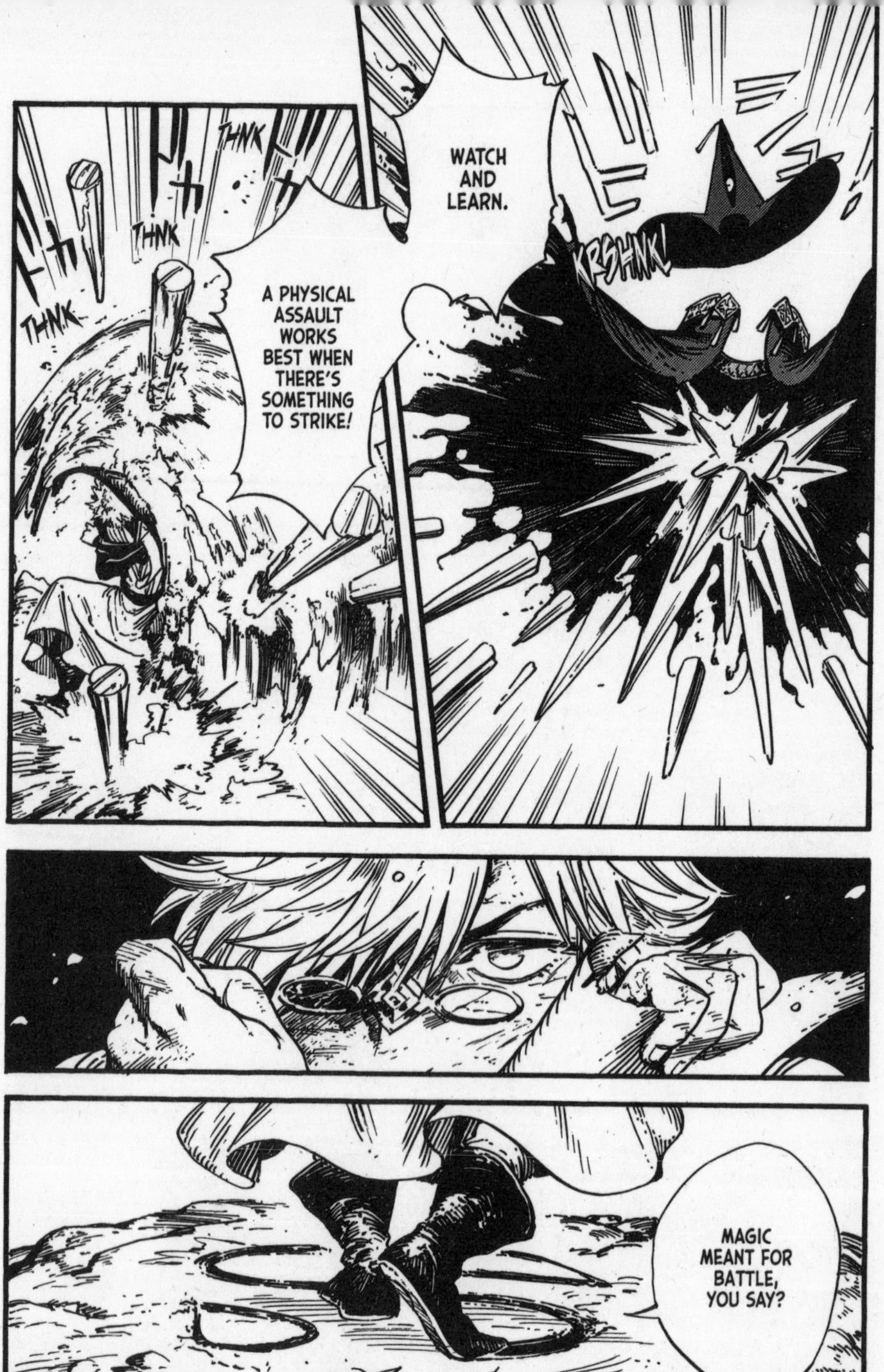
WATCH AND LEARN.
KRSHNK!
THNK
THNK
THNK
A PHYSICAL ASSAULT WORKS BEST WHEN THERE'S SOMETHING TO STRIKE!
MAGIC MEANT FOR BATTLE, YOU SAY?
ZSH

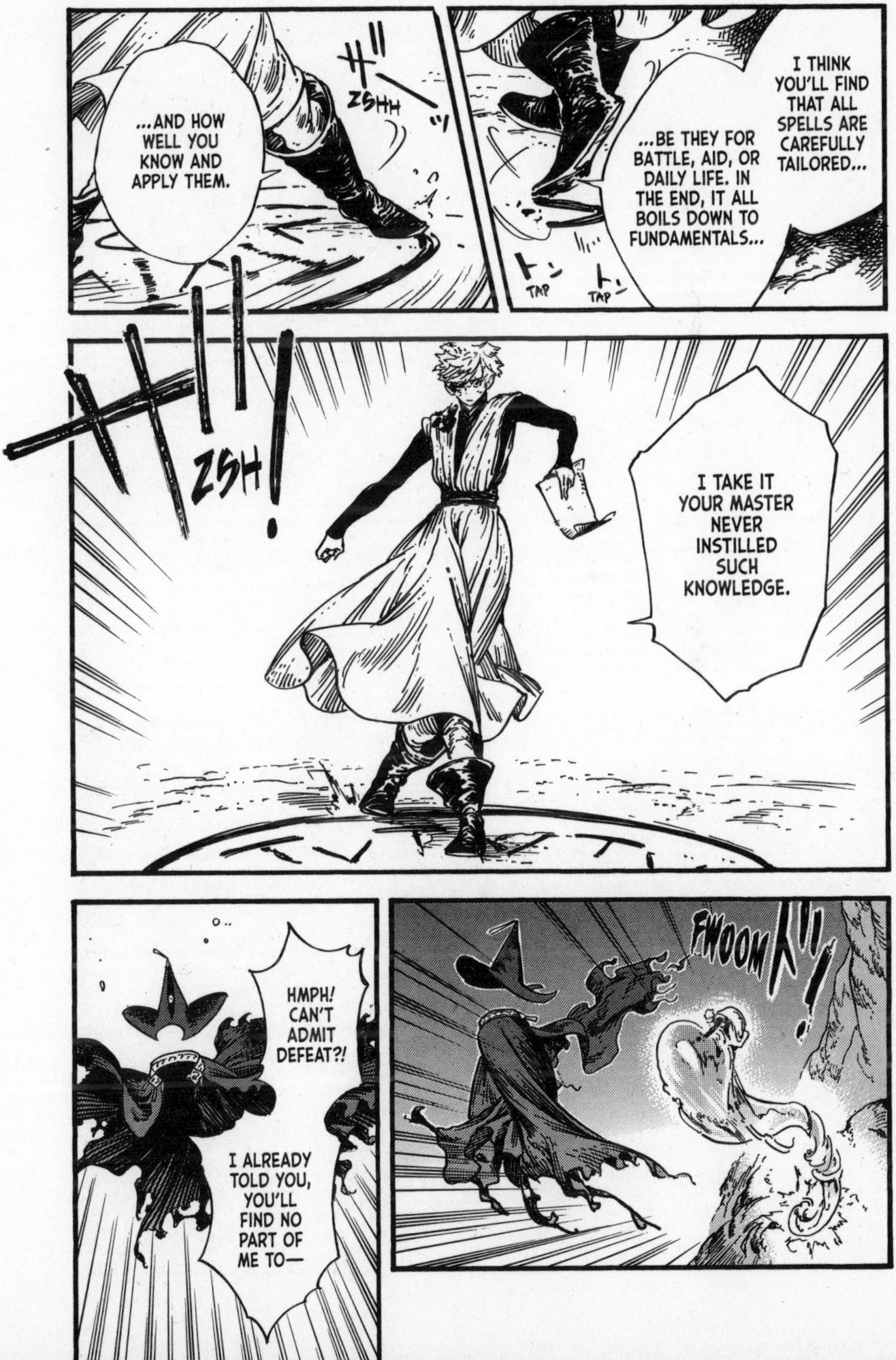
I THINK YOU'LL FIND THAT ALL SPELLS ARE CAREFULLY TAILORED...
...BE THEY FOR BATTLE, AID, OR DAILY LIFE. IN THE END, IT ALL BOILS DOWN TO FUNDAMENTALS...
TAP
TAP
ZSHH
...AND HOW WELL YOU KNOW AND APPLY THEM.
ZSH!
I TAKE IT YOUR MASTER NEVER INSTILLED SUCH KNOWLEDGE.
FWOOM
HMPH! CAN'T ADMIT DEFEAT?!
I ALREADY TOLD YOU, YOU'LL FIND NO PART OF ME TO—

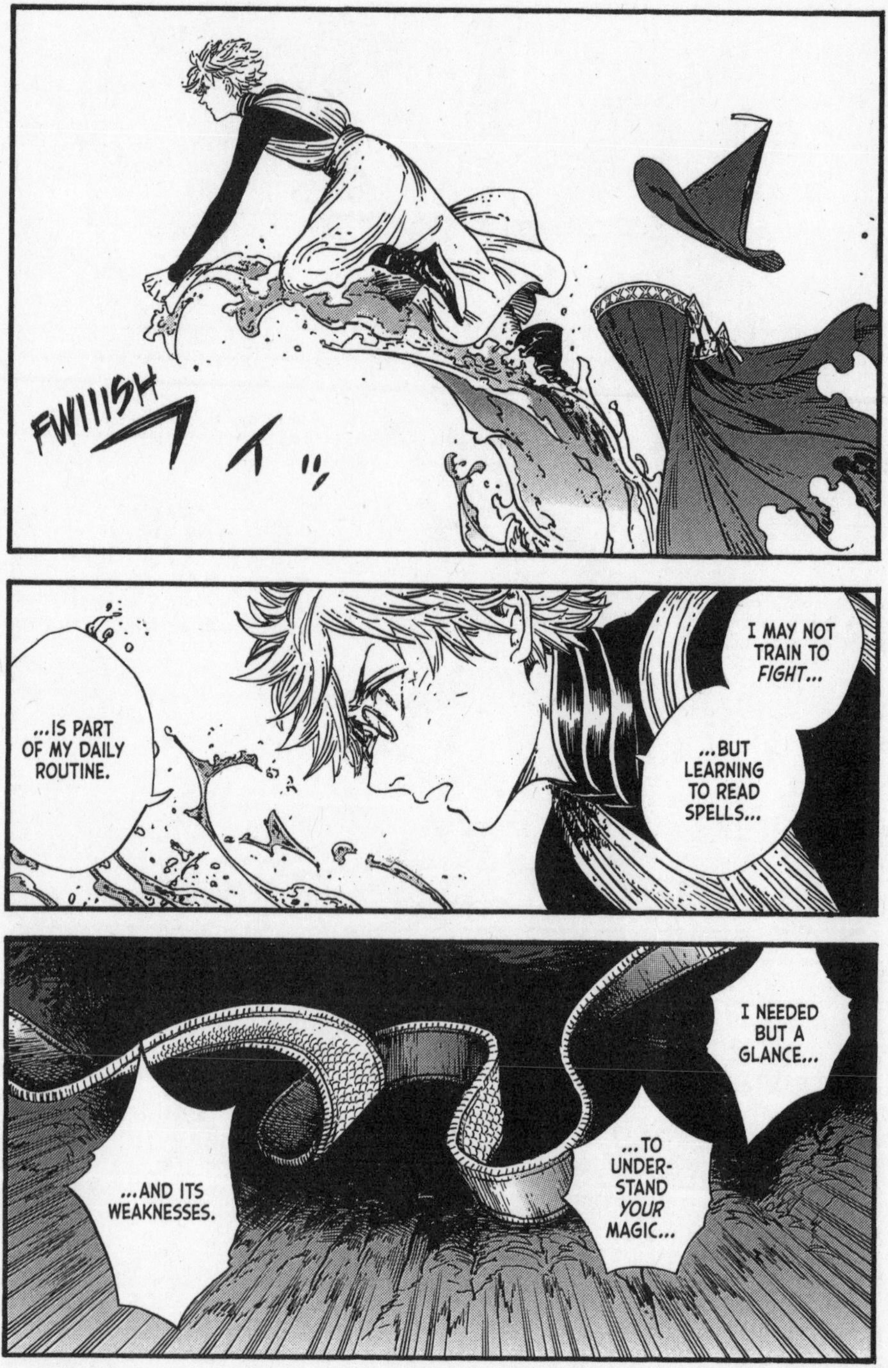
FWIIISH
I MAY NOT TRAIN TO *FIGHT*...
...BUT LEARNING TO READ SPELLS...
...IS PART OF MY DAILY ROUTINE.
I NEEDED BUT A GLANCE...
...TO UNDER-STAND *YOUR* MAGIC...
...AND ITS WEAKNESSES.

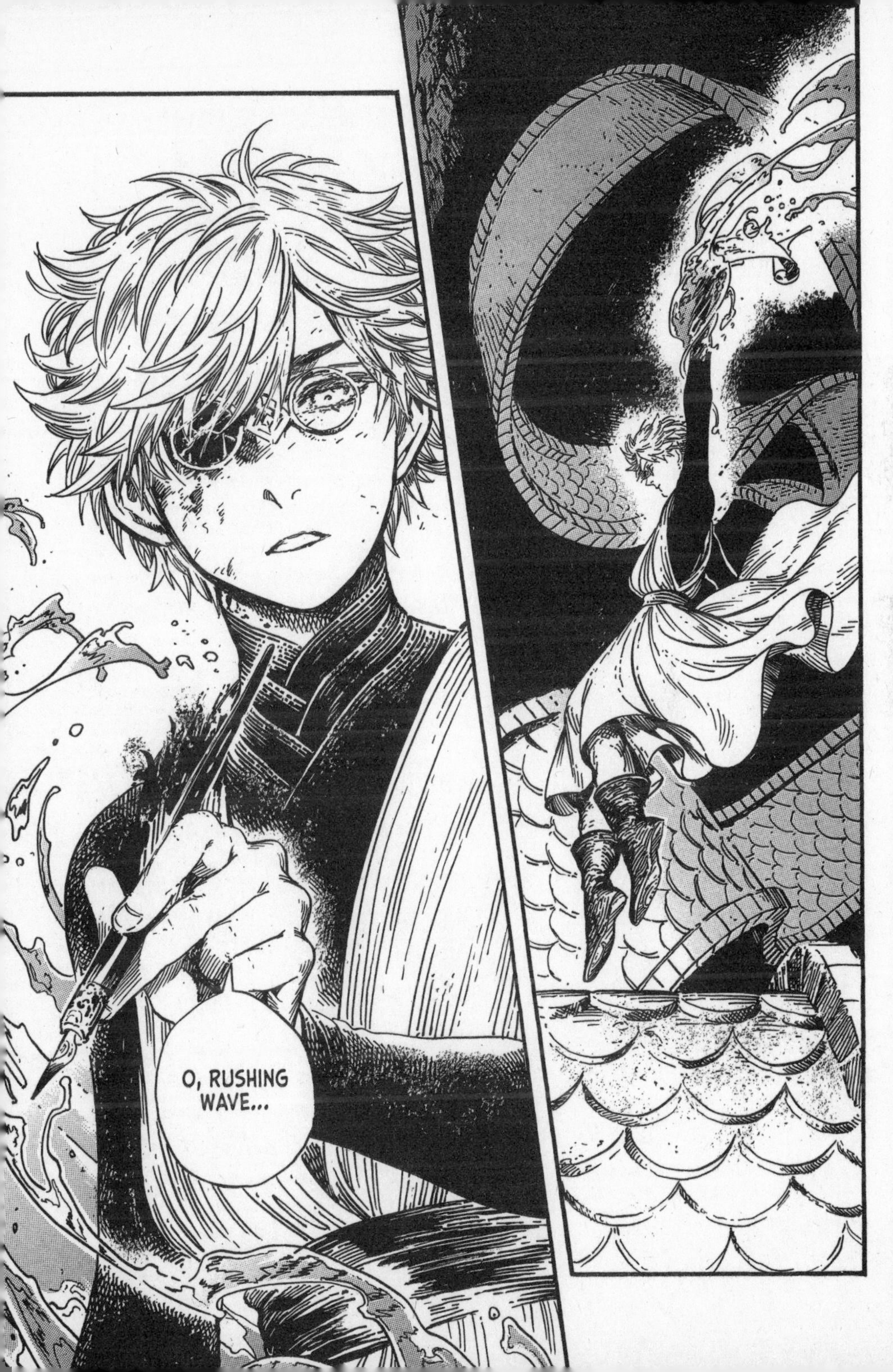
O, RUSHING WAVE...

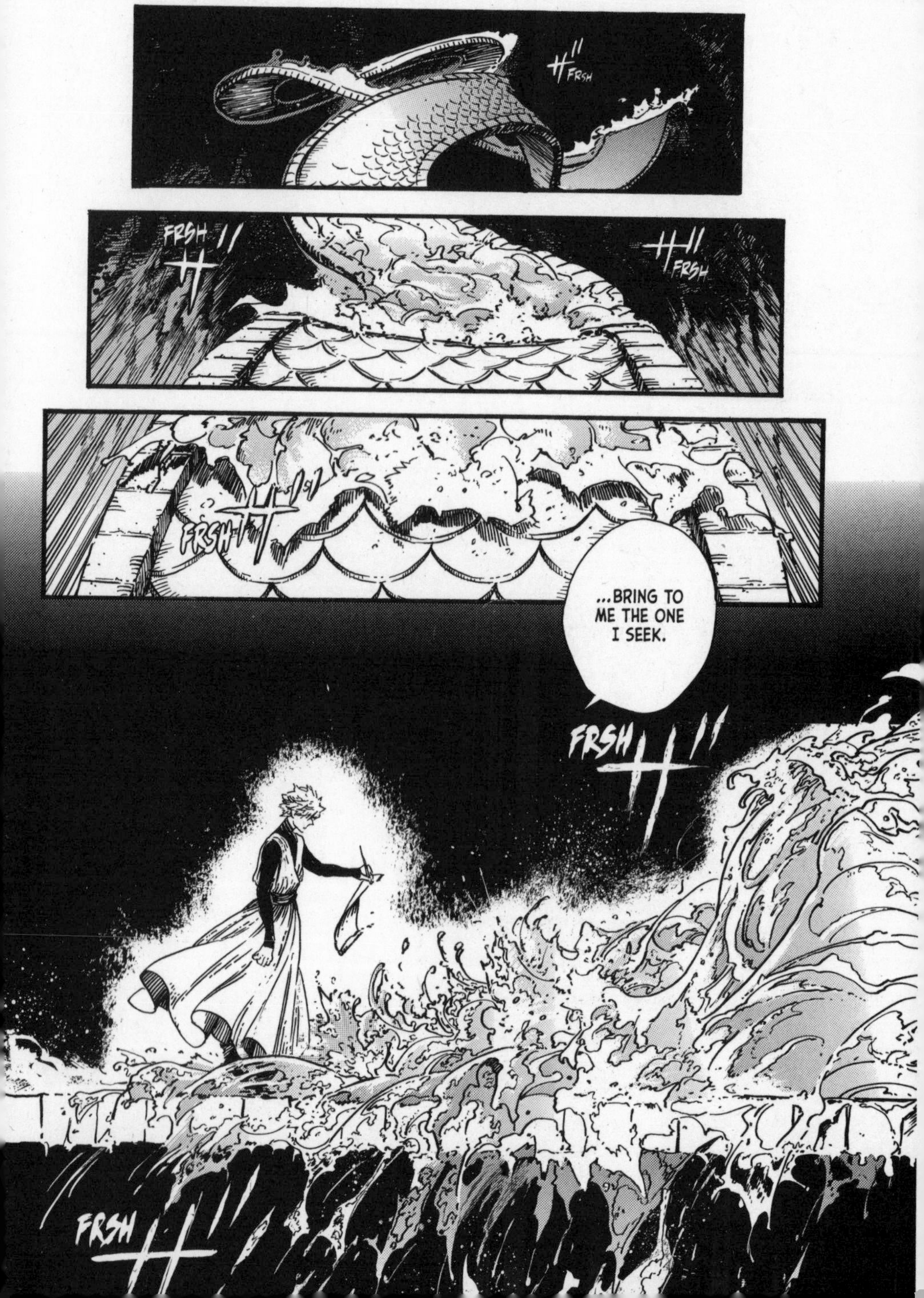
FRSH
FRSH
FRSH
FRSH
...BRING TO ME THE ONE I SEEK.
FRSH
FRSH

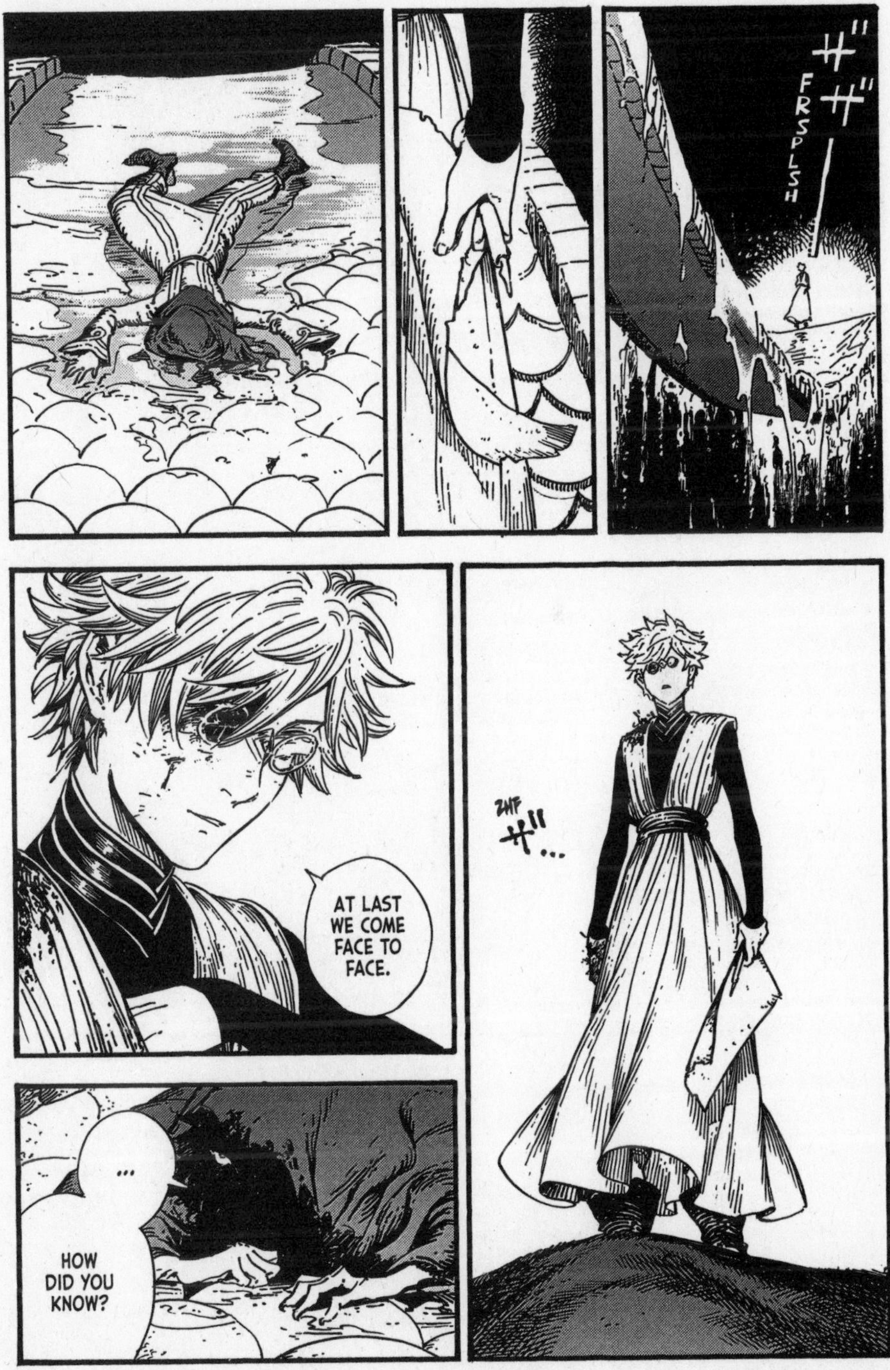
FRSPLSH
ZHF
AT LAST WE COME FACE TO FACE.
...
HOW DID YOU KNOW?

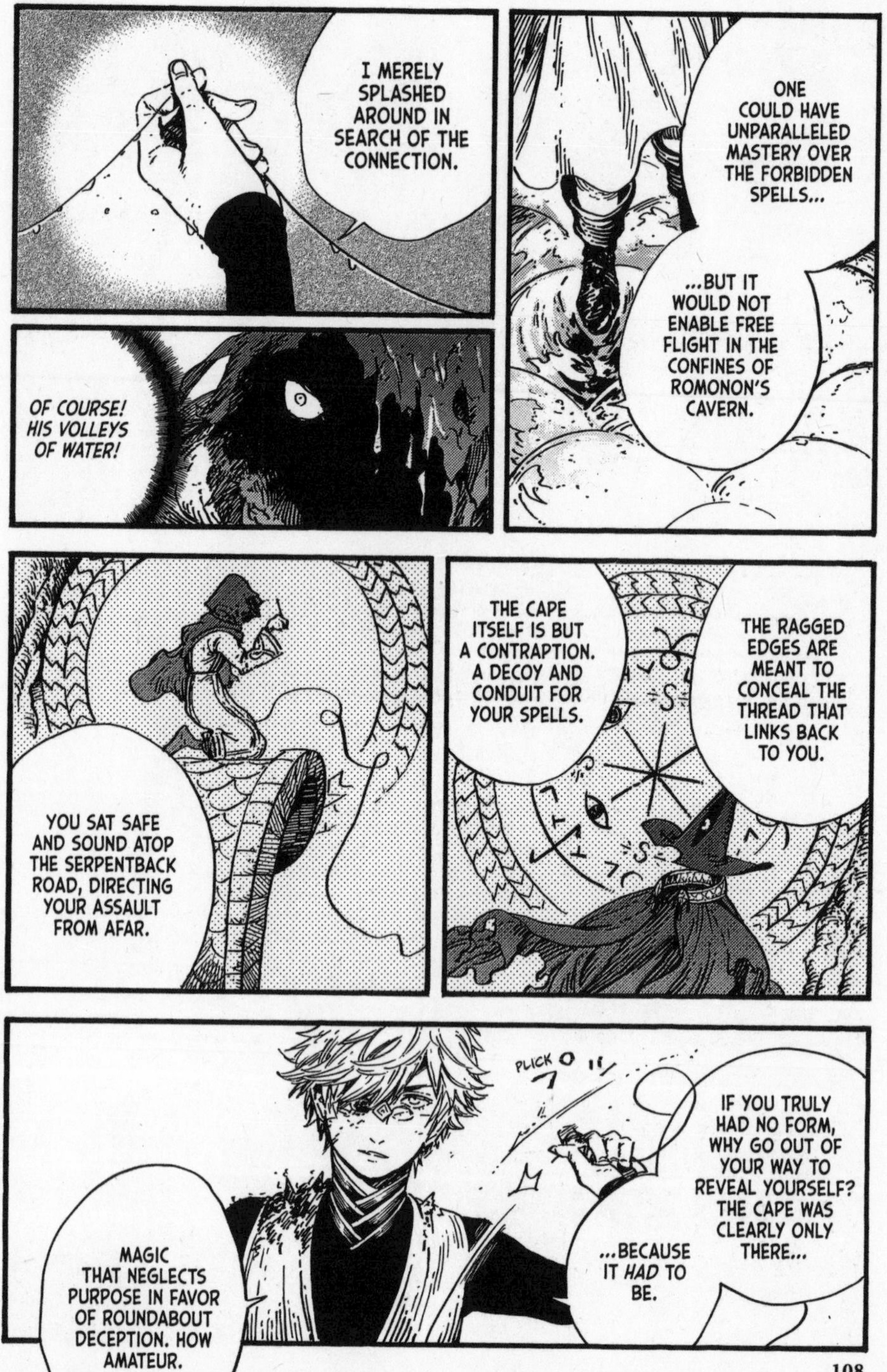
ONE COULD HAVE UNPARALLELED MASTERY OVER THE FORBIDDEN SPELLS...
...BUT IT WOULD NOT ENABLE FREE FLIGHT IN THE CONFINES OF ROMONON'S CAVERN.
I MERELY SPLASHED AROUND IN SEARCH OF THE CONNECTION.
OF COURSE! HIS VOLLEYS OF WATER!
THE RAGGED EDGES ARE MEANT TO CONCEAL THE THREAD THAT LINKS BACK TO YOU.
THE CAPE ITSELF IS BUT A CONTRAPTION. A DECOY AND CONDUIT FOR YOUR SPELLS.
YOU SAT SAFE AND SOUND ATOP THE SERPENTBACK ROAD, DIRECTING YOUR ASSAULT FROM AFAR.
IF YOU TRULY HAD NO FORM, WHY GO OUT OF YOUR WAY TO REVEAL YOURSELF? THE CAPE WAS CLEARLY ONLY THERE...
PLICK
...BECAUSE IT *HAD* TO BE.
MAGIC THAT NEGLECTS PURPOSE IN FAVOR OF ROUNDABOUT DECEPTION. HOW AMATEUR.

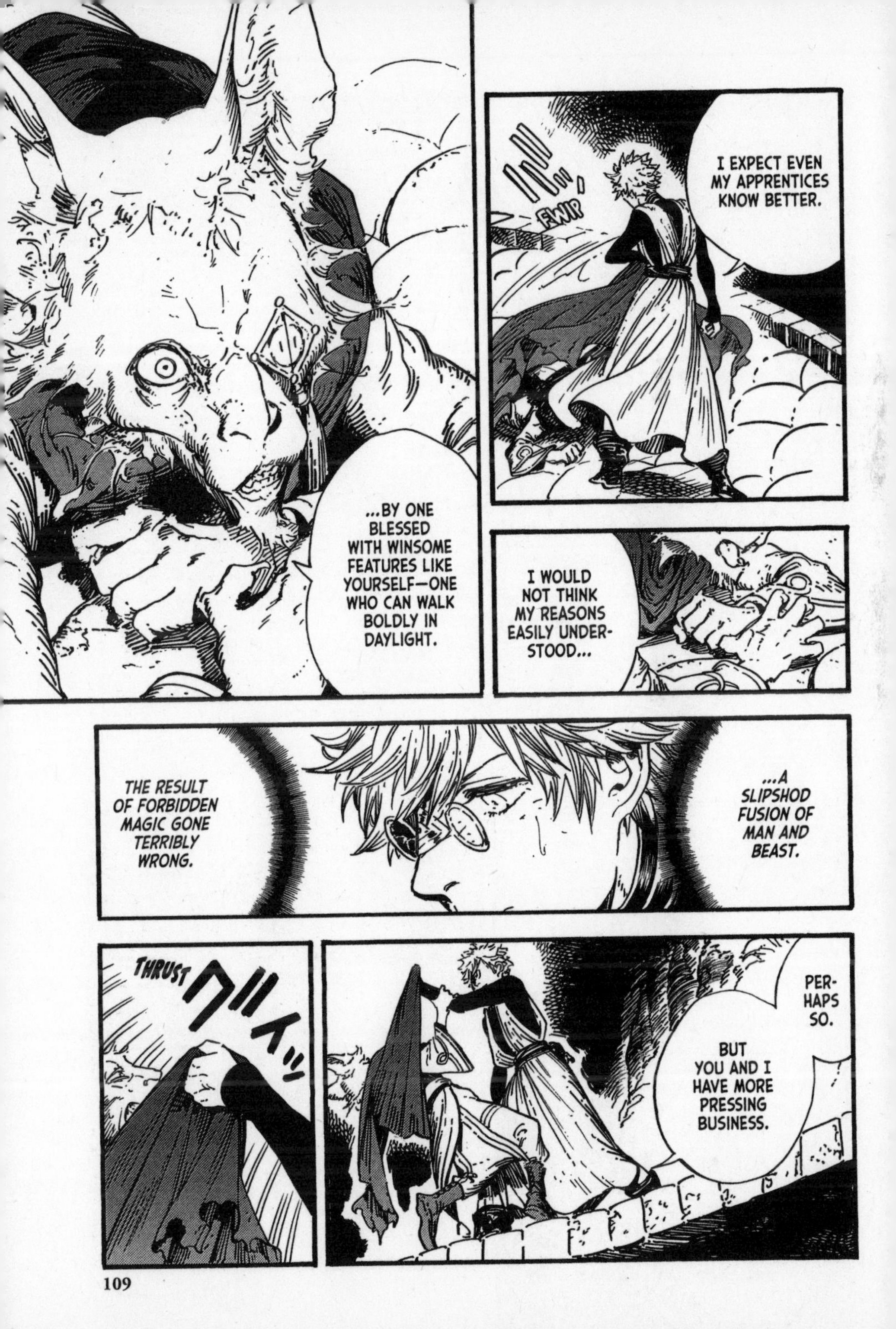
FWIP
I EXPECT EVEN MY APPRENTICES KNOW BETTER.
I WOULD NOT THINK MY REASONS EASILY UNDER-STOOD...
...BY ONE BLESSED WITH WINSOME FEATURES LIKE YOURSELF—ONE WHO CAN WALK BOLDLY IN DAYLIGHT.
...A SLIPSHOD FUSION OF MAN AND BEAST.
THE RESULT OF FORBIDDEN MAGIC GONE TERRIBLY WRONG.
PER-HAPS SO.
BUT YOU AND I HAVE MORE PRESSING BUSINESS.
THRUST

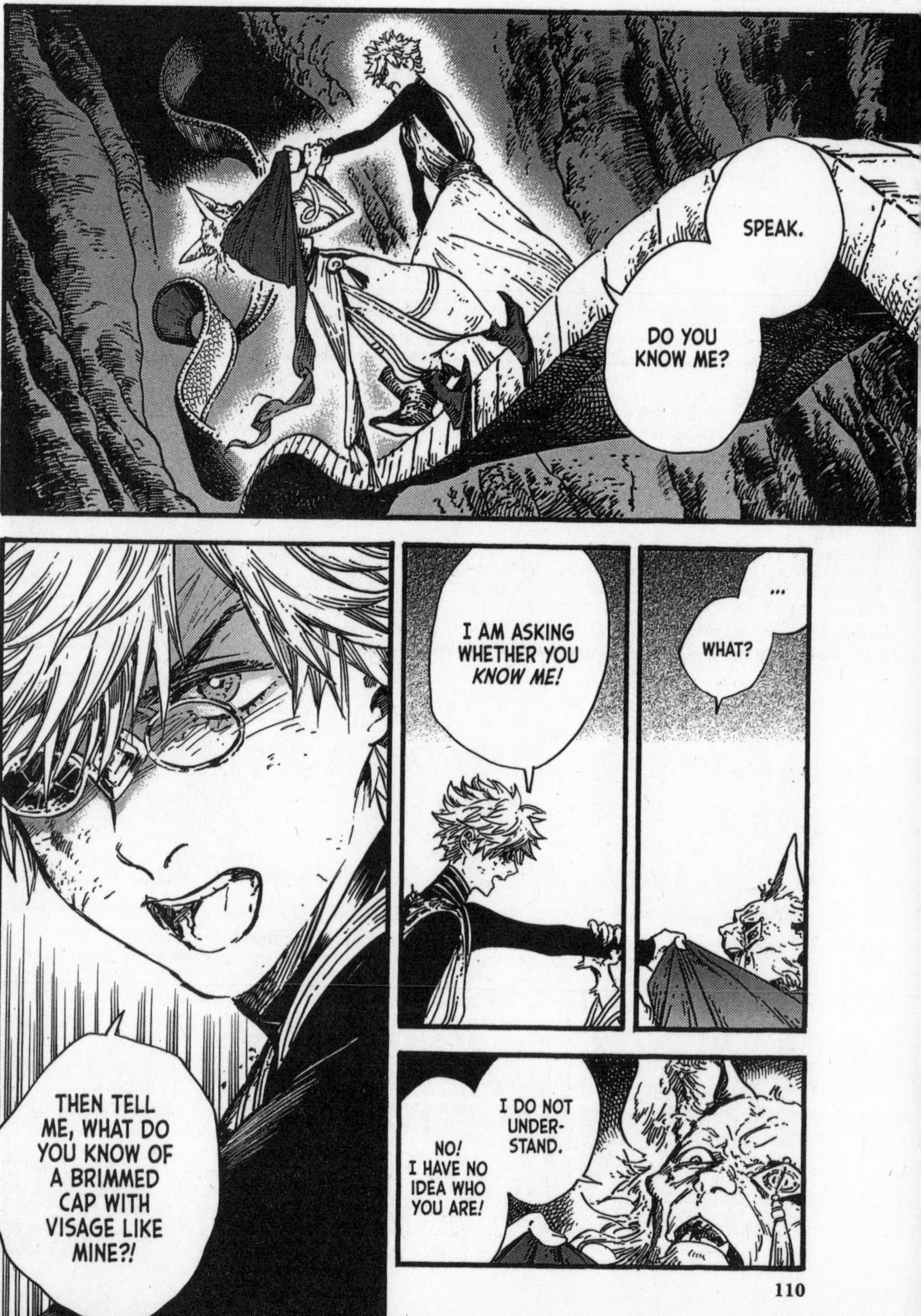
SPEAK.
DO YOU KNOW ME?
...
WHAT?
I AM ASKING WHETHER YOU *KNOW ME!*
I DO NOT UNDER-STAND.
NO! I HAVE NO IDEA WHO YOU ARE!
THEN TELL ME, WHAT DO YOU KNOW OF A BRIMMED CAP WITH VISAGE LIKE MINE?!

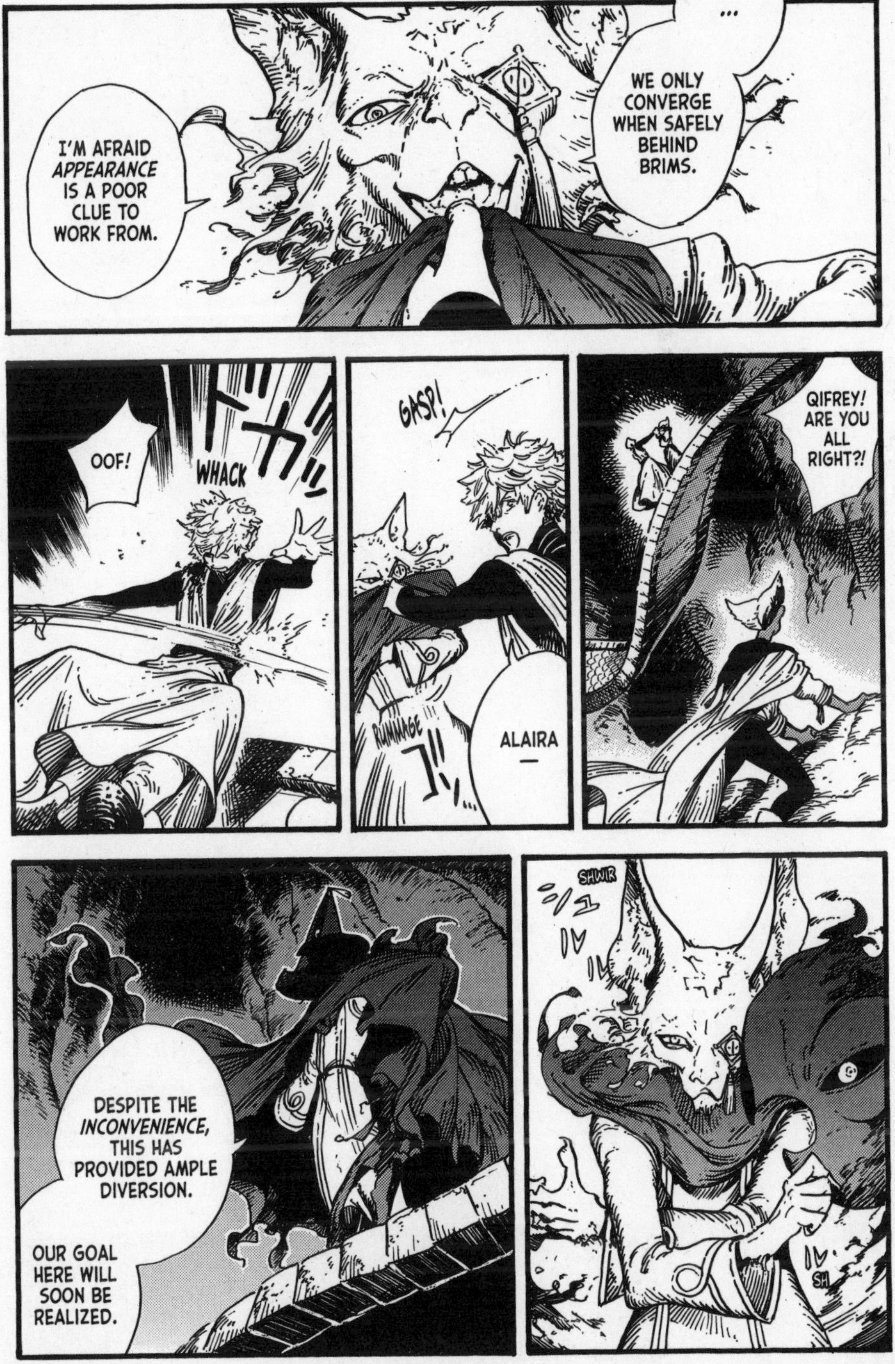
...
WE ONLY CONVERGE WHEN SAFELY BEHIND BRIMS.
I'M AFRAID *APPEARANCE* IS A POOR CLUE TO WORK FROM.
QIFREY! ARE YOU ALL RIGHT?!
GASP!
ALAIRA —
RUMMAGE
OOF!
WHACK
SHWIR
SH
DESPITE THE *INCONVENIENCE,* THIS HAS PROVIDED AMPLE DIVERSION.
OUR GOAL HERE WILL SOON BE REALIZED.

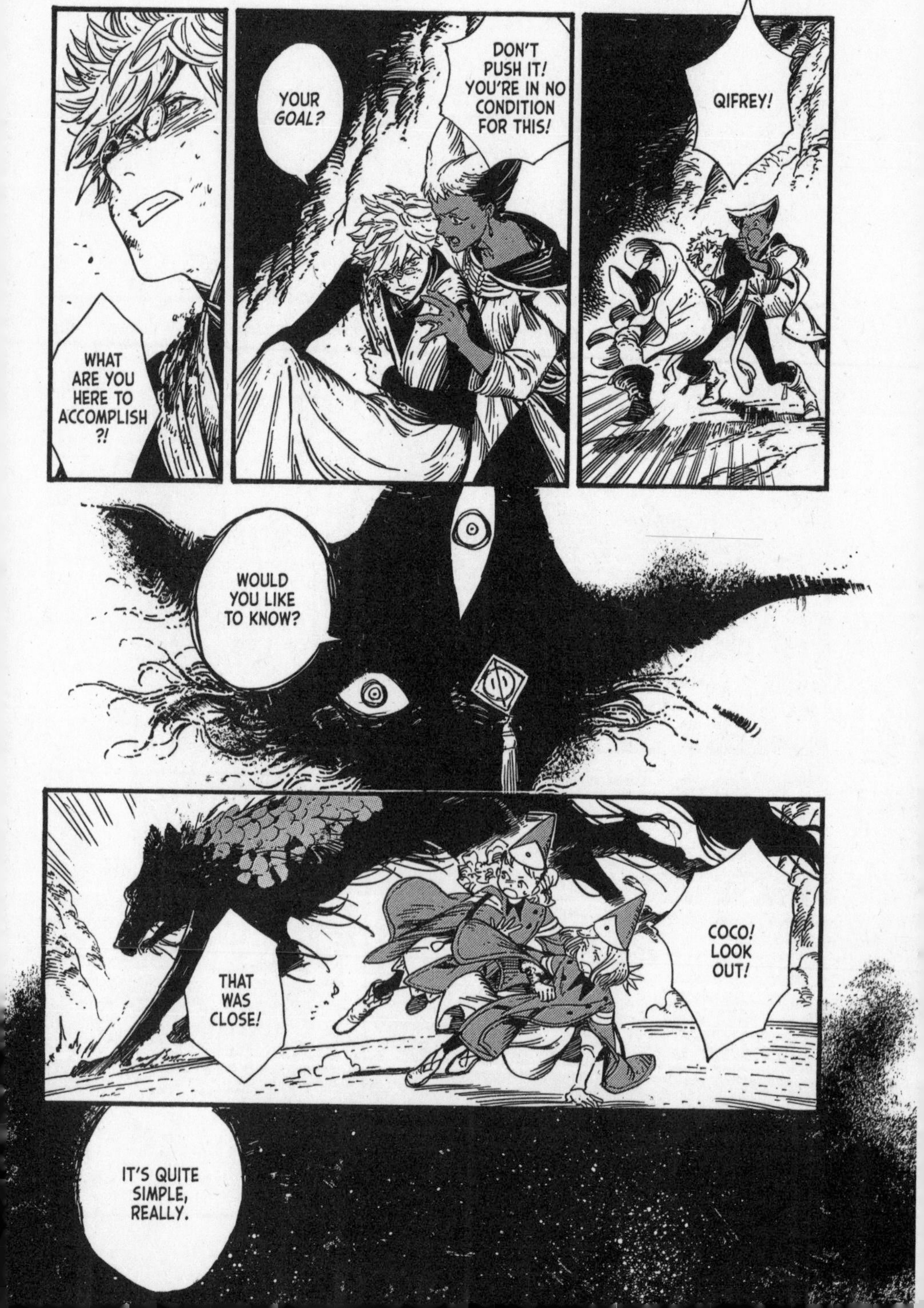
QIFREY!
DON'T PUSH IT! YOU'RE IN NO CONDITION FOR THIS!
YOUR GOAL?
WHAT ARE YOU HERE TO ACCOMPLISH?!
WOULD YOU LIKE TO KNOW?
COCO! LOOK OUT!
THAT WAS CLOSE!
IT'S QUITE SIMPLE, REALLY.

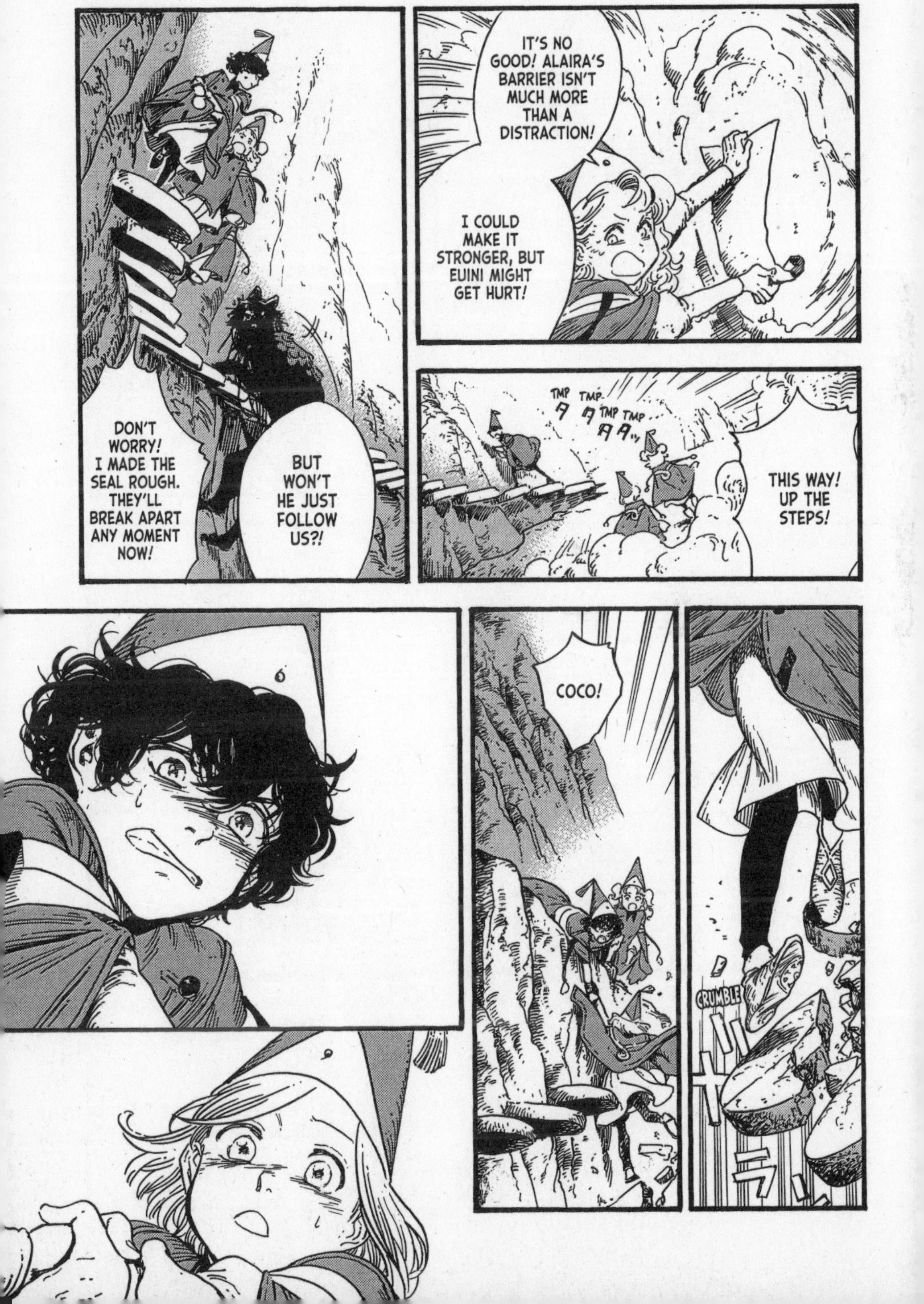
IT'S NO GOOD! ALAIRA'S BARRIER ISN'T MUCH MORE THAN A DISTRACTION!
I COULD MAKE IT STRONGER, BUT EUINI MIGHT GET HURT!
TMP TMP TMP TMP
THIS WAY! UP THE STEPS!
BUT WON'T HE JUST FOLLOW US?!
DON'T WORRY! I MADE THE SEAL ROUGH. THEY'LL BREAK APART ANY MOMENT NOW!
CRUMBLE
COCO!

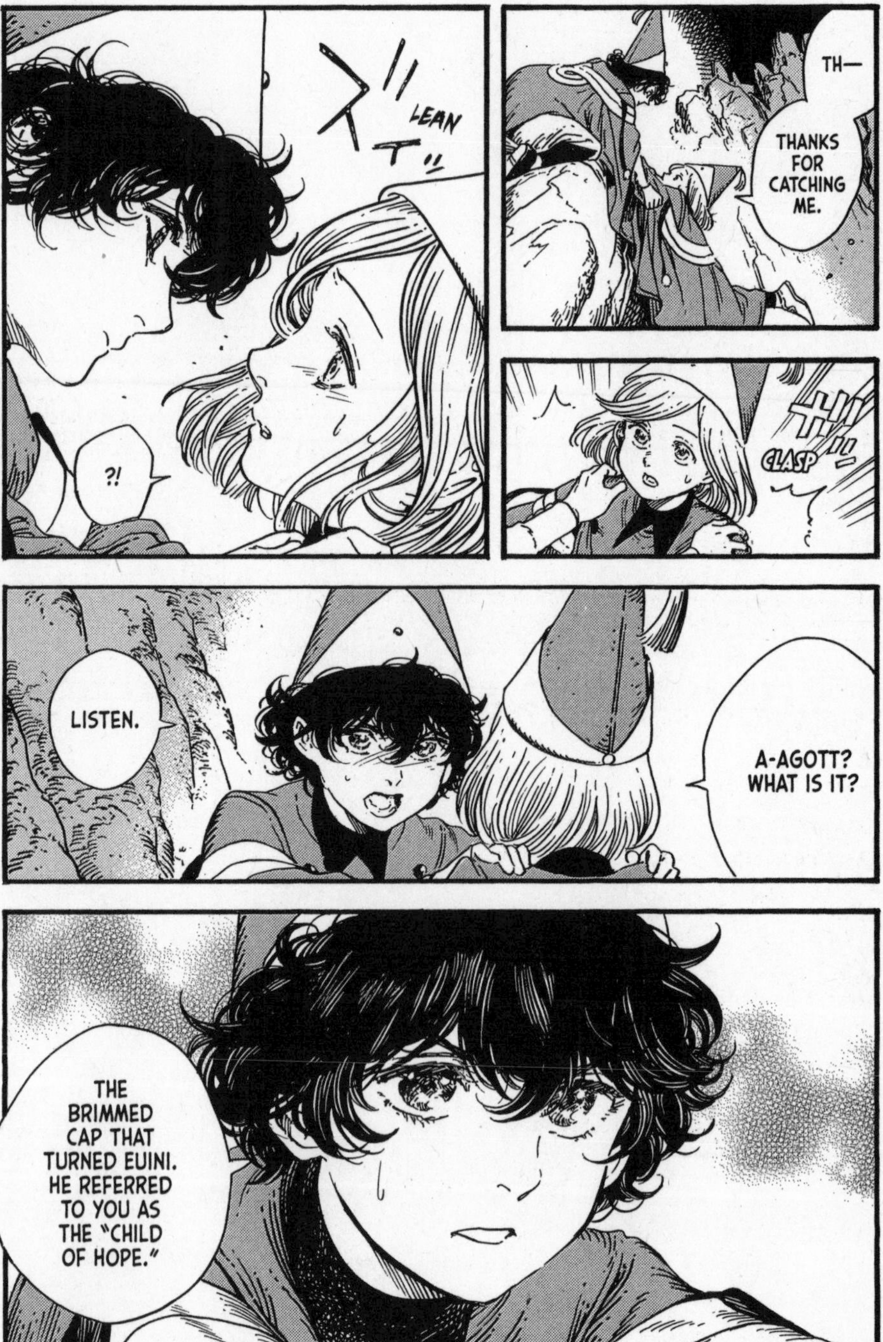
TH—
THANKS FOR CATCHING ME.
CLASP
LEAN
?!
A-AGOTT? WHAT IS IT?
LISTEN.
THE BRIMMED CAP THAT TURNED EUINI. HE REFERRED TO YOU AS THE "CHILD OF HOPE."

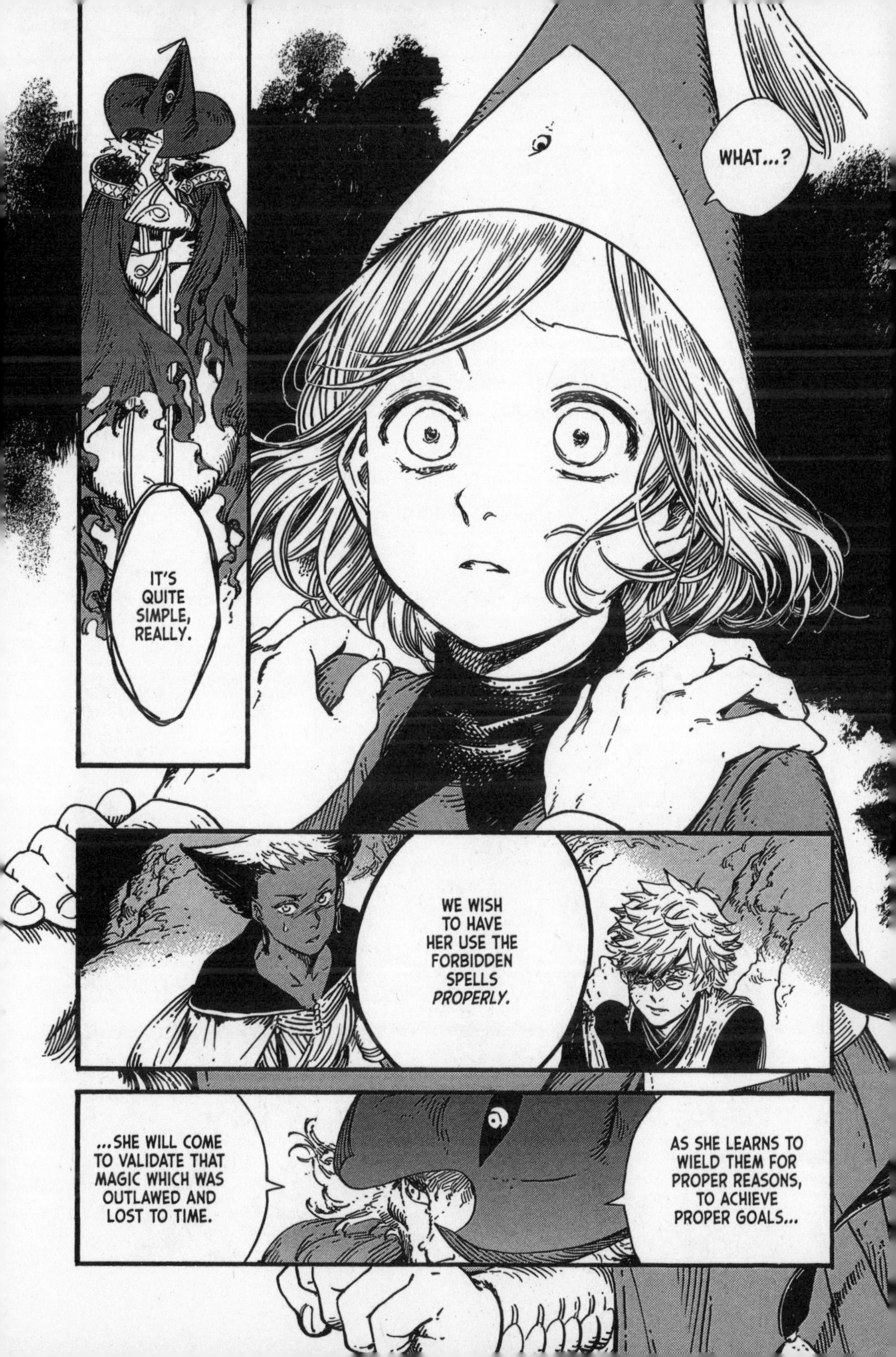
WHAT...?
IT'S QUITE SIMPLE, REALLY.
WE WISH TO HAVE HER USE THE FORBIDDEN SPELLS *PROPERLY.*
AS SHE LEARNS TO WIELD THEM FOR PROPER REASONS, TO ACHIEVE PROPER GOALS...
...SHE WILL COME TO VALIDATE THAT MAGIC WHICH WAS OUTLAWED AND LOST TO TIME.

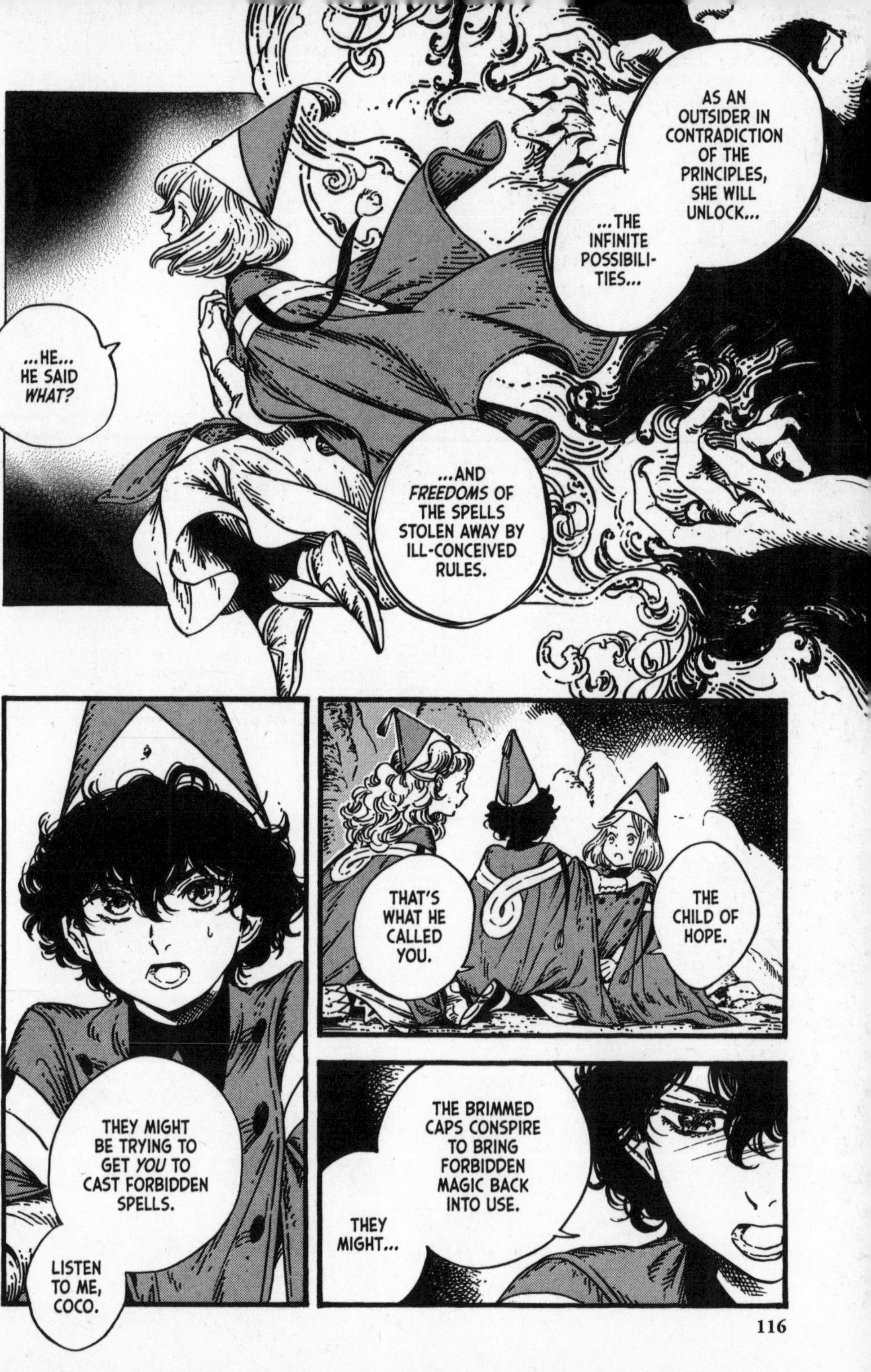
AS AN OUTSIDER IN CONTRADICTION OF THE PRINCIPLES, SHE WILL UNLOCK...
...THE INFINITE POSSIBILITIES...
...AND *FREEDOMS* OF THE SPELLS STOLEN AWAY BY ILL-CONCEIVED RULES.
...HE... HE SAID *WHAT?*
THE CHILD OF HOPE.
THAT'S WHAT HE CALLED YOU.
THE BRIMMED CAPS CONSPIRE TO BRING FORBIDDEN MAGIC BACK INTO USE.
THEY MIGHT...
THEY MIGHT BE TRYING TO GET *YOU* TO CAST FORBIDDEN SPELLS.
LISTEN TO ME, COCO.

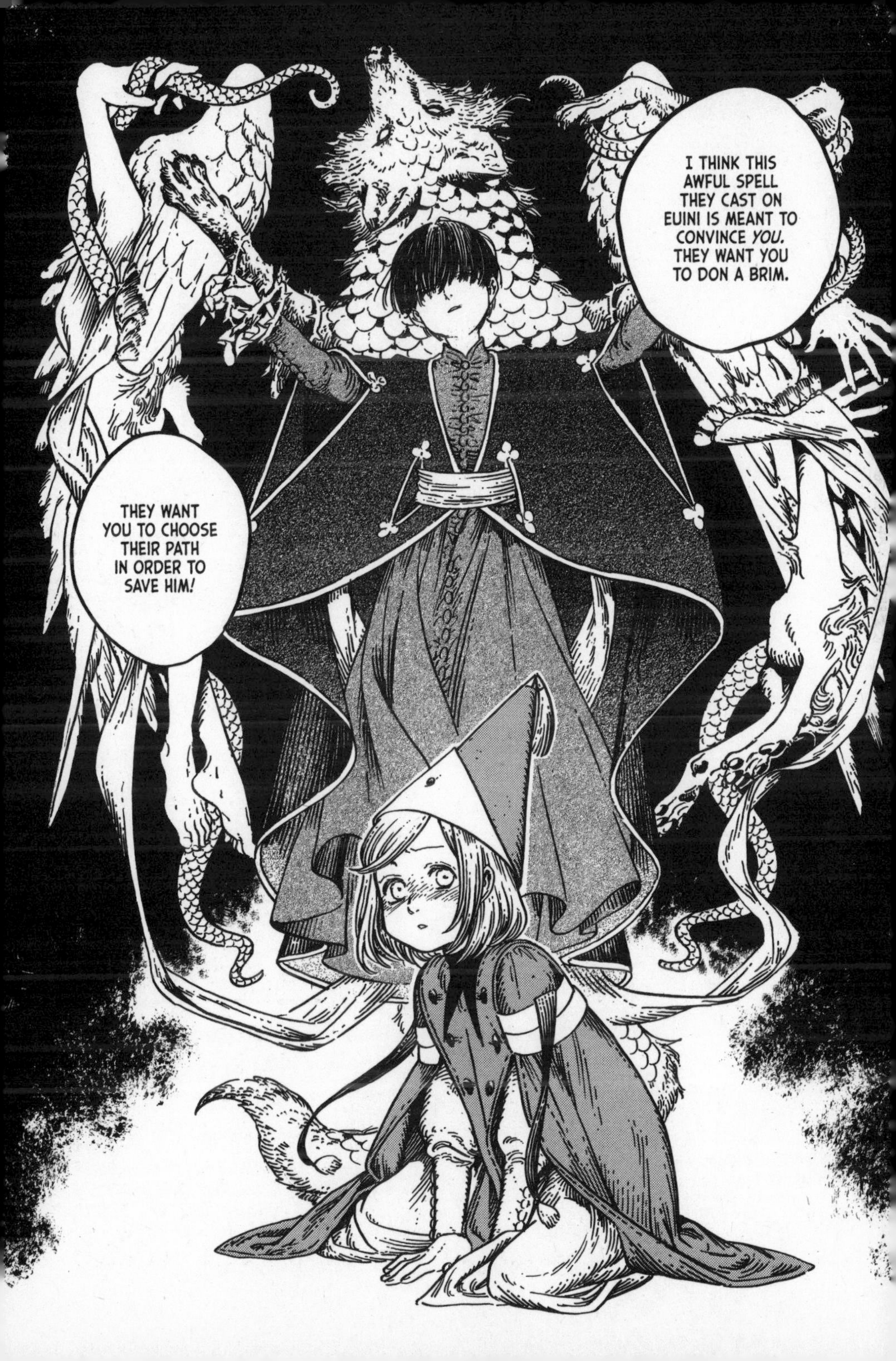
I THINK THIS AWFUL SPELL THEY CAST ON EUINI IS MEANT TO CONVINCE *YOU*. THEY WANT YOU TO DON A BRIM.
THEY WANT YOU TO CHOOSE THEIR PATH IN ORDER TO SAVE HIM!

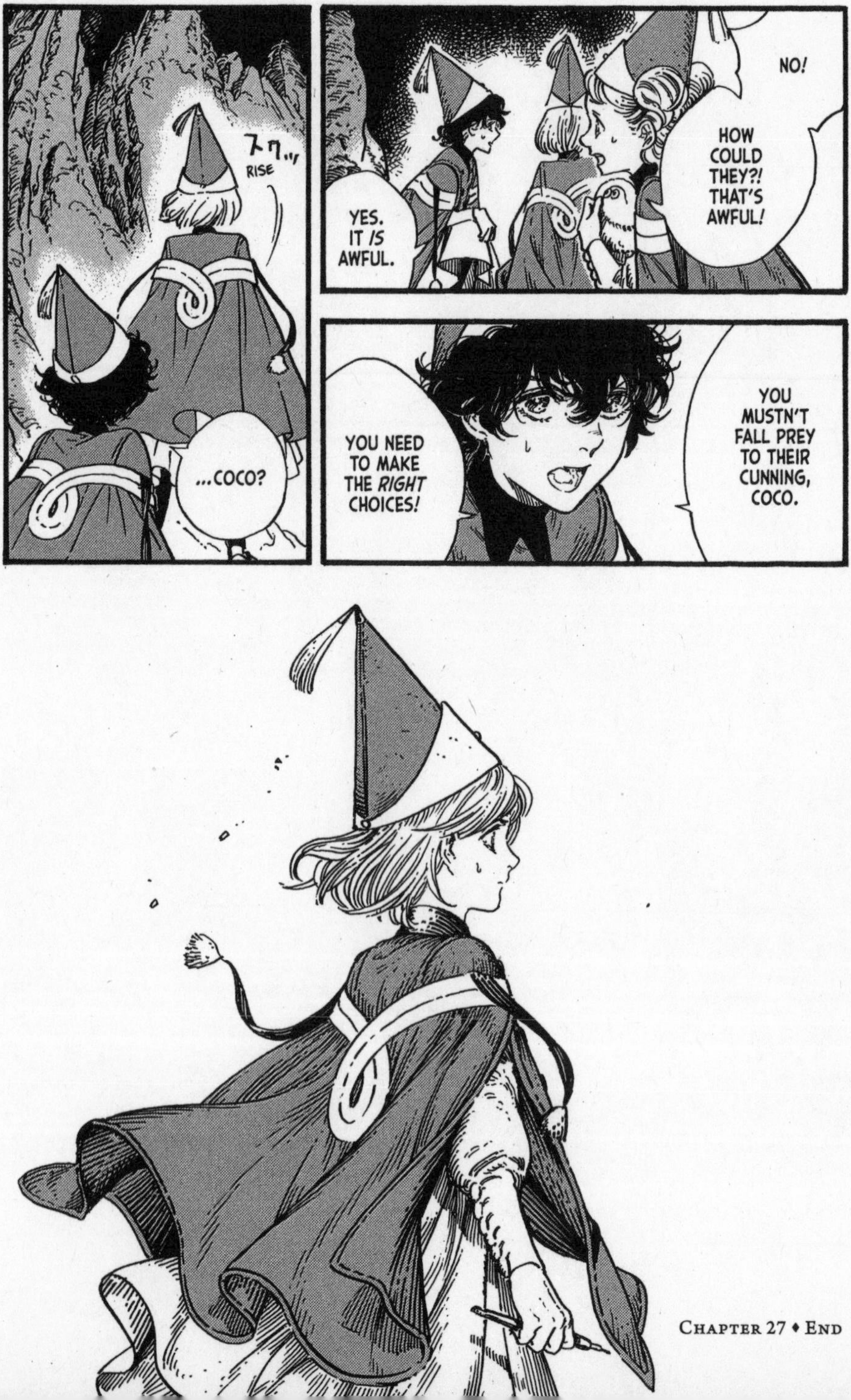
NO!
HOW COULD THEY?! THAT'S AWFUL!
YES. IT *IS* AWFUL.
YOU MUSTN'T FALL PREY TO THEIR CUNNING, COCO.
YOU NEED TO MAKE THE *RIGHT* CHOICES!
RISE
...COCO?

Chapter 27 ♦ End

Witch Hat Atelier

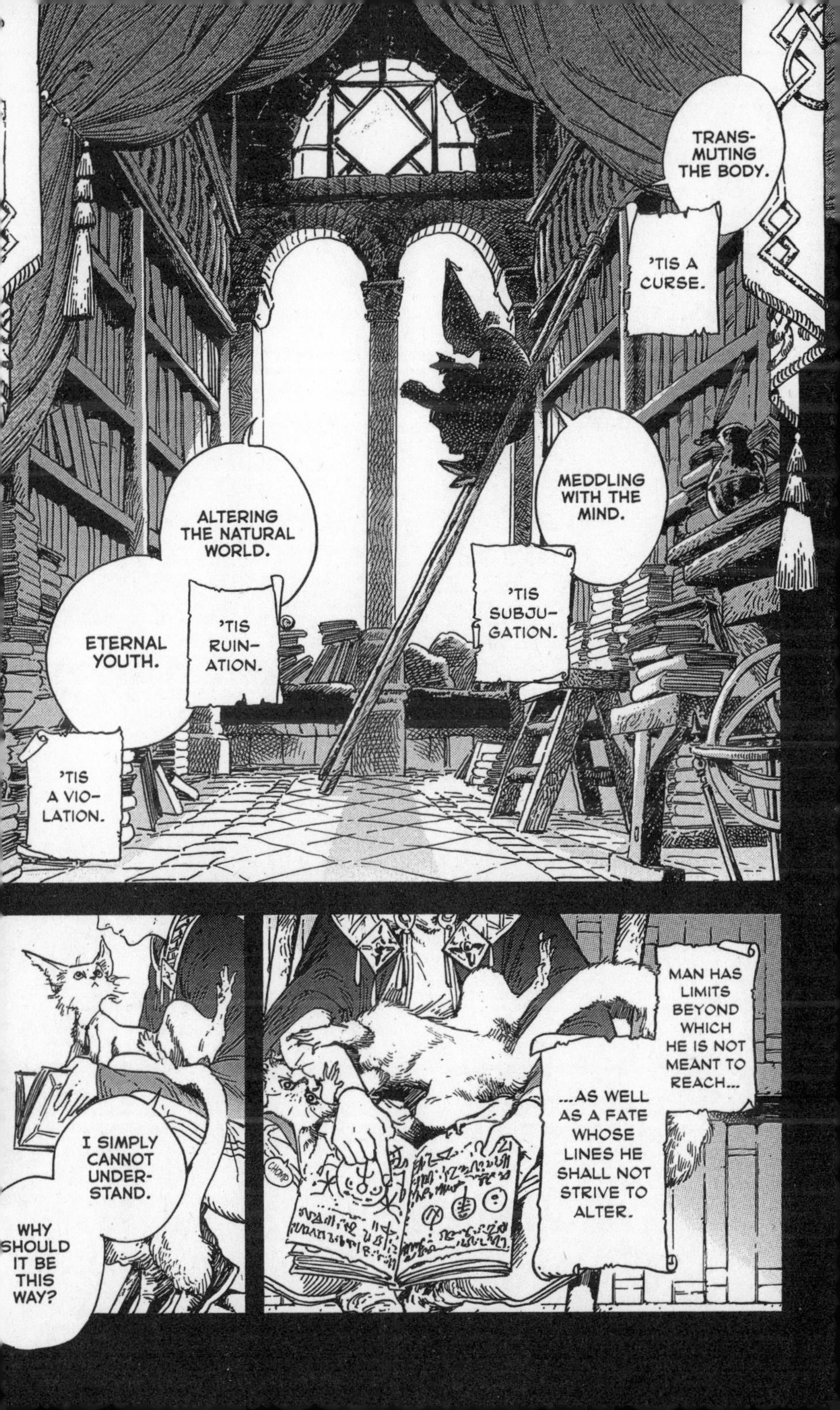
TRANSMUTING THE BODY.
'TIS A CURSE.
MEDDLING WITH THE MIND.
'TIS SUBJUGATION.
ALTERING THE NATURAL WORLD.
'TIS RUINATION.
ETERNAL YOUTH.
'TIS A VIOLATION.
MAN HAS LIMITS BEYOND WHICH HE IS NOT MEANT TO REACH...
...AS WELL AS A FATE WHOSE LINES HE SHALL NOT STRIVE TO ALTER.
CHOMP
I SIMPLY CANNOT UNDERSTAND.
WHY SHOULD IT BE THIS WAY?

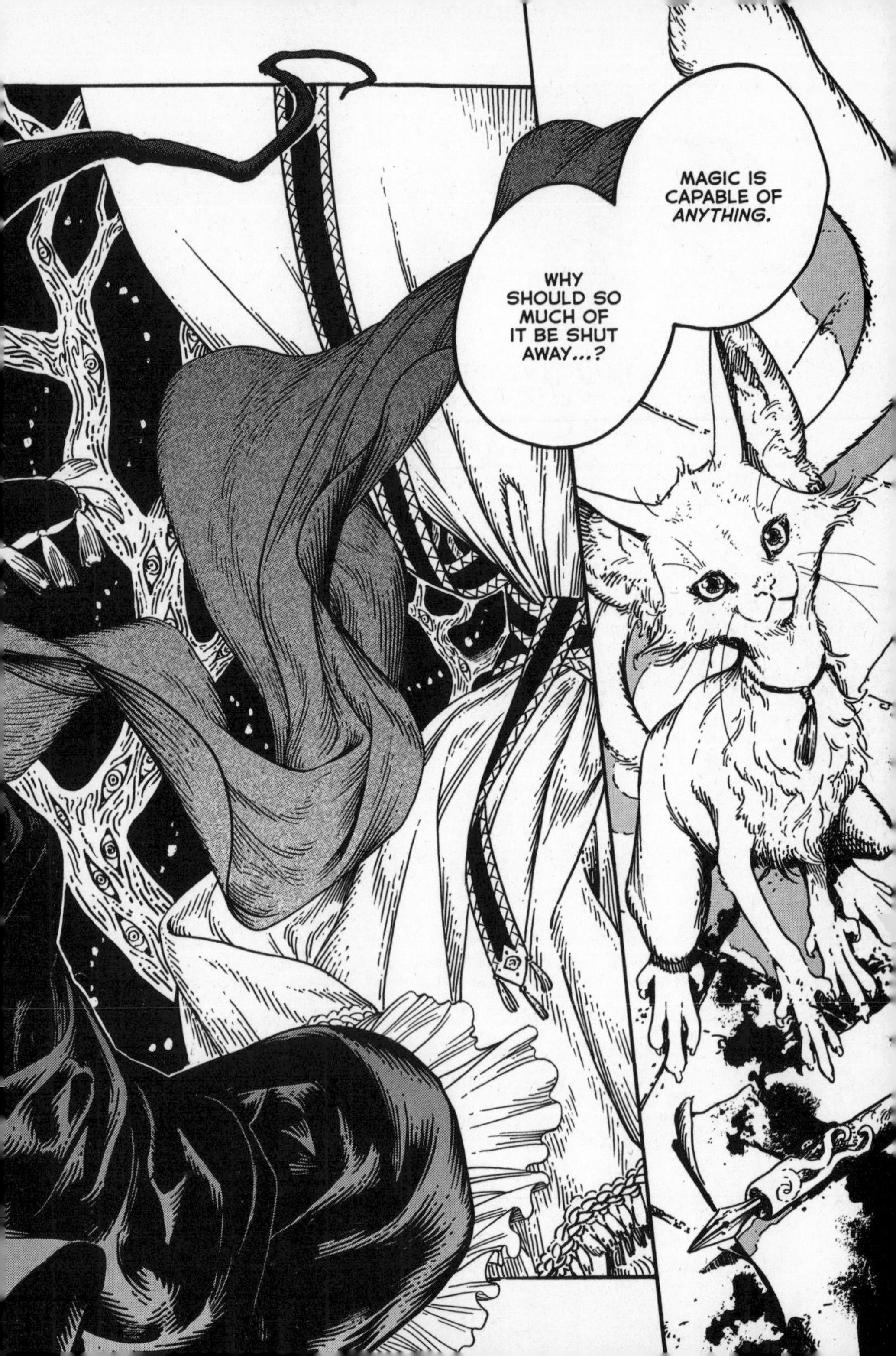
MAGIC IS CAPABLE OF *ANYTHING.*
WHY SHOULD SO MUCH OF IT BE SHUT AWAY...?

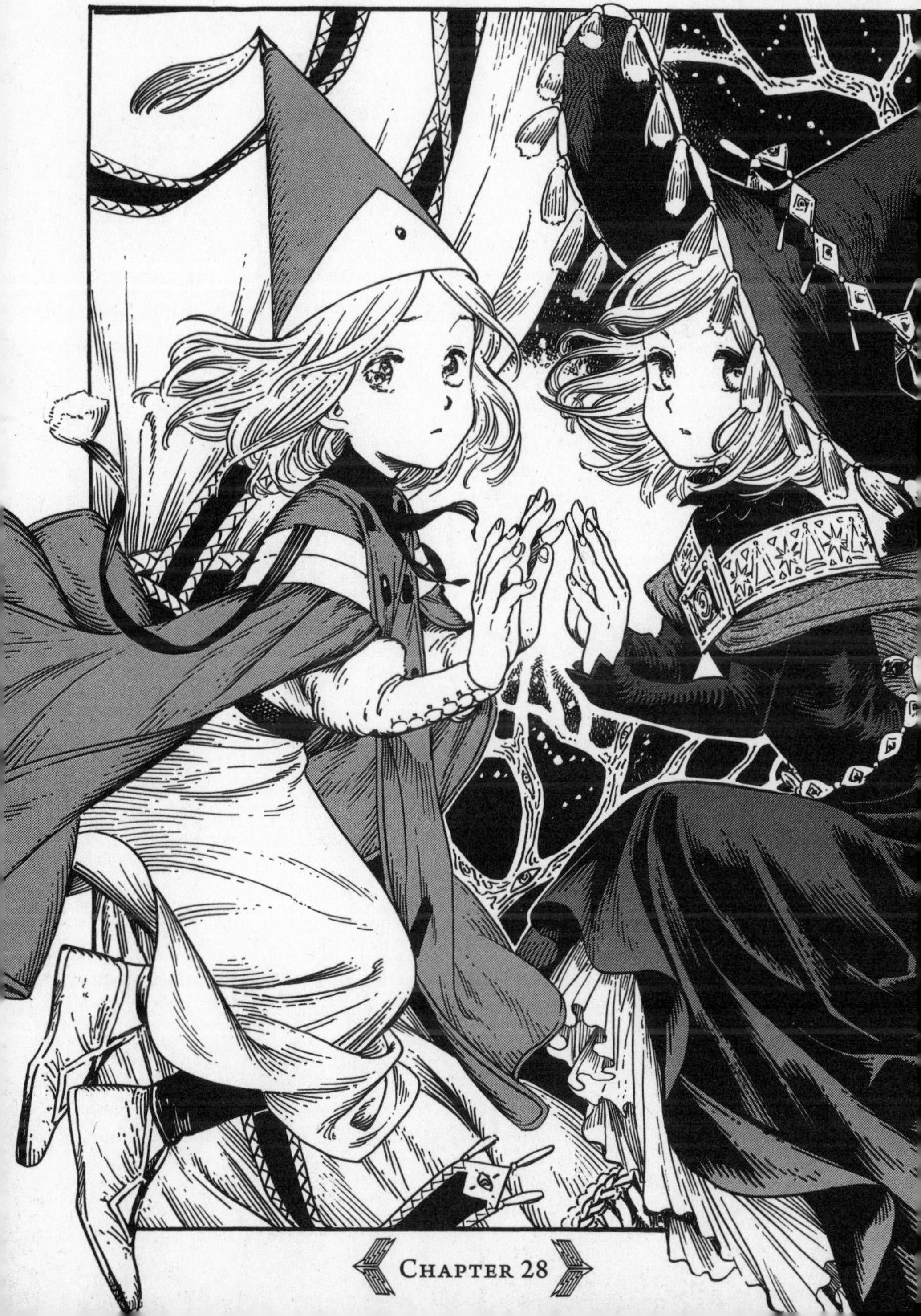

Chapter 28

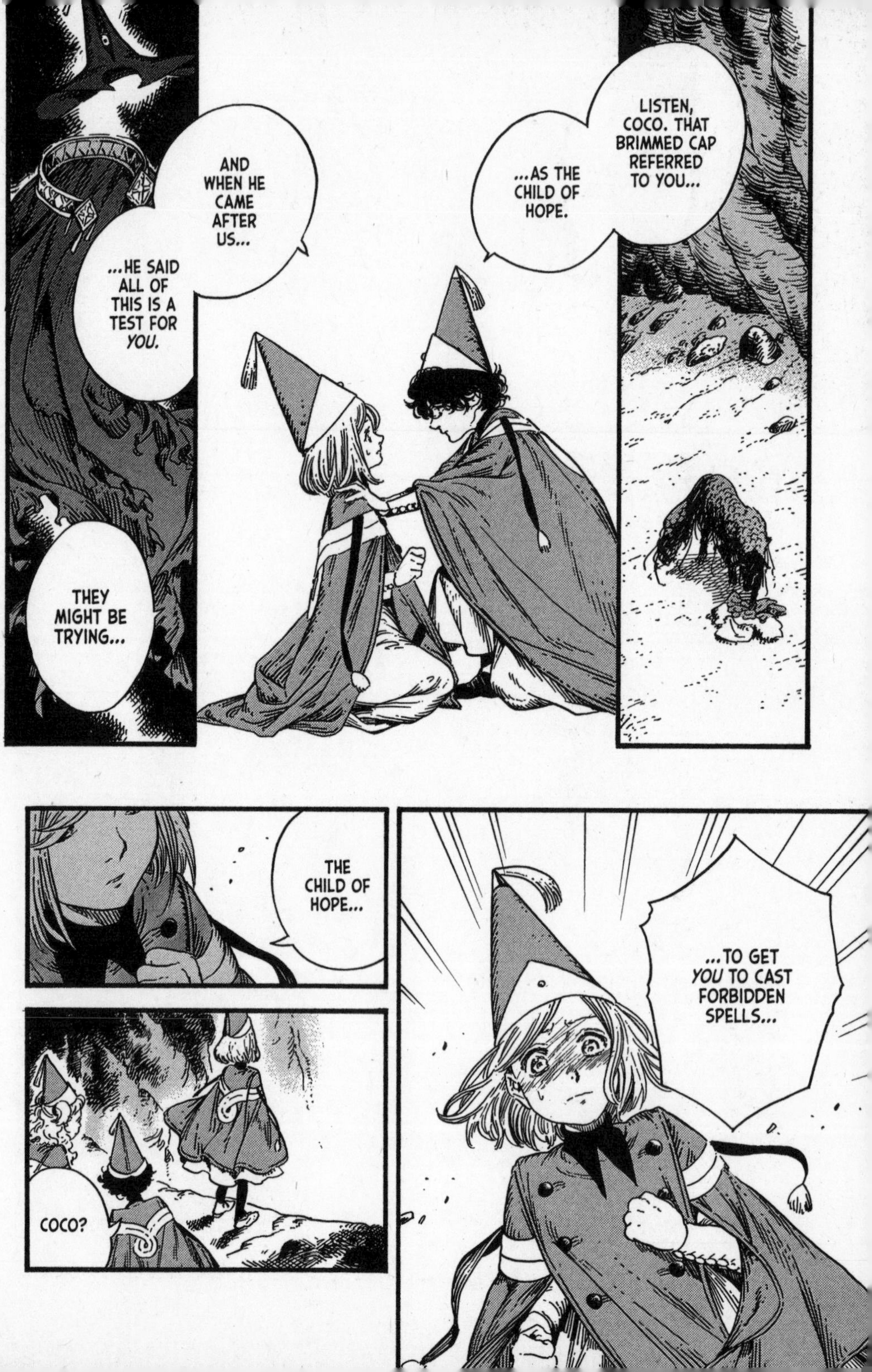
LISTEN, COCO. THAT BRIMMED CAP REFERRED TO YOU...
...AS THE CHILD OF HOPE.
AND WHEN HE CAME AFTER US...
...HE SAID ALL OF THIS IS A TEST FOR *YOU.*
THEY MIGHT BE TRYING...
...TO GET *YOU* TO CAST FORBIDDEN SPELLS...
THE CHILD OF HOPE...
COCO?

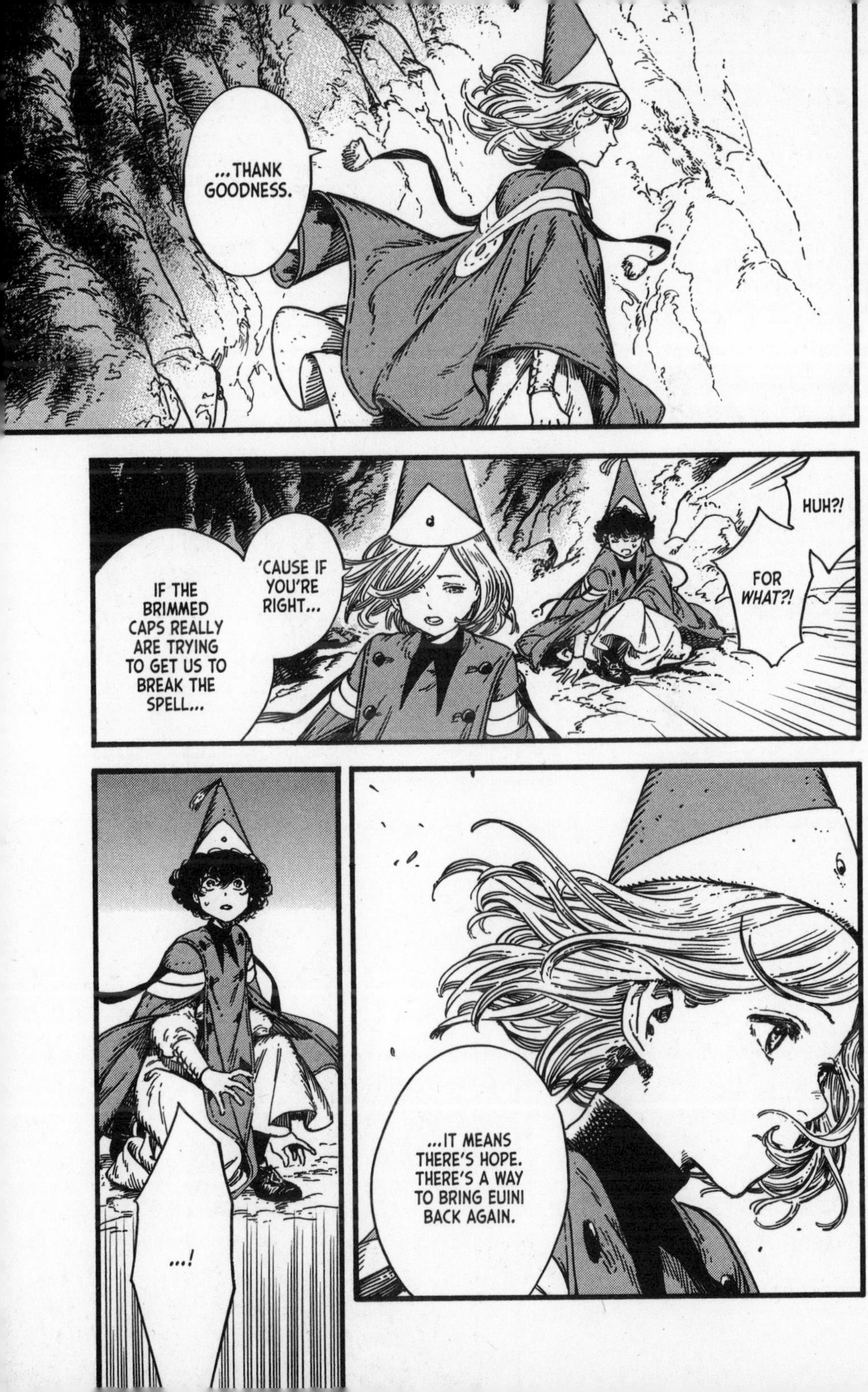
...THANK GOODNESS.
HUH?!
FOR WHAT?!
'CAUSE IF YOU'RE RIGHT...
IF THE BRIMMED CAPS REALLY ARE TRYING TO GET US TO BREAK THE SPELL...
...IT MEANS THERE'S HOPE. THERE'S A WAY TO BRING EUINI BACK AGAIN.
...!

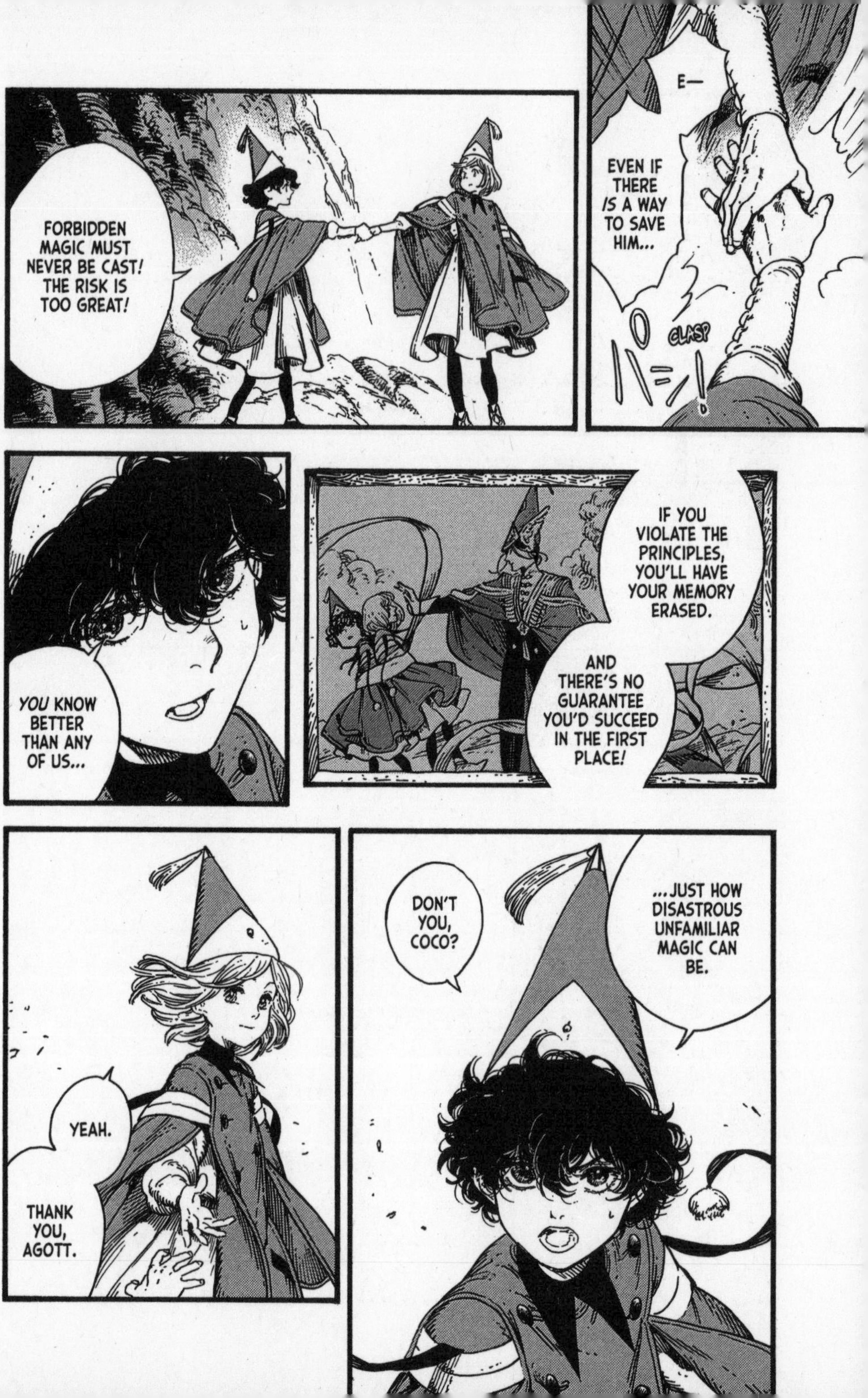
E—
EVEN IF THERE IS A WAY TO SAVE HIM...
CLASP
FORBIDDEN MAGIC MUST NEVER BE CAST! THE RISK IS TOO GREAT!
IF YOU VIOLATE THE PRINCIPLES, YOU'LL HAVE YOUR MEMORY ERASED.
AND THERE'S NO GUARANTEE YOU'D SUCCEED IN THE FIRST PLACE!
YOU KNOW BETTER THAN ANY OF US...
...JUST HOW DISASTROUS UNFAMILIAR MAGIC CAN BE.
DON'T YOU, COCO?
YEAH.
THANK YOU, AGOTT.

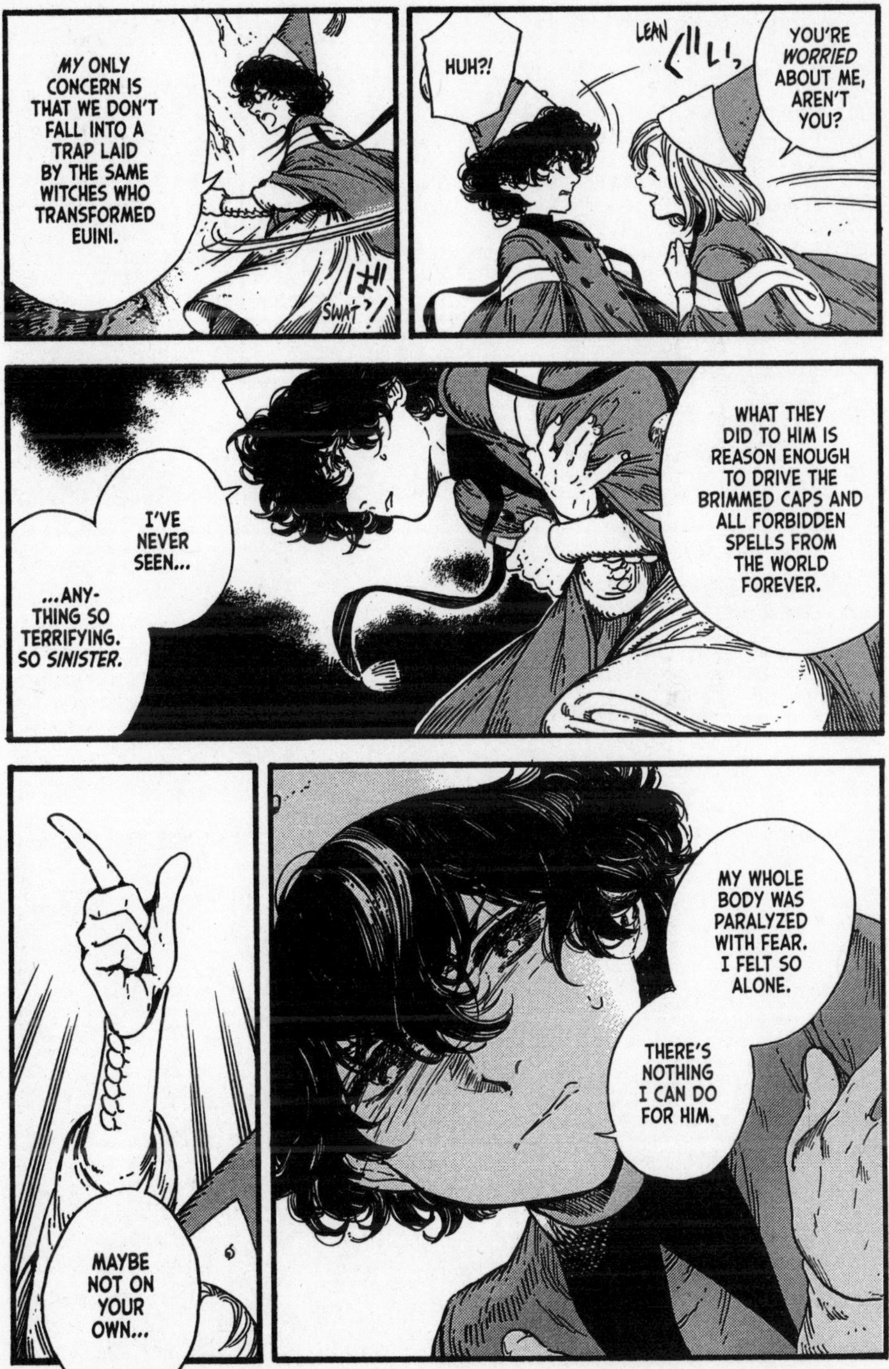
LEAN
YOU'RE WORRIED ABOUT ME, AREN'T YOU?
HUH?!
MY ONLY CONCERN IS THAT WE DON'T FALL INTO A TRAP LAID BY THE SAME WITCHES WHO TRANSFORMED EUINI.
SWAT
WHAT THEY DID TO HIM IS REASON ENOUGH TO DRIVE THE BRIMMED CAPS AND ALL FORBIDDEN SPELLS FROM THE WORLD FOREVER.
I'VE NEVER SEEN...
...ANY-THING SO TERRIFYING. SO SINISTER.
MY WHOLE BODY WAS PARALYZED WITH FEAR. I FELT SO ALONE.
THERE'S NOTHING I CAN DO FOR HIM.
MAYBE NOT ON YOUR OWN...

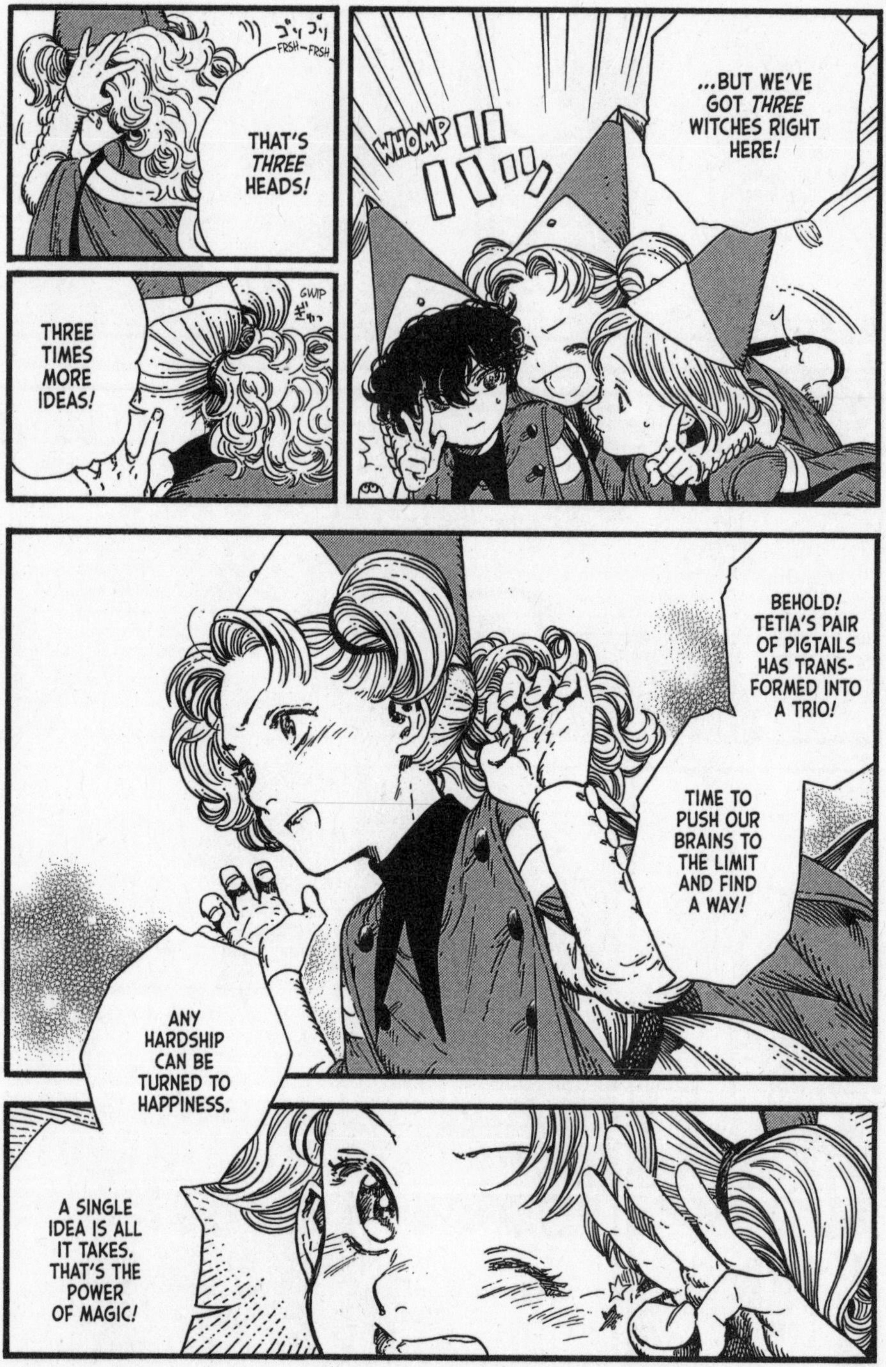

...BUT WE'VE GOT *THREE* WITCHES RIGHT HERE!
WHOMP
THAT'S *THREE* HEADS!
FRSH—FRSH
THREE TIMES MORE IDEAS!
GWIP
BEHOLD! TETIA'S PAIR OF PIGTAILS HAS TRANS-FORMED INTO A TRIO!
TIME TO PUSH OUR BRAINS TO THE LIMIT AND FIND A WAY!
ANY HARDSHIP CAN BE TURNED TO HAPPINESS.
A SINGLE IDEA IS ALL IT TAKES. THAT'S THE POWER OF MAGIC!

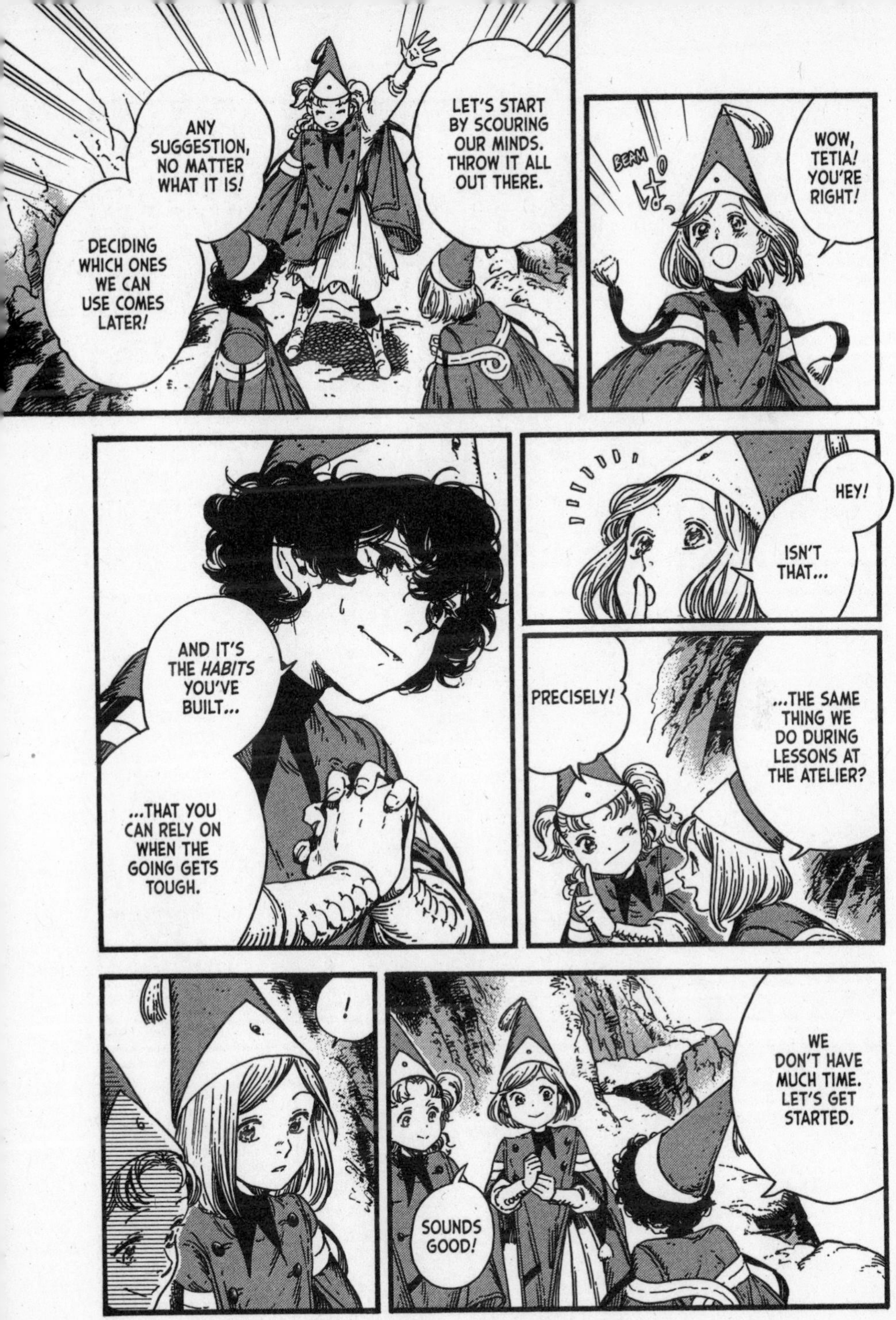
BEAM
ぱっ
WOW, TETIA! YOU'RE RIGHT!
LET'S START BY SCOURING OUR MINDS. THROW IT ALL OUT THERE.
ANY SUGGESTION, NO MATTER WHAT IT IS!
DECIDING WHICH ONES WE CAN USE COMES LATER!
HEY!
ISN'T THAT...
...THE SAME THING WE DO DURING LESSONS AT THE ATELIER?
PRECISELY!
AND IT'S THE *HABITS* YOU'VE BUILT...
...THAT YOU CAN RELY ON WHEN THE GOING GETS TOUGH.
WE DON'T HAVE MUCH TIME. LET'S GET STARTED.
SOUNDS GOOD!
!

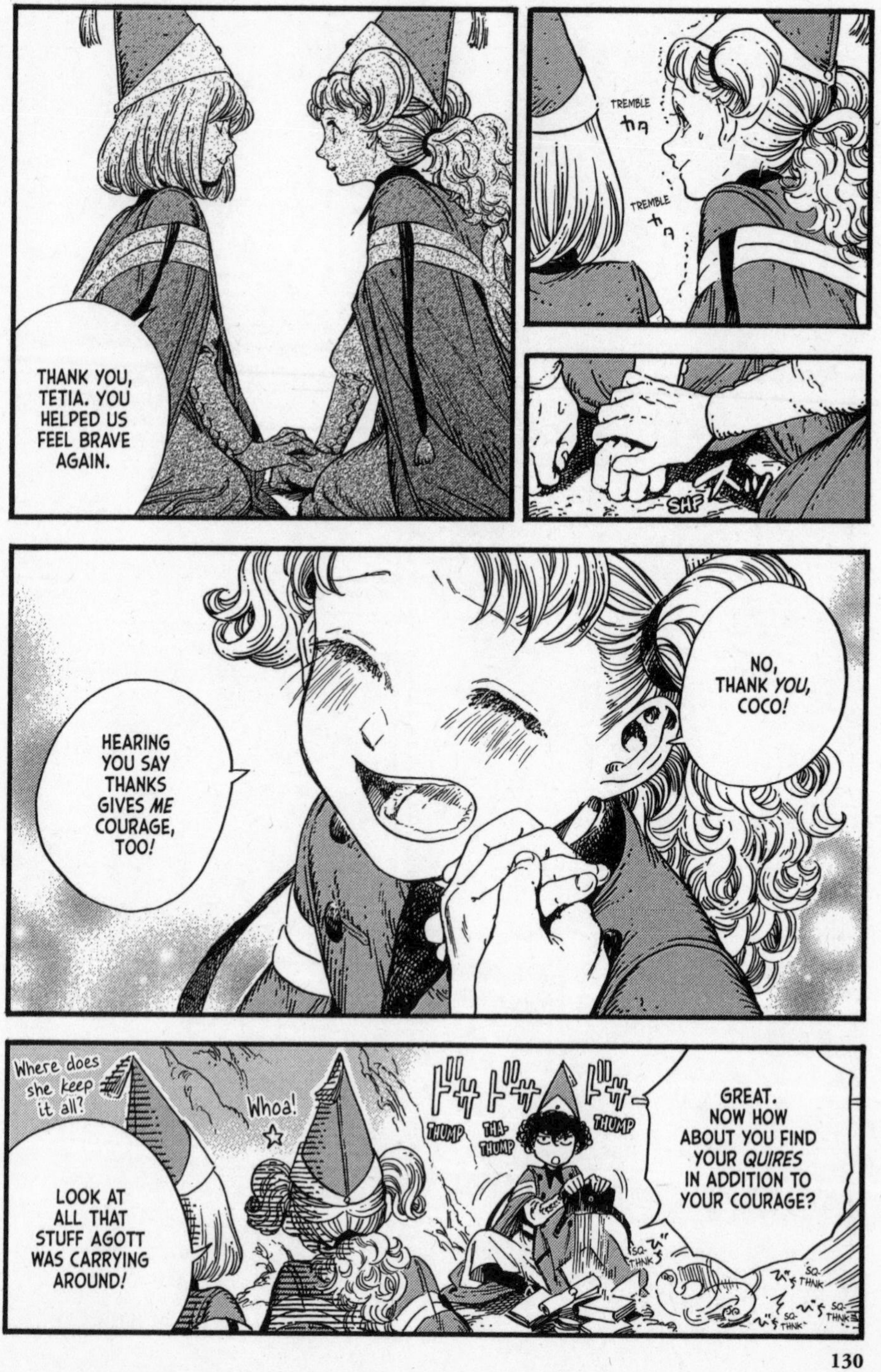
TREMBLE
TREMBLE
SHF
THANK YOU, TETIA. YOU HELPED US FEEL BRAVE AGAIN.
NO, THANK *YOU*, COCO!
HEARING YOU SAY THANKS GIVES *ME* COURAGE, TOO!
GREAT. NOW HOW ABOUT YOU FIND YOUR *QUIRES* IN ADDITION TO YOUR COURAGE?
SQ-THNK
SQ-THNK
SQ-THNK
SQ-THNK
THUMP
THA-THUMP
THUMP
Whoa!
Where does she keep it all?
LOOK AT ALL THAT STUFF AGOTT WAS CARRYING AROUND!

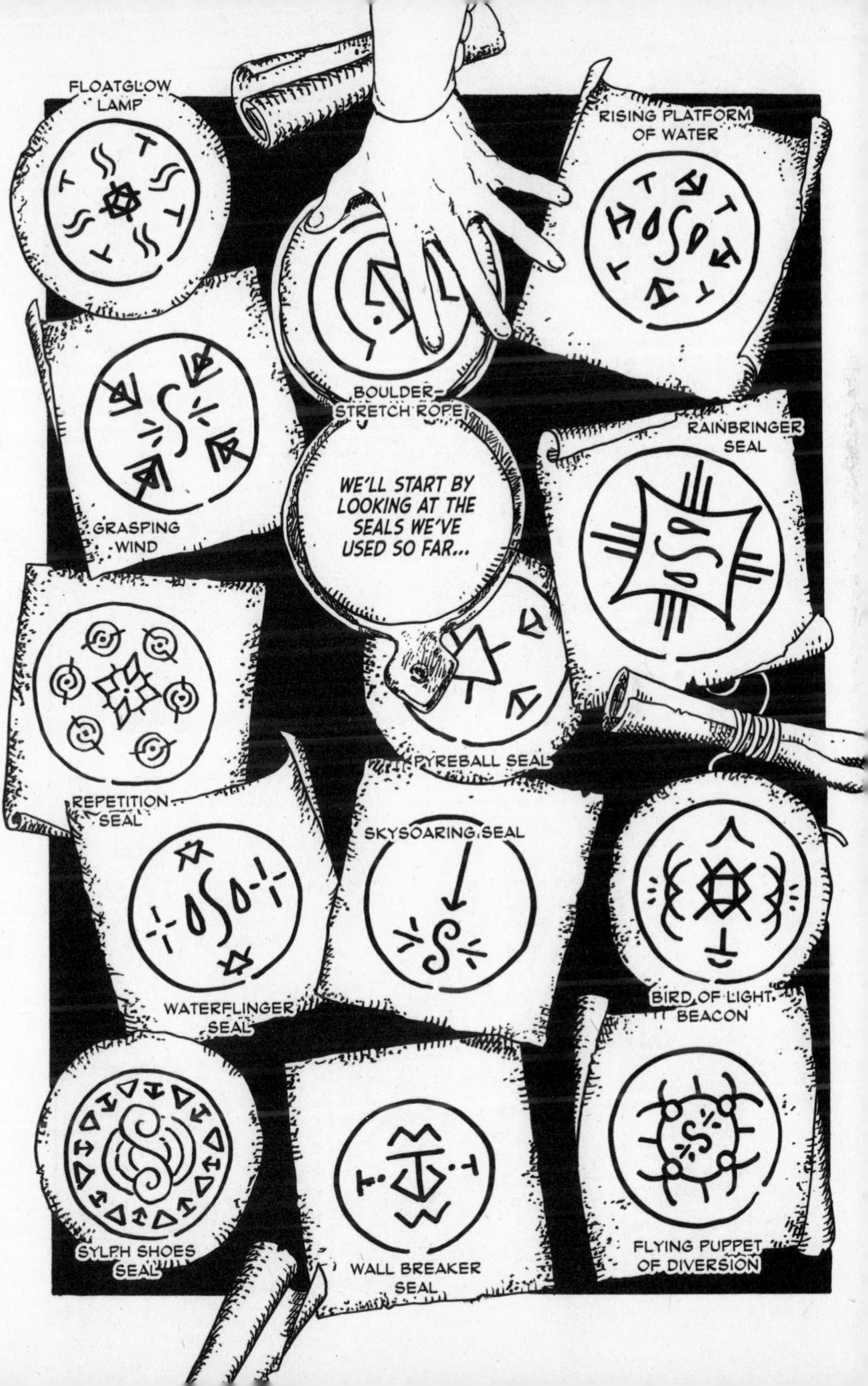
RISING PLATFORM OF WATER
FLOATGLOW LAMP
BOULDER-STRETCH ROPE
RAINBRINGER SEAL
WE'LL START BY LOOKING AT THE SEALS WE'VE USED SO FAR...
GRASPING WIND
PYREBALL SEAL
REPETITION SEAL
SKYSOARING SEAL
BIRD OF LIGHT BEACON
WATERFLINGER SEAL
FLYING PUPPET OF DIVERSION
WALL BREAKER SEAL
SYLPH SHOES SEAL

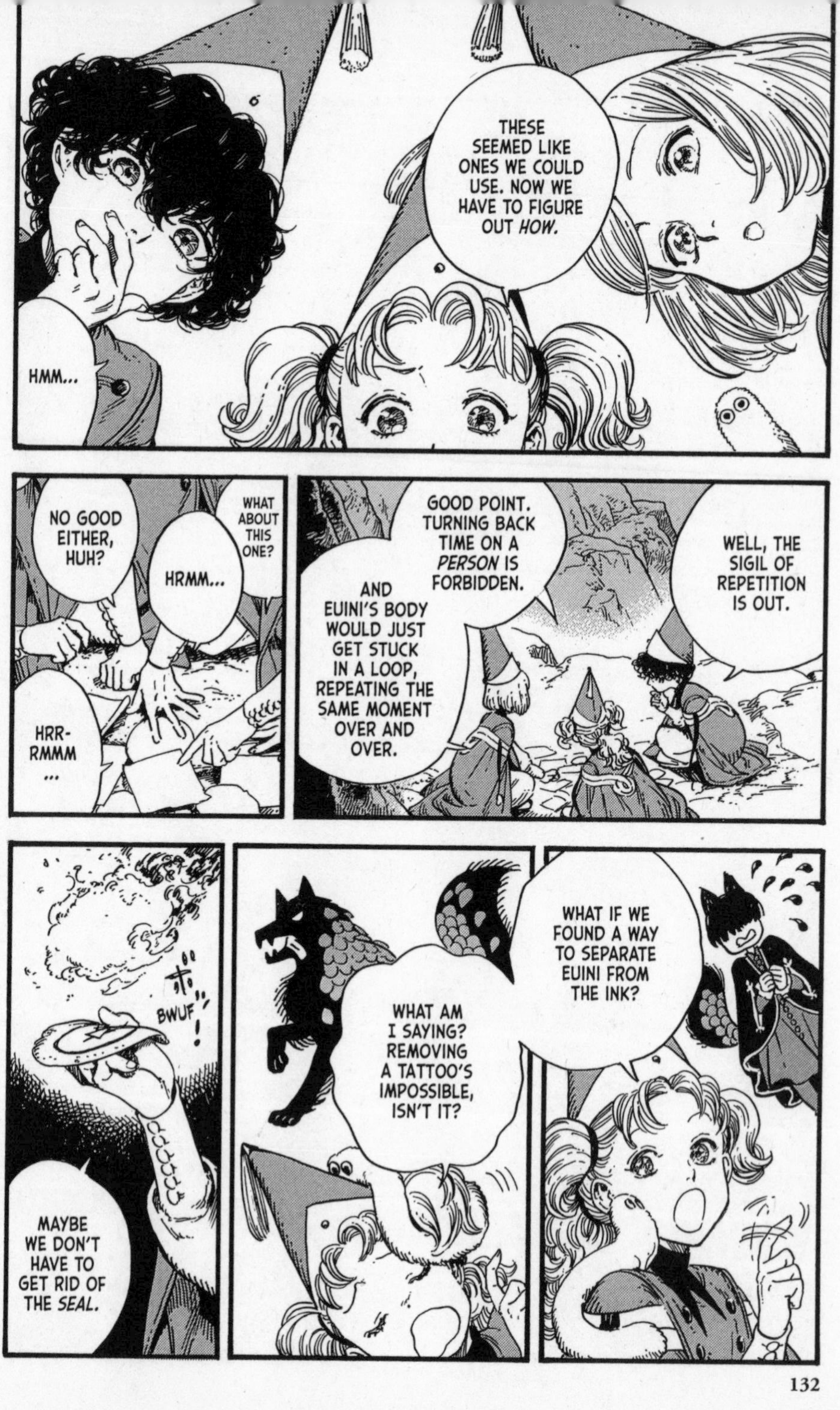
THESE SEEMED LIKE ONES WE COULD USE. NOW WE HAVE TO FIGURE OUT *HOW.*
HMM...
WELL, THE SIGIL OF REPETITION IS OUT.
GOOD POINT. TURNING BACK TIME ON A *PERSON* IS FORBIDDEN.
AND EUINI'S BODY WOULD JUST GET STUCK IN A LOOP, REPEATING THE SAME MOMENT OVER AND OVER.
WHAT ABOUT THIS ONE?
HRMM...
NO GOOD EITHER, HUH?
HRR-RMMM ...
WHAT IF WE FOUND A WAY TO SEPARATE EUINI FROM THE INK?
WHAT AM I SAYING? REMOVING A TATTOO'S IMPOSSIBLE, ISN'T IT?
BWUF!
MAYBE WE DON'T HAVE TO GET RID OF THE *SEAL.*

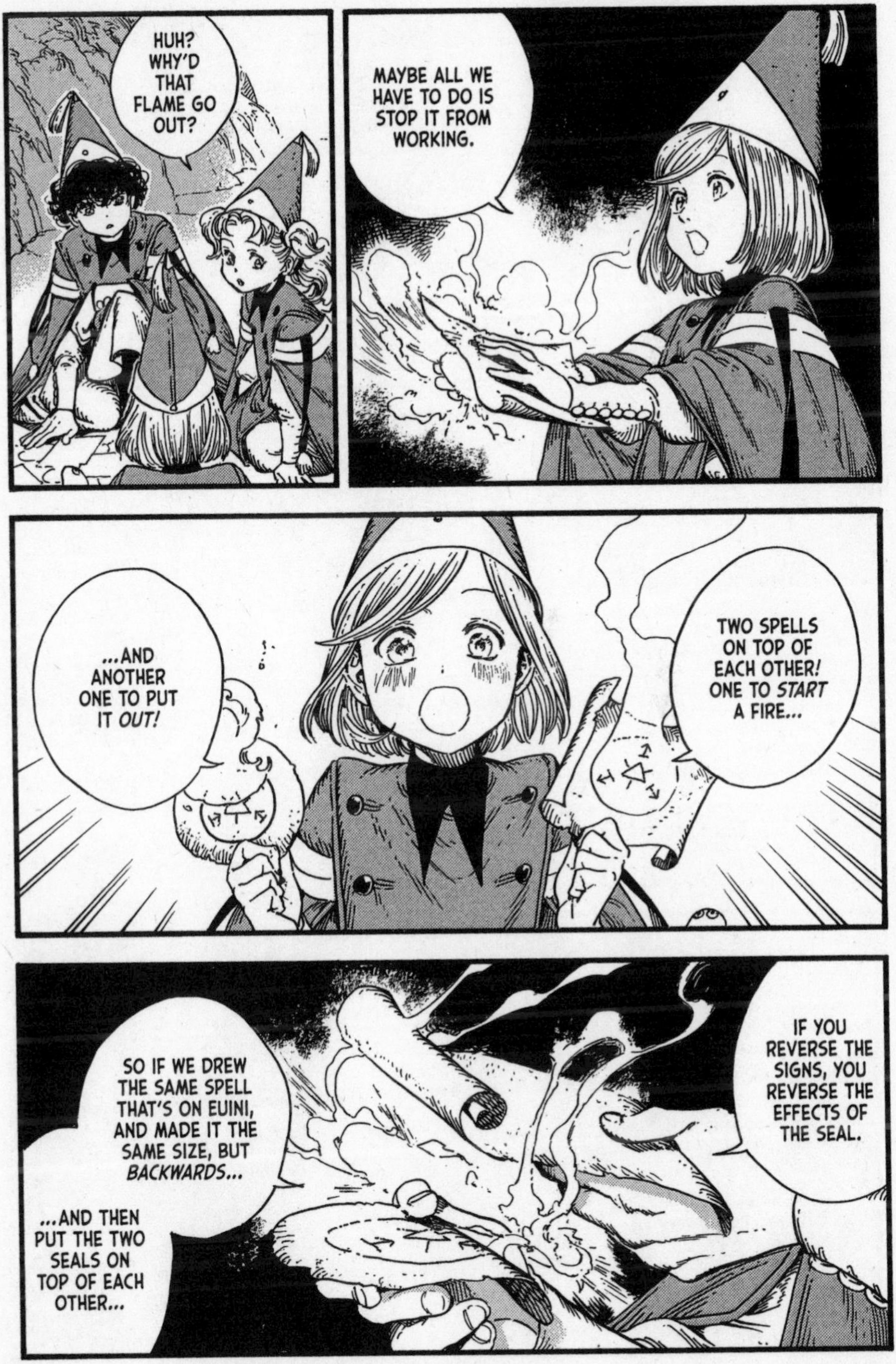
MAYBE ALL WE HAVE TO DO IS STOP IT FROM WORKING.
HUH? WHY'D THAT FLAME GO OUT?
TWO SPELLS ON TOP OF EACH OTHER! ONE TO *START* A FIRE...
...AND ANOTHER ONE TO PUT IT *OUT!*
IF YOU REVERSE THE SIGNS, YOU REVERSE THE EFFECTS OF THE SEAL.
SO IF WE DREW THE SAME SPELL THAT'S ON EUINI, AND MADE IT THE SAME SIZE, BUT *BACKWARDS*...
...AND THEN PUT THE TWO SEALS ON TOP OF EACH OTHER...

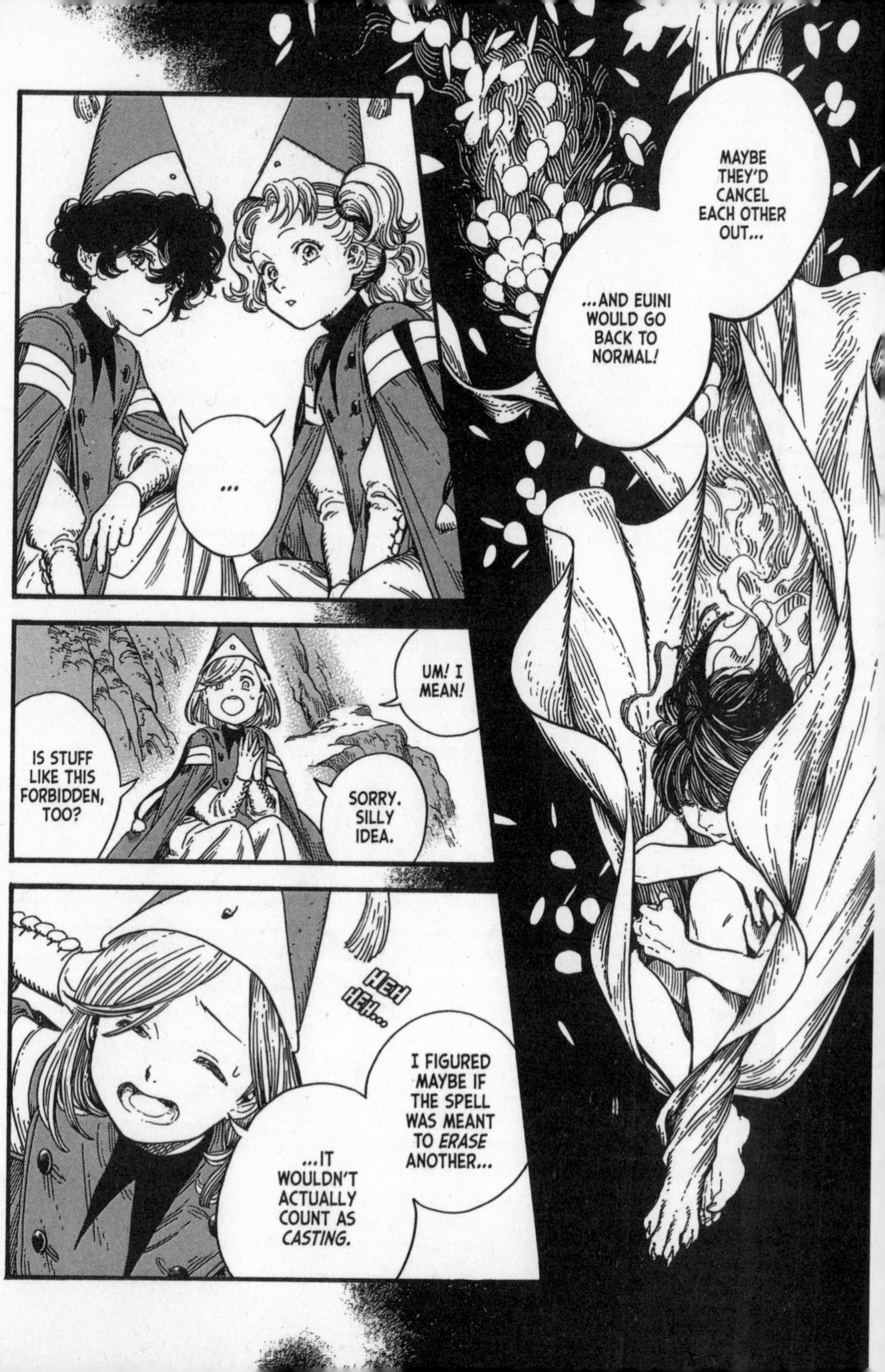
MAYBE THEY'D CANCEL EACH OTHER OUT...
...AND EUINI WOULD GO BACK TO NORMAL!
...
UM! I MEAN!
SORRY. SILLY IDEA.
IS STUFF LIKE THIS FORBIDDEN, TOO?
HEH HEH...
I FIGURED MAYBE IF THE SPELL WAS MEANT TO *ERASE* ANOTHER...
...IT WOULDN'T ACTUALLY COUNT AS *CASTING*.

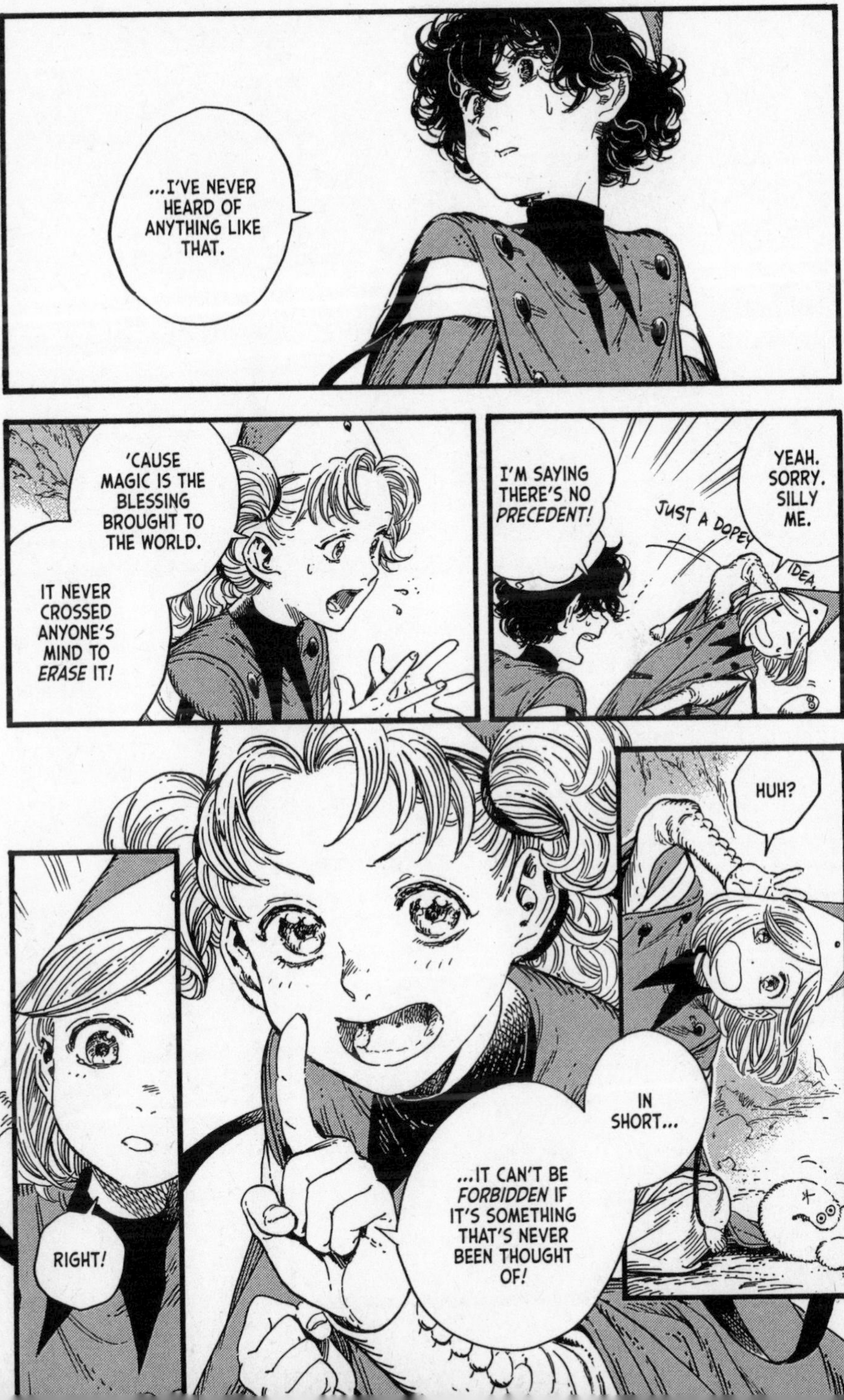

...I'VE NEVER HEARD OF ANYTHING LIKE THAT.
YEAH. SORRY. SILLY ME.
JUST A DOPEY IDEA
I'M SAYING THERE'S NO *PRECEDENT!*
'CAUSE MAGIC IS THE BLESSING BROUGHT TO THE WORLD.
IT NEVER CROSSED ANYONE'S MIND TO *ERASE* IT!
HUH?
IN SHORT...
...IT CAN'T BE *FORBIDDEN* IF IT'S SOMETHING THAT'S NEVER BEEN THOUGHT OF!
RIGHT!

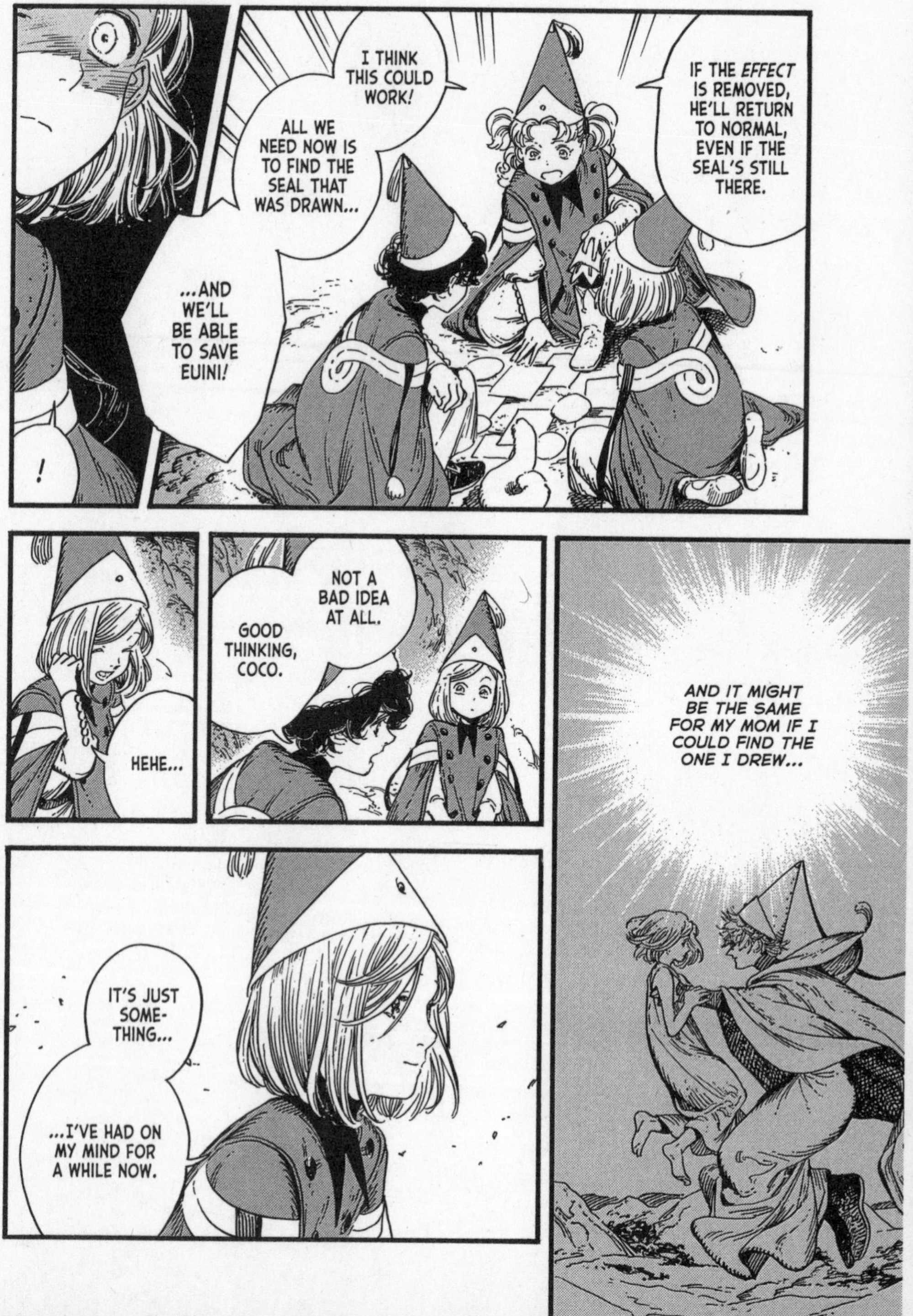
IF THE *EFFECT* IS REMOVED, HE'LL RETURN TO NORMAL, EVEN IF THE SEAL'S STILL THERE.
I THINK THIS COULD WORK!
ALL WE NEED NOW IS TO FIND THE SEAL THAT WAS DRAWN...
...AND WE'LL BE ABLE TO SAVE EUINI!
!
AND IT MIGHT BE THE SAME FOR MY MOM IF I COULD FIND THE ONE I DREW...
NOT A BAD IDEA AT ALL.
GOOD THINKING, COCO.
HEHE...
IT'S JUST SOME-THING...
...I'VE HAD ON MY MIND FOR A WHILE NOW.

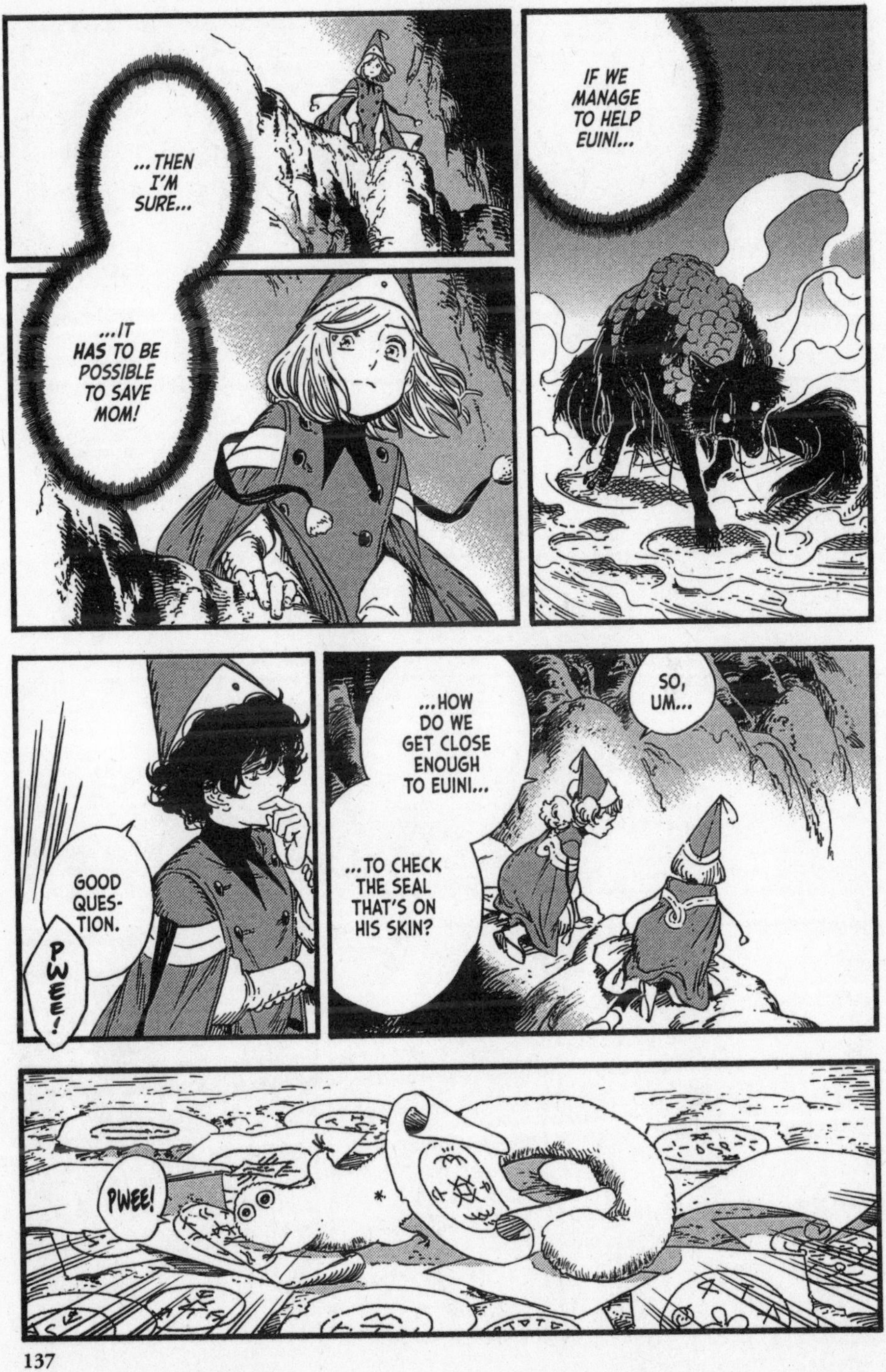
IF WE MANAGE TO HELP EUINI...
...THEN I'M SURE...
...IT HAS TO BE POSSIBLE TO SAVE MOM!
SO, UM...
...HOW DO WE GET CLOSE ENOUGH TO EUINI...
...TO CHECK THE SEAL THAT'S ON HIS SKIN?
GOOD QUES-TION.
PWEE!
PWEE!

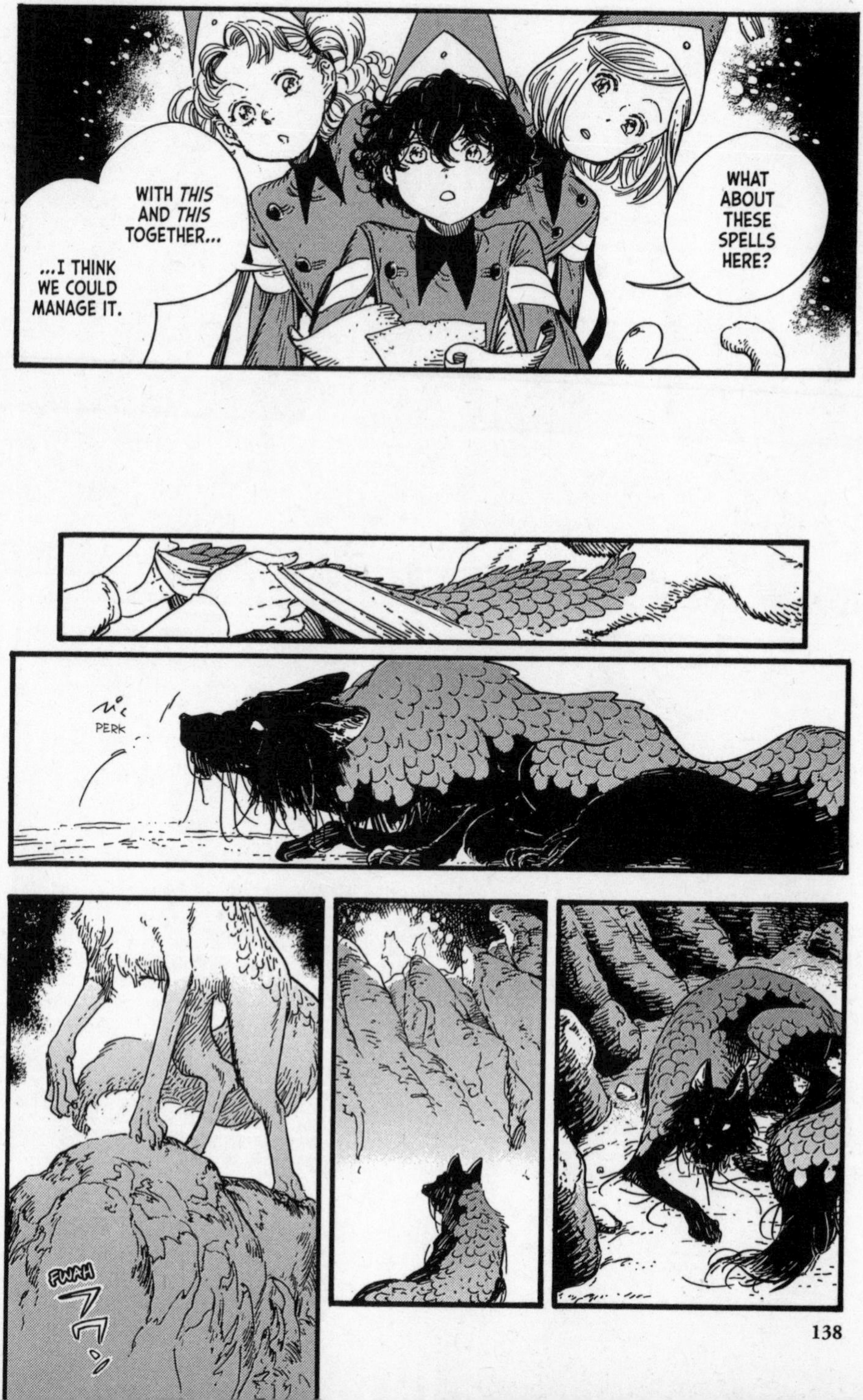
WHAT ABOUT THESE SPELLS HERE?
WITH *THIS* AND *THIS* TOGETHER...
...I THINK WE COULD MANAGE IT.
PERK
FWAH

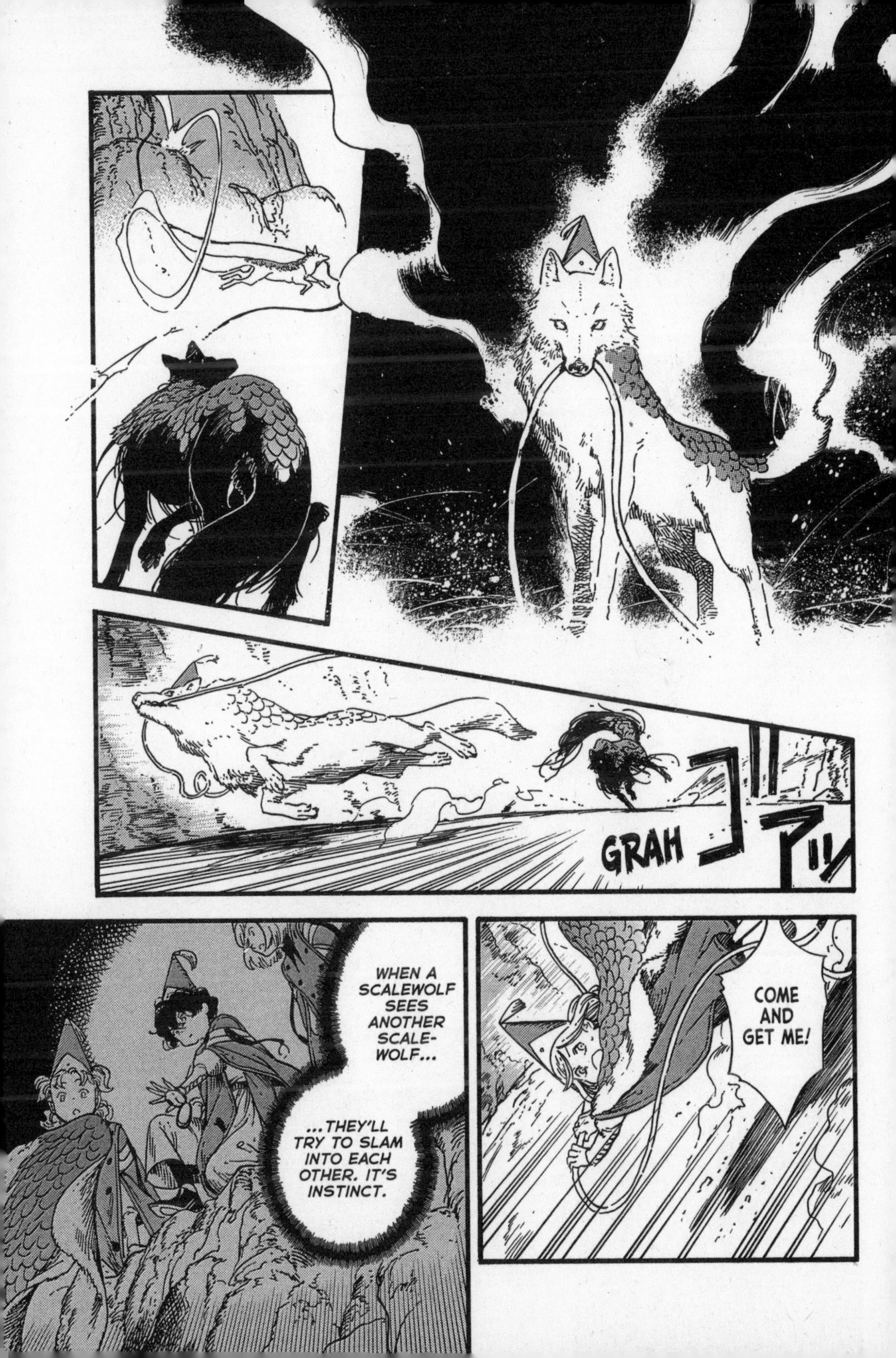
GRAH
COME AND GET ME!
WHEN A SCALEWOLF SEES ANOTHER SCALE-WOLF...
...THEY'LL TRY TO SLAM INTO EACH OTHER. IT'S INSTINCT.

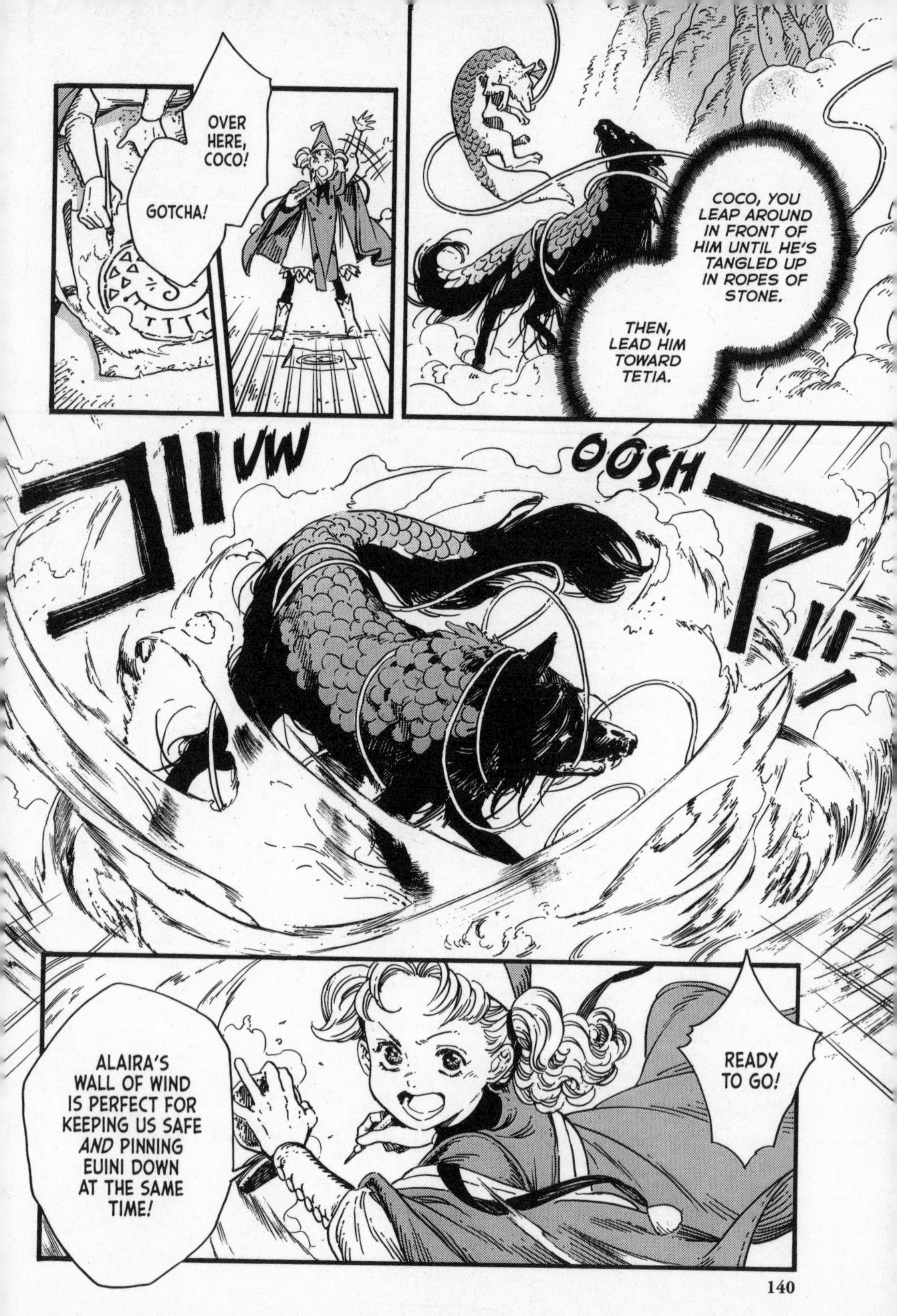

COCO, YOU LEAP AROUND IN FRONT OF HIM UNTIL HE'S TANGLED UP IN ROPES OF STONE.
THEN, LEAD HIM TOWARD TETIA.
OVER HERE, COCO!
GOTCHA!
OOSH
UW
READY TO GO!
ALAIRA'S WALL OF WIND IS PERFECT FOR KEEPING US SAFE *AND* PINNING EUINI DOWN AT THE SAME TIME!

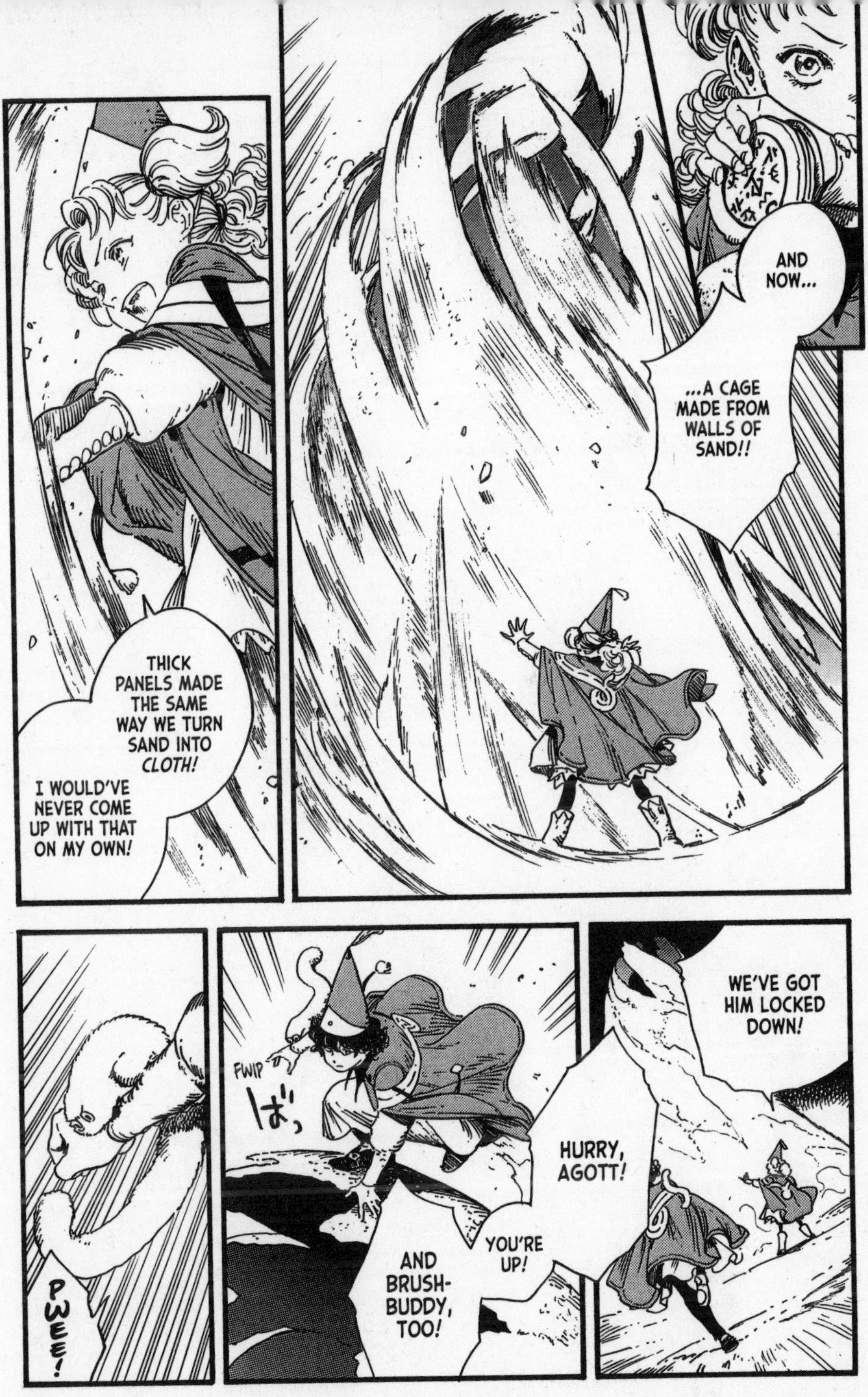
AND NOW...
...A CAGE MADE FROM WALLS OF SAND!!
THICK PANELS MADE THE SAME WAY WE TURN SAND INTO *CLOTH*!
I WOULD'VE NEVER COME UP WITH THAT ON MY OWN!
WE'VE GOT HIM LOCKED DOWN!
HURRY, AGOTT!
YOU'RE UP!
AND BRUSH-BUDDY, TOO!
FWIP
ぱっ
PWEE!

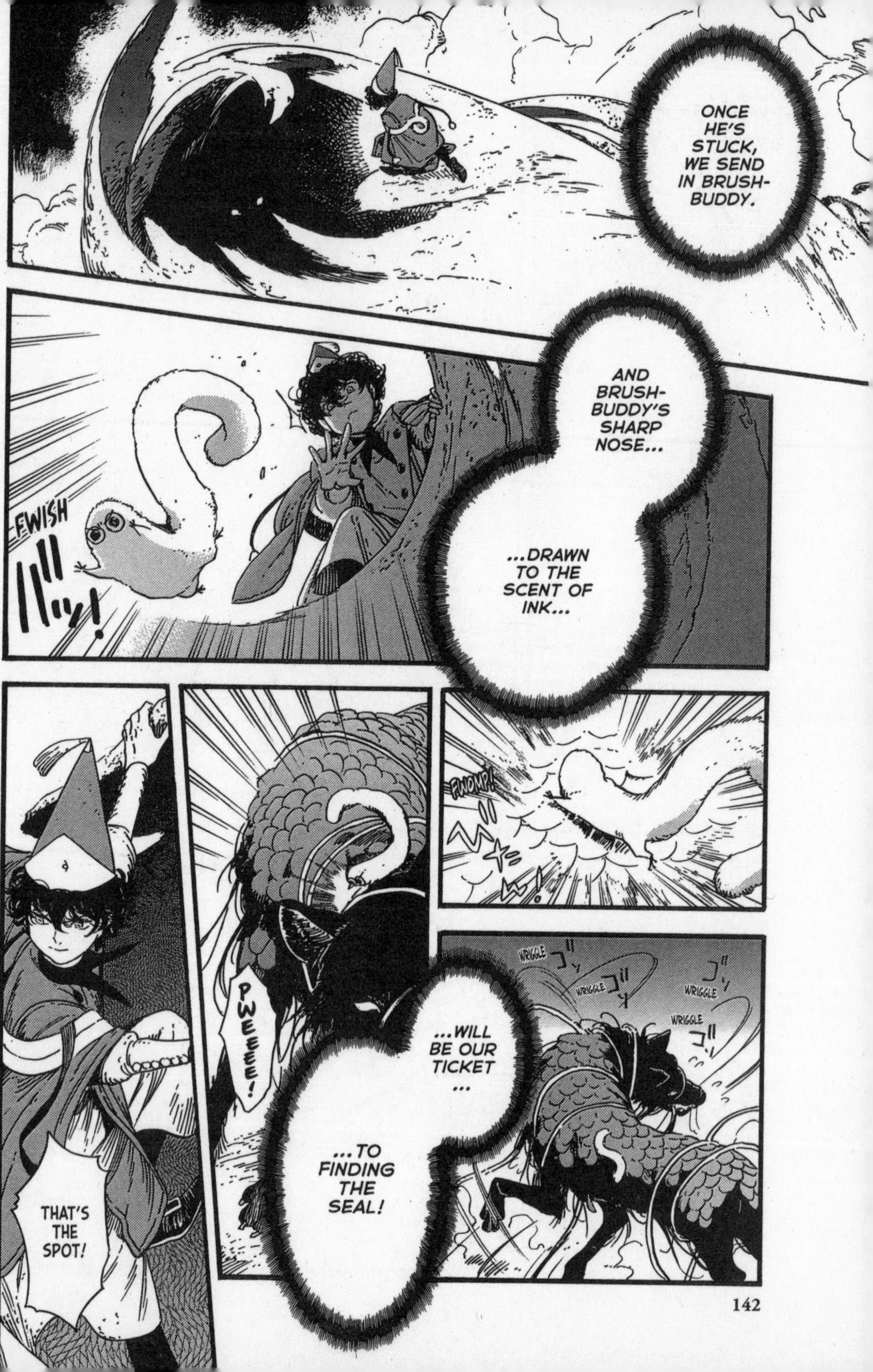
ONCE HE'S STUCK, WE SEND IN BRUSH-BUDDY.
AND BRUSH-BUDDY'S SHARP NOSE...
...DRAWN TO THE SCENT OF INK...
FWISH
FWOMP!
WRIGGLE
WRIGGLE
WRIGGLE
WRIGGLE
...WILL BE OUR TICKET...
...TO FINDING THE SEAL!
PWEEEE!
THAT'S THE SPOT!

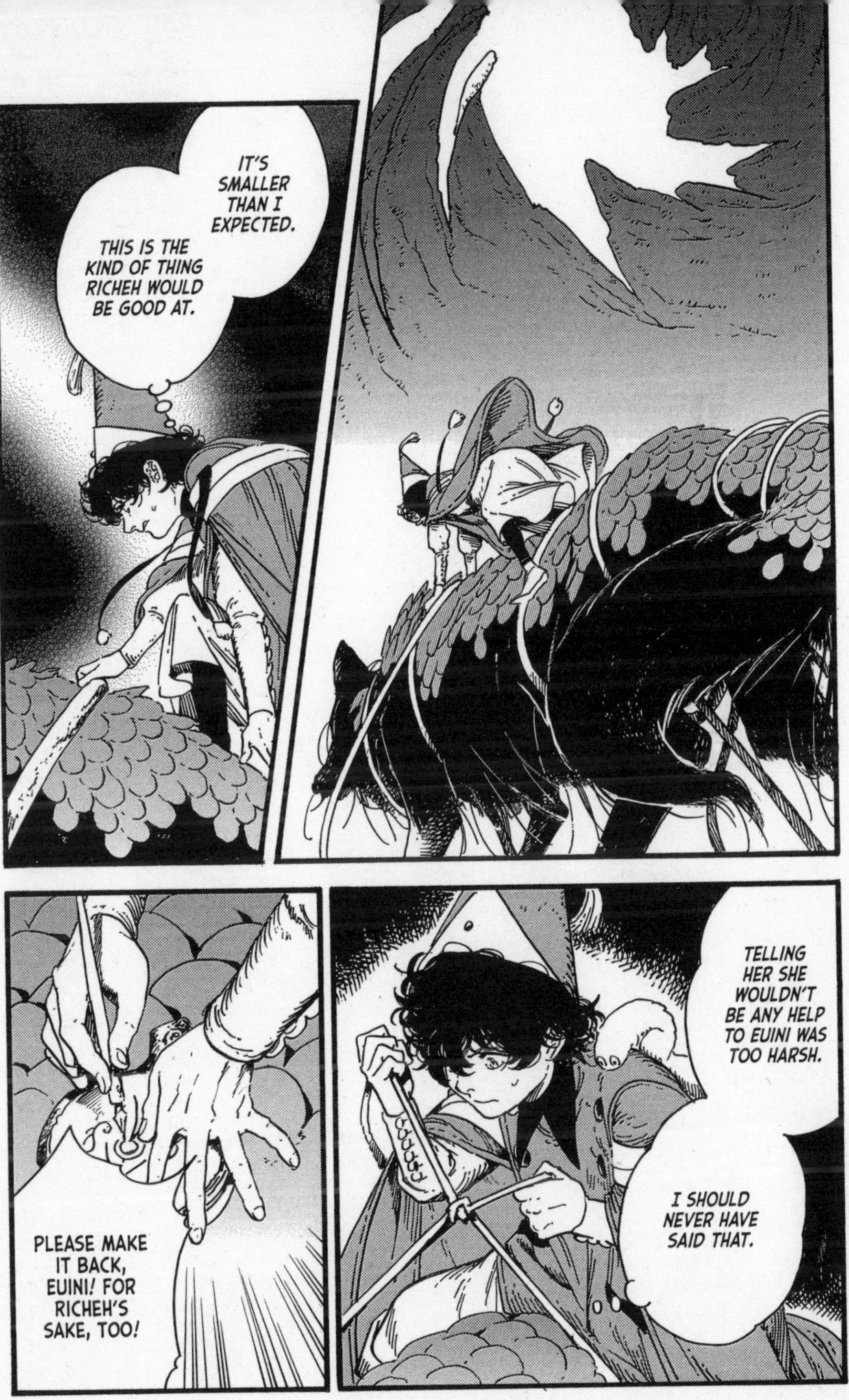
IT'S SMALLER THAN I EXPECTED.
THIS IS THE KIND OF THING RICHEH WOULD BE GOOD AT.
TELLING HER SHE WOULDN'T BE ANY HELP TO EUINI WAS TOO HARSH.
I SHOULD NEVER HAVE SAID THAT.
PLEASE MAKE IT BACK, EUINI! FOR RICHEH'S SAKE, TOO!

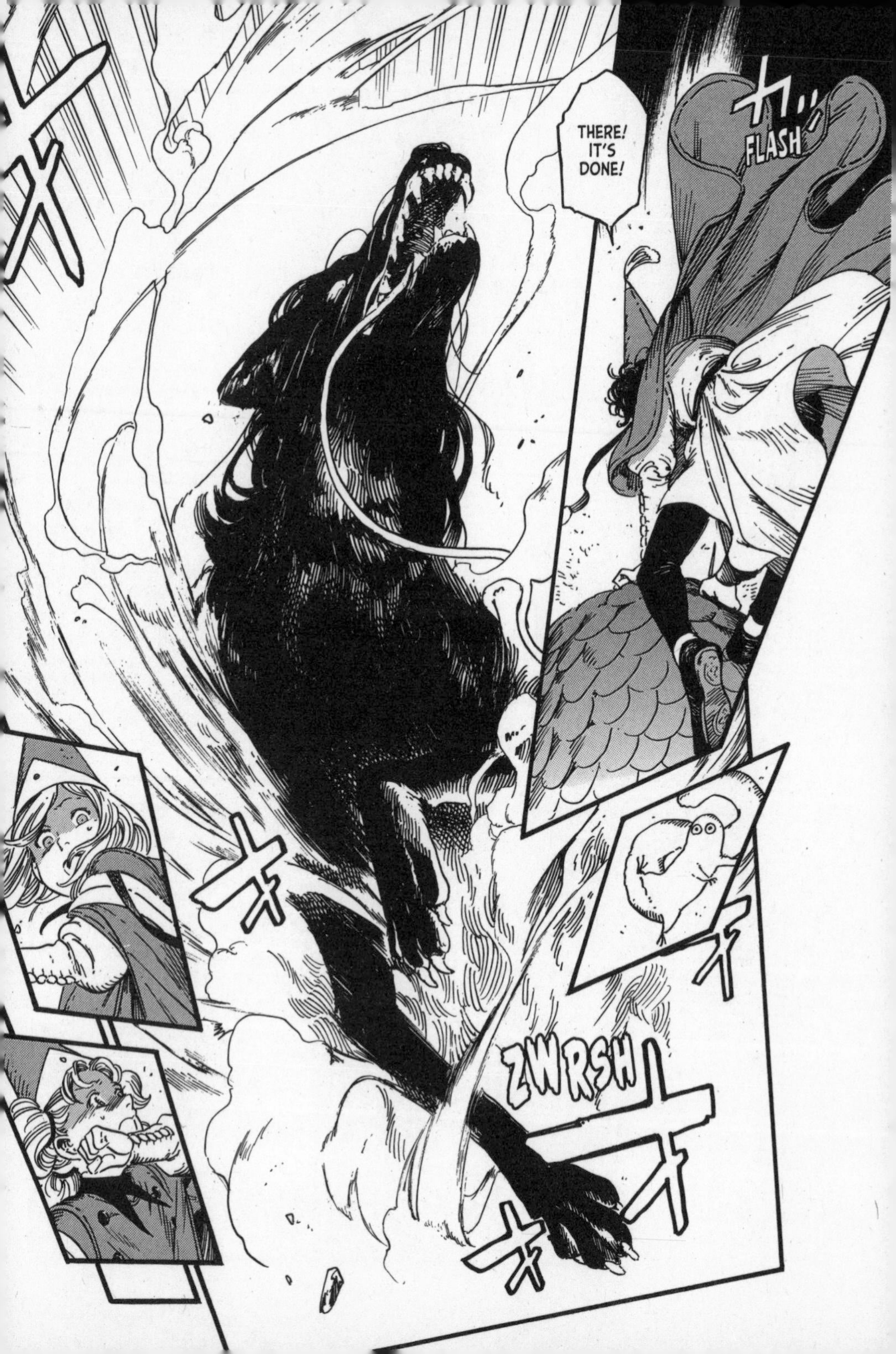
THERE! IT'S DONE!
FLASH
ZWRSH

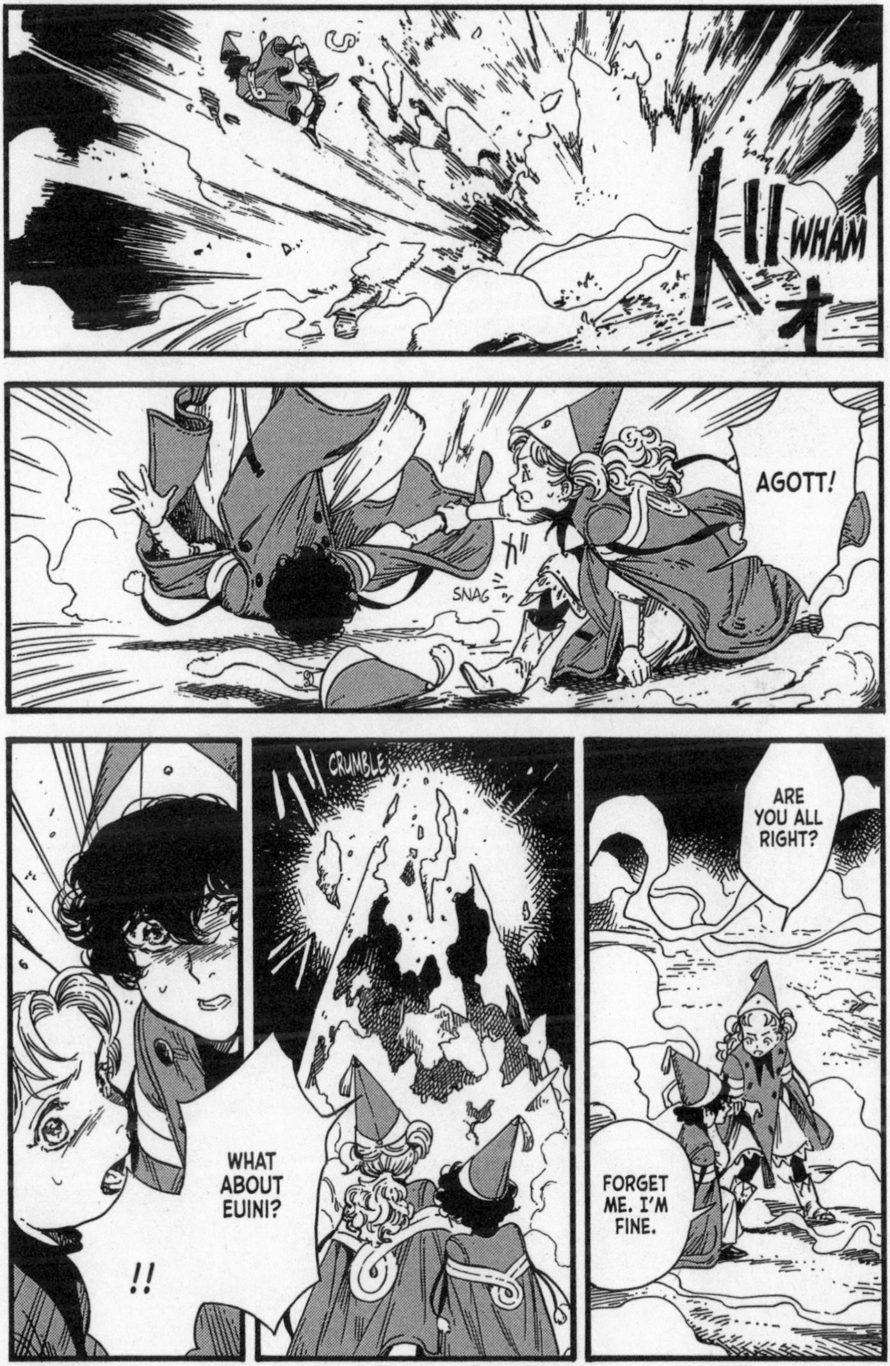
WHAM
AGOTT!
SNAG
ARE YOU ALL RIGHT?
FORGET ME. I'M FINE.
CRUMBLE
WHAT ABOUT EUINI?
!!

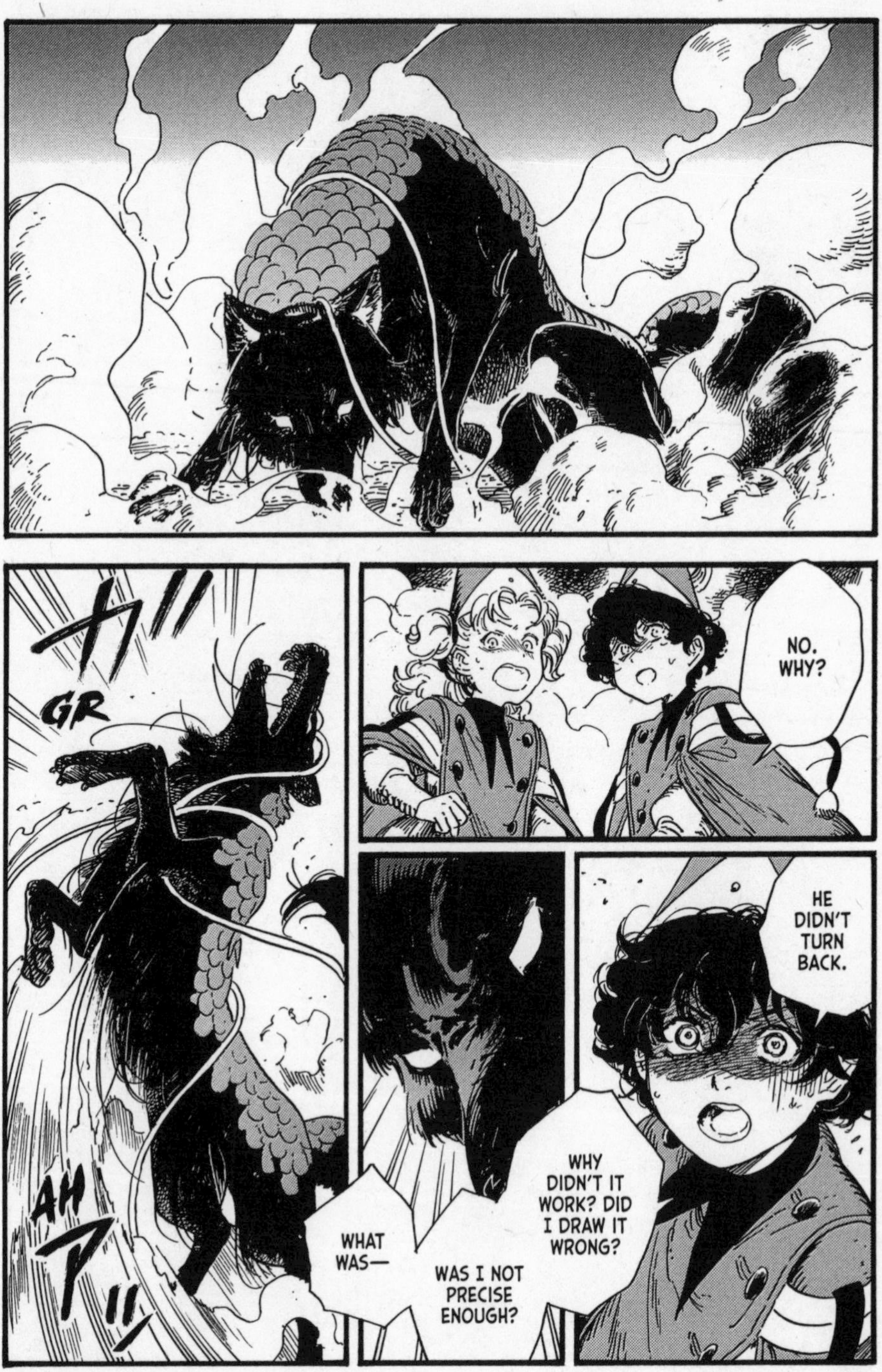
NO. WHY?
HE DIDN'T TURN BACK.
WHY DIDN'T IT WORK? DID I DRAW IT WRONG?
WAS I NOT PRECISE ENOUGH?
WHAT WAS—
GR
AH

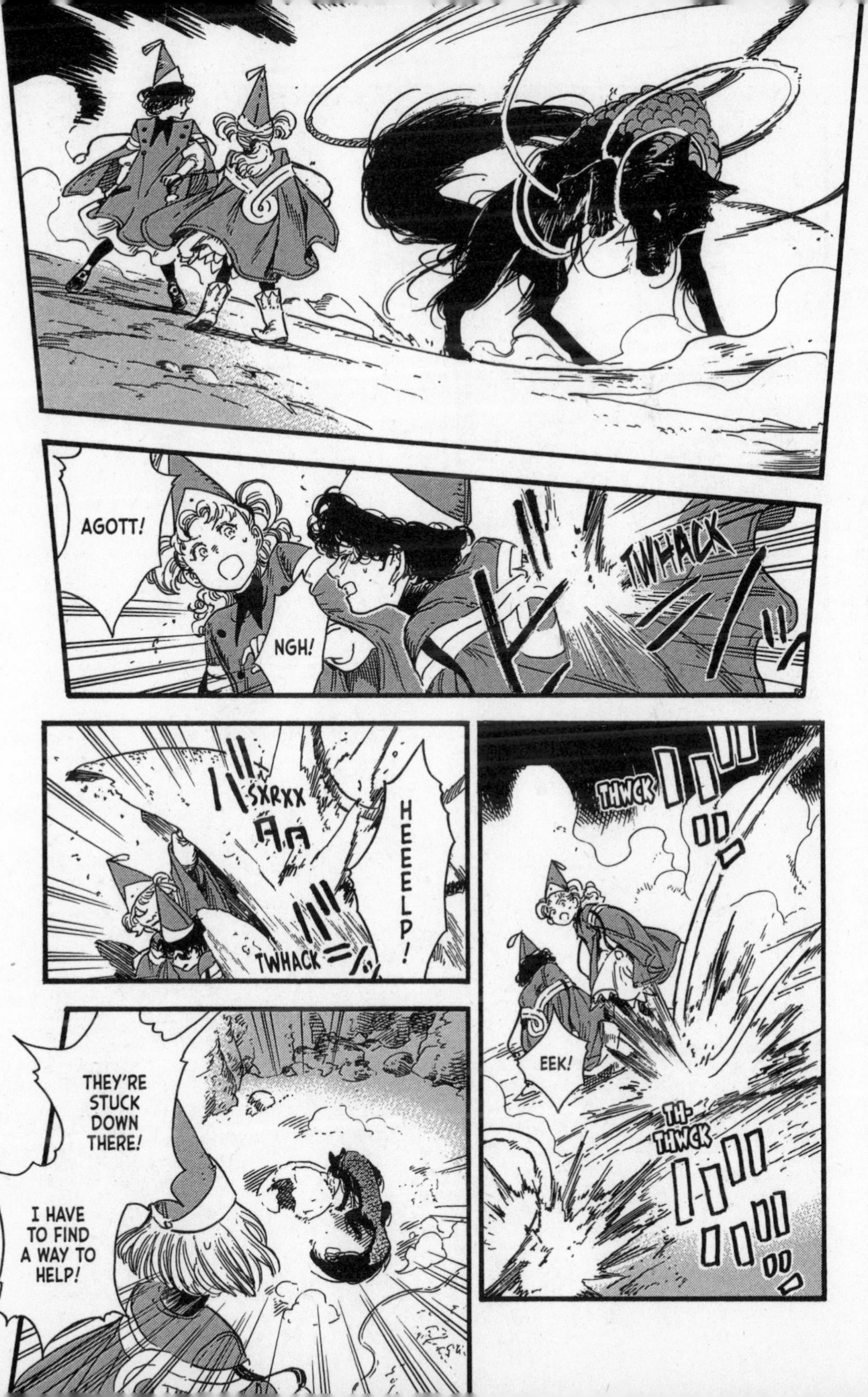
TWHACK
AGOTT!
NGH!
THWCK
EEK!
TH-THWCK
HEEEELP!
SXRXX
TWHACK
THEY'RE STUCK DOWN THERE!
I HAVE TO FIND A WAY TO HELP!

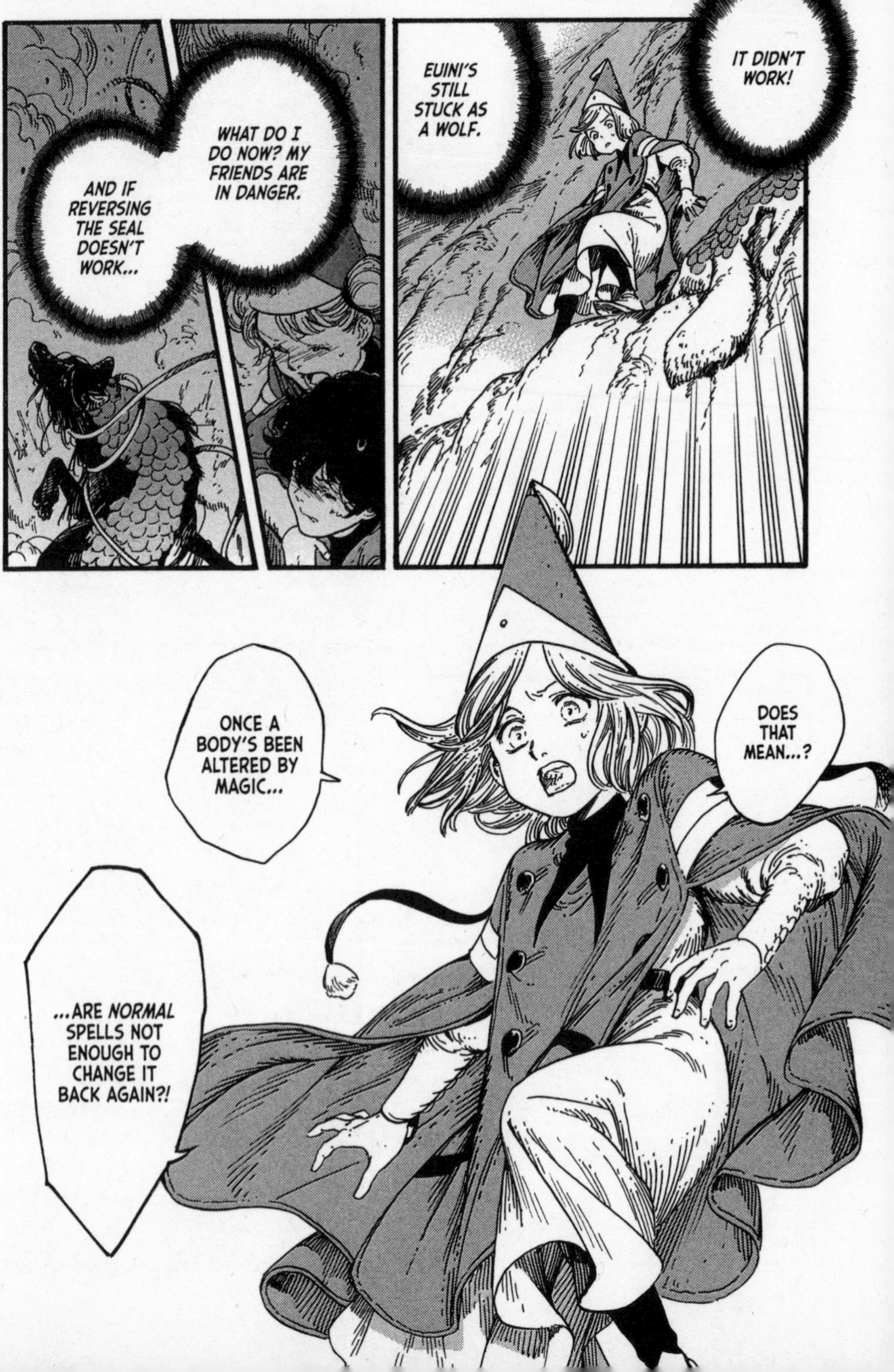
IT DIDN'T WORK!
EUINI'S STILL STUCK AS A WOLF.
WHAT DO I DO NOW? MY FRIENDS ARE IN DANGER.
AND IF REVERSING THE SEAL DOESN'T WORK...
DOES THAT MEAN...?
ONCE A BODY'S BEEN ALTERED BY MAGIC...
...ARE *NORMAL* SPELLS NOT ENOUGH TO CHANGE IT BACK AGAIN?!

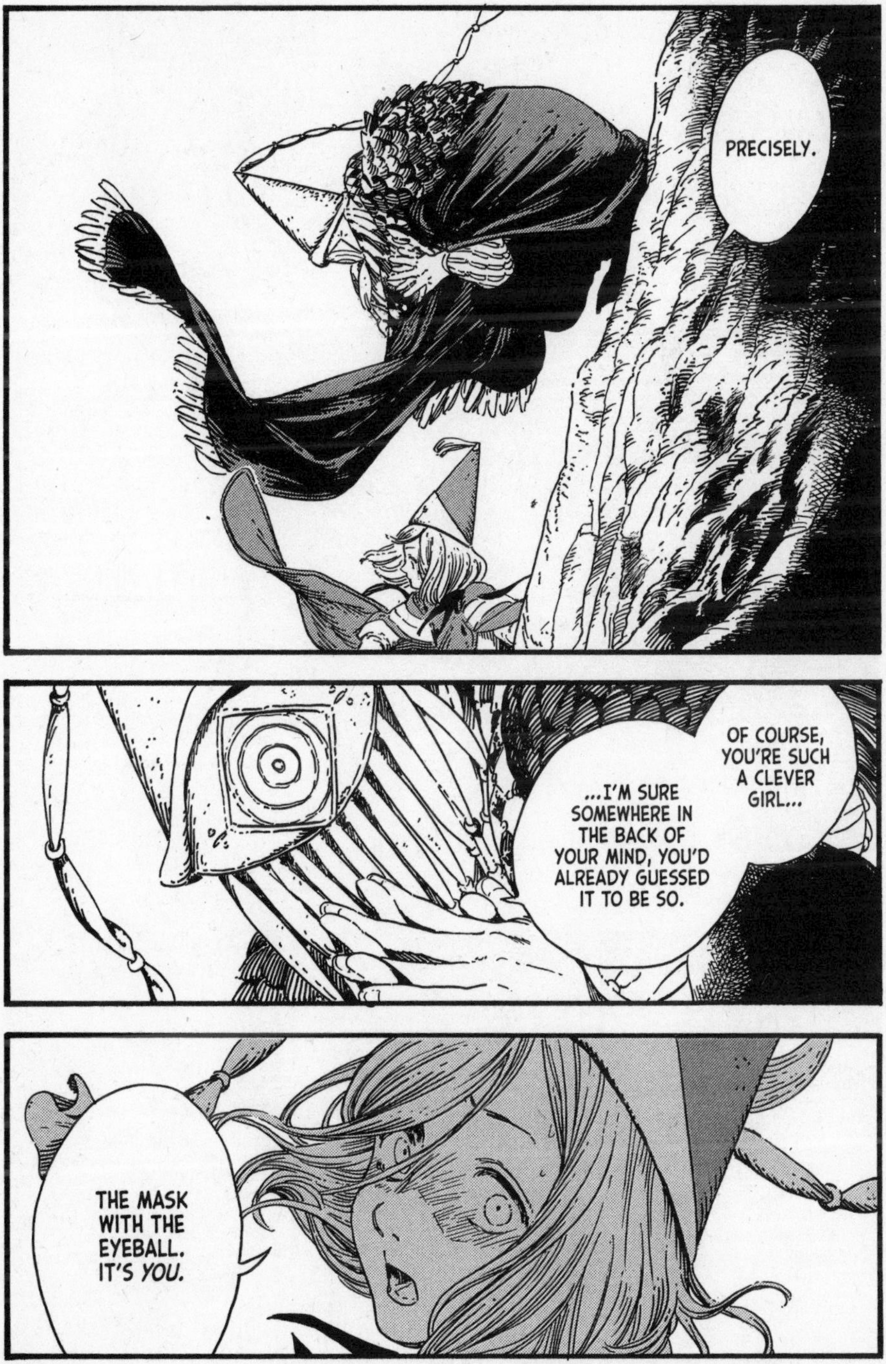
PRECISELY.
OF COURSE, YOU'RE SUCH A CLEVER GIRL...
...I'M SURE SOMEWHERE IN THE BACK OF YOUR MIND, YOU'D ALREADY GUESSED IT TO BE SO.
THE MASK WITH THE EYEBALL. IT'S *YOU.*

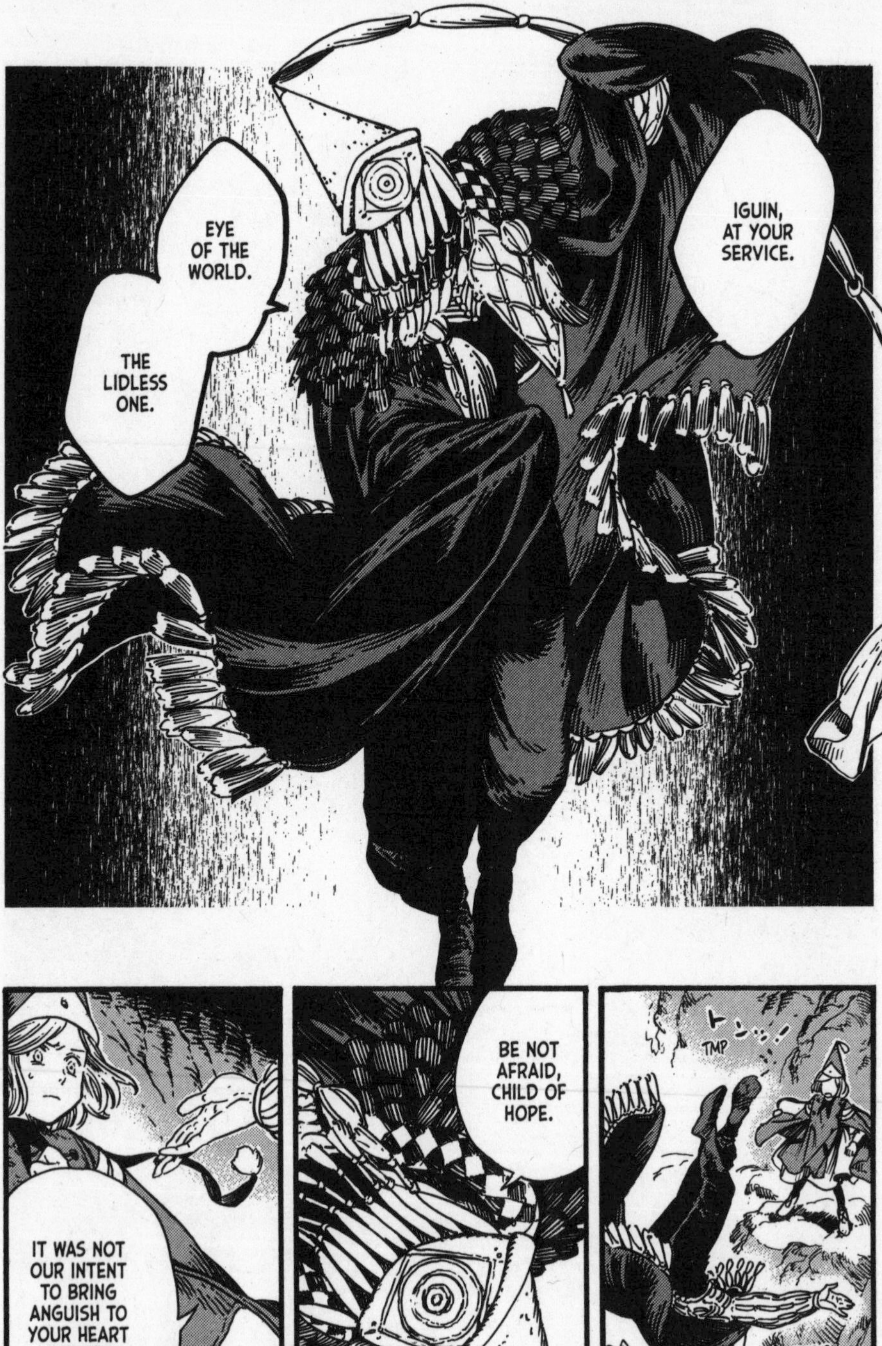
IGUIN, AT YOUR SERVICE.
EYE OF THE WORLD.
THE LIDLESS ONE.
TMP
FWAH
BE NOT AFRAID, CHILD OF HOPE.
IT WAS NOT OUR INTENT TO BRING ANGUISH TO YOUR HEART LIKE THIS.

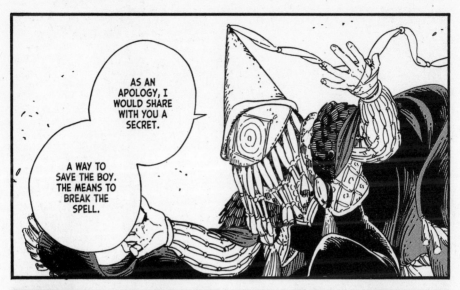

AS AN APOLOGY, I WOULD SHARE WITH YOU A SECRET.

A WAY TO SAVE THE BOY. THE MEANS TO BREAK THE SPELL.

AND LET ME GUESS.

IT INVOLVES ...

...FORBIDDEN MAGIC, DOESN'T IT?

...!

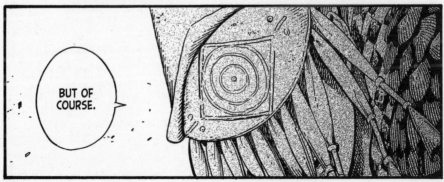

BUT OF COURSE.

151

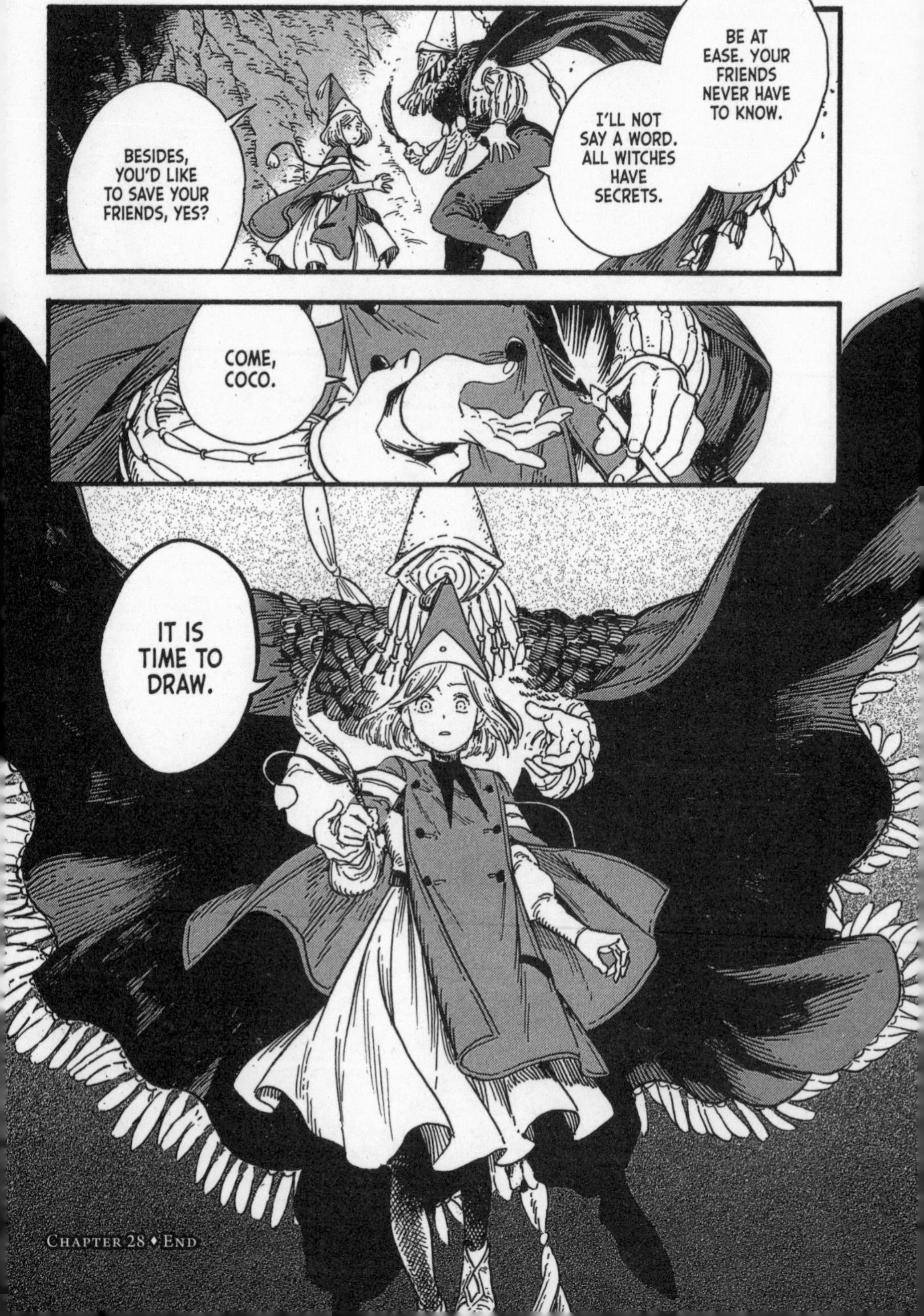
BE AT EASE. YOUR FRIENDS NEVER HAVE TO KNOW.
I'LL NOT SAY A WORD. ALL WITCHES HAVE SECRETS.
BESIDES, YOU'D LIKE TO SAVE YOUR FRIENDS, YES?
COME, COCO.
IT IS TIME TO DRAW.
CHAPTER 28 ♦ END

Witch Hat Atelier

Chapter 29

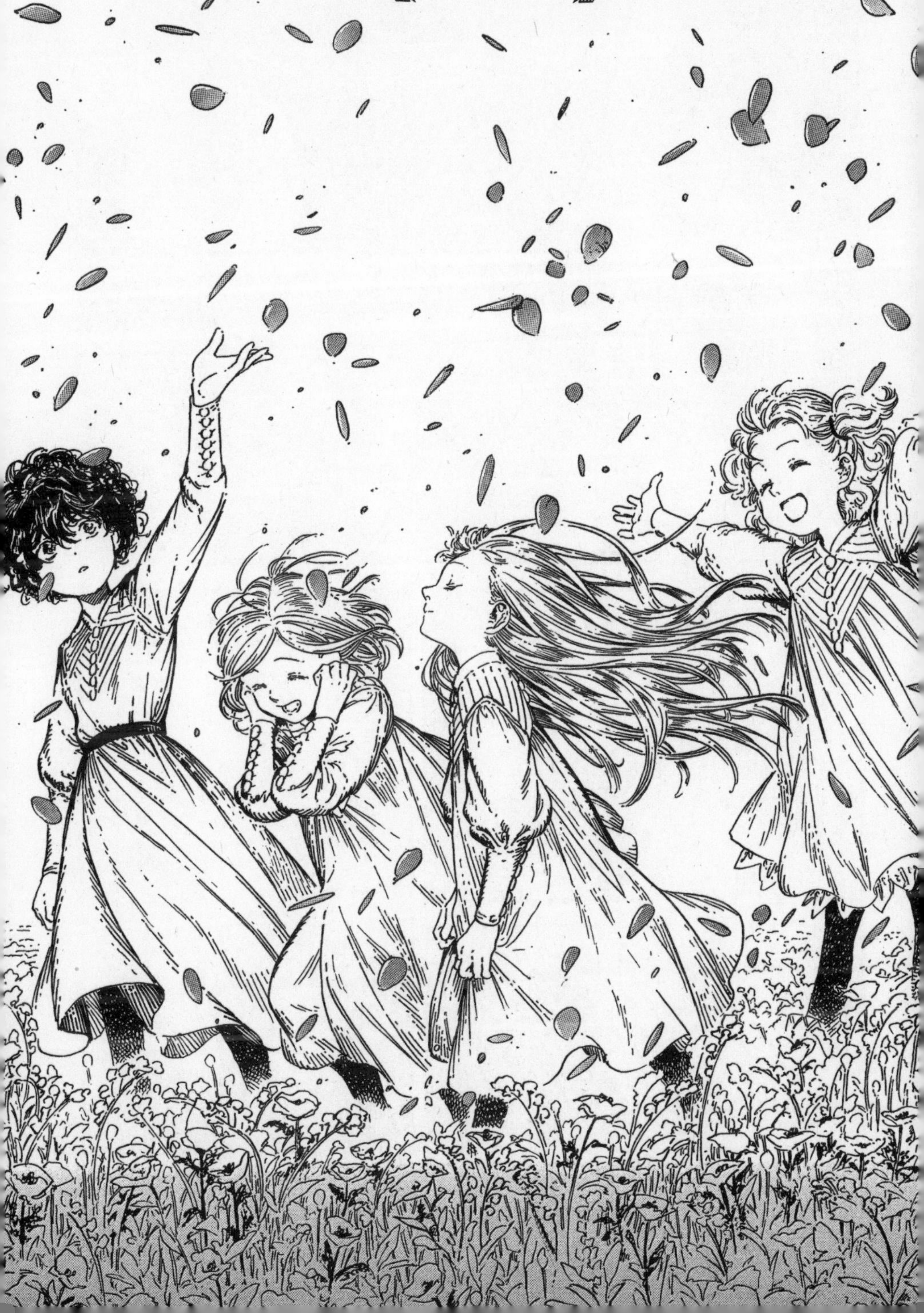

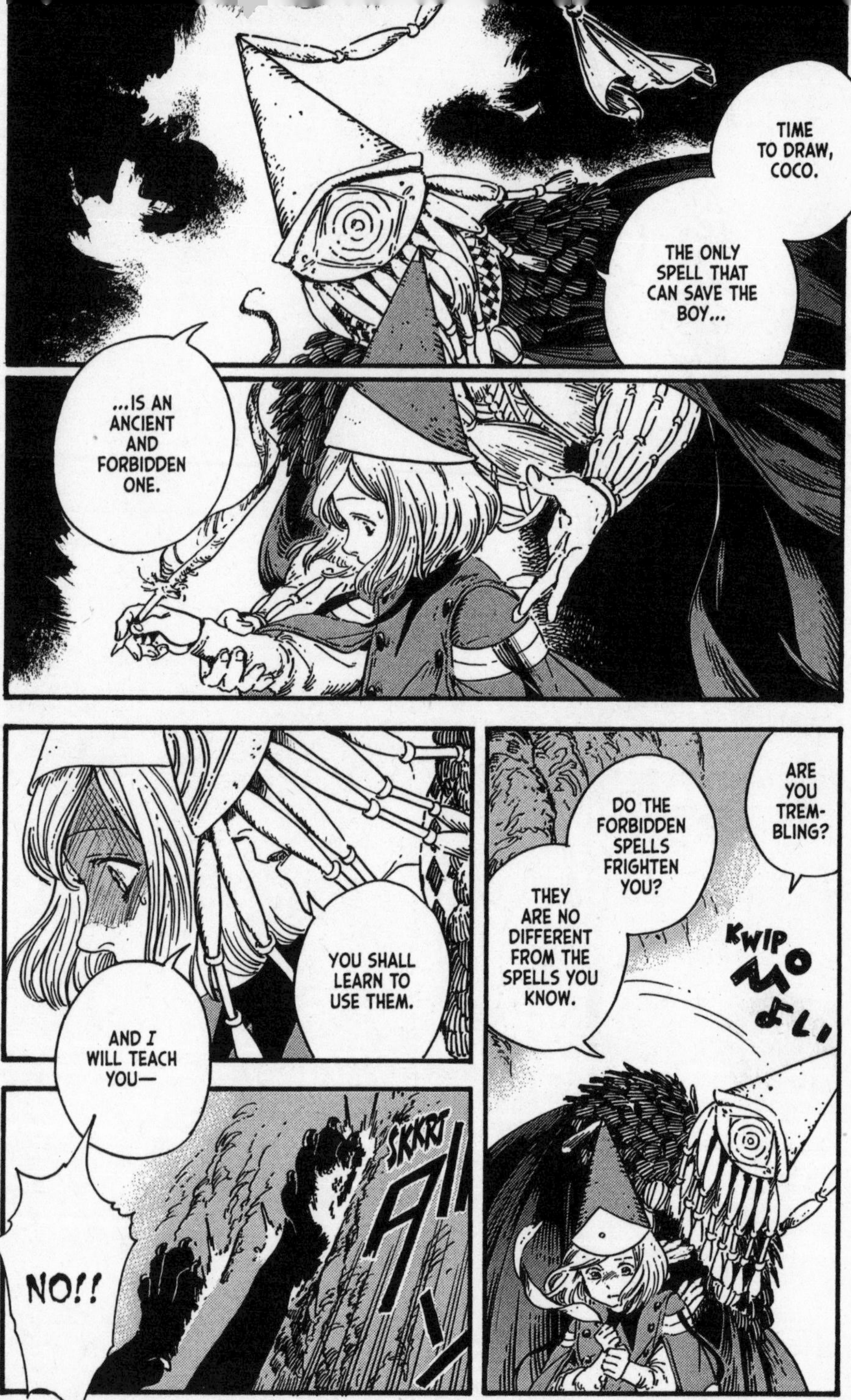
TIME TO DRAW, COCO.
THE ONLY SPELL THAT CAN SAVE THE BOY...
...IS AN ANCIENT AND FORBIDDEN ONE.
ARE YOU TREMBLING?
DO THE FORBIDDEN SPELLS FRIGHTEN YOU?
THEY ARE NO DIFFERENT FROM THE SPELLS YOU KNOW.
KWIP
YOU SHALL LEARN TO USE THEM.
AND I WILL TEACH YOU—
SKKRT
NO!!

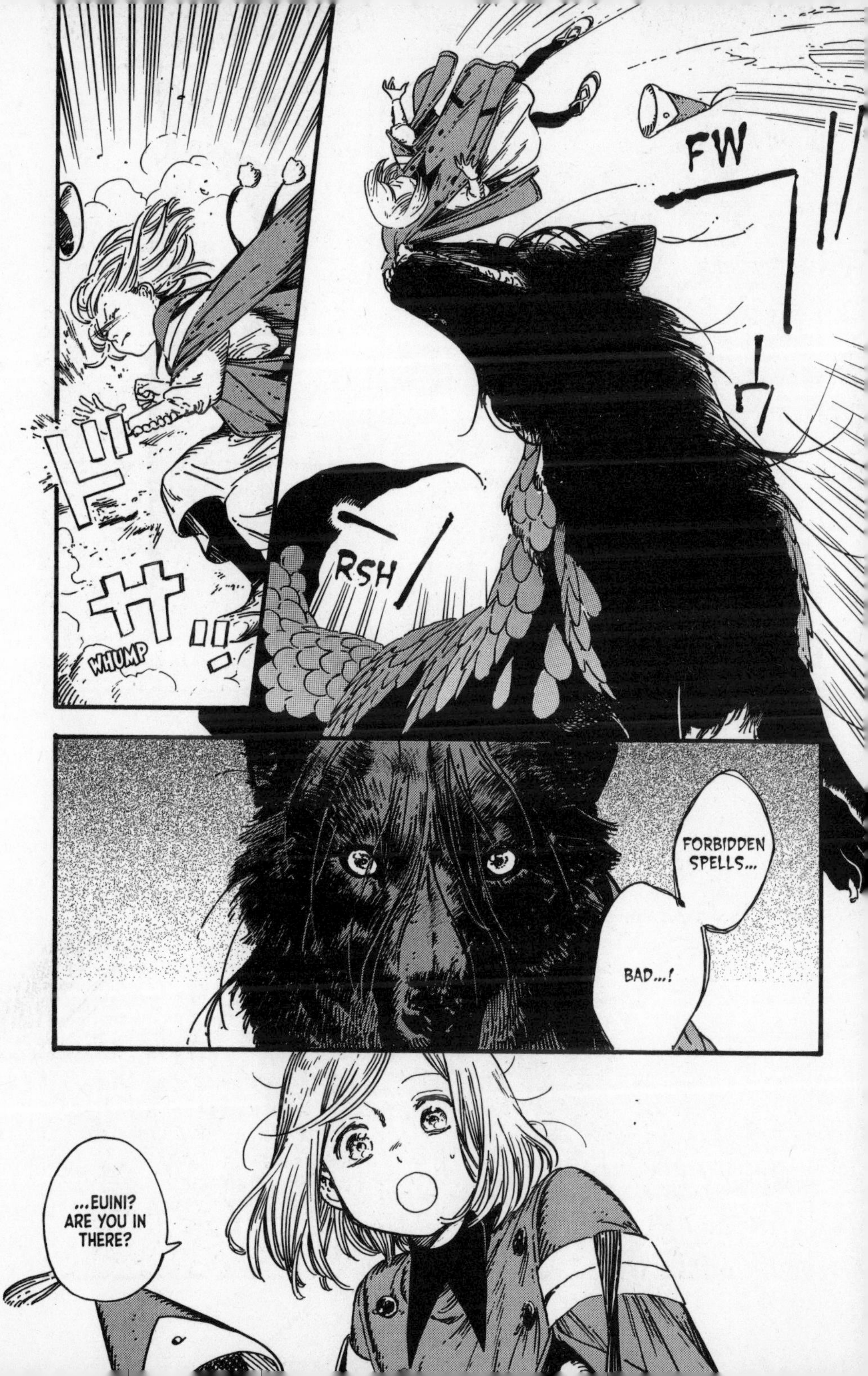
FW
RSH
ドサッ
WHUMP
FORBIDDEN SPELLS...
BAD...!
...EUINI? ARE YOU IN THERE?

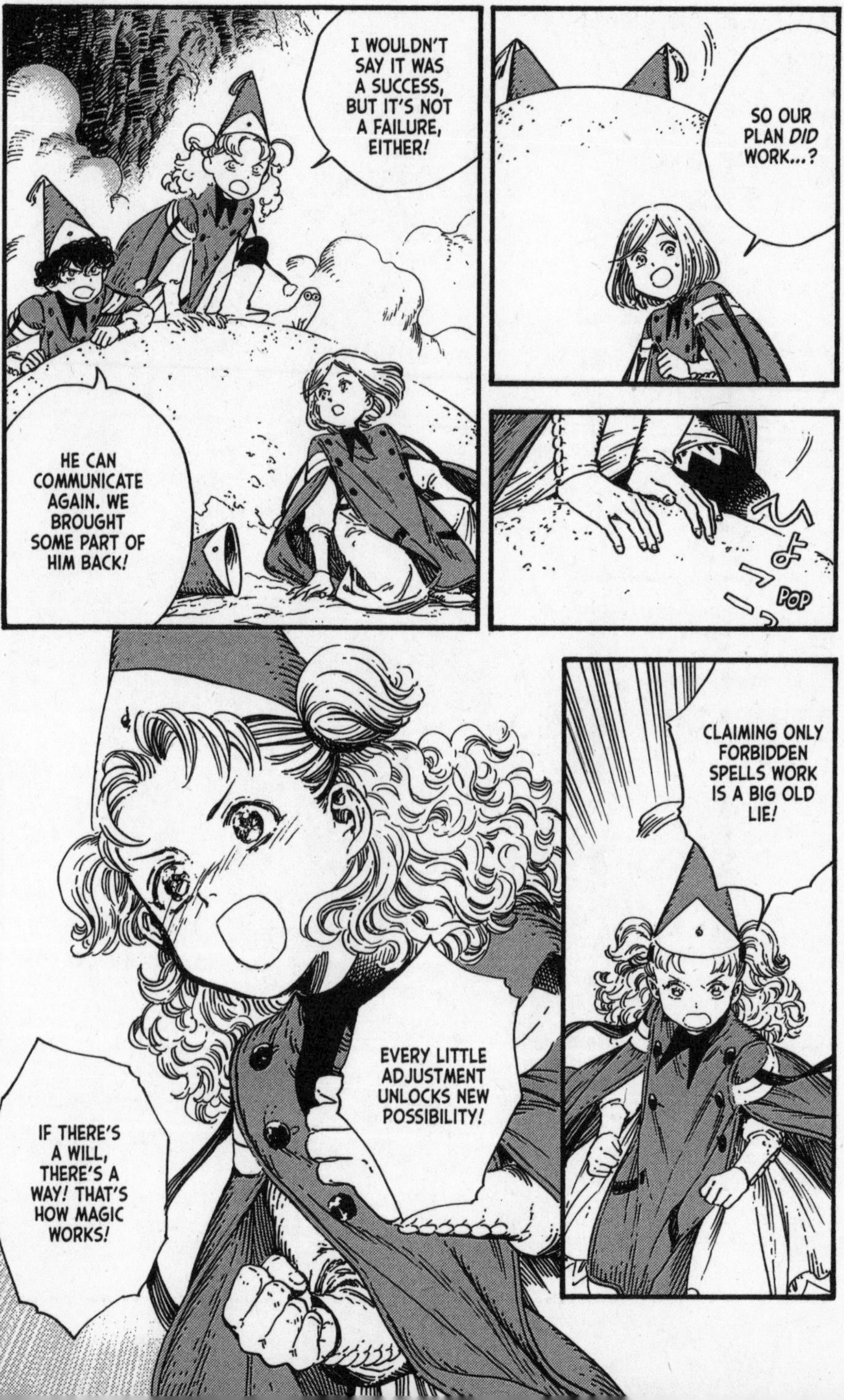
SO OUR PLAN *DID* WORK...?
POP
I WOULDN'T SAY IT WAS A SUCCESS, BUT IT'S NOT A FAILURE, EITHER!
HE CAN COMMUNICATE AGAIN. WE BROUGHT SOME PART OF HIM BACK!
CLAIMING ONLY FORBIDDEN SPELLS WORK IS A BIG OLD LIE!
EVERY LITTLE ADJUSTMENT UNLOCKS NEW POSSIBILITY!
IF THERE'S A WILL, THERE'S A WAY! THAT'S HOW MAGIC WORKS!

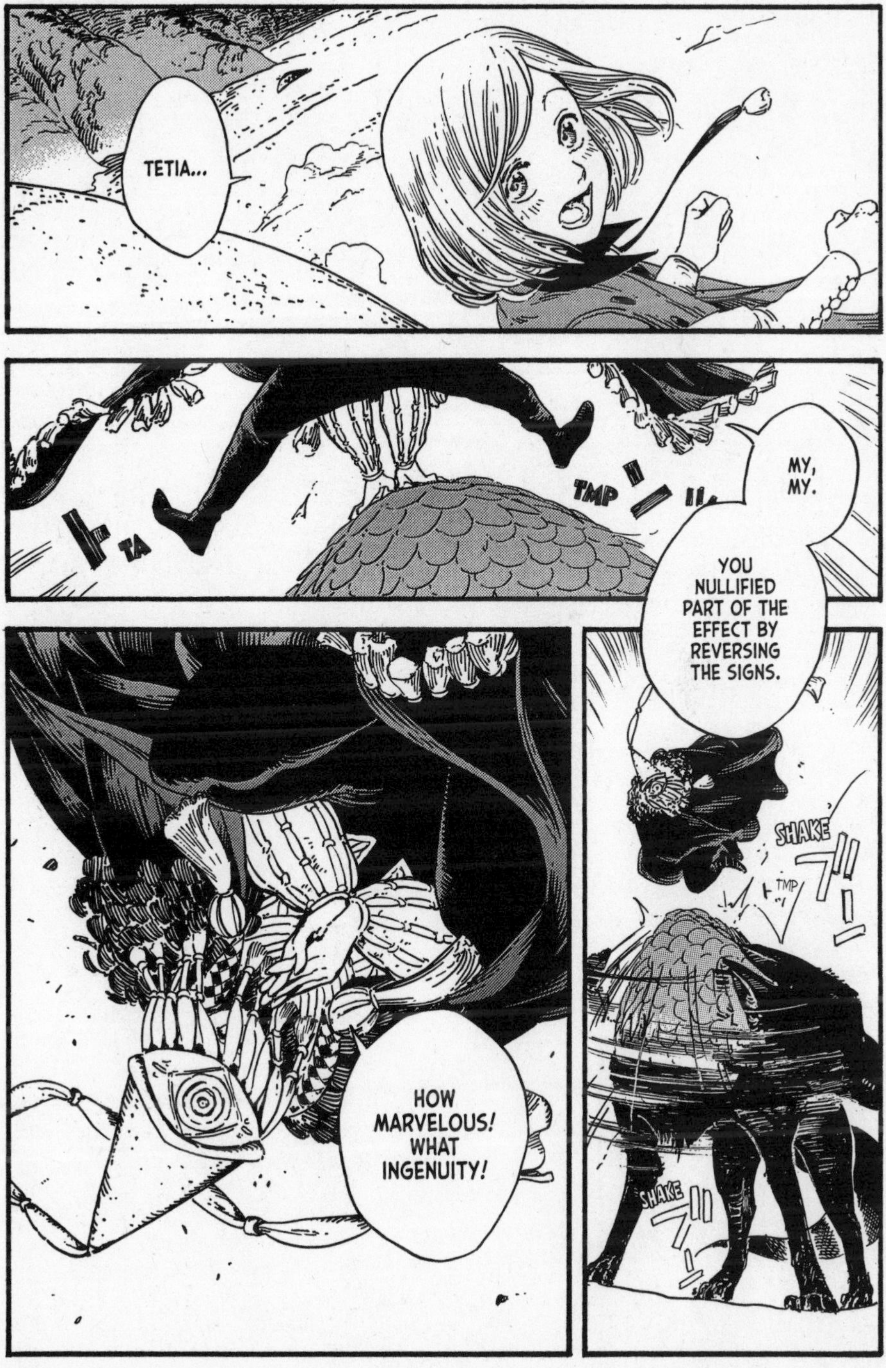
TETIA...
MY, MY.
TMP
TA
YOU NULLIFIED PART OF THE EFFECT BY REVERSING THE SIGNS.
SHAKE
TMP
SHAKE
HOW MARVELOUS! WHAT INGENUITY!

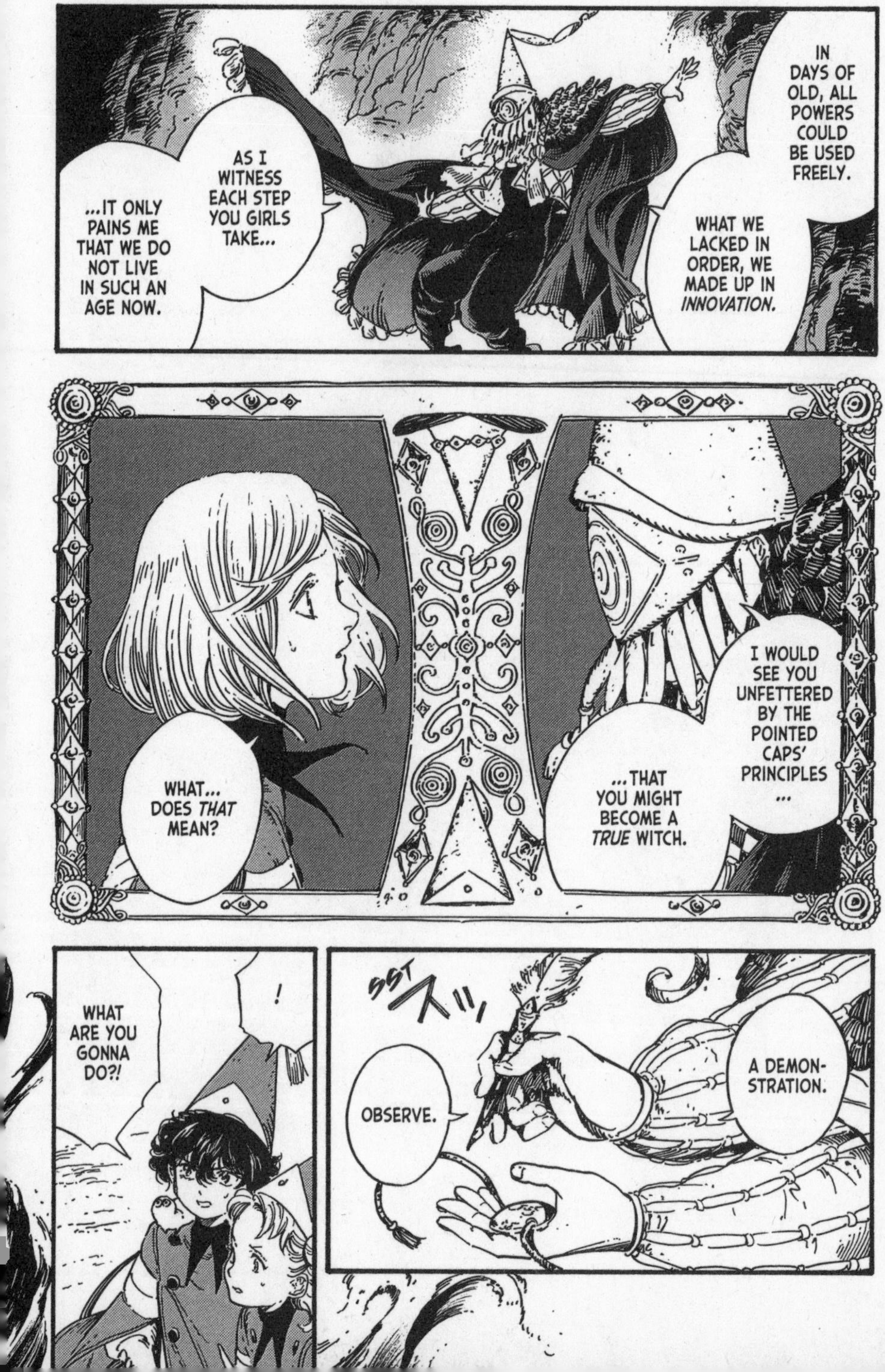
IN DAYS OF OLD, ALL POWERS COULD BE USED FREELY.
WHAT WE LACKED IN ORDER, WE MADE UP IN *INNOVATION.*
AS I WITNESS EACH STEP YOU GIRLS TAKE...
...IT ONLY PAINS ME THAT WE DO NOT LIVE IN SUCH AN AGE NOW.
I WOULD SEE YOU UNFETTERED BY THE POINTED CAPS' PRINCIPLES ...
...THAT YOU MIGHT BECOME A *TRUE* WITCH.
WHAT... DOES *THAT* MEAN?
SST
A DEMON-STRATION.
OBSERVE.
!
WHAT ARE YOU GONNA DO?!

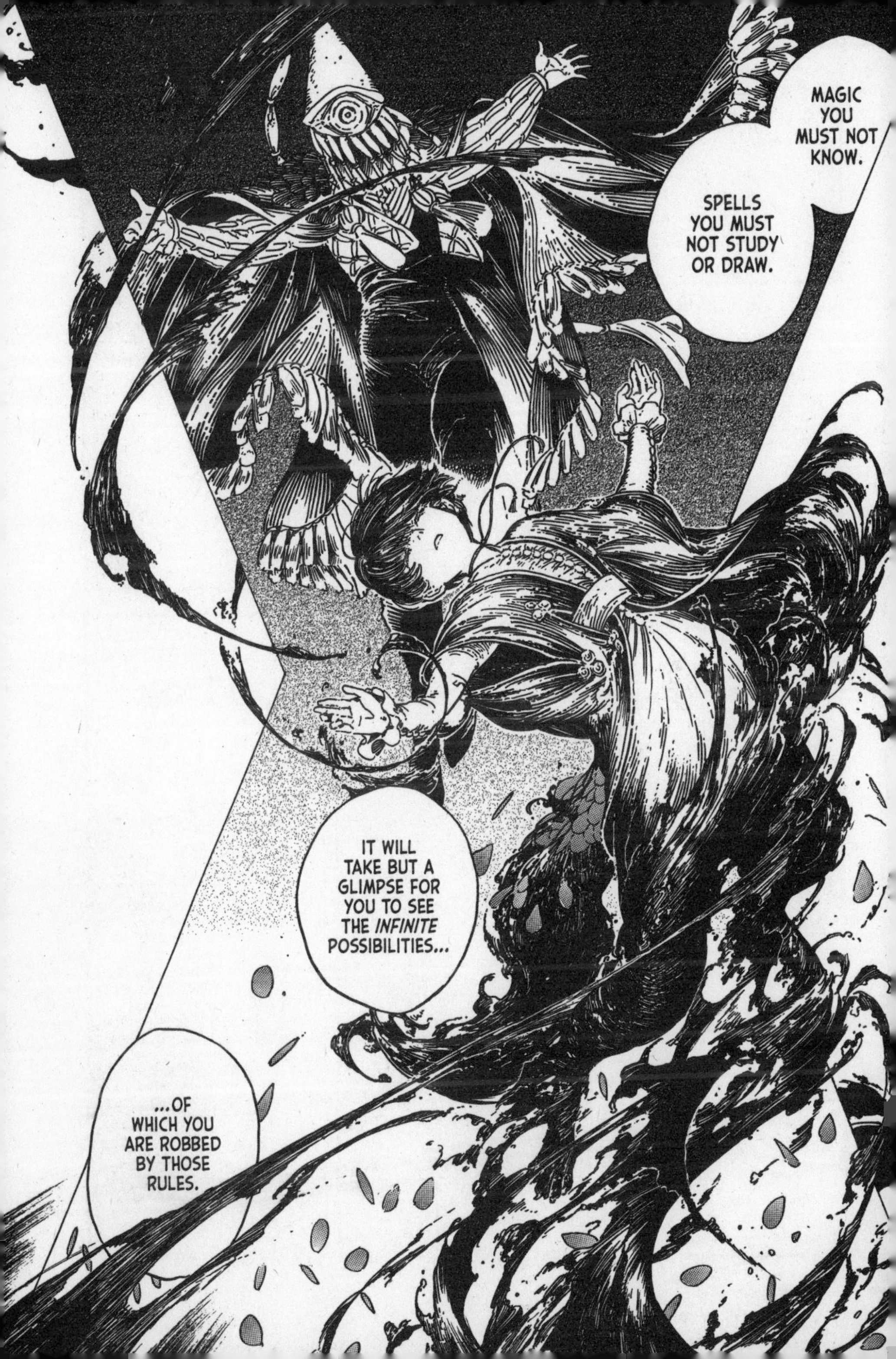
MAGIC YOU MUST NOT KNOW.
SPELLS YOU MUST NOT STUDY OR DRAW.
IT WILL TAKE BUT A GLIMPSE FOR YOU TO SEE THE *INFINITE* POSSIBILITIES...
...OF WHICH YOU ARE ROBBED BY THOSE RULES.

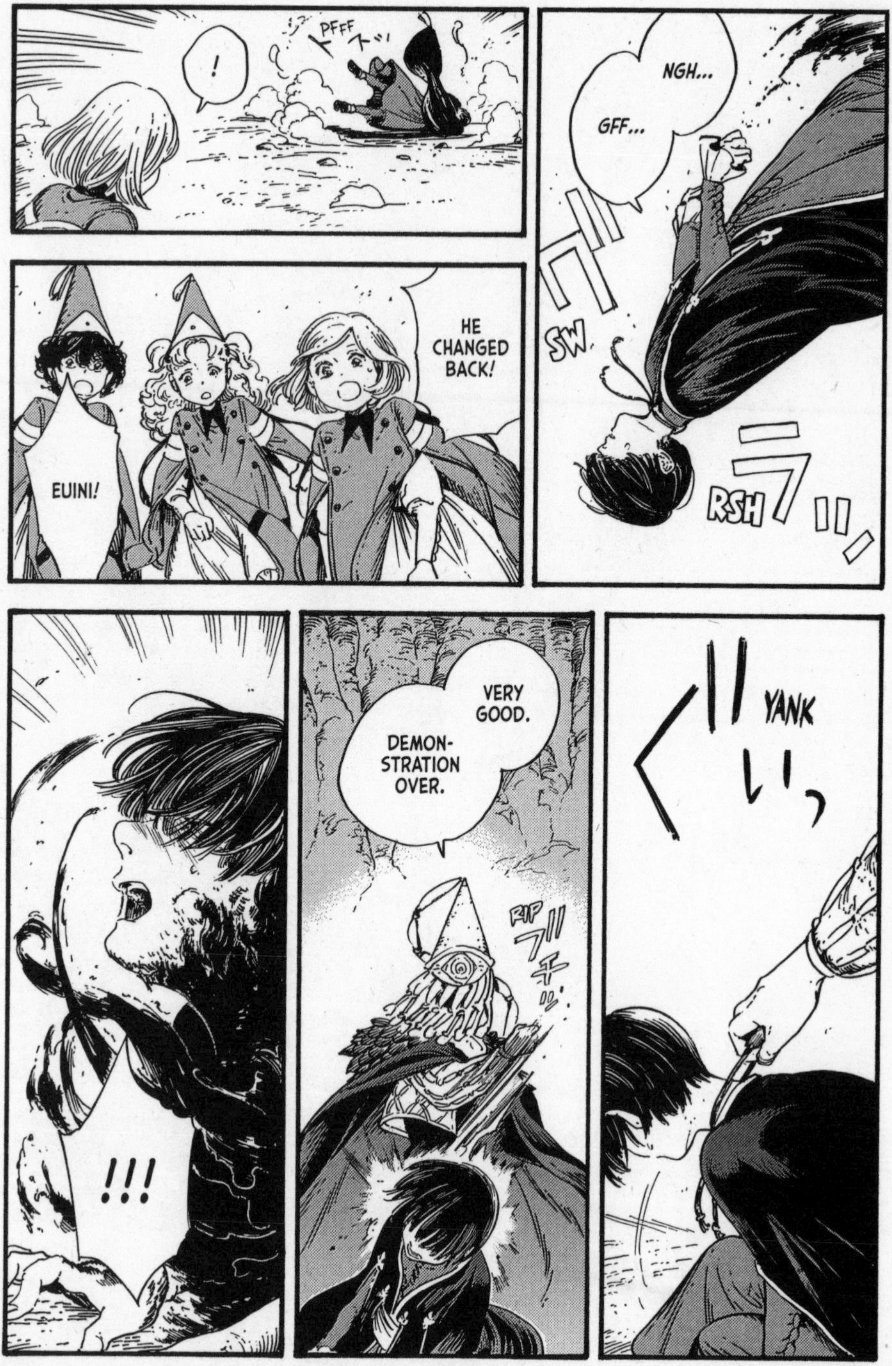
NGH...
GFF...
SW
RSH
PFFF
!
HE CHANGED BACK!
EUINI!
YANK
VERY GOOD.
DEMON-STRATION OVER.
RIP
!!!

IT MEANS NOTHING IF THE SPELL COMES FROM *ME*.

YOU MUST BE THE ONES TO DRAW IF WE ARE TO—

SHWOOP

!!

TUG

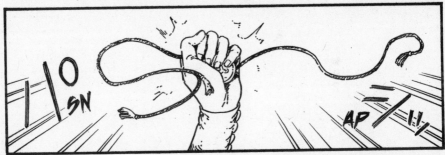

SN

AP

GRASPING WIND.

SEEMS I'VE FINALLY GOT THE HANG OF IT.

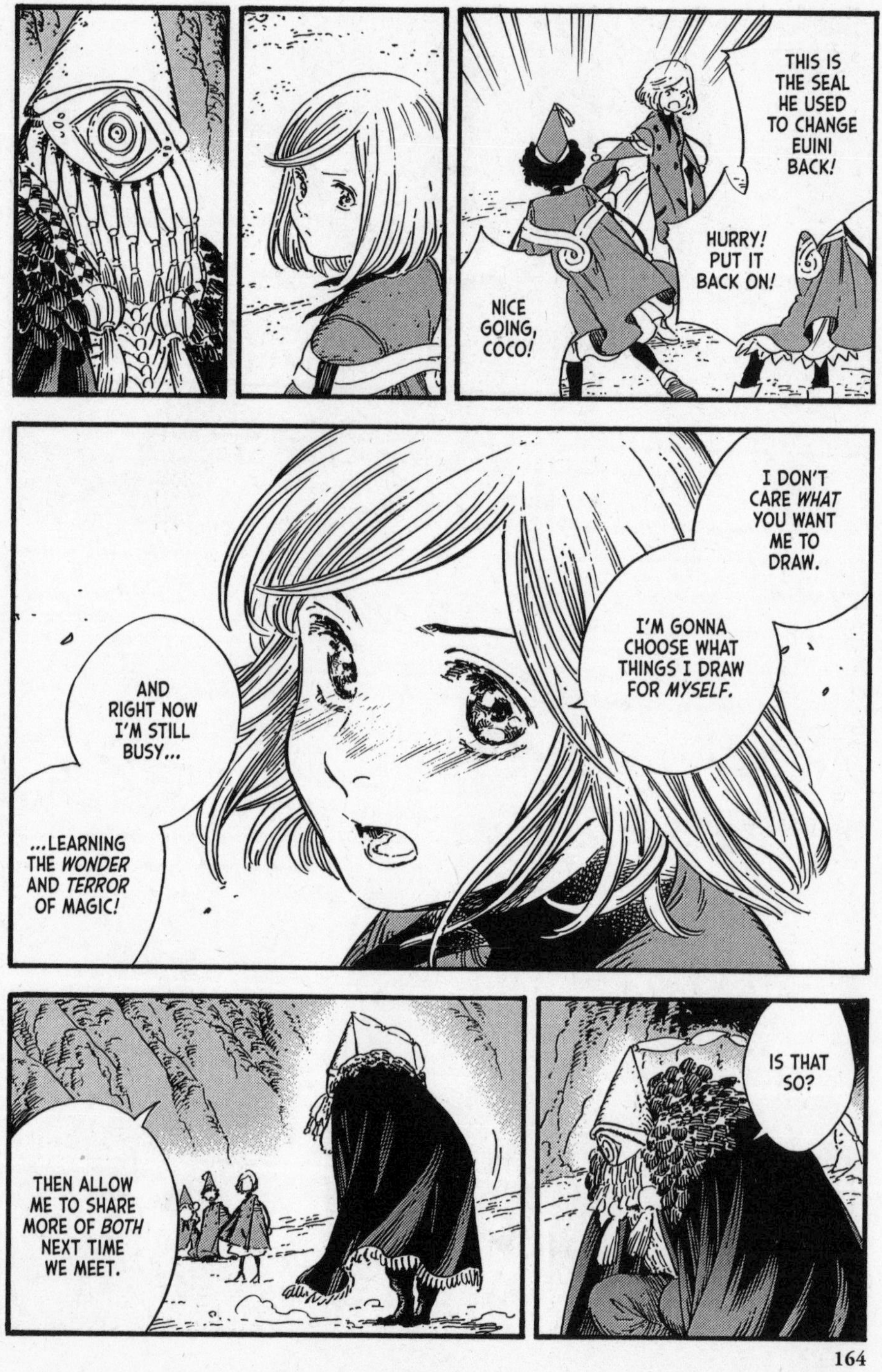
THIS IS THE SEAL HE USED TO CHANGE EUINI BACK!
HURRY! PUT IT BACK ON!
NICE GOING, COCO!
I DON'T CARE *WHAT* YOU WANT ME TO DRAW.
I'M GONNA CHOOSE WHAT THINGS I DRAW FOR *MYSELF.*
AND RIGHT NOW I'M STILL BUSY...
...LEARNING THE *WONDER* AND *TERROR* OF MAGIC!
IS THAT SO?
THEN ALLOW ME TO SHARE MORE OF *BOTH* NEXT TIME WE MEET.

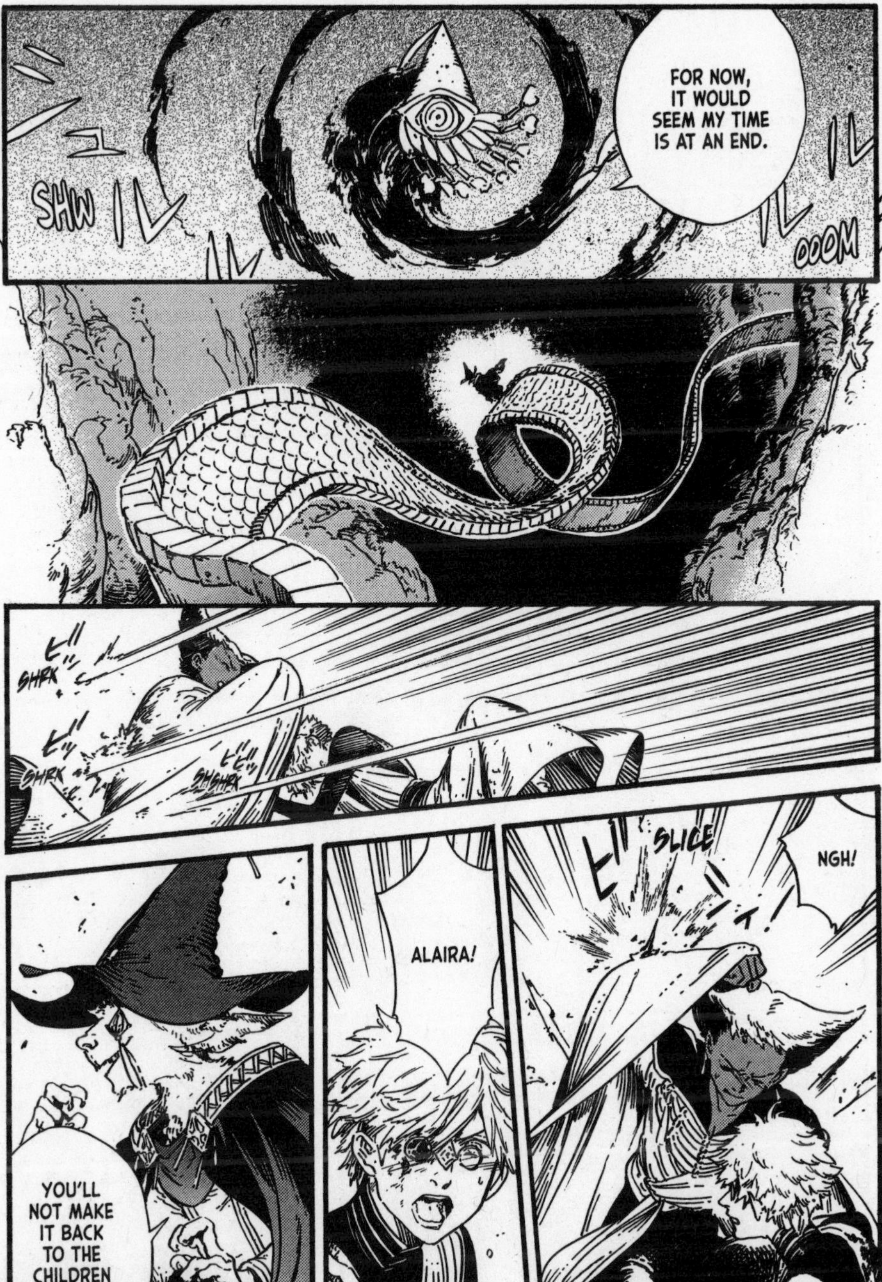
FOR NOW, IT WOULD SEEM MY TIME IS AT AN END.
OOOM
SHW
SHSHRK
SHRK
SHRK
NGH!
SLICE
ALAIRA!
YOU'LL NOT MAKE IT BACK TO THE CHILDREN ANYTIME SOON.

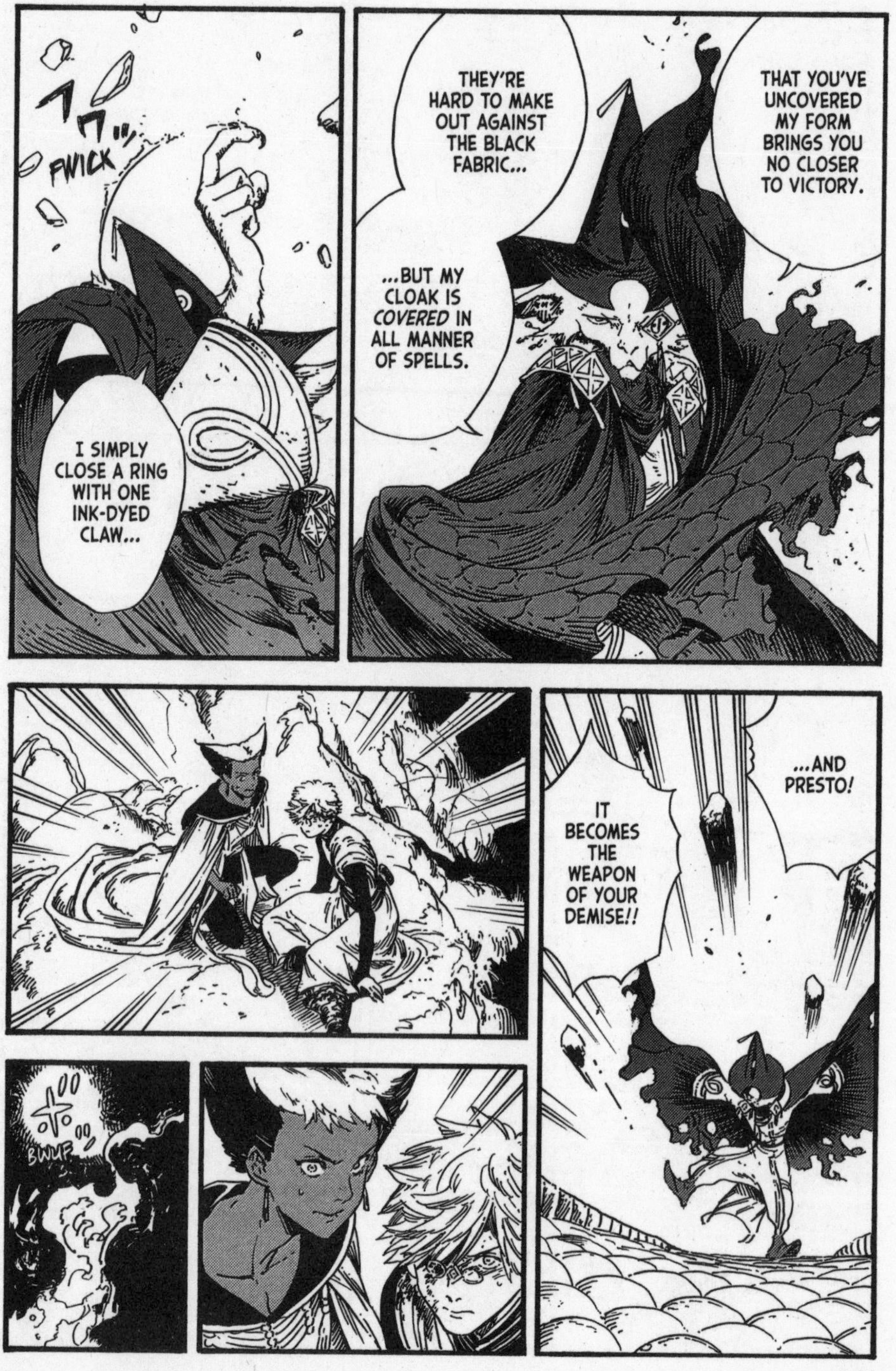
THAT YOU'VE UNCOVERED MY FORM BRINGS YOU NO CLOSER TO VICTORY.
THEY'RE HARD TO MAKE OUT AGAINST THE BLACK FABRIC...
...BUT MY CLOAK IS *COVERED* IN ALL MANNER OF SPELLS.
FWICK
I SIMPLY CLOSE A RING WITH ONE INK-DYED CLAW...
...AND PRESTO!
IT BECOMES THE WEAPON OF YOUR DEMISE!!
BWUF

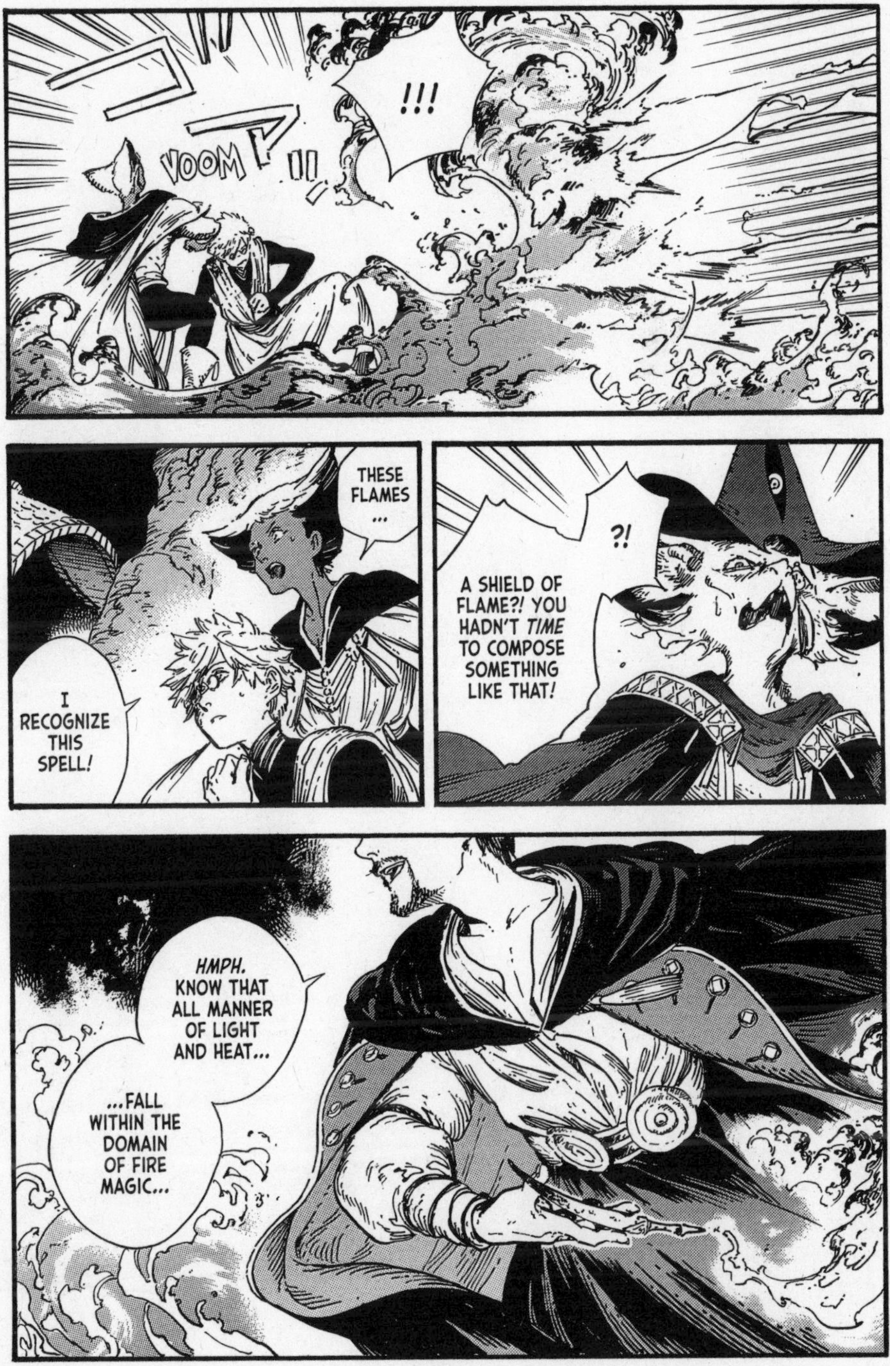
!!!
VOOM
?!
A SHIELD OF FLAME?! YOU HADN'T *TIME* TO COMPOSE SOMETHING LIKE THAT!
THESE FLAMES...
I RECOGNIZE THIS SPELL!
HMPH. KNOW THAT ALL MANNER OF LIGHT AND HEAT...
...FALL WITHIN THE DOMAIN OF FIRE MAGIC...

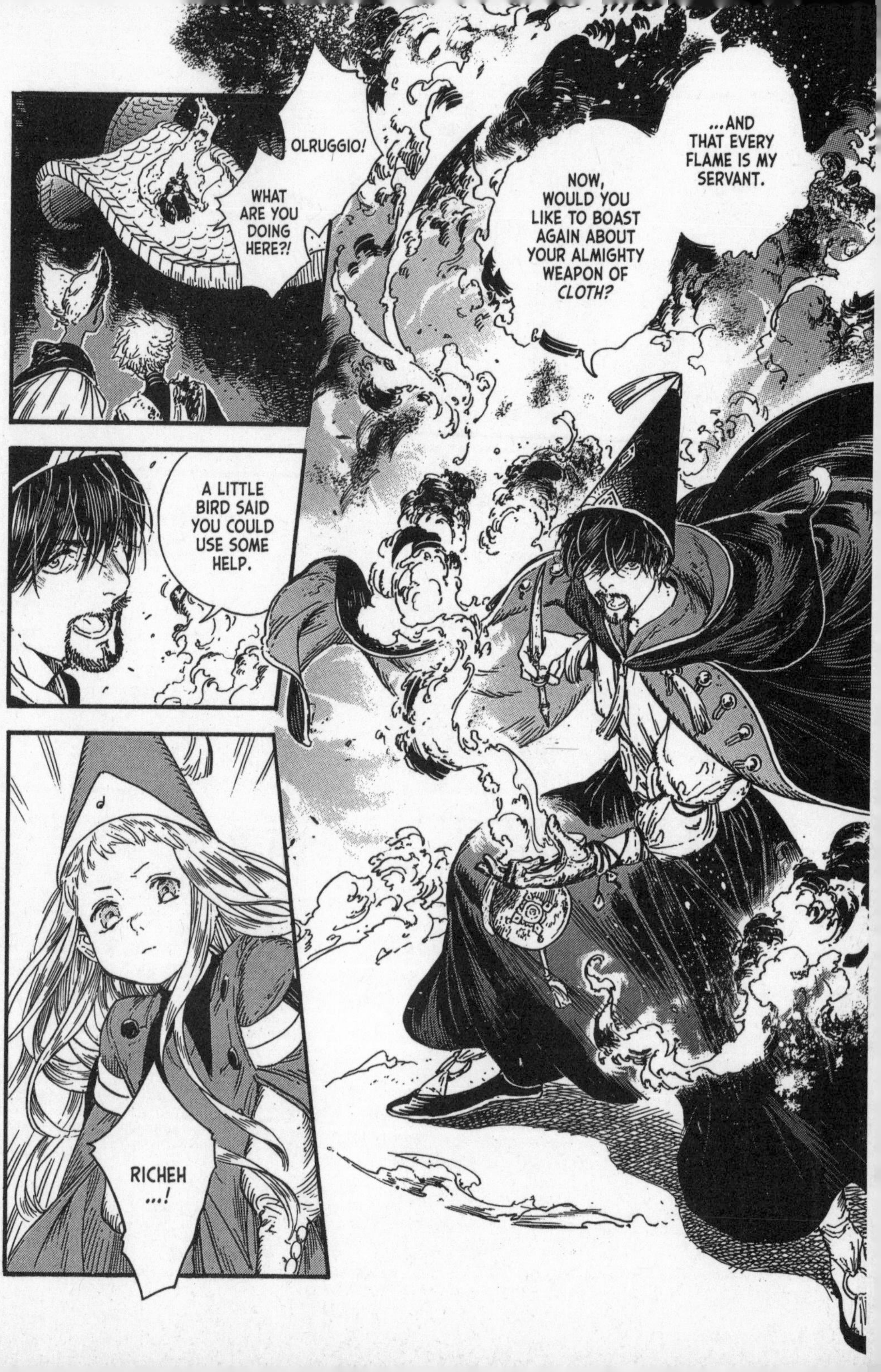
...AND THAT EVERY FLAME IS MY SERVANT.
NOW, WOULD YOU LIKE TO BOAST AGAIN ABOUT YOUR ALMIGHTY WEAPON OF *CLOTH?*
OLRUGGIO!
WHAT ARE YOU DOING HERE?!
A LITTLE BIRD SAID YOU COULD USE SOME HELP.
RICHEH ...!

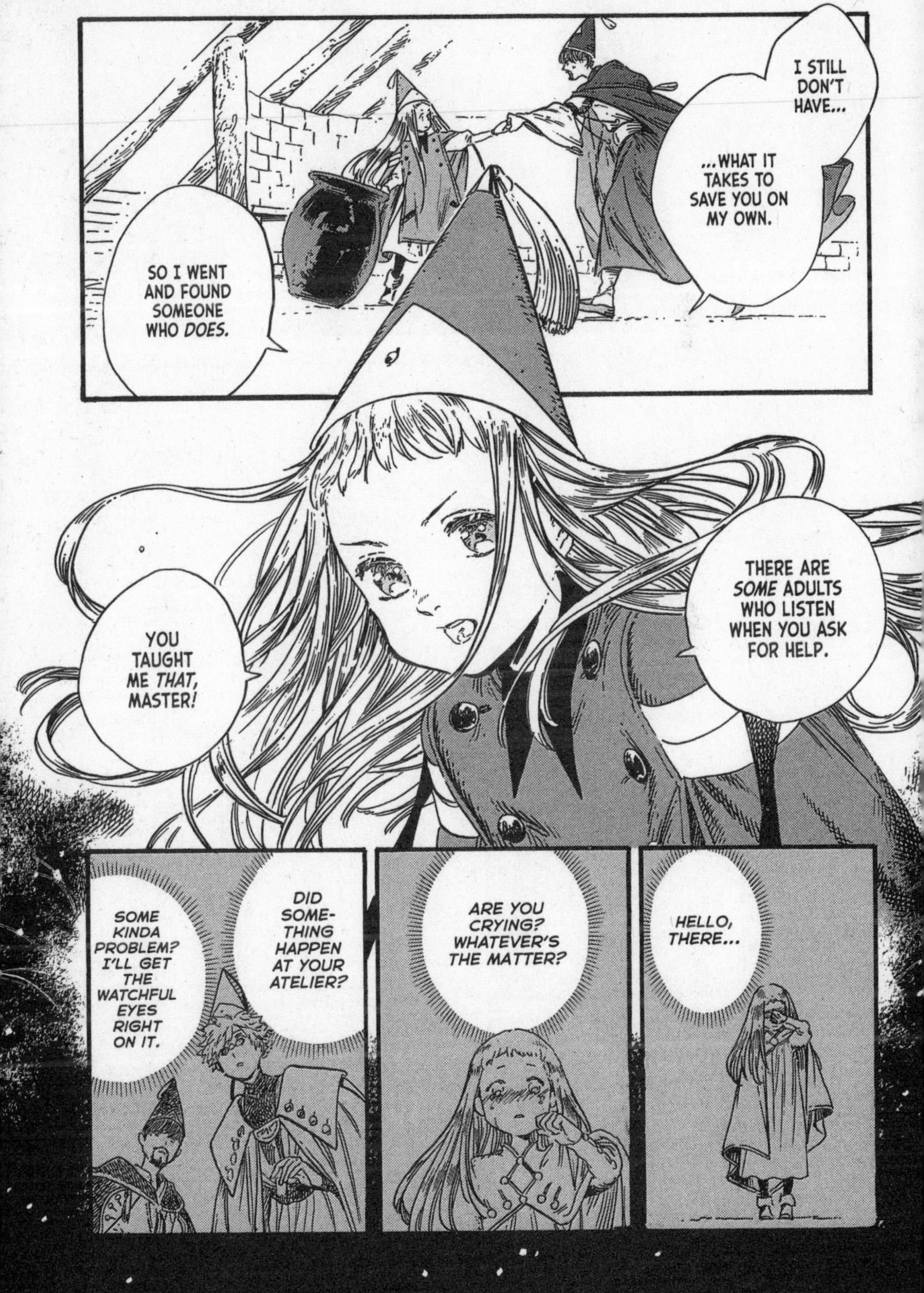
I STILL DON'T HAVE...
...WHAT IT TAKES TO SAVE YOU ON MY OWN.
SO I WENT AND FOUND SOMEONE WHO *DOES.*
THERE ARE *SOME* ADULTS WHO LISTEN WHEN YOU ASK FOR HELP.
YOU TAUGHT ME *THAT,* MASTER!
HELLO, THERE...
ARE YOU CRYING? WHATEVER'S THE MATTER?
DID SOME-THING HAPPEN AT YOUR ATELIER?
SOME KINDA PROBLEM? I'LL GET THE WATCHFUL EYES RIGHT ON IT.

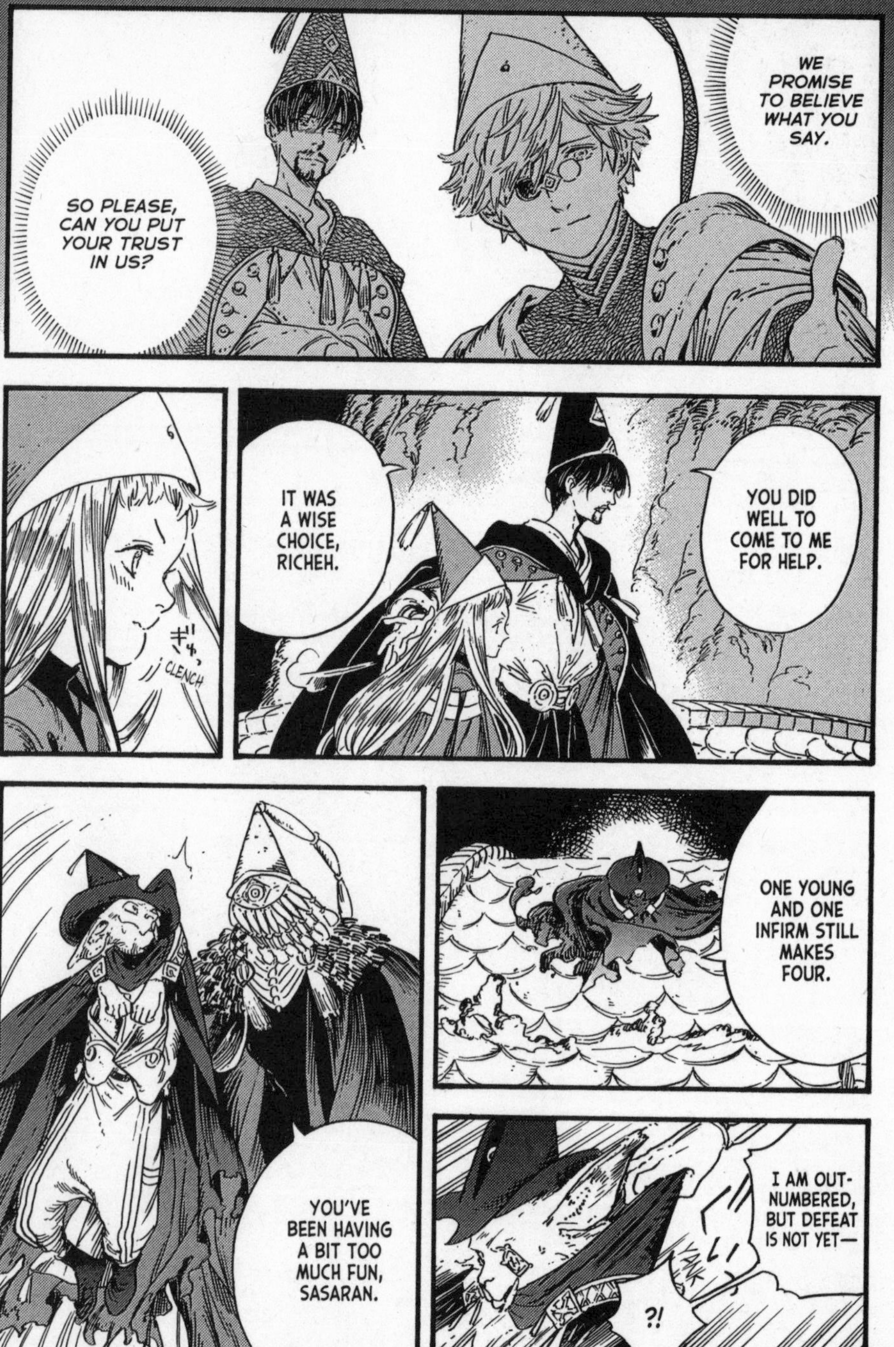
WE PROMISE TO BELIEVE WHAT YOU SAY.
SO PLEASE, CAN YOU PUT YOUR TRUST IN US?
YOU DID WELL TO COME TO ME FOR HELP.
IT WAS A WISE CHOICE, RICHEH.
CLENCH
ONE YOUNG AND ONE INFIRM STILL MAKES FOUR.
I AM OUT-NUMBERED, BUT DEFEAT IS NOT YET—
?!
YOU'VE BEEN HAVING A BIT TOO MUCH FUN, SASARAN.

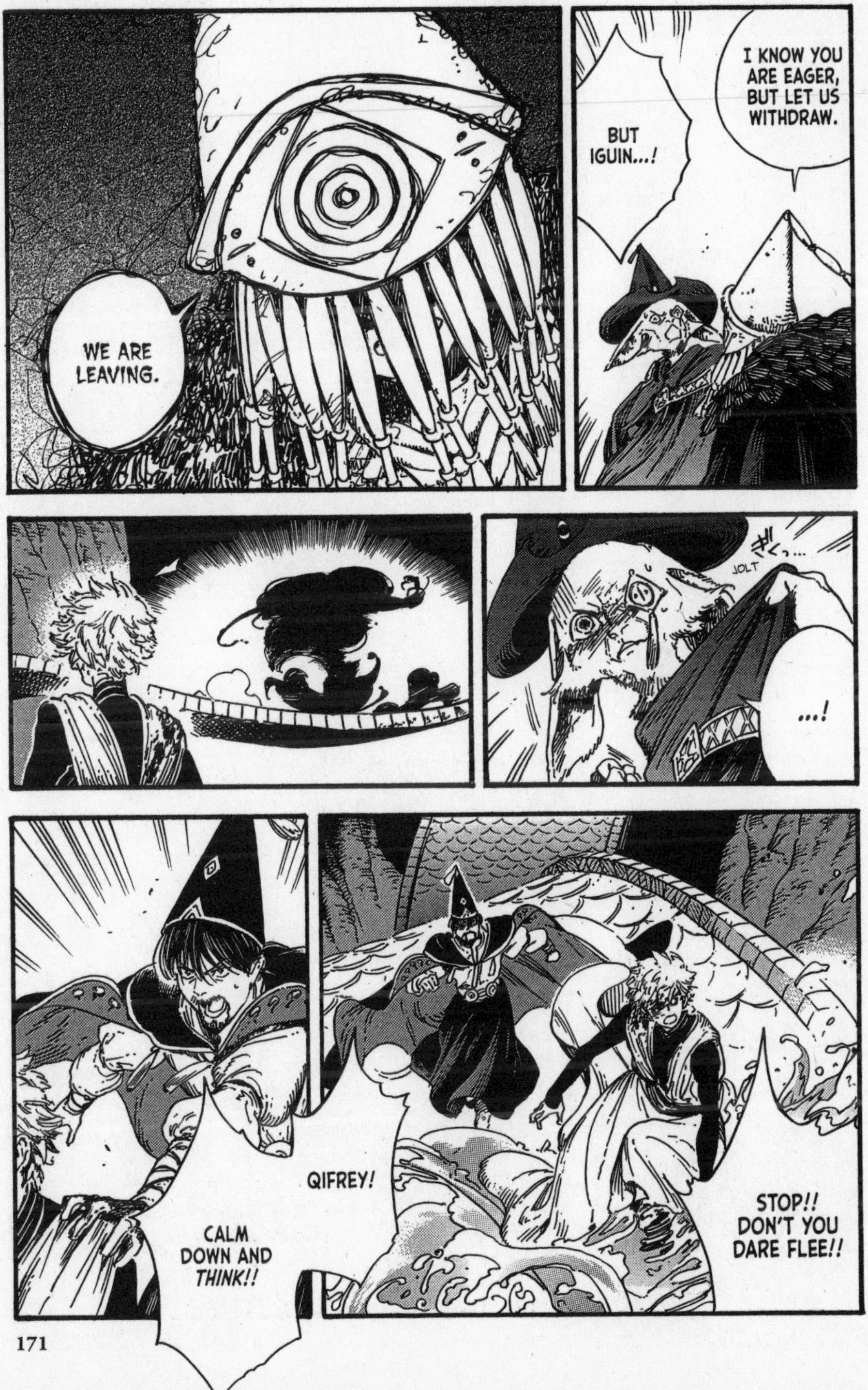
I KNOW YOU ARE EAGER, BUT LET US WITHDRAW.
BUT IGUIN...!
WE ARE LEAVING.
JOLT
...!
STOP!! DON'T YOU DARE FLEE!!
QIFREY!
CALM DOWN AND *THINK!!*

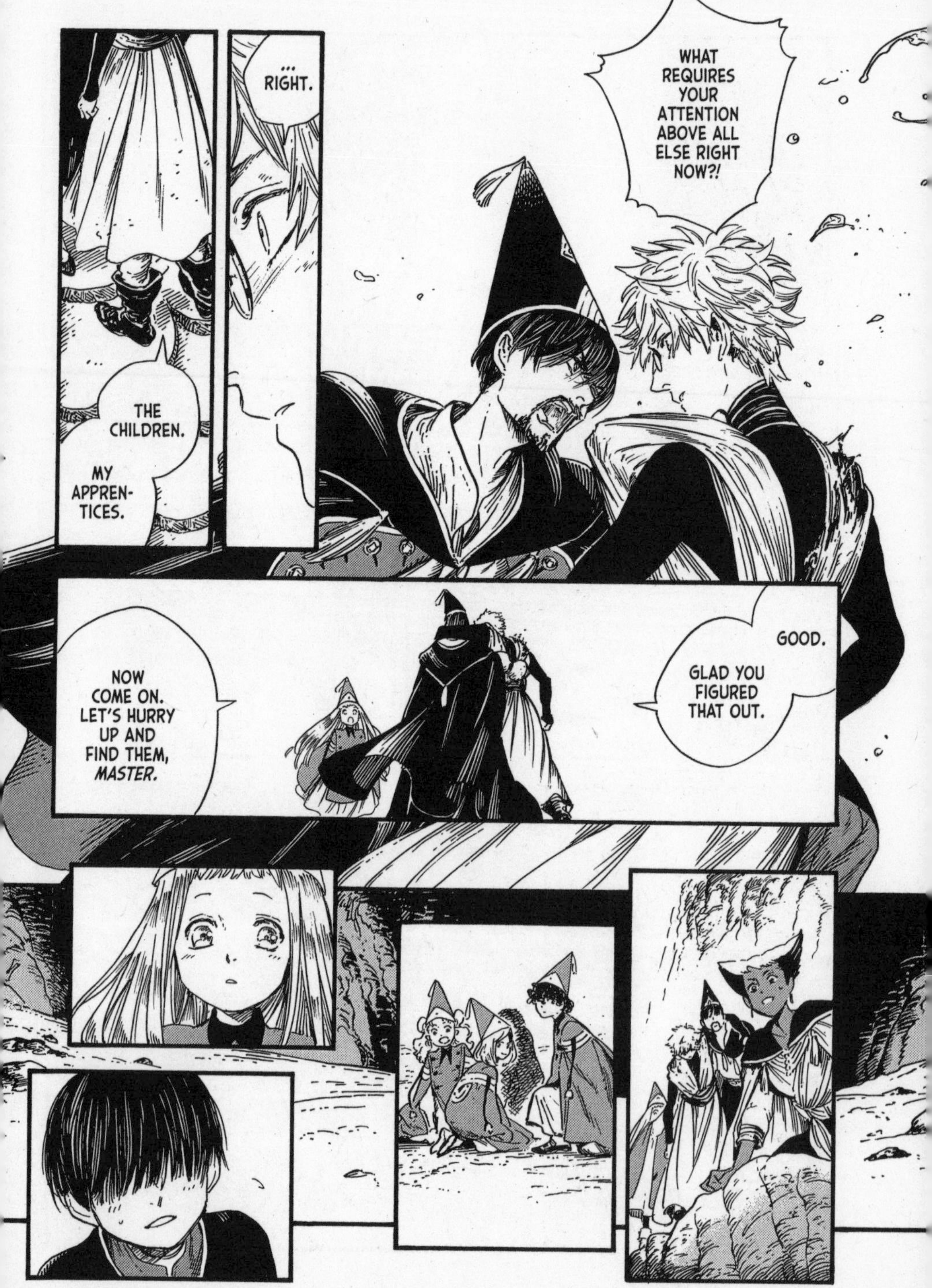
WHAT REQUIRES YOUR ATTENTION ABOVE ALL ELSE RIGHT NOW?!
... RIGHT.
...
THE CHILDREN.
MY APPREN-TICES.
GOOD.
GLAD YOU FIGURED THAT OUT.
NOW COME ON. LET'S HURRY UP AND FIND THEM, *MASTER*.

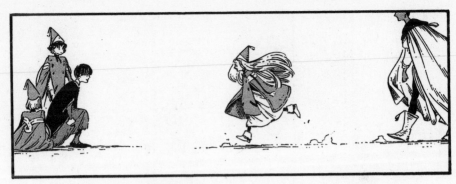

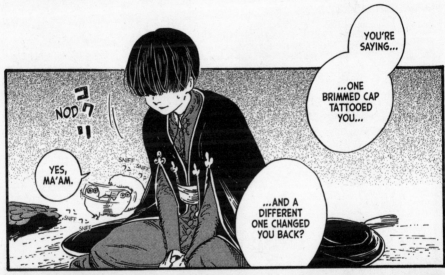

YOU'RE SAYING...
...ONE BRIMMED CAP TATTOOED YOU...
...AND A DIFFERENT ONE CHANGED YOU BACK?
NOD コクリ
YES, MA'AM.
SNIFF フン SNIFF フン
フン SNIFF フン SNIFF
PROBABLY WANTED TO SHOW YOU KIDS FORBIDDEN MAGIC.
DO THEY THINK A PERSON'S BODY IS A TOY TO SCRAWL UPON?
U-UM...
...ACTUALLY, I'M NOT EXACTLY BACK TO NORMAL.

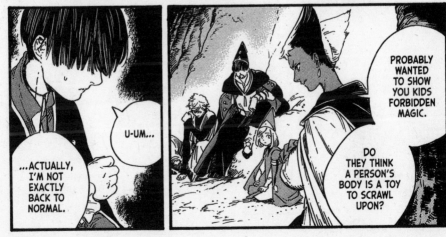

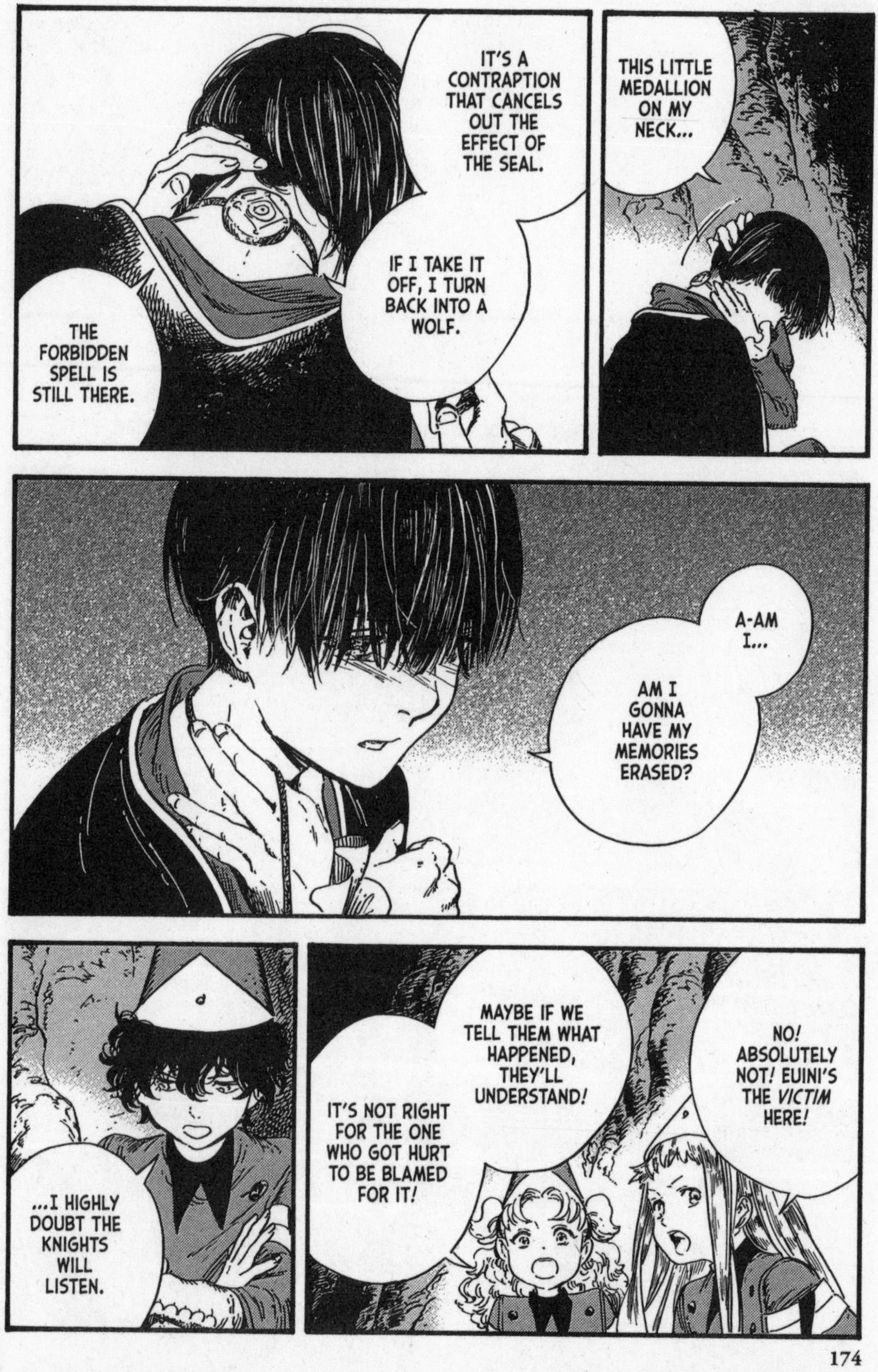
THIS LITTLE MEDALLION ON MY NECK...
IT'S A CONTRAPTION THAT CANCELS OUT THE EFFECT OF THE SEAL.
IF I TAKE IT OFF, I TURN BACK INTO A WOLF.
THE FORBIDDEN SPELL IS STILL THERE.
A-AM I...
AM I GONNA HAVE MY MEMORIES ERASED?
NO! ABSOLUTELY NOT! EUINI'S THE *VICTIM* HERE!
MAYBE IF WE TELL THEM WHAT HAPPENED, THEY'LL UNDERSTAND!
IT'S NOT RIGHT FOR THE ONE WHO GOT HURT TO BE BLAMED FOR IT!
...I HIGHLY DOUBT THE KNIGHTS WILL LISTEN.

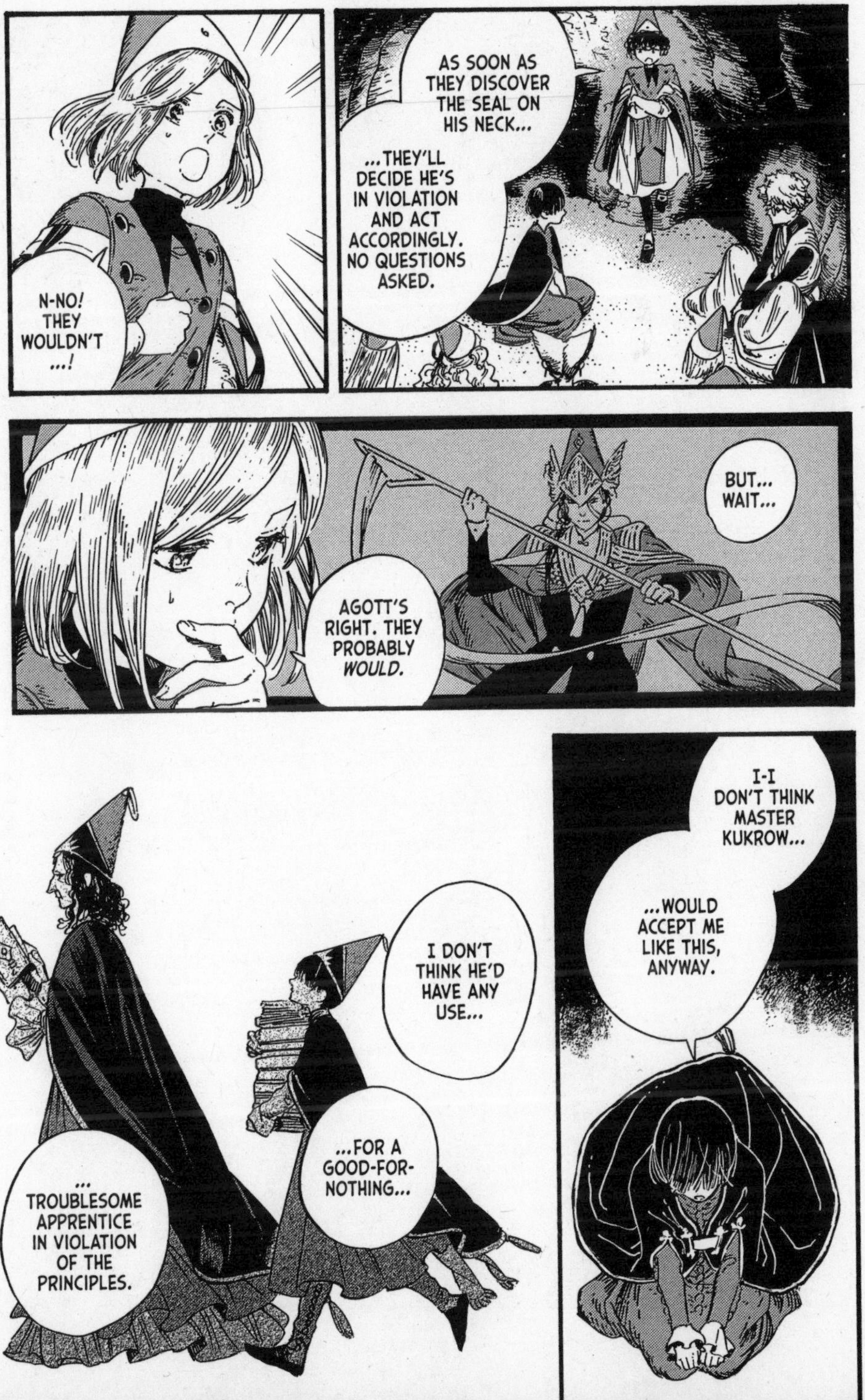
AS SOON AS THEY DISCOVER THE SEAL ON HIS NECK...
...THEY'LL DECIDE HE'S IN VIOLATION AND ACT ACCORDINGLY. NO QUESTIONS ASKED.
N-NO! THEY WOULDN'T ...!
BUT... WAIT...
AGOTT'S RIGHT. THEY PROBABLY *WOULD.*
I-I DON'T THINK MASTER KUKROW...
...WOULD ACCEPT ME LIKE THIS, ANYWAY.
I DON'T THINK HE'D HAVE ANY USE...
...FOR A GOOD-FOR-NOTHING...
... TROUBLESOME APPRENTICE IN VIOLATION OF THE PRINCIPLES.

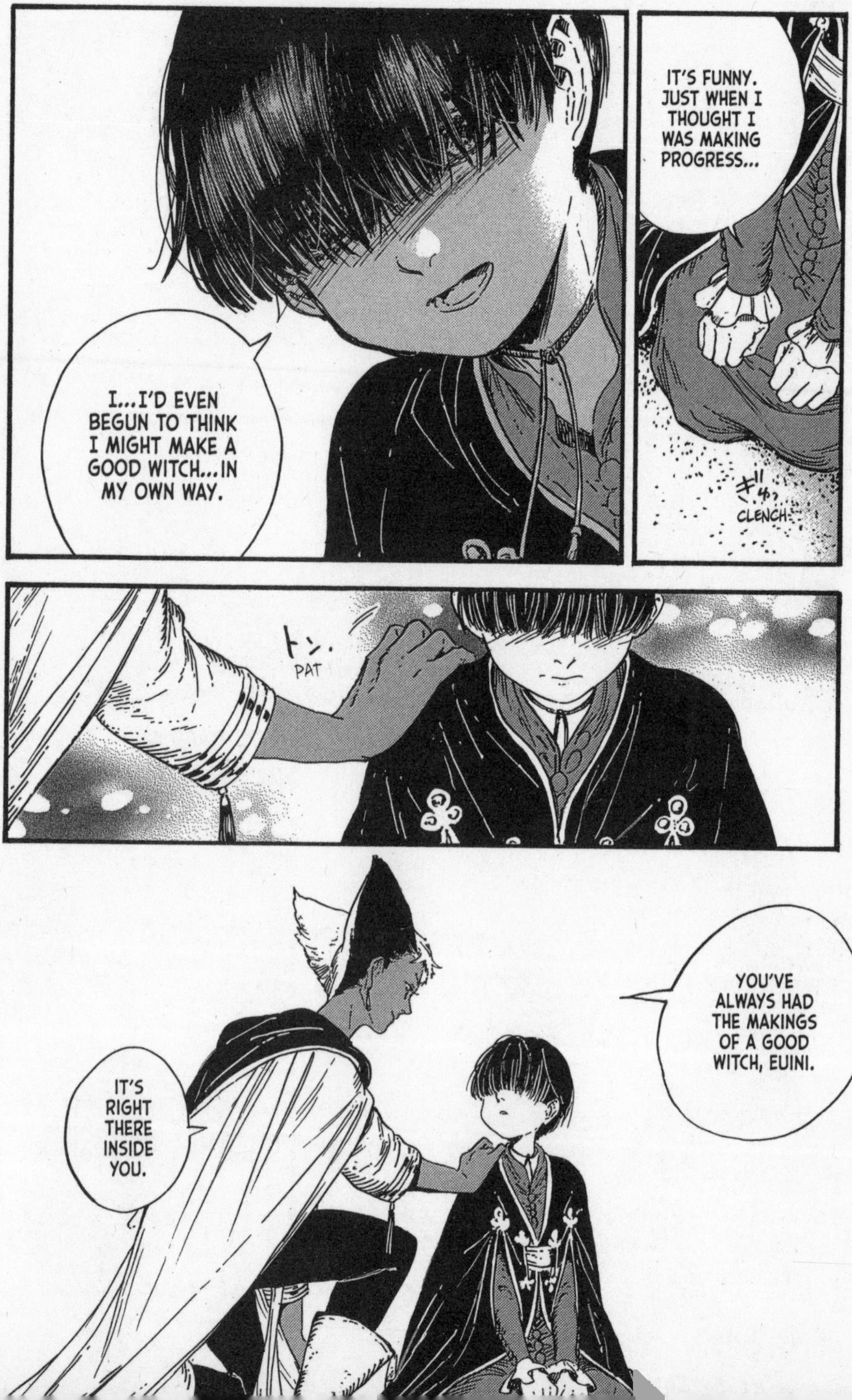
IT'S FUNNY. JUST WHEN I THOUGHT I WAS MAKING PROGRESS...
CLENCH
I...I'D EVEN BEGUN TO THINK I MIGHT MAKE A GOOD WITCH...IN MY OWN WAY.
PAT
YOU'VE ALWAYS HAD THE MAKINGS OF A GOOD WITCH, EUINI.
IT'S RIGHT THERE INSIDE YOU.

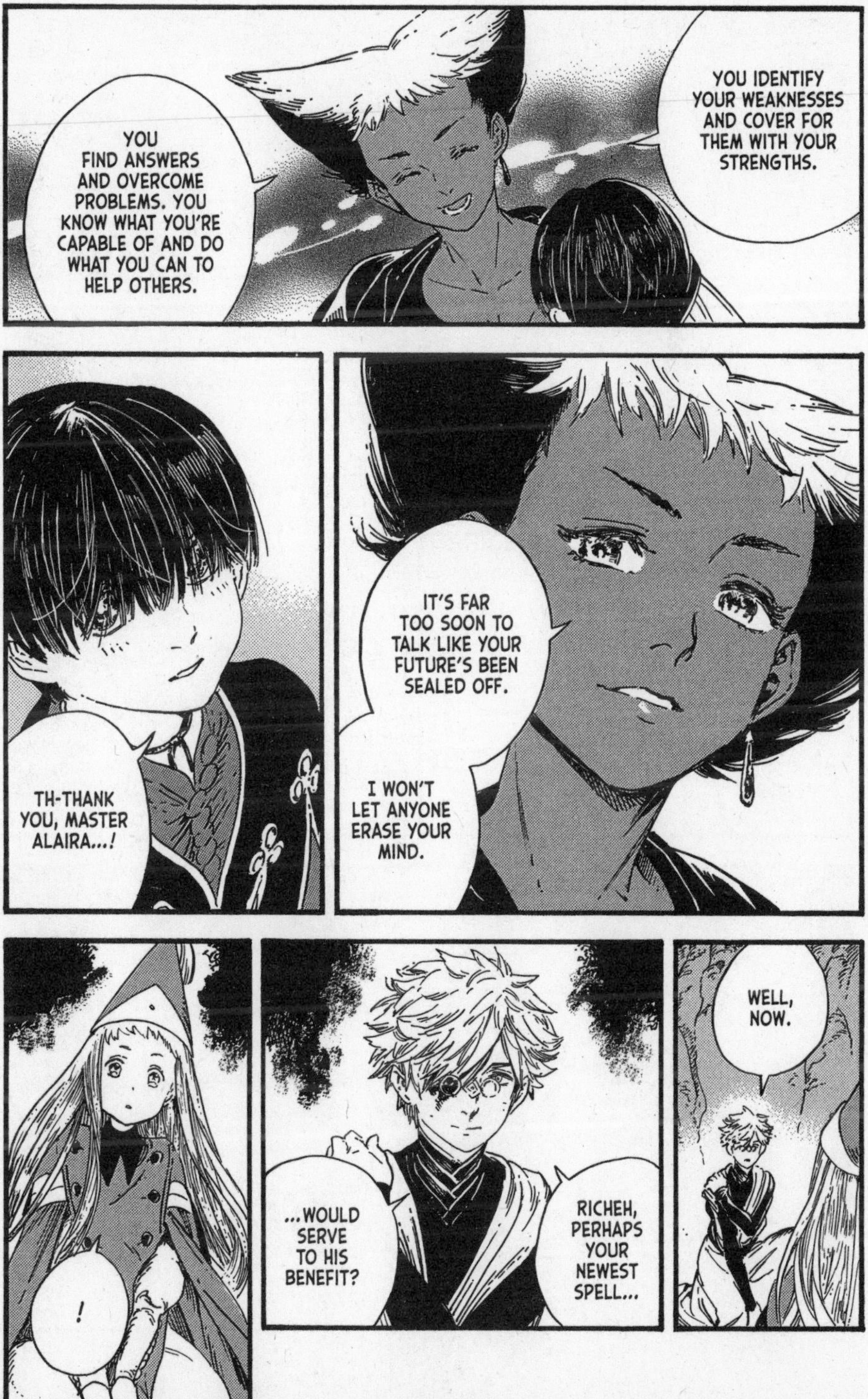
YOU IDENTIFY YOUR WEAKNESSES AND COVER FOR THEM WITH YOUR STRENGTHS.
YOU FIND ANSWERS AND OVERCOME PROBLEMS. YOU KNOW WHAT YOU'RE CAPABLE OF AND DO WHAT YOU CAN TO HELP OTHERS.
IT'S FAR TOO SOON TO TALK LIKE YOUR FUTURE'S BEEN SEALED OFF.
I WON'T LET ANYONE ERASE YOUR MIND.
TH-THANK YOU, MASTER ALAIRA...!
WELL, NOW.
RICHEH, PERHAPS YOUR NEWEST SPELL...
...WOULD SERVE TO HIS BENEFIT?
!

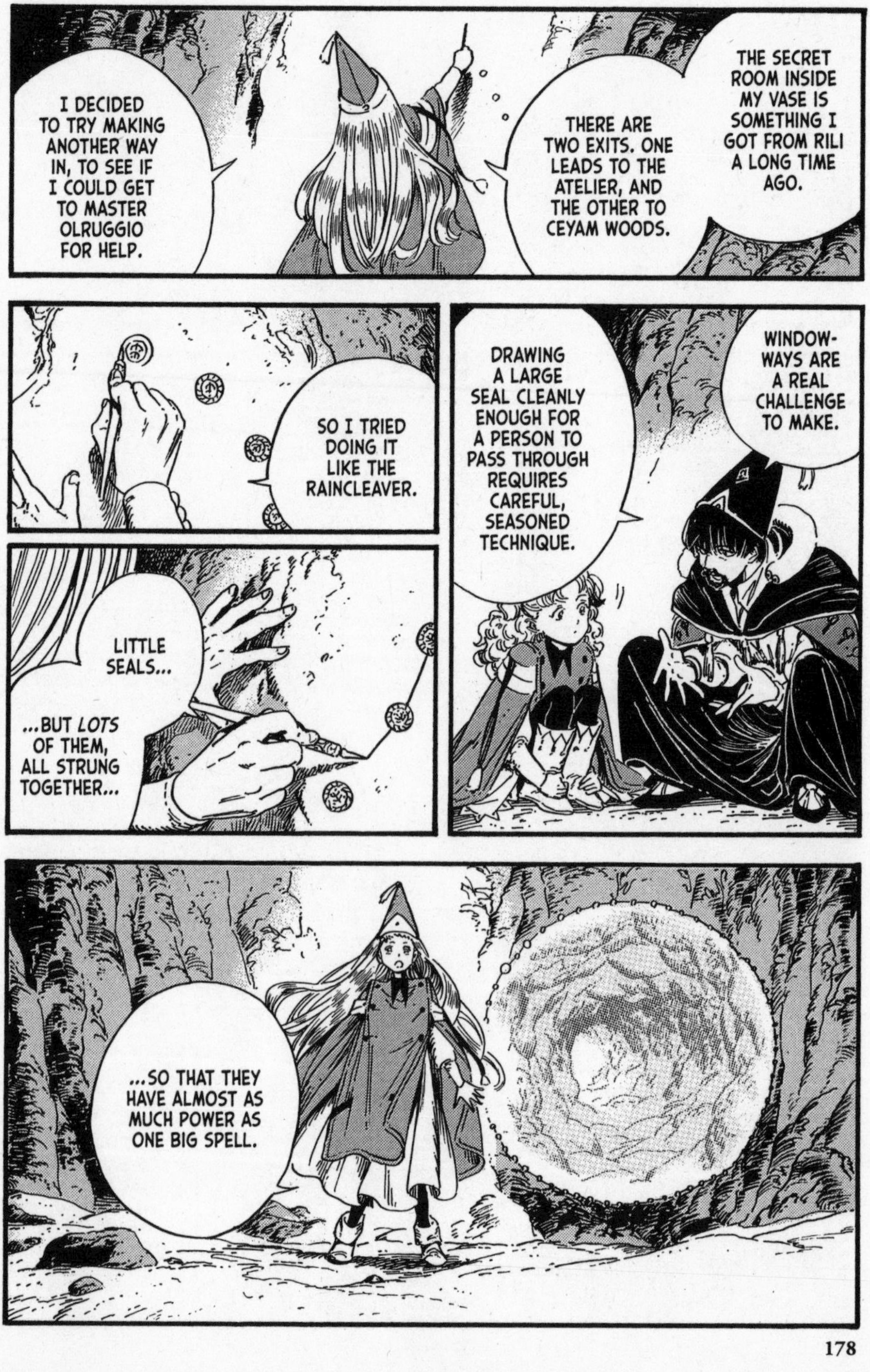
THE SECRET ROOM INSIDE MY VASE IS SOMETHING I GOT FROM RILI A LONG TIME AGO.
THERE ARE TWO EXITS. ONE LEADS TO THE ATELIER, AND THE OTHER TO CEYAM WOODS.
I DECIDED TO TRY MAKING ANOTHER WAY IN, TO SEE IF I COULD GET TO MASTER OLRUGGIO FOR HELP.
WINDOW-WAYS ARE A REAL CHALLENGE TO MAKE.
DRAWING A LARGE SEAL CLEANLY ENOUGH FOR A PERSON TO PASS THROUGH REQUIRES CAREFUL, SEASONED TECHNIQUE.
SO I TRIED DOING IT LIKE THE RAINCLEAVER.
LITTLE SEALS...
...BUT *LOTS* OF THEM, ALL STRUNG TOGETHER...
...SO THAT THEY HAVE ALMOST AS MUCH POWER AS ONE BIG SPELL.

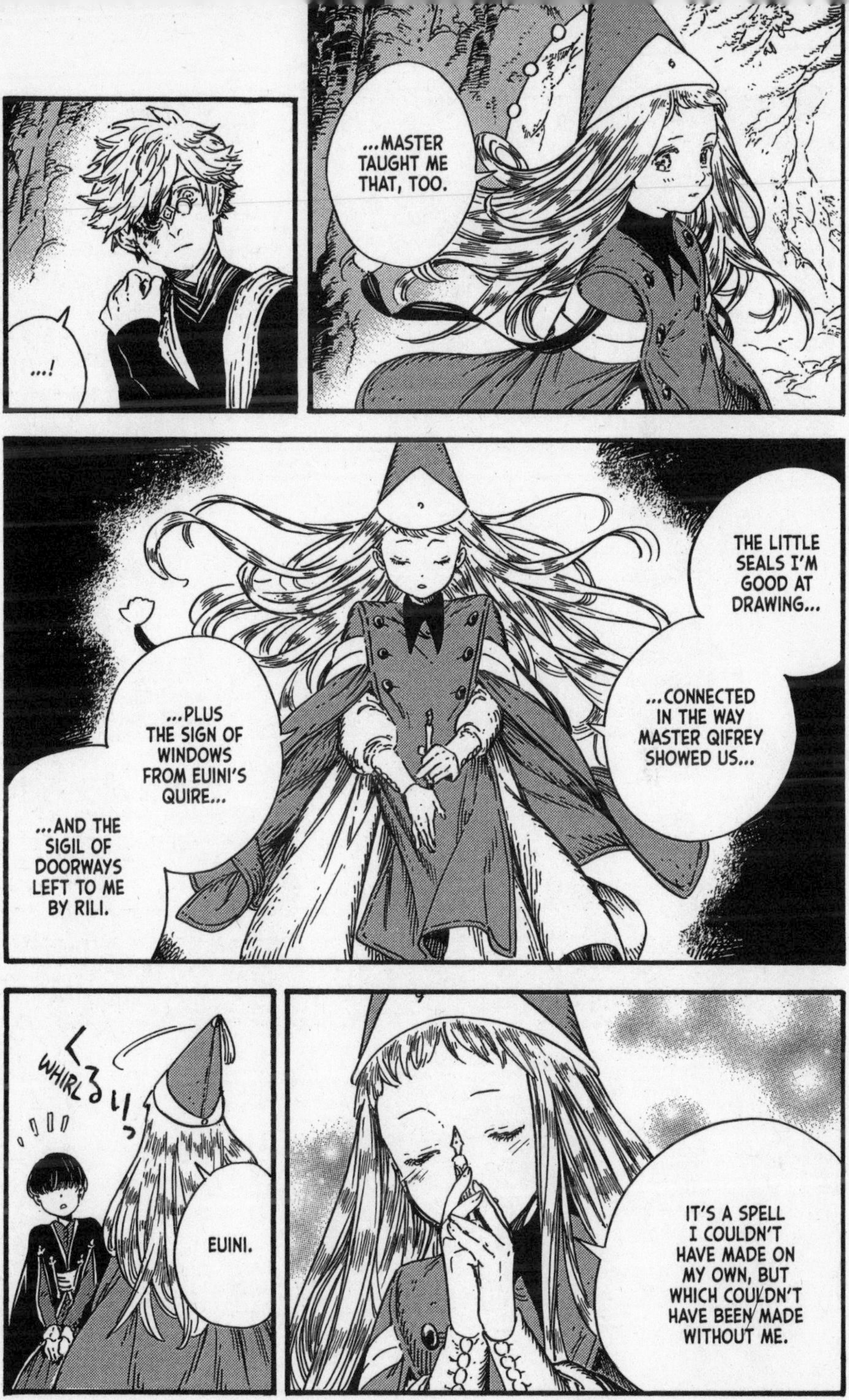
...MASTER TAUGHT ME THAT, TOO.
...!
THE LITTLE SEALS I'M GOOD AT DRAWING...
...CONNECTED IN THE WAY MASTER QIFREY SHOWED US...
...PLUS THE SIGN OF WINDOWS FROM EUINI'S QUIRE...
...AND THE SIGIL OF DOORWAYS LEFT TO ME BY RILI.
IT'S A SPELL I COULDN'T HAVE MADE ON MY OWN, BUT WHICH COULDN'T HAVE BEEN MADE WITHOUT ME.
WHIRL
EUINI.

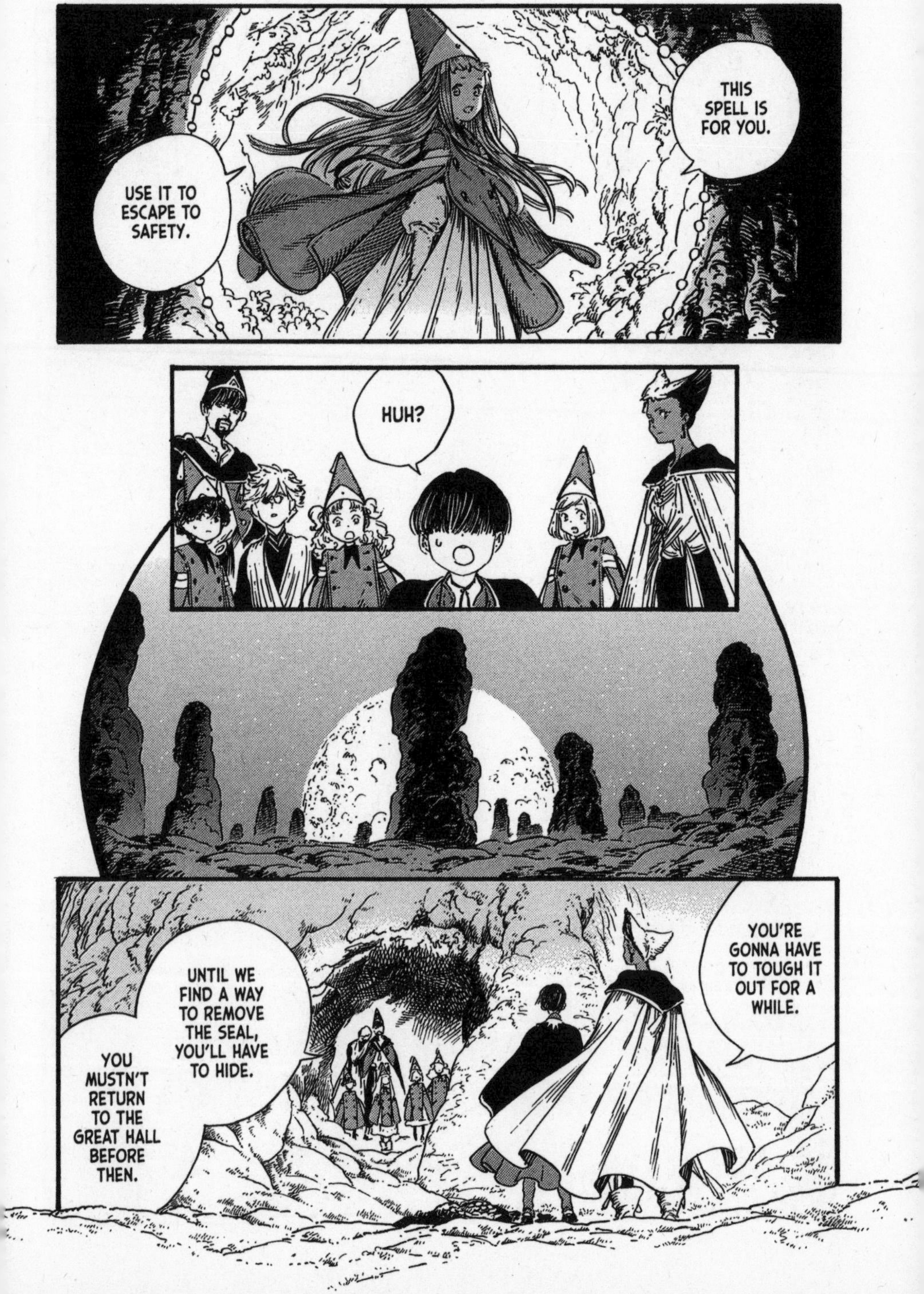
THIS SPELL IS FOR YOU.
USE IT TO ESCAPE TO SAFETY.
HUH?
YOU'RE GONNA HAVE TO TOUGH IT OUT FOR A WHILE.
UNTIL WE FIND A WAY TO REMOVE THE SEAL, YOU'LL HAVE TO HIDE.
YOU MUSTN'T RETURN TO THE GREAT HALL BEFORE THEN.

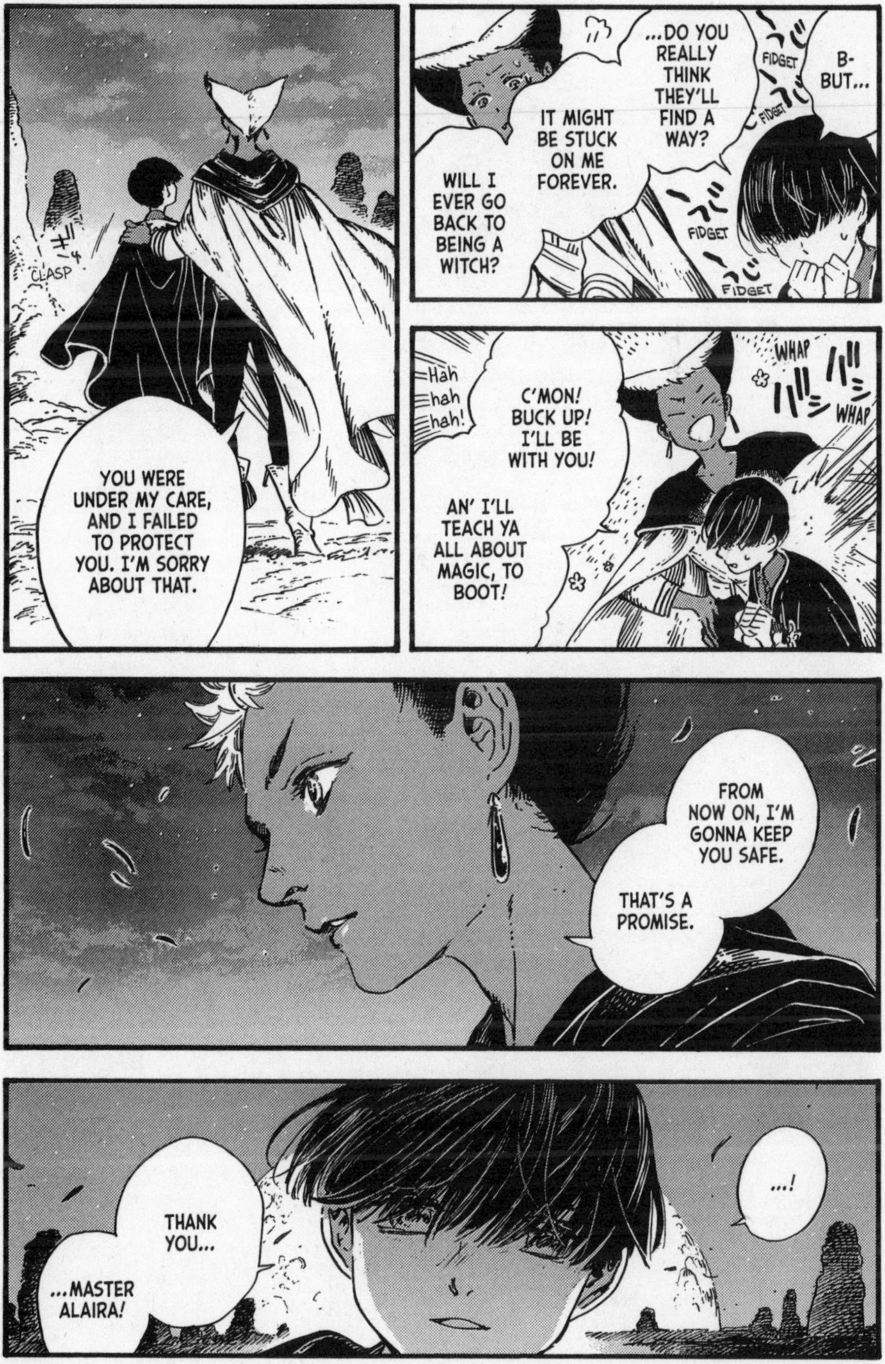
B-
BUT...
FIDGET
FIDGET
...DO YOU REALLY THINK THEY'LL FIND A WAY?
IT MIGHT BE STUCK ON ME FOREVER.
FIDGET
FIDGET
WILL I EVER GO BACK TO BEING A WITCH?
WHAP
WHAP
C'MON! BUCK UP! I'LL BE WITH YOU!
Hah hah hah!
AN' I'LL TEACH YA ALL ABOUT MAGIC, TO BOOT!
CLASP
YOU WERE UNDER MY CARE, AND I FAILED TO PROTECT YOU. I'M SORRY ABOUT THAT.
FROM NOW ON, I'M GONNA KEEP YOU SAFE.
THAT'S A PROMISE.
...!
THANK YOU...
...MASTER ALAIRA!

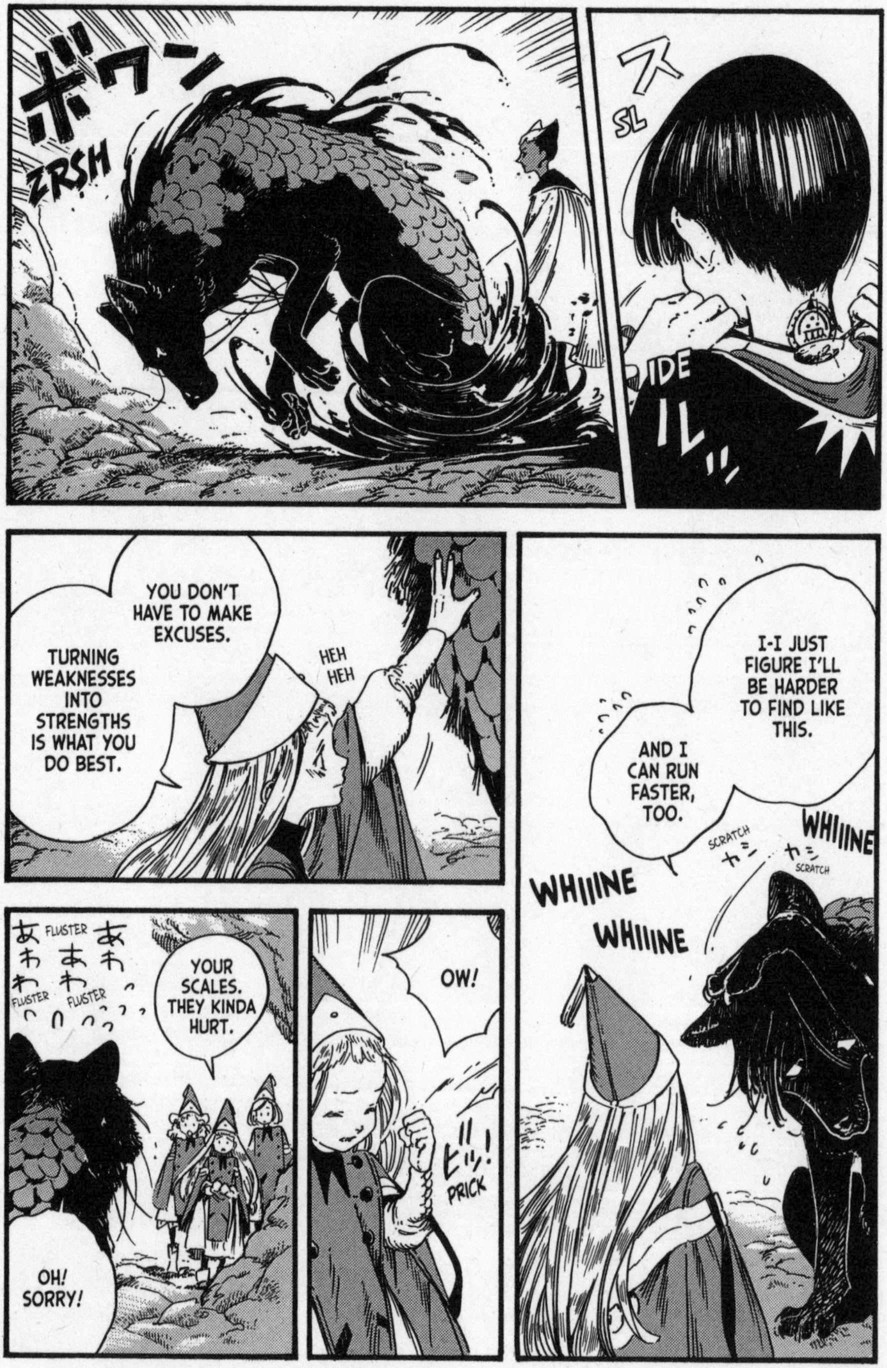

ス
SL
IDE
ル
ボワン
ZRSH
I-I JUST FIGURE I'LL BE HARDER TO FIND LIKE THIS.
AND I CAN RUN FASTER, TOO.
WHIIINE
SCRATCH
カシ
カシ
SCRATCH
WHIIINE
WHIIINE
YOU DON'T HAVE TO MAKE EXCUSES.
TURNING WEAKNESSES INTO STRENGTHS IS WHAT YOU DO BEST.
HEH HEH
OW!
ピッ
PRICK
あわ
FLUSTER
あわ
あわ
FLUSTER
FLUSTER
YOUR SCALES. THEY KINDA HURT.
OH! SORRY!

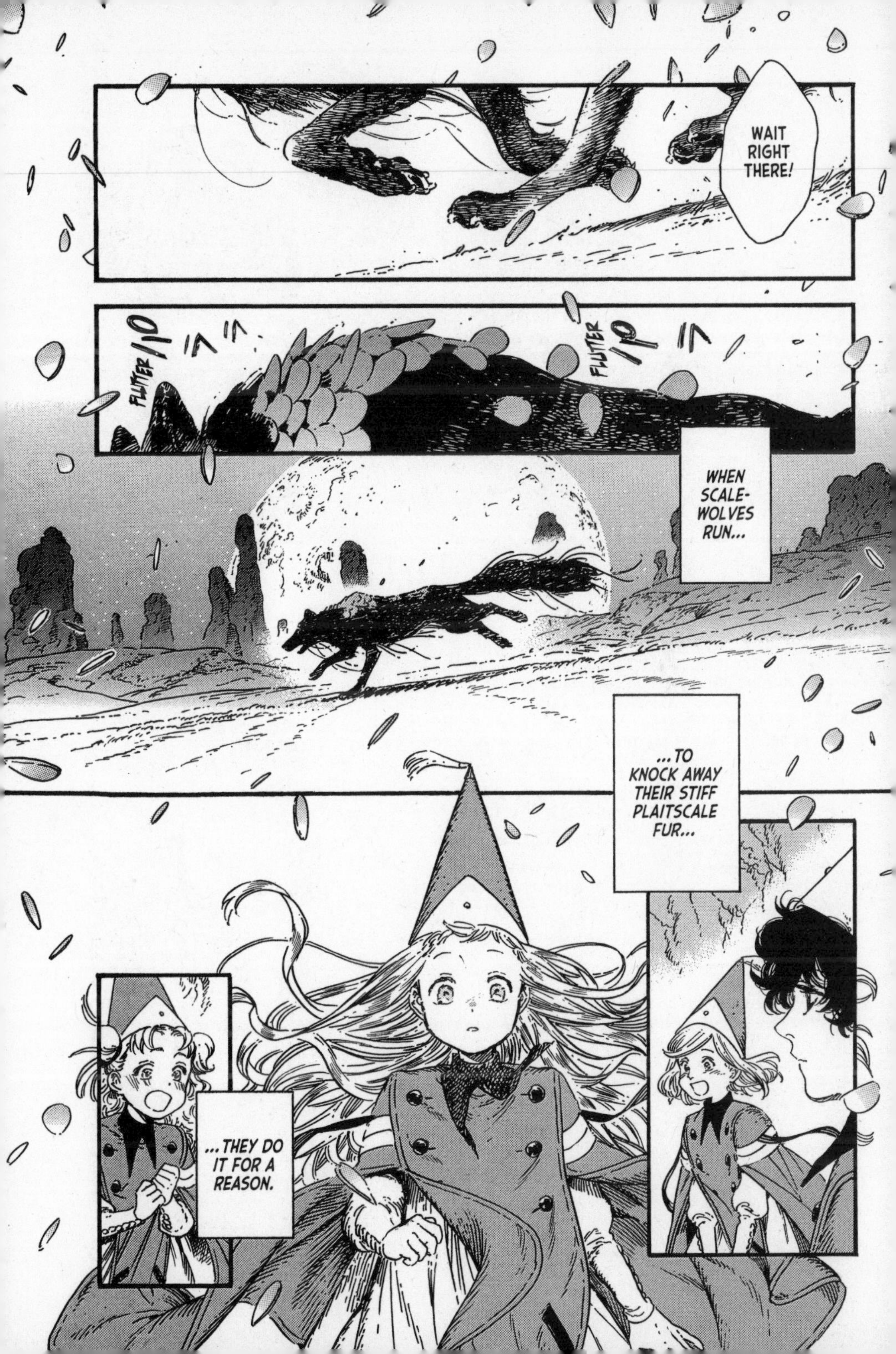
WAIT RIGHT THERE!
FLUTTER
FLUTTER
WHEN SCALE-WOLVES RUN...
...TO KNOCK AWAY THEIR STIFF PLAITSCALE FUR...
...THEY DO IT FOR A REASON.

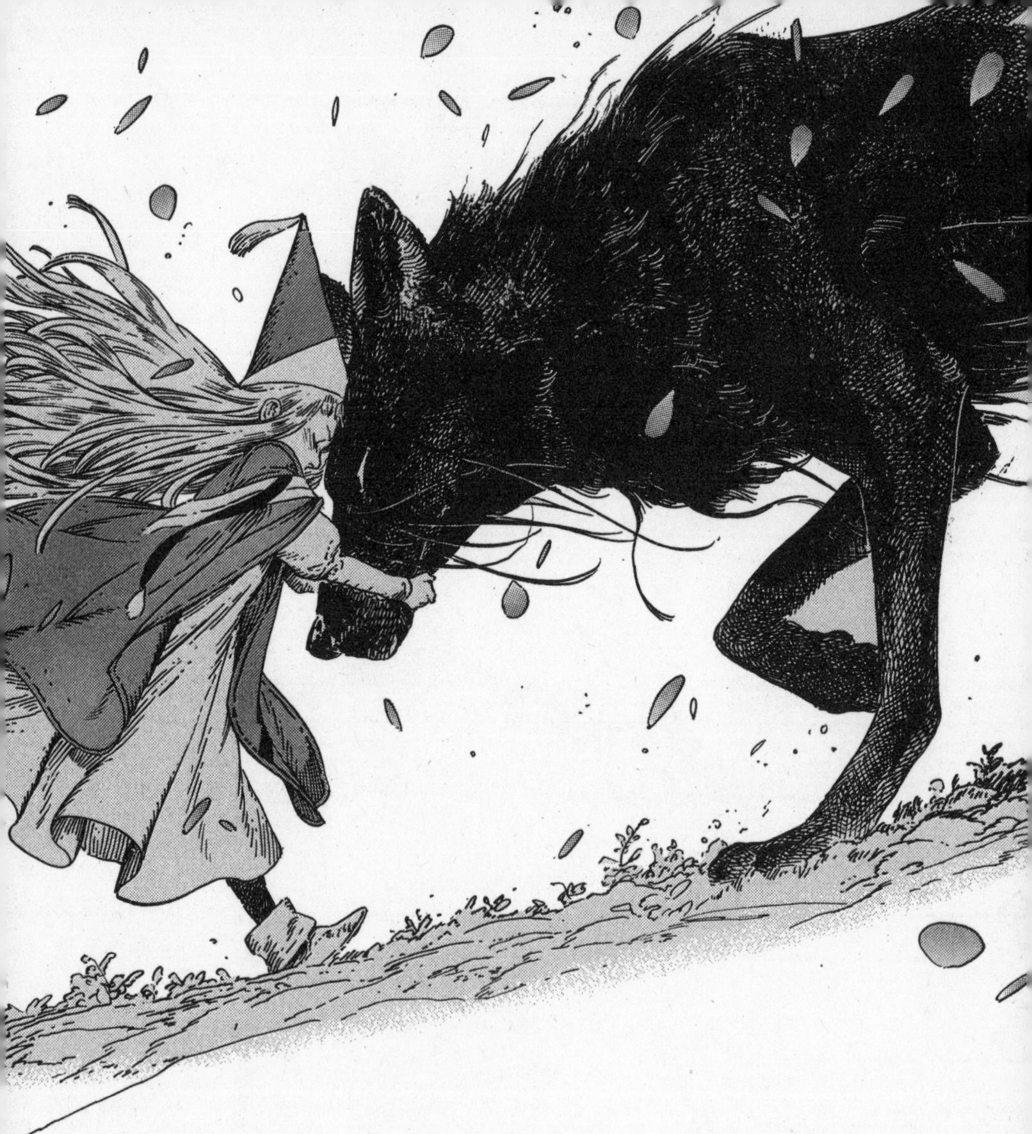

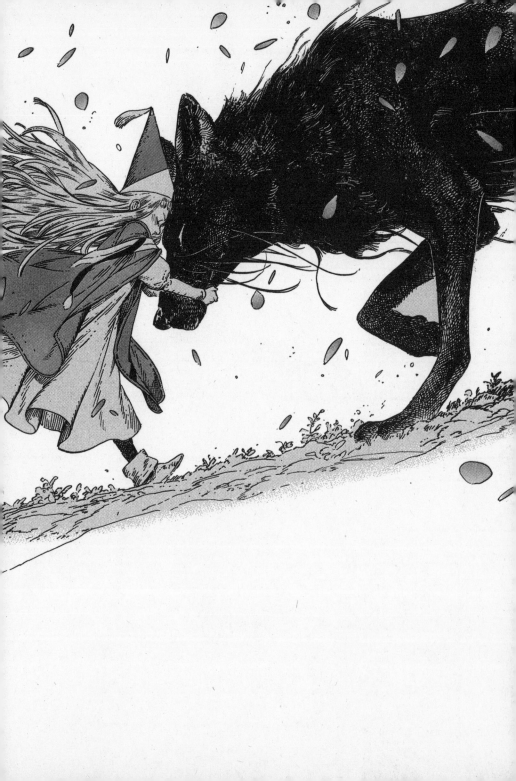

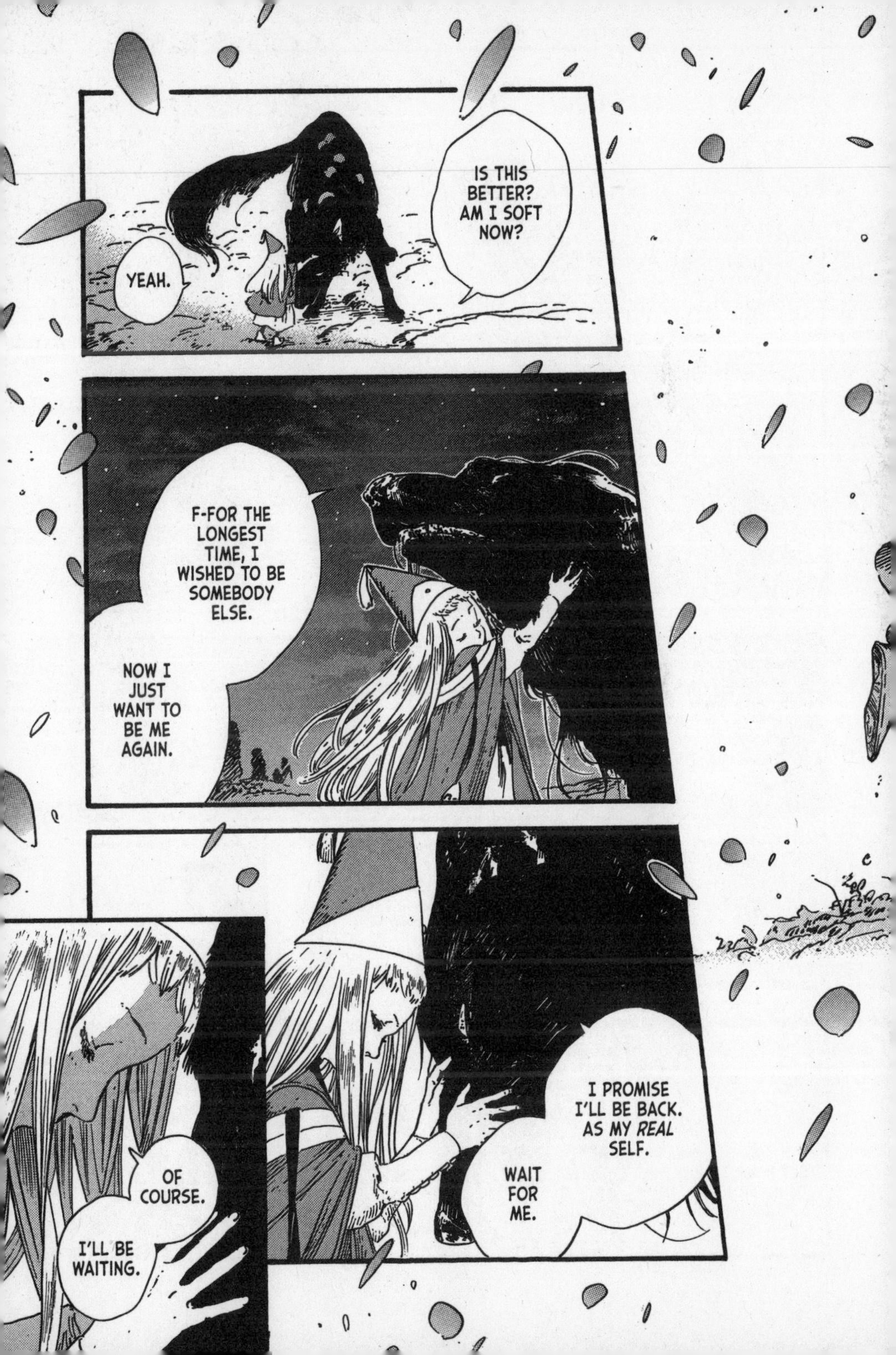
IS THIS BETTER? AM I SOFT NOW?
YEAH.
F-FOR THE LONGEST TIME, I WISHED TO BE SOMEBODY ELSE.
NOW I JUST WANT TO BE ME AGAIN.
I PROMISE I'LL BE BACK. AS MY *REAL* SELF.
WAIT FOR ME.
OF COURSE.
I'LL BE WAITING.

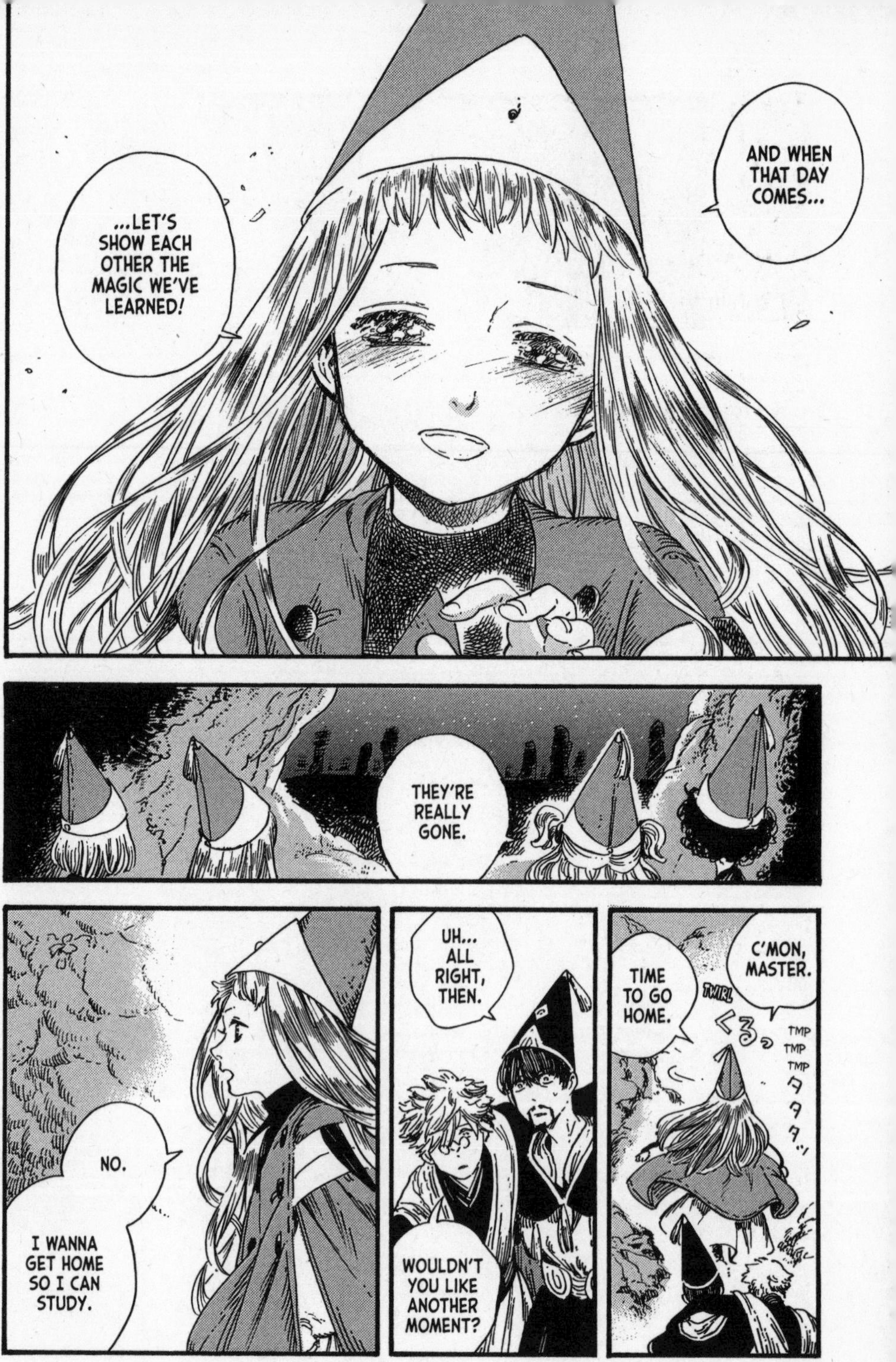
AND WHEN THAT DAY COMES...
...LET'S SHOW EACH OTHER THE MAGIC WE'VE LEARNED!
THEY'RE REALLY GONE.
C'MON, MASTER.
TIME TO GO HOME.
TWIRL くるっ
TMP TMP TMP タタタッ
UH... ALL RIGHT, THEN.
WOULDN'T YOU LIKE ANOTHER MOMENT?
NO.
...
I WANNA GET HOME SO I CAN STUDY.

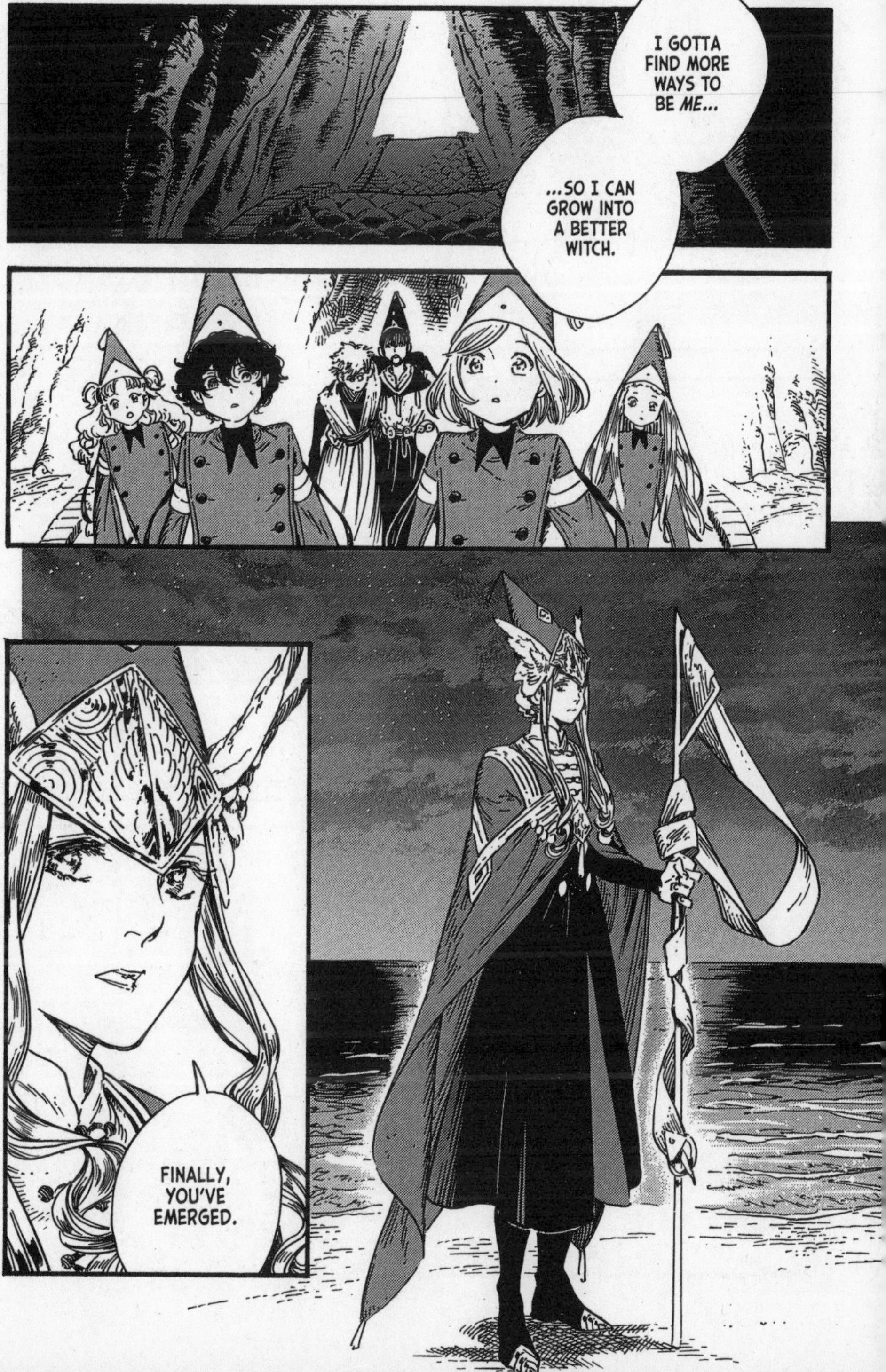
I GOTTA FIND MORE WAYS TO BE *ME*...
...SO I CAN GROW INTO A BETTER WITCH.
FINALLY, YOU'VE EMERGED.

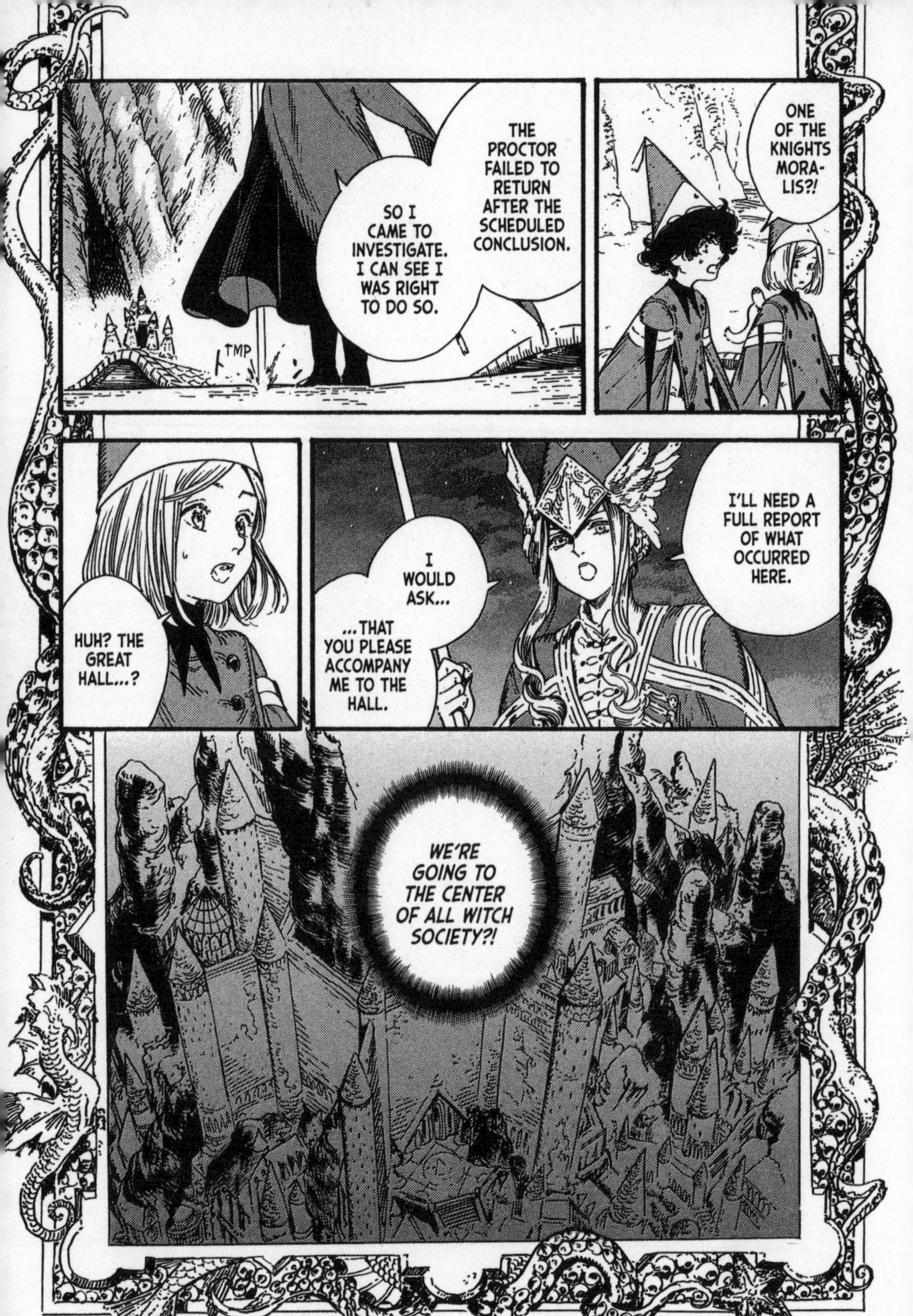
ONE OF THE KNIGHTS MORALIS?!
THE PROCTOR FAILED TO RETURN AFTER THE SCHEDULED CONCLUSION.
SO I CAME TO INVESTIGATE. I CAN SEE I WAS RIGHT TO DO SO.
TMP
I'LL NEED A FULL REPORT OF WHAT OCCURRED HERE.
I WOULD ASK...
...THAT YOU PLEASE ACCOMPANY ME TO THE HALL.
HUH? THE GREAT HALL...?
WE'RE GOING TO THE CENTER OF ALL WITCH SOCIETY?!

THE MATS OF WITCH HAT

A WITCH'S CALLING CARD IS THE POINTED CAP DONNED UPON THE HEAD. APPRENTICES ARE TYPICALLY EXPECTED TO WEAR THE CAP OF THE ATELIER TO WHICH THEY BELONG, BUT WITH GRADUATION COMES THE RIGHT TO DESIGN AND DON A HAT OF ONE'S OWN. BELOW IS A SELECTION OF THE MANY HATS THAT HAVE APPEARED IN THE STORY THUS FAR.

COCO'S HAT
FIRST APPEARS IN CHAPTER 2

STYLE WORN BY APPRENTICES OF QIFREY'S ATELIER. AGOTT, TETIA, AND RICHEH'S CAPS ARE ALL OF THE SAME DESIGN. THE WHITE FABRIC AT THE FRONT IS AFFIXED WITH A SMALL GOLDEN RIVET, AND A TASSEL EXTENDS FROM THE POINT.

QIFREY'S HAT
FIRST APPEARS IN CHAPTER 1

USES THE SAME OVERALL DESIGN AS HIS APPRENTICES' CAPS, WITH THE NOTABLE DIFFERENCES OF THE FABRIC COLOR USED FOR THE HAT'S BODY AND, IN PLACE OF THE TASSEL, A LONG RIBBON ATTACHED TO THE POINT.

ALAIRA'S HAT
FIRST APPEARS IN CHAPTER 3

THE POINT IS ADORNED WITH A DECORATIVE FEATHER. THE LENGTH OF CLOTH LOOSELY WRAPPED ABOUT THE BASE IS REMINISCENT OF A TURBAN AND IS AFFIXED AT THE FRONT BY WAY OF A GOLDEN ORNAMENT.

NOLNOA'S HAT
FIRST APPEARS IN CHAPTER 5

CONSTRUCTED OF A RELATIVELY FLEXIBLE MATERIAL, LEAVING IT PRONE TO SLIGHT FLOPPING WHEN LEFT TO STAND ON ITS OWN. THE LOWER PORTION OF CLOTH IS ATTACHED BY WAY OF STRING TIED TO A METAL RING AT THE FRONT.

OLRUGGIO'S HAT
FIRST APPEARS IN CHAPTER 10

A BODY OF BLACK CLOTH ADORNED WITH PATTERNS IN GOLD THREAD EMBROIDERY. THE TASSEL AT THE POINT IS THE SAME AS THAT OF COCO'S CAP: MANY YEARS AGO, HIS ORIGINAL ORNAMENT WAS EXCHANGED WITH QIFREY'S.

THE ORDER'S HATS
FIRST APPEAR IN CHAPTER 11

THE CAPS OF THE KNIGHTS MORALIS FEATURE CRIMSON CLOTH, WITH A METAL PLATE AT THE FRONT AND DECORATIVE WINGS AT THE SIDES. THE DESIGN IS EVOCATIVE OF THE SINSINGER, A BIRD OF LEGEND SAID TO APPEAR IN WRONGDOER'S DREAMS.

KUKROW'S HAT
FIRST APPEARS IN CHAPTER 19

THE DESIGN ALSO WORN BY EUINI. A GREEN BODY, DECORATED AT THE FRONT WITH BLACK CLOTH AND A PATTERN IN GOLD THREAD. AT THE POINT IS A METAL RING OF DESIGN SIMILAR TO A DOOR KNOCKER.

BONUS TRIVIA

TETIA'S HAT
FIRST APPEARS IN CHAPTER 14

THE CAP TETIA DREAMS OF MAKING WHEN SHE STRIKES OUT ON HER OWN. IT EXEMPLIFIES HER CONVICTION THAT EVERY SPELL BRINGS HAPPINESS FOR TWO: ONE PERSON THANKING, AND THE OTHER BEING THANKED.

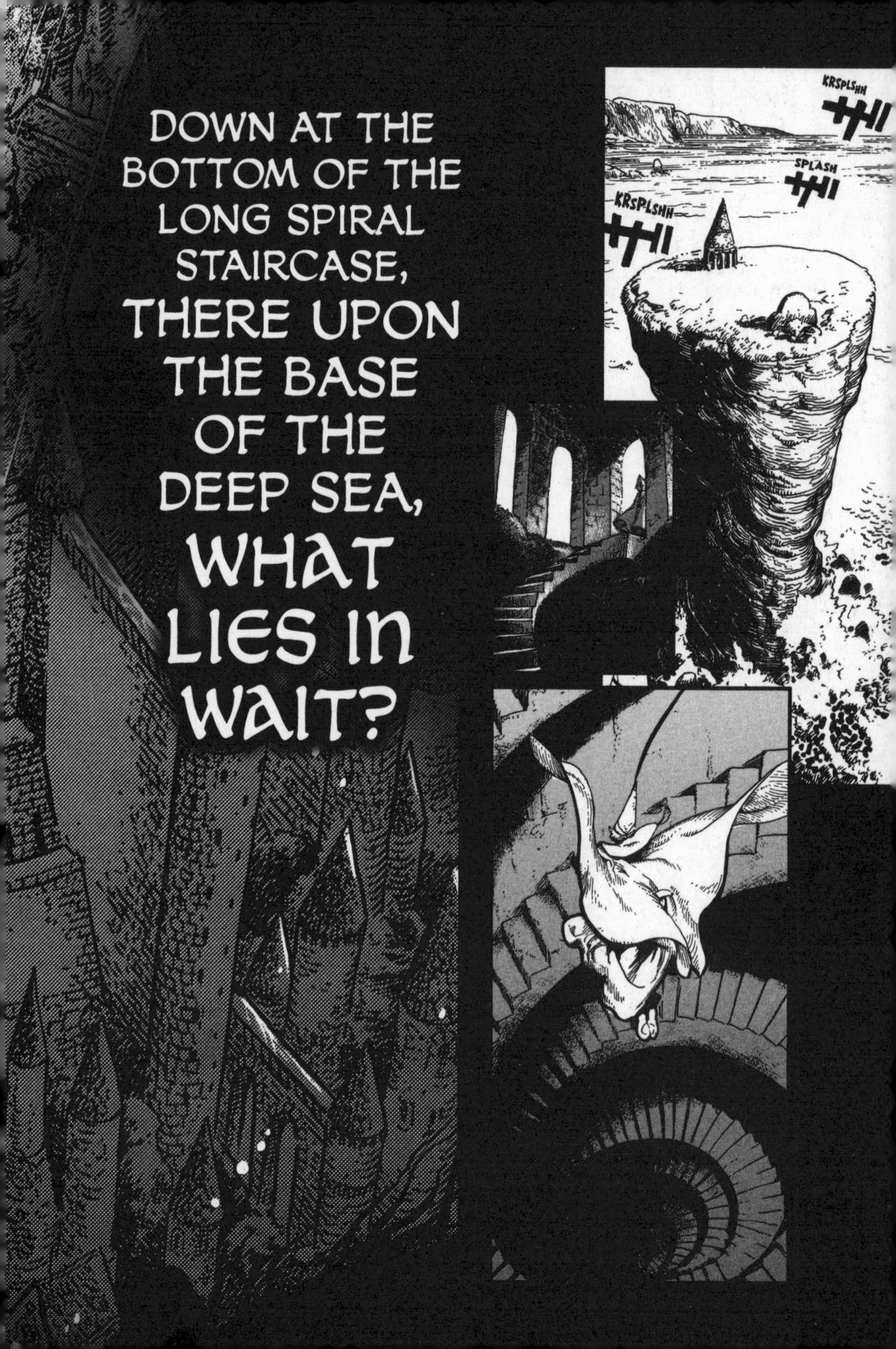
KRSPLSHH
SPLASH
KRSPLSHH
DOWN AT THE BOTTOM OF THE LONG SPIRAL STAIRCASE, THERE UPON THE BASE OF THE DEEP SEA, WHAT LIES IN WAIT?

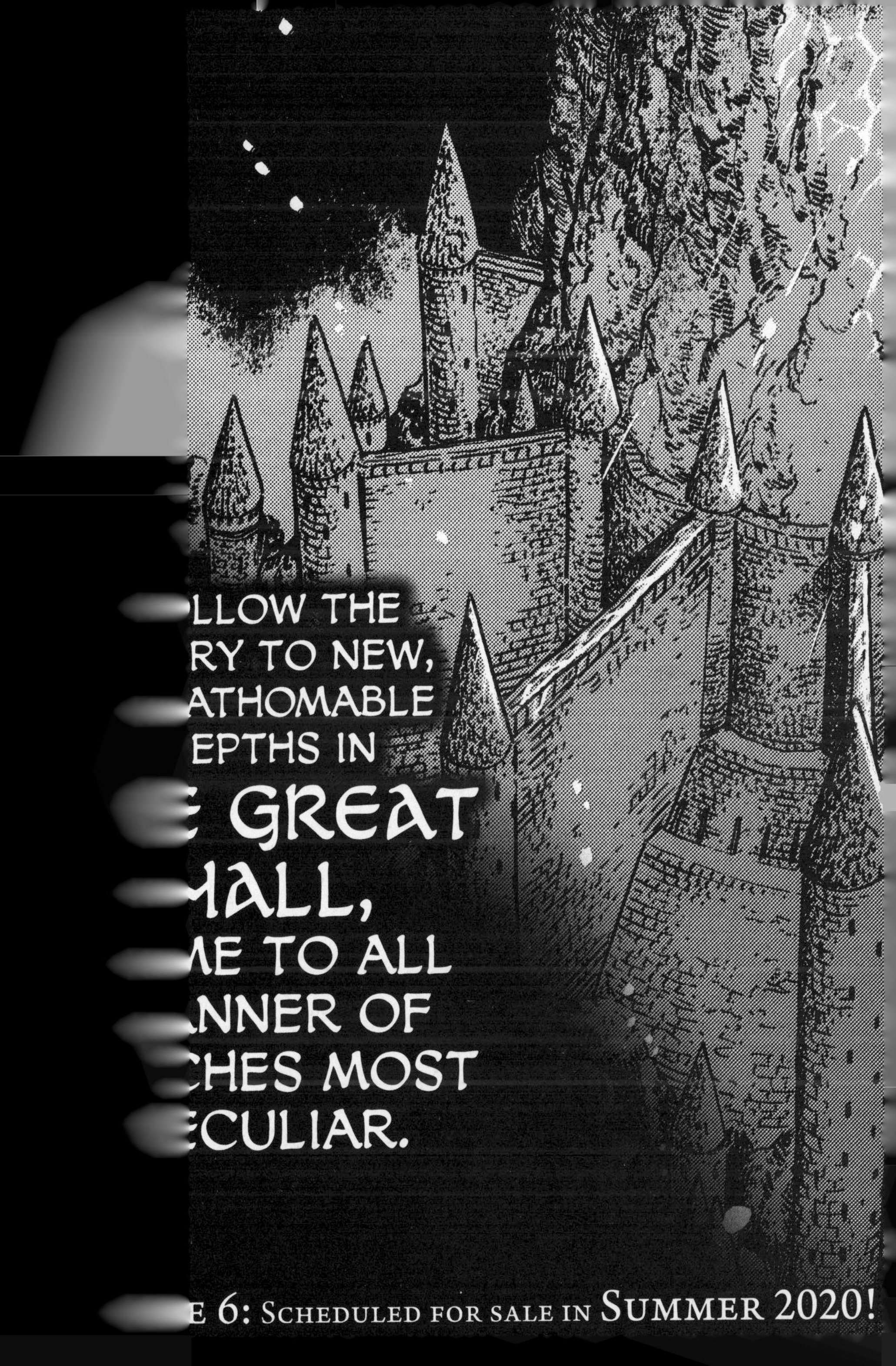
LLOW THE
RY TO NEW,
ATHOMABLE
EPTHS IN
E GREAT
HALL,
ME TO ALL
NNER OF
CHES MOST
ECULIAR.
E 6: SCHEDULED FOR SALE IN SUMMER 2020!

A Kodansha Comics Trade Paperback Original
Witch Hat Atelier 5 copyright © 2019 Kamome Shirahama
English translation copyright © 2020 Kamome Shirahama

Published in the United States by Kodansha Comics, an imprint of
Kodansha USA Publishing, LLC, New York.

Publication rights for this English edition arranged through
Kodansha Ltd., Tokyo.

First published in Japan in 2019 by Kodansha Ltd., Tokyo
as *Tongari Boshi no Atorie*, volume 5.

ISBN 978-1-63236-929-1

Original cover design by SAVA DESIGN

Printed in the United States of America.

www.kodanshacomics.com

9 8 7 6 5 4 3 2 1
Translation: Stephen Kohler
Lettering: Lys Blakeslee
Editing: Ajani Oloye
Proofreading: Jacob Friedman
Kodansha Comics edition cover design by Phil Balsman

Publisher: Kiichiro Sugawara
Vice president of marketing & publicity: Naho Yamada

Director of publishing services: Ben Applegate
Associate director of operations: Stephen Pakula
Publishing services managing editor: Noelle Webster
Assistant production manager: Emi Lotto, Angela Zurlo